Serverless Applications with Node.js

SLOBODAN STOJANOVIĆ
ALEKSANDAR SIMOVIĆ

MANNING
SHELTER ISLAND

For online information and ordering of this and other Manning books, please visit www.manning.com. The publisher offers discounts on this book when ordered in quantity.

For more information, please contact

Special Sales Department
Manning Publications Co.
20 Baldwin Road
PO Box 761
Shelter Island, NY 11964
Email: orders@manning.com

♾ Recognizing the importance of preserving what has been written, it is Manning's policy to have the books we publish printed on acid-free paper, and we exert our best efforts to that end. Recognizing also our responsibility to conserve the resources of our planet, Manning books are printed on paper that is at least 15 percent recycled and processed without the use of elemental chlorine.

 Manning Publications Co.
20 Baldwin Road
PO Box 761
Shelter Island, NY 11964

Development editor:	Toni Arritola
Review editor:	Ivan Martinović
Project manager:	Vincent Nordhaus
Copy editor:	Darren Meiss
Proofreader:	Sarah Boyer
Technical proofreader:	Valentin Crettaz
Typesetter:	Happenstance Type-O-Rama
Cover designer:	Marija Tudor

ISBN 9781617294723
Printed in the United States of America
1 2 3 4 5 6 7 8 9 10–SP–24 23 22 21 20 19

contents

foreword

Amazon forever changed IT infrastructure by making it easy to provision virtual machines back in 2007. Since then, the architectural improvements for modern applications have mostly been incremental. A decade later, by making it easy to provision functions, Amazon's Lambda platform started another tectonic wave of change. This "serverless" ecosystem is revolutionizing how we design, develop, and operate internet applications.

As an early adopter of this platform, I've had the privilege of working with Slobodan and Aleksandar and seeing first-hand the huge impact on time-to-market and on the cost of operation that "serverless" thinking brings. At the same time, the platform evolves so quickly that it's easy to get lost. To truly get the benefits of the new way of operations, developers have to rethink authentication, session management, storage, capacity planning, and distribution strategies. In *Serverless Applications with Node.js*, Slobodan and Aleksandar provide a front seat report about this revolution and an invaluable guide for JavaScript developers who want to benefit from the new generation of platforms.

What I love about this book is how it helps people get simple stuff done in AWS Lambda quickly, without trying to change the way we structure or run projects. Many serverless application frameworks abstract away AWS services, making framework lock-in a big risk because the ecosystem is still evolving rapidly. The authors don't force us to take a bet on their choice of frameworks, but explain how to use all the related services easily. For people new to AWS, this book introduces not just AWS Lambda, but also a whole host of related services such as DynamoDB (storage), Cognito (authentication), API Gateway (running web services), and Cloudwatch (event processing and scheduling). Even if you outgrow the authors' choice of tools later, you'll be able to keep all the code and just deploy it in a different way.

Another great reason to read this book is how it introduces several important real-world use cases for serverless platforms, including web APIs, chat-bots, payment processing, and order management. By incrementally building an online store for a fictional pizzeria, the authors provide almost ready-made components that most people will need to launch modern business scenarios in the cloud. This way of building up knowledge lets the book explore deeper development process topics, such as organizing automated testing and designing applications so they are easy to maintain. The last part of the book deals with migration strategies and answers some of the most common questions from people who already have applications partially running in some other cloud platform, and who want to get some quick wins and reduce time-to-market or cost of operation.

I hope you'll have as much fun with this book as I did and that you'll start finding better ways to deliver value quickly with your software in the cloud.

Gojko Adzic,
Partner, Neuri Consulting LLP

We've both been developers for over 10 years. We started with our first computers in the 90s, developing our first Pascal and BASIC functions and even went to programming competitions. But everything changed when the Web appeared. We immediately started building our first web applications and web pages playing with static HTML and CSS. When JavaScript and jQuery became the new standard, we switched almost immediately (even though, one was still playing with Flash and ActionScript). With the appearance of Node.js, it was natural to switch from languages we used such as Python and C#. Even though we're still sometimes writing a few functions in those languages, our switch to Node.js was permanent.

Approximately three years ago, we turned our attention to serverless. Gojko Adzic introduced AWS Lambda to us with his initial work on Claudia.js as a deployment tool. We were amazed how fast and how easy was it to develop and deploy serverless applications, and how easy was it to scale them, and we began working together with him on creating Claudia Bot Builder.

From one day to another, our whole perspective on building and maintaining web applications completely changed with serverless. Backend services got replaced by serverless functions and instead of writing bash scripts, logging into our servers, and planning our capacity, we stopped caring about those issues and focused more on business logic and application value.

We published our first serverless web applications into production, and developed hundreds of chat bots. Our production increased almost five-fold. It was incredible. The months spent learning how to configure and maintain application servers with bash, ssh, rsync, and so on were no longer important. Everything changed. From our starting point, the serverless ecosystem went a long way – the serverless providers are easier to use, and there are more and more serverless app components available each year (with Amazon re:Invent).

It went so fast and a huge number of things happened – we've made serverless our career. We started giving talks about serverless, holding workshops, and giving serverless consultations. We tried to gather our experience and knowledge, combined with multiple other sources and bring it together in an easy-to-learn and easy-to-follow format.

acknowledgments

It was hard writing this book, as it was our first one. Some of the chapters have been rewritten over five times to get to the point that you, as a reader, would easily grasp it and learn the most. During the process, we had lots of support from our friends and families, but we'd like to thank a few people specifically that helped us tremendously along the way.

First and foremost, we'd like to thank Gojko Adzic. He introduced the world of serverless to us several years ago. Especially for his reviews during the development of our book and comments such as "this page is worthless, delete it", "don't lie to your readers about the steps," and so on. We loved them.

Next we'd like to mention our editor at Manning, Toni Arritola. Thank you for working with us, when we struggled in the first few chapters, for being patient when we got behind schedule and supporting us with everything we needed. You always pushed for quality and made the book better for everyone who reads it. Also we'd like to thank Michael Stephens and Bert Bates, who helped us better explain all the serverless details and focus on important topics. We'd also like to thank the folks at Manning who worked on the production and promotion of the book, it was a team effort. We'd also like to thank Valentin Crettaz, our technical proofreader, and Kostas Passadis, our technical development editor, for their careful reviews of the code.

Thanks, too, to the Manning reviewers who took the time to read our manuscript at various stages and gave amazing feedback, including Arnaud Bailly, Barnaby Norman, Claudio Bernardo Rodríguez Rodríguez, Damian Esteban, Dane Balia, Deepak Bhaskaran, Jasba Simpson, Jeremy Lange, Kaj Ström, Kathleen R. Estrada, Kumar Unnikrishnan, Luca Mezzalira, Martin Dehnert, Rami Abdelwahed, Surjeet Manhas, Thomas Peklak, Umur Yilmaz, and Yvon Vieville.

Our thanks also go to Amazon and AWS teams for creating such an amazing computing service: AWS Lambda. You are changing the world.

Lastly we'd like to thank Aunt Maria and all other imaginary characters from the book!

about this book

Serverless Applications with Node.js is a book whose primary goal is to teach about and help you build serverless Node.js applications. It features a pragmatic approach, where you start with a story of your fictional Aunt Maria's Pizzeria, whose problems you're trying to solve by going serverless. The book begins by explaining serverless, tackling each problem Aunt Maria encountered by a separate serverless concept, which slowly start to form a clear picture how to build effective and clean serverless Node.js applications.

Who should read this book

Serverless Apps with Node.js is for JavaScript web developers seeking to learn how to build serverless applications and trying to understand how to properly organize, architect, and test them. Even though lots of Node.js content is already available online, as well as lots of tutorials on building basic serverless applications, this book introduces a step-by-step process for combining all those serverless topics and concepts to help you build big serverless applications and become a serverless Node.js developer.

How this book is organized

The book is organized in 3 parts with 15 chapters.

Part 1 explains the basics of serverless and how to build a serverless app with a database, how to connect to third-party services, how to debug it, how to add authorization and authentication, and how to work with files

- Chapter 1 introduces you to serverless on Amazon Web Services platform and explains serverless with simple analogies. It also introduces you to Aunt Maria, her pizzeria, and the problem she is facing. Finally, you'll learn what a common serverless Node.js app looks like and find out what Claudia.js is and how it helps you to deploy Node.js apps to AWS Lambda.

- Chapter 2 shows you how to develop a simple Pizzeria API using AWS Lambda, API Gateway, and Claudia API Builder. It also teaches you how to deploy your API with a single command using Claudia.
- Chapter 3 teaches you how databases work in serverless architecture, and it teaches you how to connect your Pizzeria API with the DynamoDB, a serverless database offered by AWS.
- Chapter 4 teaches you how to connect Pizzeria API with third-party services, such as Some Like It Hot delivery API. It also shows you some common issues you might face when using promises with Claudia API Builder.
- Chapter 5 helps you learn how to find errors in your serverless applications, how to debug them, and what debugging tools you have at your disposal.
- Chapter 6 shows you how to implement authentication and authorization in your serverless application. You'll learn the difference between authentication and authorization in a serverless environment, how to implement a web authorization mechanism using AWS Cognito, and how to identify your users using a social provider.
- Chapter 7 takes a dive into serverless file storage possibilities and examines how to create a separate file processing function that uses the storage and provides requested files to your other Lambda – your serverless API.

Part 2 covers how to create additional serverless applications that work with the same resources, how to create chatbots, voice assistants, SMS chatbots, how to add NLP, and how you should organize all those serverless applications together.

- Chapter 8 shows how to develop your first Facebook Messenger chatbot and how Claudia Bot Builder helps you do that in just several lines.
- Chapter 9 shows how to add simple NLP (natural language processing) to your chat bot, connect your chatbot to your DynamoDB database, and send delayed responses when a delivery is in progress (an asynchronous event).
- Chapter 10 shows how to develop your first Alexa skill and a Twilio SMS chatbot, and how with Claudia Bot Builder you can do that incredibly fast.

Part 3 covers the more advanced topics on how to test, architect your serverless apps, and migrate your existing applications to serverless. It also gives recommendations, general patterns, and solutions to common issues and frequent questions. It also showcases two medium scaled companies that went serverless.

- Chapter 11 teaches you about testing serverless applications, writing testable serverless functions, and running automated tests locally. Along with that, it explains Hexagonal Architecture and how to refactor your serverless applications to make them easier to test and to remove potential risks.

- Chapter 12 covers processing payments with serverless applications, implementing payments to your serverless API, and understanding the PCI compliance in payment processing.
- Chapter 13 makes sure you know all about running Express.js applications in AWS Lambda and the serverless ecosystem, serving static content from an Express.js application, connecting to MongoDB from a serverless Express.js application, and understanding the limitations and risks of Express.js apps in a serverless ecosystem.
- Chapter 14 covers how to approach migrating to serverless, structuring your app according to serverless provider characteristics, organizing your application architecture so it's business-oriented and able to grow, and dealing with the architectural differences between serverless and traditional server-hosted applications.
- Chapter 15 teaches you how CodePen uses serverless for its preprocessors ensuring hundreds of millions of requests, and how MindMup serves 400,000 active users with a two-person team and serverless.

About the code

This book contains many examples of source code both in numbered listings and inline with normal text. In both cases, source code is formatted in a fixed-width font `like this` to separate it from ordinary text. Sometimes it is also in bold to highlight code that has changed from previous steps in the chapter, such as when a new feature adds to an existing line of code.

In many cases, the original source code has been reformatted; we've added line breaks and reworked indentation to accommodate the available page space in the book. Additionally, comments in the source code have often been removed from the listings when the code is described in the text. Code annotations accompany many of the listings, highlighting important concepts.

Source code for the examples in this book is available for download from the publisher's website at https://manning.com/books/serverless-apps-with-node-and-claudiajs

Book forum

Your purchase of *Serverless Applications with Node.js* includes free access to a private web forum section run by Manning Publications where you make comments about the book, ask technical questions, and receive help from the authors and other users. To access the forum, point your web browser to https://forums.manning.com/forums/serverless-apps-with-node-and-claudiajs. You can also learn more about Manning's forums and the rules of conduct at https://forums.manning.com/forums/about.

Manning's commitment to our readers is to provide a venue where a meaningful dialog between individual readers and between readers and the authors can take place. It is not a commitment to any specific amount of participation on the part of the authors, whose contributions to the forum remain voluntary (and unpaid). We suggest you ask the authors challenging questions, lest their interest stray.

Online resources

If you need additional help, you can:

- Jump over to Claudia.js Gitter https://gitter.im/claudiajs/claudia, where the authors usually respond to technical questions regarding Claudia.js, Claudia API Builder, and Claudia Bot Builder
- See the claudiajs tag at Stack Overflow (http://stackoverflow.com/questions/tagged/claudiajs), where you can post problems and questions you have about developing serverless applications with Node.js and Claudia.js. You can also help someone else stuck on an issue, too.

about the authors

Slobodan Stojanović and Aleksandar Simović are AWS Serverless Heroes and core contributors to the Claudia.js project. They are the lead developers and maintainers of Claudia Bot Builder and co-authors of *Serverless Applications with Node.js.*

Aleksandar has been a senior software consultant and engineer for over seven years, mostly but not only, in JavaScript. He also dabbles in Swift, Python, and Rust. He is based in Belgrade and is co-organizer of the JS Belgrade meetups.

Slobodan is CTO of Cloud Horizon, a software development studio based in Montreal. He is based in Belgrade and is the JS Belgrade meetup co-organizer.

about the cover illustration

The figure on the cover of *Serverless Applications with Node.js* is captioned "Serbian from Šumadija." The illustration is taken from Vladimir Kirin's "Serbian National Costumes." Kirin (1894–1963) studied graphic design in London and attended the Academy of Arts in Vienna, and worked as an artist, draftsman, and illustrator. His work and influence are credited with improving book design in Croatia.

Throughout its rich history, the central region of Serbia, known as Šumadija, has been the cultural center of Serbia, and the traditional clothing of the area is the standard for the national costume. As shown in this image, traditional Serbian female dress consisted of *opanci*, embroidered woolen socks that reached to the knees. Skirts varied, being either plaited or gathered and embroidered linen, with the *tkanice* serving as a belt. An important part of the costume was the apron (*pregace*) decorated with floral motifs. Shirts were in the shape of tunics, richly decorated with silver thread and cords was worn over the shirt. Girls also wore collars, or a string of gold coins around their throats, earrings, bracelets, and their hair was decorated with metal coins or flowers.

At a time when it is hard to tell one computer book from another, Manning celebrates the inventiveness and initiative of the computer business with book covers based on the rich diversity of regional life of two centuries ago, brought back to life by Kirin's illustrations.

Part 1

Serverless pizzeria

Aunt Maria is a strong-willed person. For more than three decades, she has been managing her pizzeria, a gathering place for many generations in the neighborhood: Lots of people spent time there with their families, laughed, and even went on romantic dates. But recently, her pizzeria has seen some rough times. She told you she's seeing fewer and fewer customers. The rise in technology has caused her customers to prefer ordering online via websites or their phones from competitor's pizzerias.

Her pizzeria already has a website but needs a back-end application to process and store information on pizzas and orders.

In the first part of this book, your goal will be to help Aunt Maria to catch up with the competition by building a serverless API for her. But because you're still new to serverless development, you'll first learn what serverless is and how it can help you to build Pizzeria API (chapter 1). Then you'll continue by adding routes to your API and deploying it to AWS Lambda using Claudia (chapter 2). To persist and deliver all orders, you'll connect your new API to the DynamoDB table (chapter 3) and communicate with a third-party service: Some Like It Hot delivery API (chapter 4).

During the development, you'll face certain problems and learn how to debug the serverless application (chapter 5).

To make the API fully functional, you'll need to learn how to authenticate and authorize users (chapter 6) and keep and manipulate pizza images (chapter 7).

Introduction to serverless with Claudia

1

This chapter covers

- What serverless is

- The core concepts of serverless

- The difference between serverless and hosted
  web applications

- How Claudia fits

- Why use serverless

Serverless is a method of deploying and running applications on cloud infrastructure, on a pay-per-use basis and without renting or buying servers. Instead of you, the serverless platform provider is responsible for capacity planning, scaling, balancing, and monitoring; the provider is also able to treat your applications as functions.

Wait, no servers? Seems like a new buzzword, a hipster cloud trend promising to revolutionize your life for the better.

This book explains what serverless is, what problems it solves, and where it does or doesn't fit into your application development process, without fanboyishly showing off and selling serverless like some trendy cloud cult that everyone needs to follow. It does so with a pragmatic approach, explaining the concepts by teaching you how to build reliable and scalable serverless applications with Node.js and Claudia.js, while saving time and resources.

This chapter focuses on the concepts of serverless: what it is, why it matters, and how it compares to server-hosted web application development. Your main goal for this chapter is to gain a good understanding of basic serverless concepts and build a good foundation.

1.1 Servers and washing machines

To understand serverless, consider for a moment washing machines. A clothes-cleaning appliance might sound like a crazy place to start, but owning a server nowadays is similar to owning a washing machine. Everybody needs clean clothes, and the most logical solution seems to be buying a washing machine. But most of the time the washing machine is plugged in, doing nothing. At best, it's used 5 to 15 hours per week. The same goes with servers. Most of the time, your average application server is just waiting to receive a request, doing nothing.

Interestingly, servers and washing machines have many common issues. They both have a maximum weight or volume they can process. Owning a small server is similar to owning a small washing machine; if you accumulate a big pile of laundry, the machine can't process all of it at once. You can buy a bigger one that can take up to 20 pounds of clothes, but then you'll find yourself in a situation where you want to clean just one shirt, and running a 20-pound machine for a single shirt seems wasteful. Also, setting up all your applications to run safely together on one server is tricky, and sometimes impossible. A correct setup for one app can completely mess up another one with a different setting. Similarly, with washing machines you have to separate clothes by color, and then choose the proper program, detergent, and softener combinations. If you don't handle setup properly, the machine can ruin your clothing.

These issues, along with the problem that not everyone is able to own a washing machine, led to the rise of laundromats or launderettes—coin laundry machines that you rent for the time needed to wash your clothes. For servers, the same need has led many companies to start providing server rental services, either locally or in the cloud. You can rent a server, and the server provider takes care of the storage, power, and basic setup. But both laundromats and rental servers are just partial solutions.

For rentals of washing machines and servers, you still need to know how to combine your clothes or applications and set up the machines, choosing appropriate detergents or environments. You also still have to balance the number of machines and their size limitations, planning how many you will need.

In the world of dirty laundry, in the second half of the twentieth century, a new trend of "fluff and fold" services started. You can bring these services a single piece or a bag of clothes, and they will clean, dry, and fold your laundry for you. Some even deliver to your address. They usually charge by the piece, so you don't need to wait to gather a specifically sized batch to clean, and you don't have to worry about washing machines, detergents, and cleaning programs at all.

Compared to the clothes cleaning industry, the software industry is still in the era of self-service laundromats, as many of us still rent servers or use Platform as a Service (PaaS) providers. We are still estimating the number of potential requests (quantity of clothes) that we're going to handle and reserving enough servers to (we hope) deal with the load, often wasting our money on servers that either are not operating at full capacity or are overloaded and unable to process all our customer requests.

1.2 The core concepts

So how does serverless change that? The name, implying having no server at all, doesn't seem to be a logical solution. Go back to the definition:

> **What is serverless**
>
> *Serverless* is a method of deploying and running applications on cloud infrastructure, on a pay-per-use basis and without renting or buying servers.

Contrary to its name, serverless does not exclude the existence of servers; software requires hardware to run. Serverless just removes the need for companies, organizations, or developers to physically rent or buy a server.

You are probably wondering why serverless is so named. The answer lies in the serverless abstraction of the server concept. Rather than renting a server for your application, setting up the environment, and deploying it, you upload your application to your serverless provider, which takes care of assigning servers, storage, application handling, setup, and execution.

> **NOTE** Some of you may be wondering whether serverless removes a company's need for large DevOps teams. For most situations, the answer is yes.

More precisely, the provider stores your application inside a certain container. The container represents an isolated environment that contains everything your application needs to run. You can think of the container as being a pot for houseplants. The plant pot contains earth filled with all the minerals your plant needs to live.

Like the plant pot, the container allows the serverless provider to safely move and store your application, and to execute it and make copies of it depending on your needs. But the main benefit of serverless is that you don't do any server configuration, balancing, scaling—basically, any kind of server management. The serverless provider manages all of that for you while also guaranteeing that if a large number of calls to your application occur at the same time, it will clone enough containers to handle all the calls, and each clone will be an exact copy of the first. If necessary, the provider will create thousands of clones. The serverless provider decides to replicate a container only when the number of requests to your application becomes so big that the current container can't handle all incoming requests.

Unless there is a request (a call) to your application, not a single instance of your application is running, so it isn't wasting space, server time, or energy. The serverless provider is responsible for all the operational details, such as knowing where your application is stored, how and where to replicate it, when to load new containers, and when to reduce the number of replicated containers to unload the unused servers.

From the washing machine perspective, the process is like calling a fluff and fold cleaning service; the delivery guy appears at your door to pick up your dirty laundry, and the service cleans and then returns the laundry to you. No matter how much clothing you have and no matter what kinds (wool, cotton, leather, and so on), the cleaning company is responsible for all the processes of separation, detergent choice, and program selection.

Serverless and FaaS

Initially, the term *serverless* was interpreted differently from what it means now. In the early days of serverless, it was defined as a *Backend as a Service* (BaaS), because it represents applications that are partly or completely dependent on third-party services for server-based logic. Later, it was almost exclusively described as a *Function as a Service* (FaaS), because the serverless providers treat applications as functions, invoking them only when requested.

1.3 How does serverless work?

As previously described, serverless providers supply an isolated compute container for your application. The compute container is event-driven, so it's activated only when a certain event triggers.

Events are specific external actions that behave exactly like physical triggers. Take your home lights as an example: the events that turn them on can differ. A classic light switch is invoked by pressure; a motion sensor is tied to motion detection; a daylight sensor turns your lights on when the sun goes down. But containers are not limited to listening to the specified events and invoking your contained functions; they also provide a way for your functions to create events themselves, or, more precisely, to emit them. In a more technical manner, with serverless, your function containers are both *event listeners* and *event emitters*.

Finally, serverless providers offer various triggers that can run your functions. The list of triggers depends on the provider and implementation, but some of the most common triggers are HTTP requests, file uploads to file storage, database updates, and Internet of Things (IoT) events. There are many more.

NOTE A serverless function runs only when triggered, and you pay only for its execution time. After execution, the serverless provider shuts the function down, while keeping its trigger active.

1.4 Serverless in practice

The whole serverless landscape contains lots of moving parts, so we introduce it gently. We build an example application and bring in one piece at a time, so you can see how it fits. As you slowly pick up each new concept, you'll expand your example application.

This book takes a greenfield approach to its example application (it will be built from scratch), and it handles the problems of a small company—more precisely, a pizzeria. The pizzeria is managed by your fictional Aunt Maria. During the course of the book, Aunt Maria will face a lot of real-world problems, and your goal will be to help her while grasping serverless concepts along the way. Serverless, like every new technology, introduces a lot of new concepts that can be difficult to handle all at once.

> **NOTE** For a brownfield situation (migrating your current application to serverless), feel free to jump to the last part of the book. If you're not familiar with serverless, you should go through at least the first few chapters before jumping to the last part of the book.

1.4.1 *Aunt Maria's serverless pizzeria*

Aunt Maria is a strong-willed person. For more than three decades, she has been managing her pizzeria, which was the place where many generations of people from the neighborhood spent time with their families, laughed together, and even went on romantic dates. But recently, her pizzeria has seen some rough times. She's told you that she's seeing fewer and fewer customers. Many of her customers now prefer ordering online via websites or their phones rather than visiting in person. Some new companies have started stealing her customers. The new Chess's pizzeria, for example, has a mobile app with pizza previews and online ordering, and also a chatbot for ordering via various messenger applications. Your aunt's customers like her pizzeria, but most want to order from their homes, so her three-decades-old business has started to wane. The pizzeria already has a website, but it needs a back-end application to process and store information on pizzas and orders.

1.4.2 *A common approach*

Given Aunt Maria's limited resources, the easiest solution is to build a small API with a popular Node.js framework, such as Express.js or Hapi, and set up a pizza database in the same instance (most likely MongoDB, MySQL, or PostgreSQL).

A typical API would have its code structured in a few layers resembling a three-tier architecture, meaning that the code is split into presentational, business, and data tiers or layers.

Three-tier architecture

Three-tier architecture is a client/server software architecture pattern in which the user interface (presentation), functional process logic ("business rules"), and computer data storage and data access are developed and maintained as independent modules, most often on separate platforms.

To learn more about three-tier architecture, visit https://en.wikipedia.org/wiki/Multitier_architecture#Three-tier_architecture.

The typical three-tier application design would be similar to figure 1.1, with separate routes for pizzas, orders, and users. It would also have routes for webhooks for both chatbots and a payment processor. All the routes would trigger some handler functions in the business layer, and the processed data would be sent to the data layer—database and file and image storage.

This approach fits perfectly for any given small application. It would work fine for your Pizza API, at least until online pizza orders grow to a certain level. Then you would need to scale your infrastructure.

But to be able to scale a monolithic application, it's necessary to detach the data layer (because you don't want to replicate your database, for the sake of data consistency). After that, your application would look like the one shown in figure 1.2. But you'd still have one conglomerate of an application with all its API routes and the business logic for everything. Your application could be replicated if you had too many users, but each instance would have all its services replicated as well, regardless of their usage.

Monolithic application

A *monolithic application* is a software application in which the user interface and data access code are combined into a single program on a single platform. A monolithic application is self-contained and independent from other computing applications.

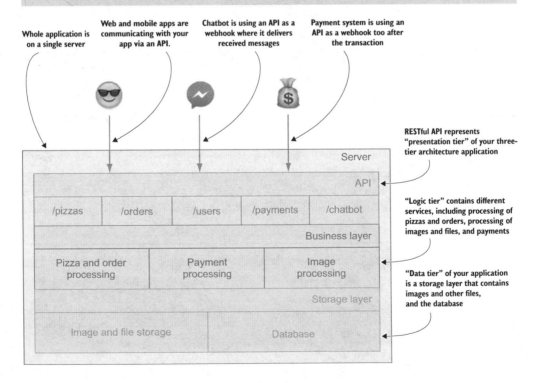

Figure 1.1 The typical three-tier design for the Pizza API

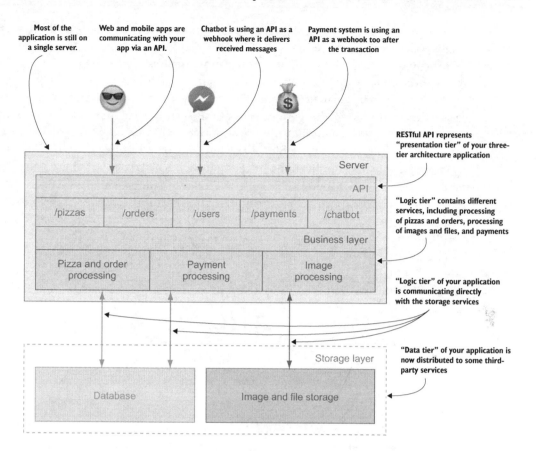

Figure 1.2 **A common approach with an external database and file storage for the Pizza API**

1.4.3 *Serverless approach*

Creating serverless applications requires a different approach, as these applications are event-driven and fully distributed.

Instead of having one server with the API endpoints and your business logic, each part of your application is isolated to independent and autoscalable containers.

In a serverless application, your requests are processed with an API router layer that has only one job: it accepts HTTP requests and routes them to the underlying business layer services. The API router in a serverless architecture is always independently managed. That means that application developers don't maintain the API router, and it's scaled automatically by the serverless provider to accept all the HTTP requests your API is receiving. Also, you pay only for the requests that are processed.

In the case of your Pizza API, the router will receive all the API requests from the mobile and web applications, and if necessary handle webhooks from chatbots and the payment processor.

After an API request is routed, it is passed to another container with the business layer service to be processed.

Instead of having one monolithic application, the business logic of a serverless application is often split into smaller units. The size of each unit depends on your preferences. A unit can be as small as a single function or as large as a monolithic application. Most of the time, its size does not directly affect the infrastructure cost, because you are paying for function execution. Units are also scaled automatically, and you won't pay for units that aren't processing anything, so owning one or a dozen of them costs the same.

However, for small applications and situations in which you don't have a lot of information, you can save money on hosting and maintenance by bundling functionalities related to one service into a single business unit. For your Pizza API, a sensible solution is to have one unit for processing pizzas and orders, one for handling payments, one for handling chatbot functionality, and one for processing images and files.

The last part of your serverless API is the data layer, which can be similar to the data layer in a scaled monolithic application, with a separately scaled database and file storage service. It would be best if the database and file storage were also independent and autoscalable.

Another benefit of a serverless application is that the data layer can trigger a serverless function out of the box. For example, when a pizza image is uploaded to the file storage, an image processing service can be triggered, and it can resize the photo and associate it with the specific pizza.

You can see the flow of the serverless Pizza API in figure 1.3.

1.5   *Serverless infrastructure — AWS*

Your serverless Pizza API needs infrastructure to run on. Serverless is very young and at the moment has several infrastructure choices. Most of these choices are owned by big vendors, because serverless requires a big infrastructure for scaling. The best-known and most advanced infrastructures are Amazon's AWS Lambda serverless compute container, Microsoft's Azure Functions, and Google's Cloud Functions.

This book focuses on AWS Lambda because AWS has the most mature serverless infrastructure available in the market, with a stable API and many successful stories behind it.

AWS Lambda is an event-driven serverless computing platform provided by Amazon as part of Amazon Web Services. It is a compute service that runs code in response to events and automatically manages the compute resources required by that code.

Google Cloud Functions and Microsoft Azure Functions

Google launched Google Cloud Functions, its answer to Amazon's AWS Lambda, in mid-2016. Google Cloud Functions are explained as lightweight event-based microservices that allow you to run JavaScript functions in a Node.js runtime. Your function can be triggered by an HTTP request, Google Cloud Storage, and other Google Cloud Pub/Sub services. At the time this book was written, Google Cloud Functions were still in alpha, so pricing was not known. You can learn more at the official website: https://cloud.google.com/functions/.

(continued)

Microsoft's implementation of serverless—Azure Functions—is part of its Azure cloud computing platform. Microsoft describes it as an event-based serverless compute experience that accelerates your development, scales based on demand, and charges you for only the resources you consume. Azure Functions allows you to develop functions in JavaScript, C#, F#, Python, and other scripting languages. Azure pricing is similar to that of AWS Lambda: You're charged 20 cents per 1 million executions and $0.000016 per GB of resource consumption per month, with a free tier for the first 1 million requests and 400,000 GB each month. For more information, visit the official website at https://azure.microsoft.com/en-us/services/functions/.

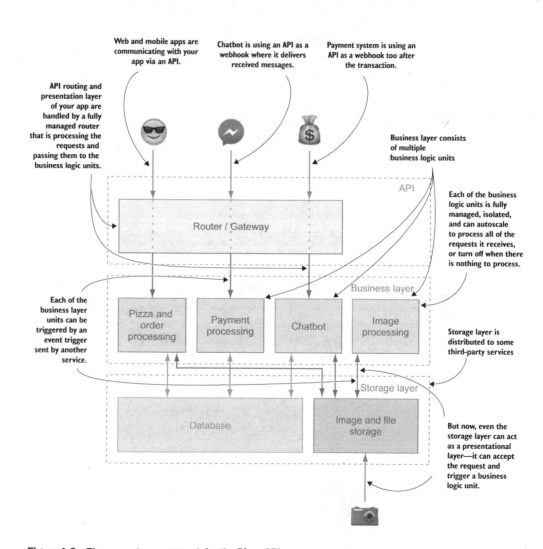

Figure 1.3   The serverless approach for the Pizza API

NOTE   Most of the things you'll learn in this book are also feasible with other serverless providers, but some services might differ, so some of the solutions might need a slightly different approach.

In the Amazon platform, the word *serverless* is usually directly related to AWS Lambda. But when you are building a serverless application such as your Pizza API, AWS Lambda is just one of the building blocks. For a full application, you often need other services, such as storage, database, and routing services. In table 1.1 you can see that AWS has fully developed services for all of them:

- Lambda is used for computing.
- API Gateway is a router that accepts HTTP requests and invokes other services depending on the routes.
- DynamoDB is an autoscalable database.
- Simple Storage Service (S3) is a storage service that abstracts the standard hard drives and offers you unlimited storage.

Table 1.1   **The building blocks of serverless applications in AWS**

Functionality	AWS service	Short description
Computing	Lambda	Computing component, used for your business logic
Router	API Gateway	Routing component, used to route HTTP request data to your Lambda function
Database	DynamoDB	Autoscalable document database
Storage	S3	Autoscalable file storage service

Lambda is the most important serverless puzzle piece you need to understand, because it contains your business logic. Lambda is AWS's serverless computing container that runs your function when an event trigger occurs. It gets scaled automatically if many events trigger the function at the same time. To develop your Pizza API as a serverless application, you will need to use AWS Lambda as its serverless compute container.

When a certain event occurs, such as an HTTP request, a Lambda function is triggered, with the data from the event, context, and a way to reply to the event as its arguments. The Lambda function is a simple function handler written in one of the supported languages. At this time of this writing, AWS Lambda support the following languages:

- Node.js
- Python
- Java (Java 8 compatible) and other JVM languages
- C# (.NET Core)

In Node.js, event data, context, and a function callback are passed as JSON objects. The `context` object contains details about your Lambda function and its current execution, such as execution time, what triggered the function, and other information. The third argument that your function receives is a callback function that allows you to reply with some payload that will be sent back to the trigger, or an error. The following listing shows a Node.js sample of a small AWS Lambda function that returns the text *Hello from AWS Lambda.*

Listing 1.1   An example of the smallest working Lambda function with Node.js

A function accepts an event, a context, and a callback function.

The callback function returns a success message.

```
function lambdaFunction(event, context, callback) {
  callback(null, 'Hello from AWS Lambda')
}

exports.handler = lambdaFunction
```

The function is exported as a handler.

> **NOTE**   As shown in listing 1.1, a function is exported with an `exports.handler` instead of the standard Node.js export, `module.exports`. This is because AWS Lambda requires the module export to be an object with a named `handler` method, rather than the function directly.

As mentioned before, the `event` in your Lambda function is the data passed by the service that triggered your Lambda function. In AWS, functions can be invoked by many things, from common events such as an HTTP request via API Gateway or file manipulation by S3, to more exotic ones such as code deployment, changes in the infrastructure, and even console commands using the AWS SDK.

Here's a list of the most important events and services that can trigger an AWS Lambda function and how they would translate to your Pizza API:

- *HTTP requests via API Gateway*—A website pizza request is sent.
- *Image uploading, deleting, and file manipulation via S3*—A new pizza image is uploaded.
- *Changes in the database via DynamoDB*—A new pizza order is received.
- *Various notifications via the Simple Notification Service (AWS SNS)*—A pizza is delivered.
- *Voice commands via Amazon Alexa*—A customer orders a pizza from home using voice commands.

For the full list of triggers, see http://docs.aws.amazon.com/lambda/latest/dg/invoking -lambda-function.html.

Lambda functions come with some limitations, such as limited execution time and memory. For example, by default, your Lambda function's execution time is up to three seconds, which means that it will time out if your code tries to process something longer. It also has 128 MB of RAM, which means that it is not suitable for complex computations.

NOTE Both of those limitations can be configured in the function settings. Time-out can be increased up to 15 minutes, and memory can be increased up to 3 GB. Increasing both of the limits can affect the cost per execution of your function.

Another important characteristic of Lambda functions is that they are stateless, and therefore state is lost between subsequent invocations.

Serverless pricing

One of the major selling points of serverless is the price. Amazon prices its standard virtual servers, Elastic Compute Cloud (Amazon EC2) servers, per hour. AWS Lambda is more expensive than EC2 in hourly cost, but by contrast, you don't pay for it unless your function is working. You pay 20 cents per million executions of your AWS Lambda function and $0.000016 per GB of resource consumption per month. Amazon also gives you a free tier with 1 million requests and 400,000 GB at no cost each month.

For your Pizza API, Aunt Maria won't have to pay anything until she reaches 1 million executions per month. If she reaches that number, you have succeeded in your goal of helping her.

For more information about pricing, visit the official website at https://aws.amazon .com/lambda/pricing/.

As you can see in figure 1.4, the flow of a Lambda function goes like this:

- A certain event happens, and the service that handles the event triggers the Lambda function.
- The function, such as the one shown in listing 1.1, starts its execution.
- The function execution ends, either with a success or error message, or by timing out.

Another important thing that can affect your serverless Pizza API is function latency. Because the Lambda function containers are managed by the provider, not the application operators, there's no way to know if a trigger will be served by an existing container or if the platform will instantiate a new one. If a container needs to be created and initialized before the function executes, it requires a bit more time and is called a *cold start*, as shown in figure 1.5. The time it takes to start a new container depends on the size of

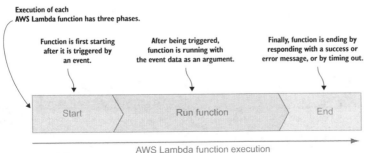

Figure 1.4   The flow of an AWS Lambda function

the application and the platform used to run it. Empirically and at the time of writing of this book, there are noticeably lower latencies with Node.js and Python than with Java.

> **COST OF THE PIZZA API** Developing the Pizza API as described in the following chapters of this book should cost less than a cup of coffee. AWS Lambda by itself will be free, but some of the services used for Pizza API development, such as DynamoDB and the Simple Storage Service, charge a small fee for the storage of your data. Both of those services and their pricing are described in later chapters. The final price of the application will depend on the amount of data and its usage, but if you are following the book's examples, it should be less than $1 per month.

Lambda functions are quite easy to understand and use. The most complex part is the deployment process.

There are a few ways to deploy your serverless application to AWS Lambda. You can deploy through the visual UI on the AWS Lambda console or the terminal via the AWS command-line interface using the AWS API, either directly or via the AWS SDK for one of the supported languages. Deploying a serverless application is simpler than deploying a traditional one, but it can be made even easier.

1.6 What is Claudia, and how does it fit?

Claudia is a Node.js library that eases the deployment of Node.js projects to AWS Lambda and API Gateway. It automates all the error-prone deployment and configuration tasks, and sets everything up the way JavaScript developers expect out of the box.

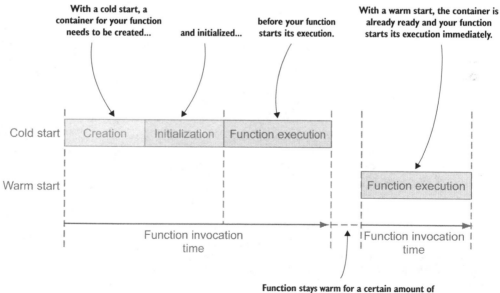

Figure 1.5 Cold start versus hot start for an AWS Lambda function

Claudia is built on top of the AWS SDK to make development easier. It is not a replacement for the AWS SDK or AWS CLI, but an extension that makes some common tasks, such as deployment and setting triggers, easy and fast.

Some of the core values of Claudia are

- Creating and updating the function with a single command (removing the need to manually zip your application and then upload the zip file via the AWS Dashboard UI)
- Not using boilerplate, which allows you to focus on your work and keep your preferred project setup
- Managing multiple versions easily
- Getting started in minutes with a very flat learning curve

Claudia acts as a command-line tool, and it allows you to create and update your functions from the terminal. But the Claudia ecosystem comes with two other useful Node.js libraries: Claudia API Builder allows you to create the API on API Gateway, and Claudia Bot Builder allows you to create chatbots for many messaging platforms.

As opposed to Claudia, which is a client-side tool never deployed to AWS, API Builder and Bot Builder are always deployed to AWS Lambda (see figure 1.6).

You can work with AWS Lambda and API Gateway without Claudia, either by using the AWS ecosystem directly or by using some of the alternatives.

The best-known alternatives are the following:

- Serverless Application Model (SAM), created by AWS, which allows you to create and deploy serverless applications via AWS CloudFormation. For more information, visit https://github.com/awslabs/serverless-application-model.
- Serverless Framework, which has a similar approach to SAM but also supports other platforms, such as Microsoft Azure. To learn more about it, visit https://serverless.com.

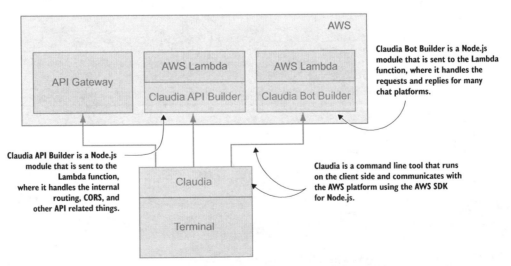

Figure 1.6   A visual representation of the relationships of Claudia, API Builder, and Bot Builder with the AWS platform

- Apex, another command-line tool that helps you deploy serverless applications but has support for more programming languages, such as Go. To learn more about it, visit http://apex.run.

NOTE   Everything written in this book can most likely be done with one of these Claudia alternatives.

You are probably wondering why we chose to use Claudia. The Claudia FAQs provide the best explanation:

- *Claudia is a deployment utility, not a framework.* It does not abstract away AWS services, but instead makes easier to get started with. As opposed to Serverless and Seneca, Claudia is not trying to change the way you structure or run projects. The optional API Builder, which simplifies web routing, is the only additional runtime dependency, and it's structured to be minimal and standalone. Microservice frameworks have many nice plugins and extensions that can help kick-start standard tasks, but Claudia intentionally focuses only on deployment. One of our key design goals is not to introduce too much magic, and let people structure the code the way they want to.
- *Claudia is focused on Node.js.* As opposed to Apex and similar deployers, Claudia has a much narrower scope. It works only for Node.js, but does so really well. Generic frameworks support more runtimes, but leave the developers to deal with language-specific issues. Because Claudia focuses on Node.js, it automatically installs templates to convert parameters and results into objects that JavaScript can consume easily, and makes things work the way JavaScript developers expect out of the box.

For more details, see https://github.com/claudiajs/claudia/blob/master/FAQ.md.

The idea of this book is to teach you how to think in a serverless way and how to easily develop and deploy quality serverless applications. Using the AWS ecosystem directly would involve a lot of distractions, such as learning how to interact with and configure different parts of the AWS platform. Rather than try to replace the AWS SDK, Claudia is built on top of it, and Claudia automates most common workflows with single commands.

Claudia favors code over configuration and as a result has almost no configuration at all. That makes it easier to learn, understand, and test. Writing a high-quality application requires proper testing; having lots of configuration doesn't mean you don't need to test it.

Claudia has a minimal set of commands that allow you to build serverless applications with a pleasant developer experience. Two of the main ideas behind Claudia are to minimize the magic and to be transparent in showing what happened when a command was invoked.

Despite its small API, Claudia enables you to develop many things: you can build serverless applications from scratch, migrate your current Express.js applications to serverless, and even build your own serverless chatbots and voice assistants.

1.7   When and where you should use it

Serverless architecture is not a silver bullet. It doesn't solve all problems, and it might not solve yours.

For example, if you are building an application that relies heavily on web sockets, serverless is not for you. AWS Lambda can work for up to 15 minutes, and it can't stay awake to listen for web socket messages after that.

If latency is critical for your application, even though waking containers is fast, there is always a price to pay for waking up them up. That price is a few dozen milliseconds, but for some applications, that can be too much.

The absence of configuration is one of the main selling points for serverless, but that advantage can be a huge setback for some application types. If you are building an application requiring a system-level configuration, you should consider the traditional approach instead. You can customize AWS Lambda to some extent; you can provide a static binary and use Node.js to invoke it, but that can be overkill in many cases.

Another important disadvantage is so-called vendor lock-in. Functions themselves are not a big problem because they are just standard Node.js functions, but if your full application is built as a serverless application, some services are not easy to migrate. However, this problem is a common one that is not related only to serverless, and it can be minimized with good application architecture.

That said, serverless has many more upsides than downsides, and the rest of this book shows you some of the good use cases.

Summary

- Serverless is abstracting servers away from software development.
- A serverless application differs from a traditional one in that serverless applications are event-driven, distributed, and autoscalable.
- There are a few choices for serverless infrastructure, and the most advanced one is Amazon's AWS Lambda.
- AWS Lambda is an event-driven, serverless computing platform that allows you to run functions written in Node.js, Python, C#, or Java and other JVM languages.
- AWS Lambda has certain limitations, such as execution time, which can be up to 15 minutes, and available memory, which can be up to 3 GB.
- The most complex parts of a serverless application in AWS are deployment and function configuration.
- Some tools and frameworks can help you deploy and configure your application more easily. The easiest one to use is Claudia, with its API Builder and Bot Builder.
- Claudia is a command-line tool that offers a minimal set of commands to allow you to build serverless applications with a pleasant developer experience.
- Serverless architecture is not a silver bullet, and there are some situations in which it isn't the best choice, such as for real-time applications with web sockets.

Building your first serverless API 2

This chapter covers

- Creating and deploying an API using Claudia
- How Claudia deploys an API to AWS
- How API Gateway works

The main goal of this chapter for you is to build your first serverless API with Claudia and deploy it to AWS Lambda and API Gateway. You'll also see the differences between a traditional and a serverless application structure and gain a better grasp of Claudia as you learn what Claudia is doing under the hood. To get the most from this chapter, you should understand the basic concepts of serverless described in chapter 1.

2.1 Assembling pizza ingredients: building the API

Your Aunt Maria is happy and grateful that you are going to help her get back on her feet. She even made you her famous pepperoni pizza! (Try not to be hungry at this moment!)

Aunt Maria already has a website, so you will build a back-end application—more precisely, an API—to enable her customers to preview and order pizzas. The API will be responsible for serving pizza and order information, as well as handling pizza orders. Later, Aunt Maria would also like to add a mobile application, which would consume your API services.

To start gently, the first API endpoints will handle some simple business logic and return static JSON objects. You can see the broad overview of your initial application structure in figure 2.1. The figure also shows the crude HTTP requests flow through your API.

Here is the list of features we cover for the initial API:

- Listing all pizzas
- Retrieving the pizza orders
- Creating a pizza order
- Updating a pizza order
- Canceling a pizza order

These features are all small and simple; therefore, you will implement them in a single Lambda function.

Even though you might feel that you should separate each feature into a separate function, for now it's simplest to put everything in the same Lambda, because the functions are tightly coupled. If you were to do inventory tracking as well, you would create that as a separate function from the start.

Each of the listed features will need to have a separate route to the corresponding handler within your function. You can implement the routing yourself, but Claudia has a tool to help you with that task: Claudia API Builder.

Claudia API Builder is an API tool that helps you handle all your incoming API Gateway requests and responses, as well as their configuration, context, and parameters, and enables you to have internal routing within your Lambda function. It has an Express-like endpoint syntax, so if you are familiar with Express, Claudia API Builder will be easy to use.

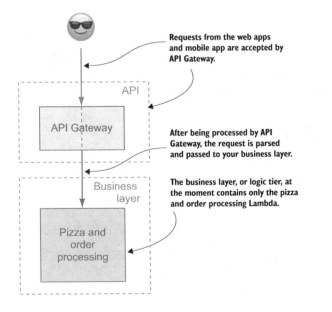

Figure 2.1   A broad overview of the Pizza API you will build in this chapter

Figure 2.2 shows a more detailed overview of how to route and handle the pizza and order features within your Lambda function by using Claudia API Builder. The figure shows that upon receiving requests from API Gateway, Claudia API Builder will redirect the requests to your defined routes and their corresponding handlers.

NOTE   At the time of this writing, you can use AWS API Gateway in two modes:

- With models and mapped templates for requests and responses
- With proxy pass-through

Claudia API Builder uses proxy pass-through to capture all the HTTP request details and structure them in a JS developer-friendly way.

To learn more about proxy pass-through and models and mapped templates, you can read the official documentation at http://docs.aws.amazon.com/apigateway/latest/developerguide/how-to-method-settings.html.

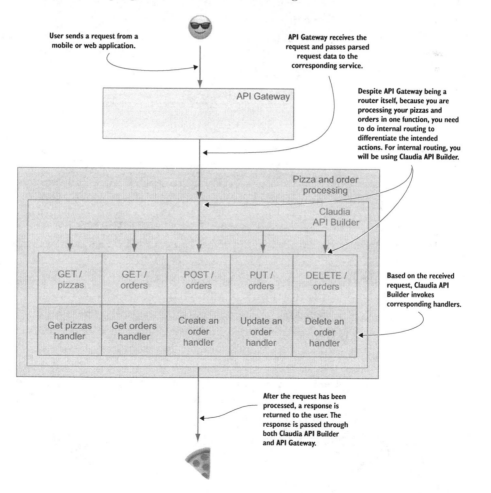

Figure 2.2   **A visual representation of the AWS Lambda function that handles pizza and order processing**

2.1.1   Which pizza can I GET?

As the first method of your Pizza API you will create a GET pizza service that lists all available pizzas. To do so, you will need to fulfill these prerequisites:

- Own an AWS account and properly set up the AWS credentials file
- Install Node.js and its package manager, NPM
- Install Claudia from NPM as a global dependency

If you're not familiar with these steps or are not sure whether you have completed them, jump to appendix A, which guides you through each setup process.

> **CODE EXAMPLES**   From this point onward, you'll see a lot of code examples. We highly recommend that you try them all, even if they feel familiar. You can use your favorite code editor unless stated otherwise.

Now that you're fully set up, you can start by creating an empty folder for your first serverless application. You can name your project folder as you like, but in this book the application folder's name is pizza-api. After you've created it, open your terminal, navigate to your new folder, and initialize the Node.js application. After your app is initialized, install the `claudia-api-builder` module from NPM as a package dependency, as explained in appendix A.

The next step is to create your application's entry point. Create a file named api.js inside your pizza-api folder, and open it with your favorite code editor.

> **ES6 SYNTAX FOR THE CODE EXAMPLES**   All the code examples in the book use the ES6/ES2015 syntax. If you are not familiar with ES6 features, such as arrow functions and/or template strings, see Manning's *ES6 in Motion*, by Wes Higbee, or the second edition of *Secrets of the JavaScript Ninja*, by John Resig.

To create an API route, you need an instance of Claudia API Builder, as it is a class and not a utility function. At the beginning of your api.js file, require and instantiate `claudia-api-builder`.

Now you're able to use Claudia API Builder's built-in router. To implement the GET /pizzas route, you need to use the get method of your Claudia API Builder instance. The get method receives two arguments: a route and a handler function. As the route parameter, pass the string /pizzas, and as the handler, pass an anonymous function.

The Claudia API Builder anonymous handler function has one major difference compared with Express.js. In Express.js, you have both the response and the request as callback function arguments, but Claudia API Builder's callback function has only the request. To send back the response, you just return the result.

Your GET /pizzas route should show a list of pizzas, so for now, you will return a static array of pizzas from Aunt Maria's pizzeria: Capricciosa, Quattro Formaggi, Napoletana, and Margherita.

Finally, you need to export your API instance, which Claudia API Builder is fitting into your Lambda function as middleware.

At this point, your code should look like the following listing.

Listing 2.1　The `GET /pizzas` handler of your Pizza API

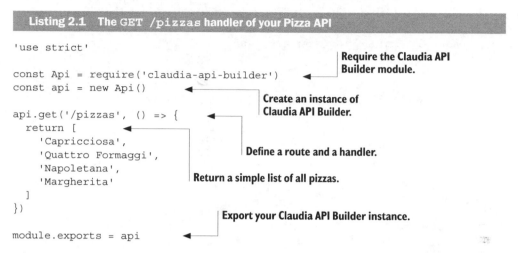

```
'use strict'

const Api = require('claudia-api-builder')
const api = new Api()

api.get('/pizzas', () => {
  return [
    'Capricciosa',
    'Quattro Formaggi',
    'Napoletana',
    'Margherita'
  ]
})

module.exports = api
```

Require the Claudia API Builder module.

Create an instance of Claudia API Builder.

Define a route and a handler.

Return a simple list of all pizzas.

Export your Claudia API Builder instance.

That's all it takes to make a simple serverless function. Before popping a champagne bottle in celebration, however, you should deploy your code to your Lambda function. To do so, jump back to your terminal and unleash the power of Claudia.

Because one of Claudia's main goals is single-command deployment, deploying your API takes just a simple `claudia create` command. This command requires only two options: the AWS region where you want your API to be deployed, and your application's entry point. The options are passed as flags, so to deploy your API, just execute the `claudia create` command with `--region` and `--api-module` flags, as shown in listing 2.2. The intricacies of the `claudia create` command are explained in more detail in section 2.2.

> **SHELL COMMANDS FOR WINDOWS USERS**　Some of the commands in the book are split into multiple lines for readability and annotation purposes. If you are a Windows user, you might need to join those commands into a single line and remove backslashes (\).

Listing 2.2　Deploying an API to AWS Lambda and API Gateway using Claudia

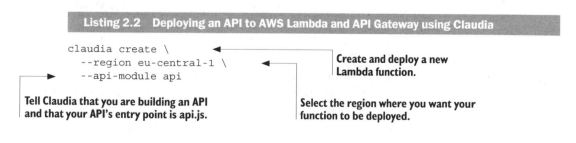

```
claudia create \
  --region eu-central-1 \
  --api-module api
```

Create and deploy a new Lambda function.

Tell Claudia that you are building an API and that your API's entry point is api.js.

Select the region where you want your function to be deployed.

For your region, choose the closest one to your users to minimize latency. The closest region to Aunt Maria's pizzeria is in Frankfurt, Germany, and it's called `eu-central-1`. You can see all the available regions in the official AWS documentation: http://docs .aws.amazon.com/general/latest/gr/rande.html#lambda_region.

Your api.js file is your API's entry point. Claudia automatically appends the .js extension, so just type `api` as your application's entry point.

> **NOTE**   The name and location of your entry point are up to you; you just need to provide a correct path to the entry point in the `claudia create` command. For example, if you name it index.js and put it in the src folder, the flag in the Claudia command should be `--api-module src/index`.

After a minute or so, Claudia will successfully deploy your API. You'll see a response similar to listing 2.3. The command response has useful information about your Lambda function and your API, such as the base URL of your API, the Lambda function's name, and the region.

> **DEPLOYMENT ISSUES**   If you encounter deployment issues, such as a credentials error, make sure you've properly set up everything as described in appendix A.

Listing 2.3   The `claudia create` command response

```
{
  "lambda": {
    "role": "pizza-api-executor",          ◄──     Lambda function information
    "name": "pizza-api",
    "region": "eu-central-1"
  },                                               API information
  "api": {                          ◄──
    "id": "g8fhlgccof",
    "module": "api",                                              Your API's base URL
    "url": "https://whpcvzntil.execute-api.eu-central-1.amazonaws.com/latest"     ◄──
  }
}
```

During the deployment, Claudia created a claudia.json file in the root of your project along with some similar information, but without your base API URL. This file is for Claudia to relate your code to a certain Lambda function and API Gateway instance. The file is intended for Claudia only; don't change it by hand.

Now it's time to "taste" your API. You can try it directly from your favorite browser. Just visit the base URL from your `claudia create` response, remembering to append your route to the base URL. It should look similar to https://whpcvzntil.execute-api .eu-central-1.amazonaws.com/latest/pizzas. When you open your modified base URL link in your browser, you should see the following:

```
["Capricciosa","Quattro Formaggi","Napoletana","Margherita"]
```

URLS FOR THE EXAMPLES FROM THE BOOK   Instead of latest, each example from the book will contain different versions in the following format: chapterX_Y, where X is the number of the chapter and Y is the number of the example in that chapter. We did this so you can run the examples simply by copying the URL from the book. When you run the code by yourself, the output URL will contain latest as a version, instead of chapterX_Y that you'll see in the book.

For example, the first example can be accessed at the following URL: https://whp-cvzntil.execute-api.eu-central-1.amazonaws.com/chapter2_1/pizzas.

Congratulations—you just built a serverless API with Claudia! If this was your first time, you should be proud of yourself, and this is a good time to pause.

2.1.2   *Structuring your API*

Before rushing to add more features, you should always try to spend a few minutes rethinking your API structure and organization. Adding all the route processors directly into the main file makes it difficult to understand and maintain, so you should ideally split handlers from routing/wiring. Smaller code files are easier to understand and work with than with one monster file.

Considering application organization, at the time of this writing there aren't any specific best practices. Also, Claudia gives you complete freedom on that topic. For your Pizza API, because the part for handling pizzas and orders isn't going to be huge, you can move all route handlers to a separate folder and keep only the routes within your

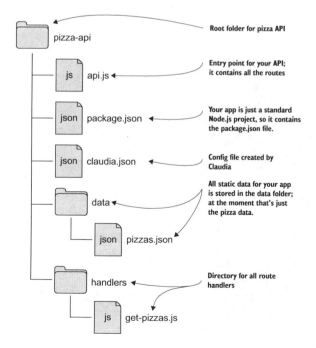

Figure 2.3   The file structure of the Pizza API project

api.js file. After that, because the pizza list should have more pizza attributes than just pizza names, you should move it to a separate file. You can even go a step further and create a folder for the data, as you did for the pizza list we mentioned earlier. After you apply these recommendations, your code structure should look similar to figure 2.3.

The first modification is moving the list of pizzas to a separate file and extending the list with additional information, such as pizza IDs and ingredients. To do so, create a folder in the root of your Pizza API project, and name it data. Then create a file in your new folder, and name it pizzas.json. Add the content from the following listing to the new file.

Listing 2.4   JSON containing the pizza info

Each pizza object has a pizza ID, name, and ingredients.

```
[
    {                        This JSON file is an array of pizza objects.
      "id": 1,
      "name": "Capricciosa",
      "ingredients": [
        "tomato sauce", "mozzarella", "mushrooms", "ham", "olives"
      ]
    },
    {
      "id": 2,
      "name": "Quattro Formaggi",
      "ingredients": [
        "tomato sauce", "mozzarella", "parmesan cheese", "blue cheese", "goat
       cheese"
      ]
    },
    {
      "id": 3,
      "name": "Napoletana",
      "ingredients": [
        "tomato sauce", "anchovies", "olives", "capers"
      ]
    },
    {
      "id": 4,
      "name": "Margherita",
      "ingredients": [
        "tomato sauce", "mozzarella"
      ]
    }
]
```

Your next step is to move the getPizzas handler to a separate file. Create a folder called handlers in your project root, and create a get-pizzas.js file inside it.

In your new get-pizzas.js file will be the getPizzas handler, which returns the list of pizzas from listing 2.4. First, you need to import the pizza list from the JSON file you created. Second, you need to create a getPizzas handler function and export it so that you can require it from your entry file. Then, instead of just returning the pizza list, go a step further and return just one pizza if a pizza ID was passed as a parameter to your getPizzas handler. To return just one pizza, you can use the Array.find method, which searches for a pizza by the pizza ID from your pizza list. If it finds a pizza, return it as a handler result. If there aren't any pizzas with that ID, have your application throw an error.

The updated code of your new pizza handler should look similar to the next listing.

Listing 2.5   Your getPizzas handler with a pizza ID filter in a separate file

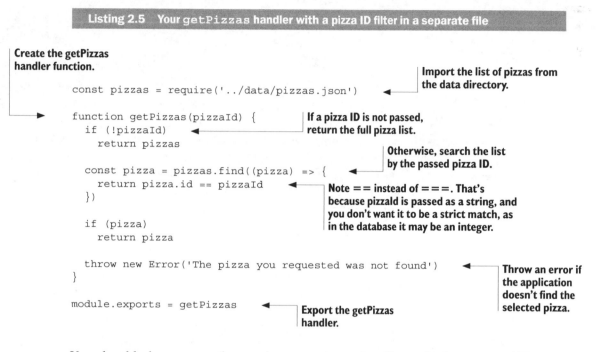

Create the getPizzas handler function.

Import the list of pizzas from the data directory.

```
const pizzas = require('../data/pizzas.json')

function getPizzas(pizzaId) {
  if (!pizzaId)
    return pizzas

  const pizza = pizzas.find((pizza) => {
    return pizza.id == pizzaId
  })

  if (pizza)
    return pizza

  throw new Error('The pizza you requested was not found')
}

module.exports = getPizzas
```

If a pizza ID is not passed, return the full pizza list.

Otherwise, search the list by the passed pizza ID.

Note == instead of ===. That's because pizzaId is passed as a string, and you don't want it to be a strict match, as in the database it may be an integer.

Throw an error if the application doesn't find the selected pizza.

Export the getPizzas handler.

You should also remove the previous getPizzas handler code from your API entry point file, api.js. Delete everything between importing Claudia API Builder and the end, where you're exporting your Claudia API Builder instance.

After the line where you're importing Claudia API Builder, import the new get-pizzas handler from your handlers folder:

```
const getPizzas = require('./handlers/get-pizzas')
```

> **NOTE** You should also create a handler for the GET route for the root path, /, which should return a static message to the user. Though this is optional, we highly recommend it. Your API is more user-friendly when it returns some friendly message instead of an error when someone is querying just your API's base URL.

Next you should add the route for getting the pizza list, but this time, you'll use the get-pizzas handler you created for the route handling. You should import the file at the beginning of your api.js entry file. If you remember, your get-pizzas handler can also filter pizzas by ID, so you should add another route that returns a single pizza. Write that route so that it accepts a GET request for the /pizzas/{id} url. The /{id} part is the dynamic route parameter that tells your handler which pizza ID the user requested. Like Express.js, Claudia API Builder supports dynamic route parameters, but it uses a different syntax, which is why it has /{id} instead of /:id. The dynamic path parameters are available in the request.pathParams object. Finally, if your handler hasn't found the pizza you wanted, return a 404 error:

```
api.get('/pizzas/{id}', (request) => {
  return getPizzas(request.pathParams.id)
}, {
  error: 404
})
```

By default, API Gateway returns HTTP status 200 for all requests. Claudia API Builder helps you by setting some sane defaults, such as status 500 for errors, so your client application can handle request errors in promise catch blocks.

To customize the error status, you can pass a third parameter to the api.get function. For example, in your get /pizza/{id} function handler, besides the path and your handler function, you can pass an object with custom headers and statuses. To set the status error to 404, pass an object with the error: 404 value in it.

You can see how your fully updated api.js file should look in the following listing.

Listing 2.6   The updated api.js

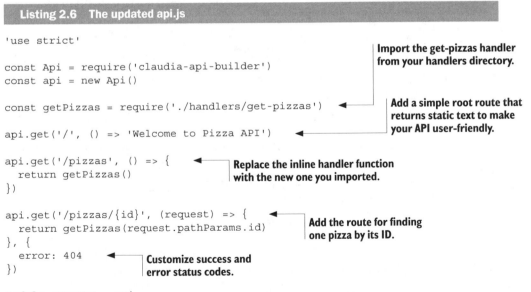

```
'use strict'

const Api = require('claudia-api-builder')
const api = new Api()

const getPizzas = require('./handlers/get-pizzas')        ◄──  Import the get-pizzas handler
                                                               from your handlers directory.

api.get('/', () => 'Welcome to Pizza API')                ◄──  Add a simple root route that
                                                               returns static text to make
                                                               your API user-friendly.

api.get('/pizzas', () => {          ◄──  Replace the inline handler function
  return getPizzas()                      with the new one you imported.
})

api.get('/pizzas/{id}', (request) => {     ◄──  Add the route for finding
  return getPizzas(request.pathParams.id)        one pizza by its ID.
}, {
  error: 404          ◄──  Customize success and
})                         error status codes.

module.exports = api
```

Now deploy your API again. To update your existing Lambda function along with its API Gateway routes, run the Claudia update command from your terminal:

```
claudia update
```

NOTE Because of the claudia.json file, the `claudia update` command knows exactly which Lambda function the files are deployed to. The command can be customized with a `--config` flag. For more information, see the official documentation at https://github.com/claudiajs/claudia/blob/master/docs/update.md.

After a minute or so, you should see a response similar to the one in listing 2.7. After processing the command and redeploying your application, Claudia will print out some useful information about your Lambda function and your API in the terminal. That information includes the function name, Node.js runtime, timeout, function memory size, and base URL of your API.

Listing 2.7 **The printed information after running the** `claudia update` **command**

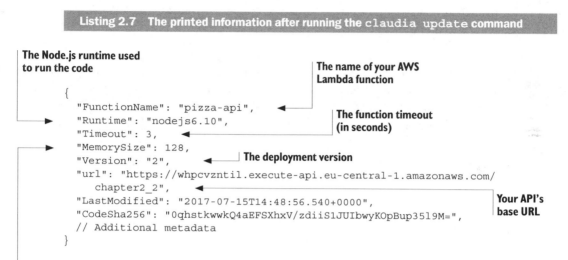

The Node.js runtime used to run the code

The name of your AWS Lambda function

The function timeout (in seconds)

```
{
    "FunctionName": "pizza-api",
    "Runtime": "nodejs6.10",
    "Timeout": 3,
    "MemorySize": 128,
    "Version": "2",
    "url": "https://whpcvzntil.execute-api.eu-central-1.amazonaws.com/
        chapter2_2",
    "LastModified": "2017-07-15T14:48:56.540+0000",
    "CodeSha256": "0qhstkwwkQ4aEFSXhxV/zdiiS1JUIbwyKOpBup3519M=",
    // Additional metadata
}
```

The deployment version

Your API's base URL

The maximum amount of memory your function can use

If you open this route link again from your browser (which should look similar to https://whpcvzntil.execute-api.eu-central-1.amazonaws.com/chapter2_2/pizzas), you see the array of all pizza objects from your data/pizza.js file.

When you open the other route link (something similar to https://whpcvzntil.execute-api.eu-central-1.amazonaws.com/chapter2_2/pizzas/1), you see only the first pizza. This response should look something like this:

```
{"id":1,"name":"Capricciosa","ingredients":["tomato
    sauce","mozzarella","mushrooms","ham","olives"]}
```

To test whether your API is working as expected, you should also try to get a pizza that doesn't exist. Visit your API URL with a nonexistent pizza ID, such as this one: https://whpcvzntil.execute-api.eu-central-1.amazonaws.com/chapter2_2/pizzas/42. In this case, the response should look similar to this:

```
{"errorMessage" : "The pizza you requested wasn't found"}
```

Congratulations—your Pizza API is now capable of showing a list of pizzas to Aunt Maria's customers! This will make your Aunt Maria happy, but your API is not done yet. You need to implement the core feature of the API: creating a pizza order.

2.1.3   POSTing an order

Being able to create a pizza order via your API is important to Aunt Maria. Even though she is not as technically proficient as you are, she's aware that it will speed up pizza ordering and help her to quickly serve all the customers from her whole neighborhood, or even the whole town.

> **NOTE**   In this example, you will learn about basic application structure, so to simplify things you will not store the orders anywhere. You will work with persistent storage in chapter 3.

To implement pizza order creation, you need to have a "create pizza order" route and a "create an order" handler, which means that you will need to create a new file in the handlers folder in your Pizza API project. As always, try to create simple and readable filenames. In this case, a good name for your handler file would be create-order.js.

First, create the new handler file, and open it in your favorite code editor. Next, create the `createOrder` function, and export it at the end of the file. Your handler function needs to accept some order data or an `order` object. At this moment, this `order` object should have only two attributes: the ID of the pizza a customer ordered and the customer address where the pizza should be delivered.

As a first step, check whether those two values have been passed within the `order` object. If not, throw an error.

The following part should implement storing the order to the database, but at the moment, you will just return an empty object if the `order` object is valid. You could store the object in a file, but a Lambda function can be deployed on multiple containers, and you have no control over that, so it's important not to rely on the local state. In the next chapter, you will learn how to connect your serverless function to a database and actually save an order.

Your create-order.js file should look like the one in the next listing.

Listing 2.8   Creating a pizza order handler

If the order object doesn't contain a pizzaId or a customer address, **throw an error.**

The createOrder handler function accepts the order object.

```
function createOrder(order) {
   if (!order || !order.pizzaId || !order.address)
     throw new Error('To order pizza please provide pizza type and address
       where pizza should be delivered')

   return {}          Otherwise, return an empty object.
}

module.exports = createOrder          Export the handler function.
```

Now that you have the handler for creating an order, it's time to create a route—but this one should accept POST requests. To do that, you'll need to go back to your api.js file. Like api.get, Claudia API Builder has an api.post method that receives three parameters: path, handler function, and options.

NOTE Besides GET, Claudia API Builder supports POST, PUT, and DELETE as HTTP verbs.

For the route path, you should write /orders, as your app is creating a new order. As the route handler function, import the create-order.js file you just made in your handlers folder. Finally, for the options parameter, pass customized statuses for both success and error: 201 and 400, respectively. Use the success attribute to add a custom status for success.

The POST request body is automatically parsed for you and available in the request .body attribute, which means that you don't need to use any additional middleware to parse the received data, such as the Express.js body_parser.

Parsing POST request body

The body of the POST request is automatically parsed by API Gateway. Claudia checks the body and normalizes it. For example, if the content type of the request is application/json, Claudia converts the empty body to an empty JSON object.

After you add the new route, your api.js file should look like the following listing.

Listing 2.9 Main API file updated with the new routes

```
'use strict'

const Api = require('claudia-api-builder')
const api = new Api()

const getPizzas = require('./handlers/get-pizzas')
const createOrder = require('./handlers/create-order')

api.get('/', () => 'Welcome to Pizza API')

api.get('/pizzas', () => {
  return getPizzas()
})

api.get('/pizzas/{id}', (request) => {
  return getPizzas(request.pathParams.id)
}, {
  error: 404
})

api.post('/orders', (request) => {
  return createOrder(request.body)
}, {
```

Import the create-order handler from the handlers directory.

Add the POST /orders route to create an order and pass the request.body to the handler.

**Return the status "400 Bad Request"
in case of an error.**

**Return the status "20I Created"
for a successful request.**

```
        success: 201,
        error: 400
})
```

```
module.exports = api
```

Again, deploy the API by running the `claudia update` command.

Trying out a POST request can be a bit trickier than testing a GET. You can't test it by opening the route URL in the browser. Hence, for the POST routes, you should use one of the free HTTP testing tools, such as `curl` or Postman.

> **NOTE**   From now on, you will see `curl` commands for all examples where you should try out your API endpoints. They aren't obligatory; you are free to use any tool you prefer.

---

curl and Postman

`curl` is a tool used in command lines or scripts to transfer data. It is also used in cars, television sets, routers, printers, audio equipment, mobile phones, tablets, set-top boxes, and media players, and is the internet transfer backbone for thousands of software applications affecting billions of humans daily. `curl` is designed to work without user interaction.

Postman is an application with a graphical user interface (GUI) that can also help you test your APIs. It can also speed up development, as you can build API requests and documentation through testing. It is available as an application for Mac, Windows, and Linux and as a Chrome plug-in.

You are going to test your POST /orders endpoint by using a `curl` command. In this command, you'll send an empty request body so you can check the validation error. Besides the POST body, you need to specify the method, provide a header to tell your API you are sending a JSON request, and specify the full URL you want to send the request to.

> **NOTE**   By default, `curl` doesn't print out the response HTTP status code. To check if your API is returning the correct status, use the `-w` flag and append the HTTP status after the API response.

You can see the command format in the following listing. This command has an empty body so you can test the error response.

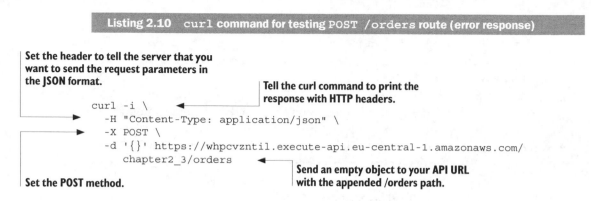

After you run the `curl` command from listing 2.10 in your terminal, the response should look like this, with a few additional headers:

```
HTTP/1.1 400 Bad Request
Content-Type: application/json
Content-Length: 104
Date: Mon, 25 Sep 2017 06:53:36 GMT
```

```
{"errorMessage":"To order pizza please provide pizza type and address where
    pizza should be delivered"}
```

Now that you've verified the returned error when no order data is passed, you should also test a successful response. To do so, run a similar `curl` command from your terminal; change only the request body, as now it needs to contain a pizza ID and an address. The following listing shows the updated `curl` command. This command has a valid body so you can test the successful response.

Listing 2.11   `curl` **command for testing the** POST /orders **route (successful response)**

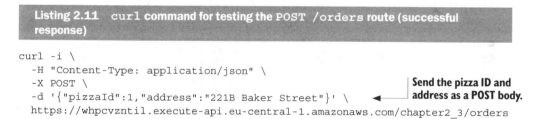

This command returns the following:

```
HTTP/1.1 201 Created
Content-Type: application/json
Content-Length: 2
Date: Mon, 25 Sep 2017 06:53:36 GMT
```

```
{}
```

This confirms that your API works correctly.

Now that you've learned the serverless API basics, it's time to take a look at what Claudia did when you ran the `claudia create` command.

2.2 *How Claudia deploys your API*

The previous examples demonstrated one of the main ideas of Claudia: single-command application deployment. There is no magic behind the tool, so every command can be explained easily.

Figure 2.4 represents the flow of events that happened when you ran the `claudia create` command. This simplified diagram is focused on the most important parts of the process for easier understanding. Also, some of the events described in this flow can be skipped or modified if you provide some flags with the `create` command. For example, Claudia can skip the first step and copy your code with all the local dependencies if you provide the flag `--use-local-dependencies`. For the full list of options, see https://github.com/claudiajs/claudia/blob/master/docs/create.md.

When you run the `claudia create` command, the first thing that Claudia does is zip your code without the dependencies and hidden files, using the `npm pack` command. Then it creates a copy of your project in a temporary folder in your system. This action ensures a clean and reproducible release, always starting from a well-known point and preventing problems caused by potential local dependencies. During this step, Claudia ignores your node_modules folder and all files ignored by Git or NPM. It also installs your production and optional dependencies using the `npm install --production` command.

Because the Lambda function requires the code with all its dependencies to be uploaded as a zip file, Claudia installs all production and optional NPM dependencies before compressing your project into a zip file.

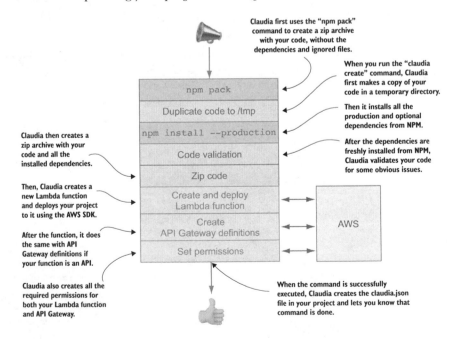

Figure 2.4   The `claudia create` **process**

Also, because debugging Lambda functions isn't straightforward, as you will see in chapter 5, Claudia also verifies that your project doesn't have any obvious issues, such as typos or your application invoking an undefined module. Take this step with a grain of salt, because it will do just a shallow validation. If you have a typo or an undefined function or module invocation inside the function or handler body, this step won't catch it.

As the next step, Claudia creates a zip file with your code with all the dependencies installed in the first step.

The last three steps in figure 2.4 aren't executed sequentially, but in parallel.

When the zip file is created, Claudia invokes the AWS API to create your Lambda function and uploads the archive. The interaction with the AWS platform is done through the AWS SDK module for Node.js. Before the code is uploaded, Claudia creates a new IAM user and assigns to the IAM user certain permissions to allow it to interact with AWS Lambda and API Gateway.

AWS IAM users, roles, and permissions

AWS Identity and Access Management (IAM) enables you to securely control access to AWS services and resources for your users. Using IAM, you can create and manage AWS users and groups, as well as use permissions to allow or deny any user or group access to your AWS resources.

A deeper explanation of IAM is beyond the scope of this book, but we highly recommend that you read more about it before progressing to the next few chapters. You can start with the official documentation: https://aws.amazon.com/iam/.

After your Lambda function is fully set up, Claudia sets up an API Gateway instance to it, defines all the routes, and sets their required permissions.

The `claudia update` command flow is almost identical to that of the `claudia create` command, but without some steps that have already been completed, such as role creation and permissions setup.

If you want to dive even deeper into Claudia and its commands, you can see its source code here: https://github.com/claudiajs/claudia.

Now that you know how Claudia works under the hood, the last piece of the API puzzle is understanding how API Gateway does the routing for your Pizza API.

2.3 *Traffic control: How API Gateway works*

In chapter 1 you learned that users can't interact with AWS Lambda outside of the AWS platform unless a trigger wakes up the function. One of Lambda's most important triggers is API Gateway.

As you can see in figure 2.5, API Gateway acts like a router or a traffic controller. It accepts HTTP requests (such as Pizza API requests from your web or mobile application), parses them to a common format, and routes them to one of your connected AWS services.

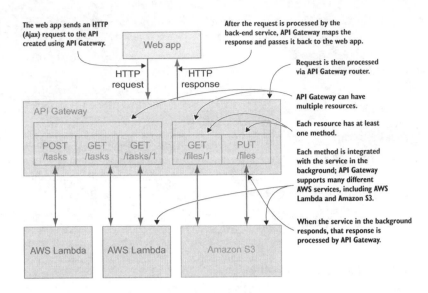

The web app sends an HTTP (Ajax) request to the API created using API Gateway.

After the request is processed by the back-end service, API Gateway maps the response and passes it back to the web app.

Web app

HTTP request   HTTP response

Request is then processed via API Gateway router.

API Gateway

API Gateway can have multiple resources.

Each resource has at least one method.

POST /tasks   GET /tasks   GET /tasks/1   GET /files/1   PUT /files

Each method is integrated with the service in the background; API Gateway supports many different AWS services, including AWS Lambda and Amazon S3.

When the service in the background responds, that response is processed by API Gateway.

AWS Lambda   AWS Lambda   Amazon S3

Figure 2.5   API Gateway routes requests to your AWS services.

API Gateway can be integrated with many AWS services, including AWS Lambda and Amazon S3. Each API on API Gateway can be connected to multiple services. For example, certain routes can invoke Lambda functions, whereas others can interact with some other service.

API Gateway offers another approach to HTTP request routing, called a *proxy router*. Instead of creating each route, a proxy router sends all requests to a single AWS Lambda function. This approach can be useful when you are creating a small API or when you want to speed up your deployment, because creating and updating multiple routes on API Gateway can take a few minutes, depending on your internet connection speed and the number of routes.

2.4   *When a serverless API is not the solution*

Even though we've just scratched the surface, you can already see how easy it is to build serverless APIs with Claudia.js and Claudia API Builder. Serverless APIs can be powerful and incredibly scalable, but in certain situations traditional APIs are a much better solution, such as the following:

- When request time and latency are critical. You can't guarantee minimal latency with serverless applications.
- When you need to guarantee a certain level of availability. In most cases, AWS will provide a pretty good level of availability, but sometimes that's not enough.
- When your application requires intensive and complex computing.
- When your API requires compliance with a specific standard. AWS Lambda and API Gateway might not be flexible enough.

2.5   *Taste it!*

After going through each chapter, have a "do it yourself" session. Most of the chapters give you a certain task, and you should try to implement it yourself. We provide a few useful hints, and the solutions are in the next section.

2.5.1   *Exercise*

In this chapter, you implemented the GET /pizzas and POST /orders API routes. To make your API more useful, there are two routes left: PUT /orders and DELETE / orders.

For the first exercise, do the following:

1 Create a handler for updating a pizza order, and add an API route for it.
2 Create a handler for deleting a pizza order, and add an API route for it.

In case you need some hints, here are a few:

- To add a PUT route, use the api.put method provided by Claudia API Builder.
- To add a DELETE route, use the api.delete method provided by Claudia API Builder.
- Both methods accept three arguments: a route path, a handler function, and an options object.
- Both paths require a dynamic parameter: an order ID.
- The updateOrder handler also requires a body with the new order details.
- Because you don't have the database yet, just return an empty object or a simple text message as a response.

When you finish the exercise, the file structure of your Pizza API should look like the one in figure 2.6.

If this exercise is too easy for you, and you want an additional challenge, try to add an API route for listing the pizza orders. There's no solution for this challenge in the next section, but that handler exists in the source code of Pizza API included with this book, so feel free to check the source and compare the solutions.

2.5.2   *Solution*

We hope you managed to finish the exercise on your own. Here are our solutions, so you can compare.

The first part of the exercise was to create a handler to update an order. To begin, you needed to create a file in your handlers folder, and name it update-order.js. In the file, you needed to create and export an updateOrder function that accepts an ID and the updated order details. The function should throw an error if the order ID or the updated order details object is not provided, or return a success message if successful. The code should look like the following listing.

Listing 2.12   Updating an order handler

If the ID or updates object is not passed,
throw an error.

A handler function accepts the
order ID and the order updates.

```
function updateOrder(id, updates) {
  if (!id || !updates)
    throw new Error('Order ID and updates object are required for updating
      the order')
  return {
    message: `Order ${id} was successfully updated`
  }
}

module.exports = updateOrder
```

Otherwise, return a
success message.

Export the handler function.

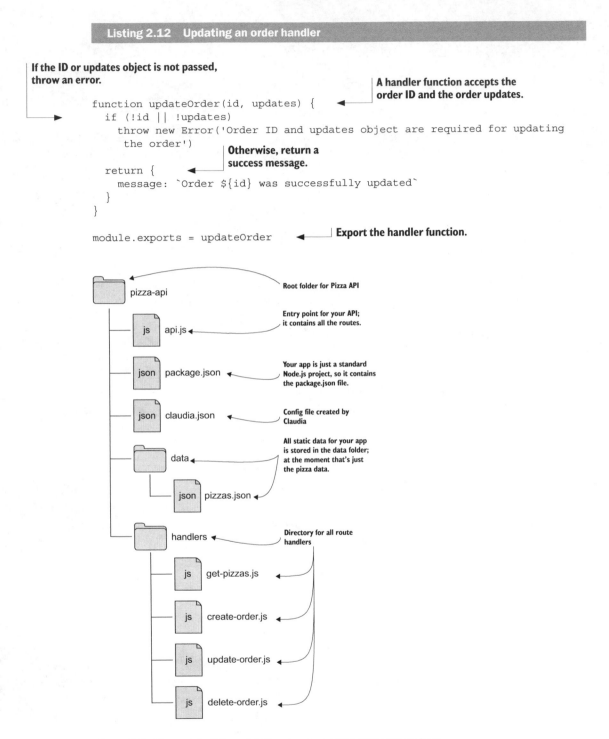

Root folder for Pizza API

Entry point for your API;
it contains all the routes.

Your app is just a standard
Node.js project, so it contains
the package.json file.

Config file created by
Claudia

All static data for your app
is stored in the data folder;
at the moment that's just
the pizza data.

Directory for all route
handlers

Figure 2.6   The updated file and folder structure of the Pizza API project

After you created the `updateOrder` function, you should have done the same for the handler to delete an order. First, you needed to create the delete-order.js file in your handlers folder. Then you should have created an exported `deleteOrder` function in the file. That function should accept an order ID. If the order ID isn't passed, the handler should throw an error; otherwise, it should return an empty object. The code should look like the following listing.

Listing 2.13 Deleting an order handler

If an ID is not passed, throw an error.

A handler function accepts the order ID.

```
function deleteOrder(id) {
  if (!id)
    throw new Error('Order ID is required for deleting the order')

  return {}
}

module.exports = deleteOrder
```

Otherwise, return an empty object.

Export the handler function.

Now, with the handlers implemented, your next step is to import them to api.js and create routes for updating and deleting the orders.

To update an order, use the `api.put` method, and use the `/orders/{id}` URL as the path; then set the handler function and the options with 400 as the status code for errors. You can't just pass the handler function you created in the previous step because it doesn't accept the full request object; instead, pass an anonymous function that invokes the `updateOrder` handler with an order ID from the received request body. The `DELETE /orders` route is the same except for two differences: it uses the `api.delete` method, and it doesn't pass the request body to the `deleteOrder` handler function.

After this step, your api.js file should look like the following listing.

Listing 2.14 The Pizza API with `PUT /orders` and `DELETE /orders` routes

```
'use strict'

const Api = require('claudia-api-builder')
const api = new Api()

const getPizzas = require('./handlers/get-pizzas')
const createOrder = require('./handlers/create-order')
const updateOrder = require('./handlers/update-order')
const deleteOrder = require('./handlers/delete-order')

// Define routes
api.get('/', () => 'Welcome to Pizza API')

api.get('/pizzas', () => {
  return getPizzas()
})
api.get('/pizzas/{id}', (request) => {
```

Import the update-order handler from the handlers directory.

Import the delete-order handler from the handlers directory.

```
    return getPizzas(request.pathParams.id)
}, {
  error: 404
})

api.post('/orders', (request) => {
  return createOrder(request.body)
}, {
  success: 201,
  error: 400
})
api.put('/orders/{id}', (request) => {
  return updateOrder(request.pathParams.id, request.body)
}, {
  error: 400
})
api.delete('/orders/{id}', (request) => {
  return deleteOrder(request.pathParams.id)
}, {
  error: 400
})

module.exports = api
```

Add a route for PUT /orders and connect a handler.

Add a route for DELETE /orders and connect a handler.

Both routes return status 400 in case of an error.

As always, open your terminal, navigate to your pizza-api folder, and run the `claudia update` command from it to update your Lambda function and API Gateway definition.

When Claudia updates your Pizza API, you can use the `curl` commands from listings 2.15 and 2.16 to test your new API endpoints. These commands are almost the same as the command you used for the POST request, with the following differences:

- The HTTP method is different: You use PUT for updating and DELETE for deleting the order.
- Updating the order needs to pass the body with the updates.
- Deleting the order doesn't require the request body.

These commands each have a valid body and should return a successful response.

Listing 2.15   `curl` command for testing PUT `/orders/{id}` route

Add extra pepperoni to your order.

Send the PUT request.

```
curl -i \
  -H "Content-Type: application/json" \
  -X PUT \
  -d '{"pizzaId":2}' \
  https://whpcvzntil.execute-api.eu-central-1.amazonaws.com/chapter2_4/
      orders/42
```

Add an order ID as a path parameter.

> **Listing 2.16 `curl` command for testing `DELETE` `/orders/{id}` route**

```
curl -i \
  -H "Content-Type: application/json" \
  -X DELETE \
  https://whpcvzntil.execute-api.eu-central-1.amazonaws.com/chapter2_4/
    orders/42
```

Provide an order ID as the URL parameter.

Send the DELETE request.

When you execute the commands in your terminal, they return the responses `{"message":"Order 42 was successfully updated"}` and `{}`, respectively, both with status 200.

Summary

- Claudia enables you to deploy your API to API Gateway and AWS Lambda in a single command.
- Updating your API takes a single Claudia command, too.
- A serverless API on AWS Lambda doesn't require any specific folder structure or organization.
- API Gateway acts as a router and can invoke various services.
- If you want to bundle more routes into a single AWS Lambda function, you need internal routing.
- Claudia API Builder has a router identical to the routers in other popular Node.js web API libraries.
- Serverless APIs are powerful, but they are not a silver bullet, so depending on your case, a traditional API might work better.

Asynchronous work is easy, we Promise()

This chapter covers

- Handling asynchronous operations with Claudia

- The basics of JavaScript promises

- Connecting to DynamoDB from Claudia and AWS Lambda

In the previous chapter, you created a simple API for handling pizza information and orders. You also learned that unlike with a traditional Node.js server, AWS Lambda state is lost between subsequent invocations. Therefore, a database or an external service is required to store Aunt Maria's pizza orders or any other data you want to keep.

As Node.js executes asynchronously, you will first learn how serverless affects asynchronous communication: how it works with Claudia, and, more importantly, the recommended way of developing your serverless applications. As you grasp these concepts, you will see how easy it is to connect AWS Lambda to an external service, and you will learn how to use it to store your pizza orders by using AWS DynamoDB.

Because our brains aren't good at asynchronous reading, and books are written in a synchronous manner, let's go step by step.

3.1   *Storing the orders*

Ring, ring! You just had a short phone call with Aunt Maria. She is impressed by your speed, though she still can't use your application, as you aren't storing any of her pizza orders. She still needs to use the old pen-and-paper method. To complete the basic version of your Pizza API, you need to store your orders somewhere.

Before starting development, you should always have an idea of which details you want to store. In your case, the most elementary pizza order is defined by the selected pizza, the delivery address, and the order status. For clarity, this kind of information is usually drawn as a diagram. So as a small exercise, take a minute to try to draw it yourself.

Your diagram should be similar to figure 3.1.

Now that you have an idea of what to store, let's see how you should structure it for the database. As you previously learned, you can't rely on AWS Lambda to store state, which means that storing order information in your Lambda filesystem is off the table.

In a traditional Node.js application, you would use some popular database, such as MongoDB, MySQL, or PostgreSQL. In the serverless world, each of the serverless providers has a different combination of data storage systems. AWS doesn't have an out-of-the-box solution for any of those databases.

As the easiest alternative, you can use Amazon DynamoDB, a popular NoSQL database that can be connected to AWS Lambda easily.

> **NOTE**   AWS Lambda is not limited to DynamoDB, and you can use it with other databases, but that's beyond the scope of this book.

> ### So what is DynamoDB?
> DynamoDB is a fully managed, proprietary NoSQL database service offered by Amazon as part of its AWS portfolio. DynamoDB exposes a similar data model to and derives its name from Dynamo, a highly available key-value structured storage system with a different underlying implementation.

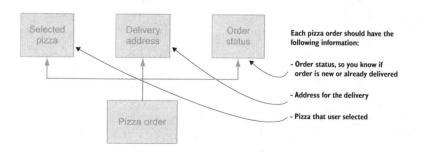

Figure 3.1   The most basic pizza order

To put it simply, DynamoDB is just a database building block for serverless applications. DynamoDB is to NoSQL databases what AWS Lambda is to computing functions: a fully managed, autoscaled, and relatively cheap cloud database solution.

DynamoDB stores the data in its data tables. A data table represents a collection of data. Each table contains multiple items. An item represents a single concept described by a group of attributes. You can think of an item as a JSON object, because it has the following similar characteristics:

- Its keys are unique.
- It doesn't limit how many attributes you can have.
- Values can be different types of data, including numbers, strings, and objects.

The table is just the storage representation of the model you previously defined, as shown in figure 3.1.

Now you need to transform your previously defined model to the structure your database understands: a database table. While you are doing that, keep in mind that DynamoDB is almost schemaless, which means that you need to define only your primary key and can add everything else later. As a first step, you'll design a minimum viable table for your orders.

Ready?

As in any other database, you want to store each order as one item in the database table. For your pizza order storage, you'll use a single DynamoDB table, which will be a collection of your orders. You want to receive your orders via an API and store them to the DynamoDB table. Each order can be described by a set of its characteristics:

- Unique order ID
- Pizza selection
- Delivery address
- Order status

You can use those characteristics as keys in your table. Your orders table should look like table 3.1.

Table 3.1   The structure of an orders table in DynamoDB

Order ID	Order status	Pizza	Address
1	pending	Capricciosa	221B Baker Street
2	pending	Napoletana	29 Acacia Road

The next step is to create your table—let's name it `pizza-orders`. As with most things in AWS, you can do this several ways; our preferred method is to use the AWS CLI. To create a table for the orders, you can use the `aws dynamodb create-table` command, as shown in listing 3.1.

You need to supply a few required parameters when creating the table. First, you need to define your table name; in your case, it will be `pizza-orders`. Then you need to define your attributes. As we mentioned, DynamoDB requires only primary key definition, so you can define only the `orderId` attribute and tell DynamoDB that it will be of type string. You also need to tell DynamoDB that `orderId` will be your primary key (or, in DynamoDB's world, *hash key*).

After that, you need to define the provisioned throughput, which tells DynamoDB what read and write capacity it should reserve for your application. Because this is a development version of your application, setting both read and write capacity to 1 will work perfectly fine, and you can change that later through the AWS CLI. DynamoDB supports autoscaling, but it requires the definition of the minimum and maximum capacity. At this point, you won't need to use autoscaling, but if you want to learn more about it, visit http://docs.aws.amazon.com/amazondynamodb/latest/developerguide/AutoScaling.html.

Finally, you need to select the region where you want to create your table. Pick the same region as you did with your Lambda function to decrease latency in database communication. The following listing shows the complete command.

Listing 3.1 Create a DynamoDB table using the AWS CLI

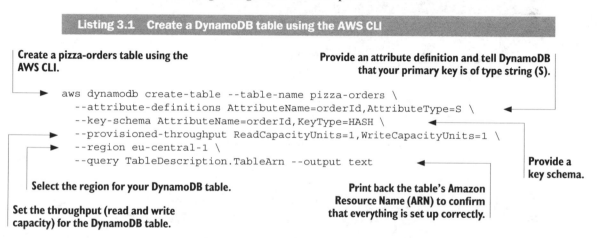

Create a pizza-orders table using the AWS CLI.

Provide an attribute definition and tell DynamoDB that your primary key is of type string (S).

```
aws dynamodb create-table --table-name pizza-orders \
    --attribute-definitions AttributeName=orderId,AttributeType=S \
    --key-schema AttributeName=orderId,KeyType=HASH \
    --provisioned-throughput ReadCapacityUnits=1,WriteCapacityUnits=1 \
    --region eu-central-1 \
    --query TableDescription.TableArn --output text
```

Provide a key schema.

Select the region for your DynamoDB table.

Set the throughput (read and write capacity) for the DynamoDB table.

Print back the table's Amazon Resource Name (ARN) to confirm that everything is set up correctly.

TIP Adding the `--query` attribute in AWS CLI commands will filter the output and return only the values you need. For example, `--query TableDescription.TableArn` returns only the table's ARN.

You can also define the type of your output by using the `--output` attribute along with the value. For example, `--output text` returns the result as plain text.

When you run the command in listing 3.1, it prints the ARN of your DynamoDB table and looks similar to this:

```
arn:aws:dynamodb:eu-central-1:123456789101:table/pizza-orders
```

That's it! Now you have the `pizza-orders` DynamoDB table. Let's see how you can connect it to your API's route handlers.

To be able to connect to your DynamoDB table from Node.js, you need to install the AWS SDK for Node.js. You can get the aws-sdk from NPM, as you would any other module. In case you are unfamiliar with that process, see appendix A.

You now have all the ingredients, and it's time for the most important step: combine all the pieces, just as you would prepare a pizza. (Fortunately for you, we have a pizza recipe in the last appendix.)

The easiest way to communicate with DynamoDB from your Node.js application is through the DocumentClient class, which requires asynchronous communication. DocumentClient, like any part of the AWS SDK, works perfectly with Claudia, and you will use it in the API route handlers you made in chapter 2.

> **DynamoDB DocumentClient**
>
> DocumentClient is a class of the DynamoDB subset of the AWS SDK. Its goal is to simplify working with table items by abstracting the operations. It exposes a simple API, and we'll cover only the pieces you need later in this chapter. In case you want to see the API documentation, it's available here: http://docs.aws.amazon.com/AWSJavaScriptSDK/latest/AWS/DynamoDB/DocumentClient.html.

Connecting your pizza order API to the newly created database is easy. Storing an order to your DynamoDB table takes just two steps:

1 Import the AWS SDK, and initialize the DynamoDB DocumentClient.
2 Update your POST method to save an order.

Because you split your code into separate files in chapter 2, let's start with the create -order.js file in the handlers folder. The following listing shows how to update create -order.js to save a new order to the pizza-orders DynamoDB table.

Listing 3.2   Saving an order to the DynamoDB table

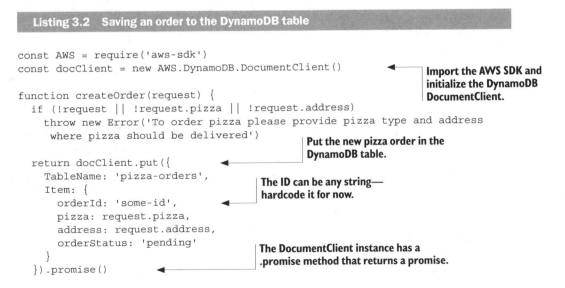

```
const AWS = require('aws-sdk')
const docClient = new AWS.DynamoDB.DocumentClient()          ← Import the AWS SDK and
                                                               initialize the DynamoDB
                                                               DocumentClient.
function createOrder(request) {
  if (!request || !request.pizza || !request.address)
    throw new Error('To order pizza please provide pizza type and address
      where pizza should be delivered')
                                                  Put the new pizza order in the
                                                  DynamoDB table.
  return docClient.put({                ←
    TableName: 'pizza-orders',
    Item: {                             The ID can be any string—
      orderId: 'some-id',               hardcode it for now.
      pizza: request.pizza,      ←
      address: request.address,
      orderStatus: 'pending'
    }                                   The DocumentClient instance has a
  }).promise()          ←              .promise method that returns a promise.
```

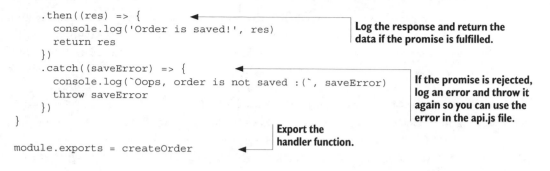

```
  .then((res) => {
    console.log('Order is saved!', res)
    return res
  })
  .catch((saveError) => {
    console.log(`Oops, order is not saved :(`, saveError)
    throw saveError
  })
}

module.exports = createOrder
```

Log the response and return the data if the promise is fulfilled.

If the promise is rejected, log an error and throw it again so you can use the error in the api.js file.

Export the handler function.

When you finish this step, the POST /orders method of your Pizza API should look and work the way it is presented in figure 3.2.

Let's explain what happens here. After importing the AWS SDK, you need to initialize the DynamoDB DocumentClient. Then you can replace the empty object you are returning on line 7 of your create-order.js handler with the code that saves an order to your table, using the DocumentClient you imported previously.

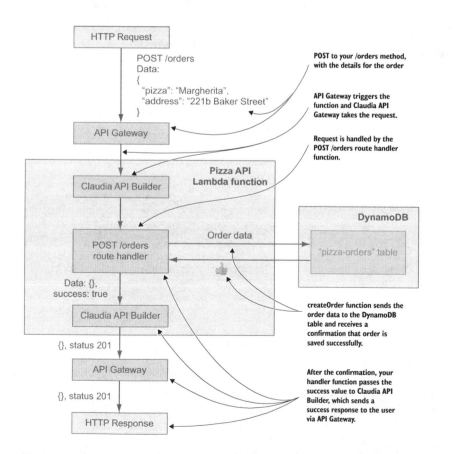

Figure 3.2 The flow of the POST /orders method of your Pizza API with DynamoDB integration

To save an order to DynamoDB, you use the `DocumentClient.put` method that puts a new item in the database, either by creating a new one or replacing an existing item with the same ID. The `put` method expects an object that describes your table by providing the `TableName` attribute and the item by providing the following `Item` attribute as an object. In your database table plan, you decided that your item should have four attributes—ID, pizza, address, and order status—and that's exactly what you want to add to the `Item` object you are passing to the `DocumentClient.put` method.

As Claudia API Builder expects a promise for async operations, you should use the `.promise` method of `DocumentClient.put`. The `.promise` method converts a reply to a JavaScript promise. Some of you are probably wondering if there are any differences in how promises work in serverless applications and how Claudia handles asynchronous communication. The following section gives a short explanation of promises and how they work with Claudia and Claudia API Builder. If you are already familiar with these concepts, jump to section 3.3.

3.2   *Promising to deliver in less than 30 minutes!*

The pizzeria processes include dough rising, baking, pizza ordering, and so on. These are asynchronous operations. If they were synchronous, Aunt Maria's pizzeria would be blocked and stopped from working on anything else until the operation in progress finished. For example, you would wait until the dough had risen, and then do something else. And for such time-wasting, Aunt Maria would fire anyone, even you! Because most of the JavaScript runtimes are single-threaded, many longer operations, such as network requests, are executed asynchronously. Asynchronous code execution is handled by two known concepts: callbacks and promises. At the time of this writing, promises are the recommended way to go in all Node.js applications. We do not explain callbacks, as you are most likely already familiar with them.

> **Asynchronous promise**
>
> A *promise* represents an eventual result of an asynchronous operation.

A promise is like a real-world promise made to partners, friends, parents, and kids:

- "Honey, will you please take out the garbage?"
- "Yes, dear, I promise!"

And a couple of hours later, guess who took out the garbage?

Promises are just pretty wrappers around callbacks. In real-world situations, you wrap a promise around a certain action or operation. A promise can have two possible outcomes: it can be *resolved* (fulfilled) or *rejected* (unfulfilled).

Promises can have conditions related to them, and this is where their asynchronous power comes into play:

- "Johnny, when you finish your homework, you will be able to go out and play!"

This example displays how certain actions can occur only after fulfilling a certain asynchronous operation. In the same way, the execution of certain code blocks waits for the completion of a defined promise.

The following listing is a JavaScript promise representation of the example sentence.

Listing 3.3   Johnny's play—the promise way

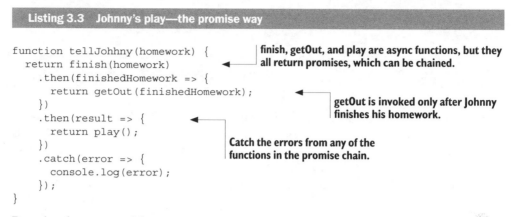

```
function tellJohhny(homework) {
  return finish(homework)            finish, getOut, and play are async functions, but they
    .then(finishedHomework => {      all return promises, which can be chained.
      return getOut(finishedHomework);
    })                                          getOut is invoked only after Johnny
    .then(result => {                           finishes his homework.
      return play();
    })                               Catch the errors from any of the
    .catch(error => {                functions in the promise chain.
      console.log(error);
    });
}
```

Promises have several features:

- *Promise chaining*—As in listing 3.3, you can easily *chain* one promise to another, passing the results from one code block to the next without any hassle.
- *Parallel execution*—You can execute two functions at the same time and get the results of both just once.
- *Proper asynchronous operation rejection*—If a function gives an error or doesn't give a good result, you can reject it and stop its execution at any time. By contrast, with callbacks, rejecting the promise stops the full chain of promises.
- *Error recovery*—The promise `catch` block allows you to easily and properly manage errors and propagate them to the responsible error handler.

Some customers order multiple pizzas in one order, but those pizzas are not delivered one by one. If they were, customers would be furious with such an inefficient process. Instead, the pizza chef usually bakes them all at the same time; then the delivery person waits until *all* of them are finished before delivery.

The following listing is a code representation of this process.

Listing 3.4   Pizza parallel baking

```
function preparePizza(pizzaName) {
  return new Promise((resolve, reject) => {
    // prepare pizza
    resolve(bakedPizza);
  });
}

function processOrder(pizzas) {
  return Promise.all([
```

```
      preparePizza('extra-cheese'),
      preparePizza('anchovies')
  ]);
}

return processOrder(pizzas)
  .then((readyPizzas) => {
    console.log(readyPizzas[0]); // prints out the result from the extra-
      cheese pizza
    console.log(readyPizzas[1]); // prints out the result from the anchovies
      pizza
    return readyPizzas;
  })
```

As you can see in listings 3.3 and 3.4, promises help a lot. They allow you to handle any situation Aunt Maria's pizzeria could have and also help you properly describe all the processes. Claudia fully supports all promise features, so you can easily use them.

In the next listing, you can see a simple Claudia example of a handler replying after one second. Because `setTimeout` is not returning a promise, you need to wrap it by using a `new Promise` statement.

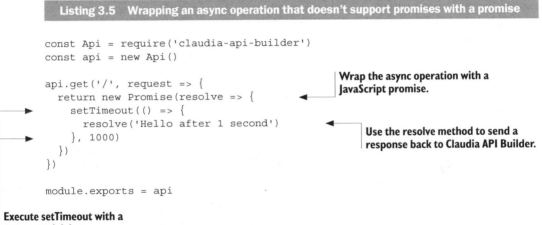

Listing 3.5   **Wrapping an async operation that doesn't support promises with a promise**

```
const Api = require('claudia-api-builder')
const api = new Api()

api.get('/', request => {                        Wrap the async operation with a
  return new Promise(resolve => {                 JavaScript promise.
    setTimeout(() => {
      resolve('Hello after 1 second')            Use the resolve method to send a
    }, 1000)                                      response back to Claudia API Builder.
  })
})

module.exports = api
```

Execute setTimeout with a
one-second delay.

As you see in listing 3.5, as opposed to some popular Node.js frameworks, Claudia API Builder only exposes the request in the route handler. In chapter 2, to reply to it you would return a value, but in the case of an asynchronous operation, you should return a JavaScript promise. Claudia API Builder receives it, waits for it to be resolved, and uses the value returned as a reply.

> **NOTE**   The AWS SDK has out-of-the-box support for JavaScript promises. All the SDK classes have a `promise` method that can, instead of default callback behavior, return a promise.

3.3   *Trying out your API*

After the small detour into the world of promises, run `claudia update` again from
your pizza-api folder and deploy the code. In less than a minute, you'll be able to test
your API and see if it works.

To test your API, reuse the `curl` command from chapter 2:

```
curl -i \
  -H "Content-Type: application/json" \
  -X POST \
  -d '{"pizza":4,"address":"221b Baker Street"}'
  https://whpcvzntil.execute-api.eu-central-1.amazonaws.com/chapter3_1/orders
```

> **NOTE** Don't forget to replace the URL in your `curl` command with the URL
> you got from the `claudia update` command.

Oh! The `curl` command returns this:

```
HTTP/1.1 400 Bad Request
Content-Type: application/json
Content-Length: 219
Date: Mon, 25 Sep 2017 06:53:36 GMT

{"errorMessage":"User: arn:aws:sts::012345678910:assumed-role/pizza-api
     -executor/book-pizza-api
is not authorized to perform: dynamodb:PutItem on resource:
arn:aws:dynamodb:eu-central-1:012345678910:table/pizza-orders"}
```

What's wrong?

This error is telling you that the role your Lambda function is using
(`arn:aws:sts::012345678910:assumed-role/pizza-api-executor/book-pizza`
`-api`) is not allowed to perform a `dynamodb:PutItem` command on your DynamoDB
database (`arn:aws:dynamodb:eu-central-1:012345678910:table/pizza-orders`).

To fix the issue, you need to add an IAM policy that allows your Lambda function to
communicate with your database. You can do that with `claudia create` by providing
a `--policies` flag. Be careful, though; that flag doesn't work with the `claudia update`
command, as Claudia never duplicates things that you can do with a single AWS CLI
command.

> **NOTE** In AWS, everything is enclosed in IAM policies, which are something
> like authorization policies. An IAM policy is similar to a passport visa. To enter
> a certain country, you need to have a valid visa.

First, define a role in a JSON file. Create a new folder in your project root, and call it
roles. Then create a role file for DynamoDB. Call it dynamodb.json, and use the content from the following listing. You want to allow your Lambda function to get, delete,
and put items in the table. Because you might have more tables in the future, apply this
rule to all tables, not just the one you have right now.

Listing 3.6   JSON file that represents DynamoDB role

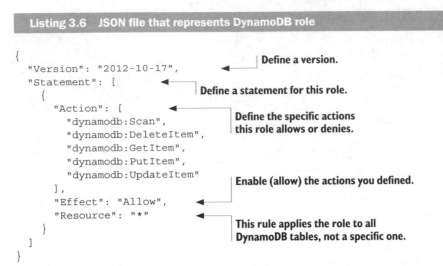

```
{
  "Version": "2012-10-17",          Define a version.
  "Statement": [                    Define a statement for this role.
    {
      "Action": [                   Define the specific actions
        "dynamodb:Scan",            this role allows or denies.
        "dynamodb:DeleteItem",
        "dynamodb:GetItem",
        "dynamodb:PutItem",
        "dynamodb:UpdateItem"       Enable (allow) the actions you defined.
      ],
      "Effect": "Allow",
      "Resource": "*"               This rule applies the role to all
    }                               DynamoDB tables, not a specific one.
  ]
}
```

TIP You probably want to have more precise roles in a production app, and you definitely don't want your Lambda function to be able to access all DynamoDB tables. To read more about roles and policies, visit http://docs.aws.amazon .com/IAM/latest/UserGuide/access_policies.html.

Now you can use the AWS CLI `put-role-policy` command to add a policy to your role, as shown in the next listing. To do so, you'll need to provide the role that your Lambda function is using, the name of your policy, and the absolute path to your dynamodb. json file. Where can you find the role? Remember the claudia.json file that Claudia created in the root folder of your project? Open that file, and you'll see the `role` attribute in the `lambda` section.

Listing 3.7   Add a policy to the Lambda role to allow it to communicate with DynamoDB tables.

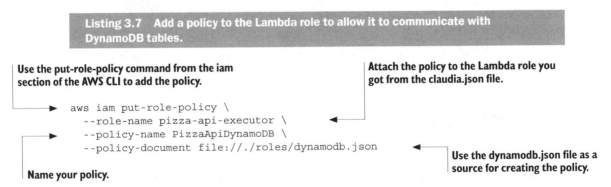

Use the put-role-policy command from the iam section of the AWS CLI to add the policy.

Attach the policy to the Lambda role you got from the claudia.json file.

```
aws iam put-role-policy \
    --role-name pizza-api-executor \
    --policy-name PizzaApiDynamoDB \
    --policy-document file://./roles/dynamodb.json
```

Name your policy.

Use the dynamodb.json file as a source for creating the policy.

NOTE You need to provide a path to dynamodb.json with the `file://` prefix. If you are providing an absolute path, keep in mind that you will have three slashes after `file:`. The first two are for `file://`, and the third one is from the absolute path, because it starts with a slash.

When you run the command from listing 3.7, you won't get any response. That's OK, because an empty response means that everything went well.

Now, rerun the same `curl` command and try to add an order:

```
curl -i \
  -H "Content-Type: application/json" \
  -X POST \
  -d '{"pizza":4,"address":"221b Baker Street"}'
  https://whpcvzntil.execute-api.eu-central-1.amazonaws.com/chapter3_1/orders
```

> **NOTE** You don't need to redeploy your code, because you didn't change it. The only thing you updated was the role for your Lambda function.

The `curl` command should return {} with status 201. If that's the case, congratulations! Your database connection is working! But how do you see whether the order was really saved to the table?

The AWS CLI has an answer to that question, too. To list all the items in your table, you can use the `scan` command in the `dynamodb` section of the AWS CLI. The `scan` command returns all the items in the table unless you provide a filter. To list all the items in the table, run the command in the following listing from your terminal.

Listing 3.8 An AWS CLI command that lists all the items from the `pizza-orders` table

The scan command lists all the items from the table.

The command requires a table name as a parameter.

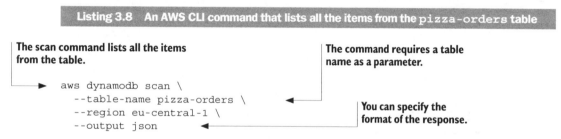

```
aws dynamodb scan \
  --table-name pizza-orders \
  --region eu-central-1 \
  --output json
```

You can specify the format of the response.

This command "scans" your `pizza-orders` table and returns the result as a JSON object. You can change the output value to `text`, and you'll get the result in text format. A few more formats are available, including XML.

The command should return something like the value in the following listing: a JSON response with the count and an array of all your table items.

Listing 3.9 Response from the `scan` command for your `pizza-orders` table

This returns a count of all table items.

Items are returned as objects in the Items array.

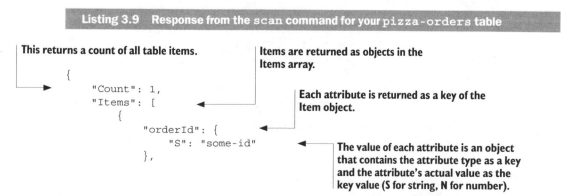

```
{
    "Count": 1,
    "Items": [
        {
            "orderId": {
                "S": "some-id"
            },
        }
```

Each attribute is returned as a key of the Item object.

The value of each attribute is an object that contains the attribute type as a key and the attribute's actual value as the key value (S for string, N for number).

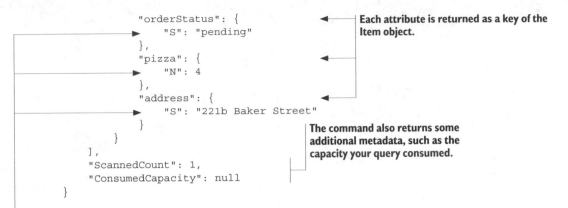

```
              "orderStatus": {                     ◄──────   Each attribute is returned as a key of the
        ──►      "S": "pending"                              Item object.
              },
              "pizza": {                           ◄──────
        ──►      "N": 4
              },
              "address": {                         ◄──────
        ──►      "S": "221b Baker Street"
              }
            }
          ],                                        The command also returns some
        "ScannedCount": 1,                          additional metadata, such as the
        "ConsumedCapacity": null                    capacity your query consumed.
  }
```

The value of each attribute is an object that contains the
attribute type as a key and the attribute's actual value as
the key value (S for string, N for number).

Awesome—it seems that your API is working as expected!

Try to add another pizza order now with the same `curl` command—for example, a Napoletana for 29 Acacia Road. If you then run the AWS CLI command from listing 3.8 again to scan the database, you'll see only one item in your table; the previous one doesn't exist anymore.

Why did that happen?

Remember that you hardcoded an `orderId` in your create-order.js handler, as shown in listing 3.2?

Each of the orders should have a unique primary key, and you used the same one, so your new entry replaced the previous one.

You can fix that by installing the `uuid` module from NPM and saving it as a dependency. `uuid` is a simple module that generates universally unique identifiers.

> ### Universally unique identifiers
>
> A *universally unique identifier* is a 128-bit value used to identify information in computer systems. It's better known by the abbreviation UUID. Sometimes it's called a globally unique identifier (GUID).
>
> UUIDs are standardized by the Open Software Foundation (OSF) as part of the Distributed Computing Environment (DCE). To learn more about the UUID standard, see RFC 4122 (the specification that describes it), available here: http://www.ietf.org/rfc/rfc4122.txt.

After you download the module, update your create-order.js handler as shown in the next listing. You can simply import and invoke the `uuid` function to get a unique ID for the order. Keep in mind that this listing shows only the part of the create-order.js file affected by this change; the rest of the file is the same as the one in listing 3.2.

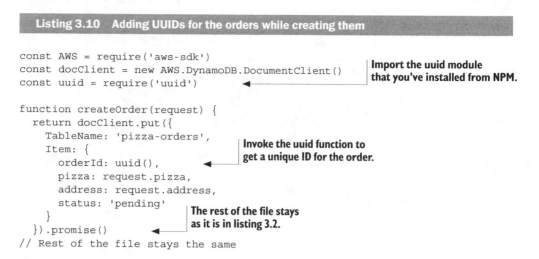

Listing 3.10   Adding UUIDs for the orders while creating them

```
const AWS = require('aws-sdk')
const docClient = new AWS.DynamoDB.DocumentClient()          Import the uuid module
const uuid = require('uuid')                                 that you've installed from NPM.

function createOrder(request) {
  return docClient.put({
    TableName: 'pizza-orders',
    Item: {                           Invoke the uuid function to
      orderId: uuid(),                get a unique ID for the order.
      pizza: request.pizza,
      address: request.address,
      status: 'pending'
    }                                 The rest of the file stays
  }).promise()                        as it is in listing 3.2.
// Rest of the file stays the same
```

After you redeploy the code by invoking the `claudia update` function, use the same `curl` command to test your API again and then scan the database with the AWS CLI command from listing 3.8. As you can see, the new `orderId` for your new order is some unique string like this one: `8c499027-a2d7-4ad9-8360-a49355021adc`. If you add more orders, you'll see that all of them are now saved in the database, as expected.

3.4   *Getting orders from the database*

After storing an order in the database, retrieving one should be fairly easy. The `DocumentClient` class has a `scan` method, which you can use to retrieve the orders.

The `scan` method works the same way as in the AWS CLI, with a small difference: You need to pass an object to it as a parameter, along with some options. In the options, the only required attribute is the name of your table.

Besides scanning the database, your get-orders.js handler can get a single item by an ID. You can do that with a scan by filtering the results, but that's inefficient. A more efficient way is to use the `get` method, which works almost the same way but requires a key for your item, too.

Let's update your get-orders.js file in the handlers folder to scan the orders from your table, or to get a single item if an order ID is provided. When you update your code, it should look like the code in the following listing. Once you've made these changes, deploy the code using the `claudia update` command.

Listing 3.11   get-orders.js handler reads the data from the `pizza-orders` table

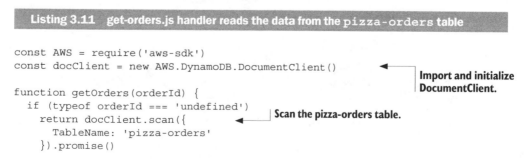

```
const AWS = require('aws-sdk')
const docClient = new AWS.DynamoDB.DocumentClient()          Import and initialize
                                                             DocumentClient.
function getOrders(orderId) {
  if (typeof orderId === 'undefined')          Scan the pizza-orders table.
    return docClient.scan({
      TableName: 'pizza-orders'
    }).promise()
```

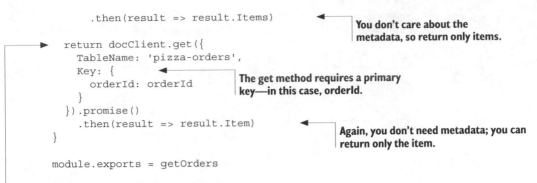

```
      .then(result => result.Items)
```
You don't care about the metadata, so return only items.

```
  return docClient.get({
    TableName: 'pizza-orders',
    Key: {
      orderId: orderId
    }
  }).promise()
    .then(result => result.Item)
}
```
The get method requires a primary key—in this case, orderId.

Again, you don't need metadata; you can return only the item.

```
module.exports = getOrders
```

If an order ID is provided, use the get method to get only one item from the table.

Let's test it! First, scan all the orders with the following `curl` command:

```
curl -i \
  -H "Content-Type: application/json" \
  https://whpcvzntil.execute-api.eu-central-1.amazonaws.com/chapter3_2/orders
```

When you run it, it should display something like this:

```
HTTP/1.1 200 OK

[{
  "address": "29 Acacia Road",
  "orderId": "629d4ab3-f25e-4110-8b76-aa6d458b1fce",
  "pizza": 4,
  "orderStatus":"pending"
}, {
  "address": "29 Acacia Road",
  "orderId": "some-id",
  "pizza": 4,
  "status": "pending"
}]
```

Don't worry if the order ID is different from yours; it should be unique.

Now try using an ID from one of the returned orders to get a single order. You can do that by running the following `curl` command from your terminal:

```
curl -i \
  -H "Content-Type: application/json" \
  https://whpcvzntil.execute-api.eu-central-1.amazonaws.com/chapter3_2/
    orders/629d4ab3-f25e-4110-8b76-aa6d458b1fce
```

The result should look something like this:

```
HTTP/1.1 200 OK

{
  "address": "29 Acacia Road",
  "orderId": "629d4ab3-f25e-4110-8b76-aa6d458b1fce",
  "pizza": 4,
  "status": "pending"
}
```

It works! Awesome and easy, right?

3.5 *Taste it!*

As you've seen, saving orders to the database and retrieving them is easy. But Aunt Maria has told you that sometimes customers make mistakes and order the wrong pizza, so she wants the capability to change or cancel a pizza order.

3.5.1 *Exercise*

To fulfill Aunt Maria's request, you need to connect two more API endpoints to the database:

1 Update the update-order.js handler to update an existing order in the `pizza -orders` DynamoDB table.
2 Update the delete-order.js handler to delete an order from the `pizza-orders` DynamoDB table.

When you finish both endpoints, your API should have the same structure as the one in figure 3.3.

The solution's code is in the next section. Before looking at it, try to complete the exercise yourself, but if you're struggling, peek a little.

A few hints:

- You should use DynamoDB's `DocumentClient` for both updates and deletions.
- To update an existing order, use the `DocumentClient.update` method. Besides `TableName`, this method requires a few more items in the object you are providing, including `Key`, `UpdateExpression`, and others. See the official documentation

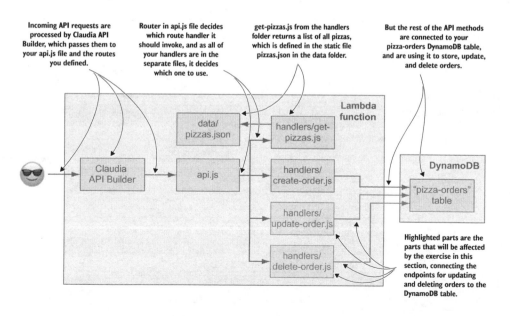

Figure 3.3 The Pizza API after connecting all order endpoints to the DynamoDB table, with the parts of the app that need to be addressed by this exercise highlighted

for the full list: http://docs.aws.amazon.com/AWSJavaScriptSDK/latest/AWS/
DynamoDB/DocumentClient.html#update-property.

- If the `update` method seems too complex for you, remember that `DocumentClient` `.put` will replace an existing order with a new one, so you can try using that one.
- To delete an existing order, use the `DocumentClient.delete` method. To delete an item, you need to provide an object that contains the `TableName` and the `Key` for that item. For more information, see the official documentation: http://docs.aws .amazon.com/AWSJavaScriptSDK/latest/AWS/DynamoDB/DocumentClient .html#delete-property.
- Don't forget to return a promise and to pass the value.

In case this is too easy, here are a few additional things you can do:

- Update update-order.js and delete-order.js to affect pending orders only, because you don't want customers to be able to change an order if the pizza is ready and being delivered.
- Update get-orders.js to be able to filter by order status, and by default return only pending orders.

The solutions to these additional tasks are available in the final application source code, along with code annotations.

3.5.2   Solution

Finished already or peeking a little? If you're finished, that's great, but even if you weren't able to complete the exercise without any help, don't worry. DynamoDB is a bit different from the other popular noSQL databases, and you may need more time and practice to understand it.

Let's take a look at the solution. The following listing shows the updates for the update-order.js file in the handlers folder of your project.

Listing 3.12   Updating an order in the pizza-orders DynamoDB table

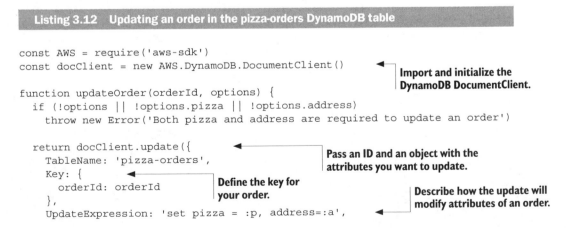

```
const AWS = require('aws-sdk')
const docClient = new AWS.DynamoDB.DocumentClient()        ◀──  Import and initialize the
                                                                 DynamoDB DocumentClient.
function updateOrder(orderId, options) {
  if (!options || !options.pizza || !options.address)
    throw new Error('Both pizza and address are required to update an order')

  return docClient.update({                ◀──  Pass an ID and an object with the
    TableName: 'pizza-orders',                  attributes you want to update.
    Key: {                    ◀── Define the key for
      orderId: orderId             your order.
    },                                                          Describe how the update will
    UpdateExpression: 'set pizza = :p, address=:a',   ◀──       modify attributes of an order.
```

```
    ExpressionAttributeValues: {
      ':p': options.pizza,
      ':a': options.address
    },
    ReturnValues: 'ALL_NEW'
  }).promise()
    .then((result) => {
      console.log('Order is updated!', result)
      return result.Attributes
    })
    .catch((updateError) => {
      console.log(`Oops, order is not updated :(`, updateError)
      throw updateError
    })
}

module.exports = updateOrder
```

Provide the values to the UpdateExpression expression.

Tell DynamoDB that you want a whole new item to be returned.

Just log the response or error and pass the value—you'll use this in chapter 5 for debugging purposes.

Export the handler.

It's not that different from create-order.js. The two major differences are

- Using the `DocumentClient.update` method with a `Key`, which is `orderId` in your case
- Passing more values to the function because you need an `orderId` and new values to update (`pizza` and `address`)

TIP Update syntax can be a bit confusing because of its `UpdateExpression`, `ExpressionAttributeValues`, and `ReturnValues` attributes. But the attributes are quite simple. The annotations of listing 3.12 provide a basic explanation. For more details, check the official documentation at http://docs.aws.amazon.com/amazondynamodb/latest/developerguide/Expressions.UpdateExpressions .html.

The following listing shows the updates for the delete-order.js file in your handlers folder. The required updates are similar to those in both the create-order.js and update-order.js files; the only difference is that you're using the `DocumentClient` `.delete` method here.

Listing 3.13 Deleting an order from the pizza-orders DynamoDB table

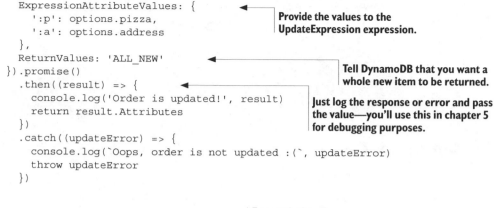

Use the DocumentClient.delete method to delete an order.

Import and initialize the DynamoDB DocumentClient.

```
const AWS = require('aws-sdk')
const docClient = new AWS.DynamoDB.DocumentClient()

function deleteOrder(orderId) {
  return docClient.delete({
    TableName: 'pizza-orders',
    Key: {
      orderId: orderId
    }
  }).promise()
    .then((result) => {
```

Pass an order ID.

Provide an orderId, the primary key for your table.

Don't forget to use the .promise method to return a promise.

```
            console.log('Order is deleted!', result)
            return result
        })
        .catch((deleteError) => {
            console.log(`Oops, order is not deleted :(`, deleteError)
            throw deleteError
        })
}

module.exports = deleteOrder          ◄──┘ Export the handler.
```

**Log the response or the error,
and pass the value.**

Seems easy, right?

Now you need to run the `claudia update` command from your pizza-api folder one more time to deploy your code. To test whether everything works, you can use the same `curl` commands you were using in chapter 2. Copy them from listings 3.14 and 3.15, and paste them in your terminal. Don't forget to update your `orderId` value. Using the one provided in those listings won't work because it's just a placeholder.

Listing 3.14 `curl` command for testing `PUT` `/orders/{orderId}` route

```
curl -i \                                    Remember to replace some-id
  -H "Content-Type: application/json" \      with the real ID of your order.
  -X PUT \
  -d '{"pizza": 3, "address": "221b Baker Street"}'
  https://whpcvzntil.execute-api.eu-central-1.amazonaws.com/chapter3_3/
      orders/some-id     ◄──
```

This command should return the following:

```
HTTP/1.1 200 OK

{
  "address": "221b Baker Street",
  "orderId": "some-id",
  "pizza": 3,
  "status": "pending"
}
```

Listing 3.15 `curl` command for testing `DELETE` `/orders/{orderId}` route

```
curl -i \                                    Remember to replace some-id
  -H "Content-Type: application/json" \      with the real ID of your order.
  -X DELETE \
  https://whpcvzntil.execute-api.eu-central-1.amazonaws.com/chapter3_3/
      orders/some-id     ◄──
```

This command should return

```
HTTP/1.1 200 OK

{}
```

Summary

- To build a useful serverless application, you'll often need to use external services—either for saving and retrieving data in a database, or to get needed information from another API.
- Communication to an external service is asynchronous.
- Claudia allows you to handle asynchronous functions by using JavaScript promises.
- JavaScript promises simplify the way you handle async operations. They also fix the problem often known as "callback hell" by allowing you to chain async operations, pass the values, and bubble the errors up.
- The simplest way to store data with AWS Lambda is to use DynamoDB, a NoSQL database offered as part of the AWS ecosystem.
- You can use DynamoDB in Node.js by installing the `aws-sdk` Node module. Among other things, the AWS SDK also exposes the DynamoDB `DocumentClient` class, which allows you to save, query, edit, and delete items in DynamoDB tables.
- DynamoDB tables are similar to collections in traditional NoSQL databases. Unfortunately, they only allow queries by primary key, which can be a combination of hash and range keys.

Pizza delivery: Connecting an external service

4

This chapter covers

- Connecting your serverless function to an external service using an HTTP API

- Dealing with common problems in async communication with Claudia API Builder

As you learned in the previous chapter, handling asynchronous operations in AWS Lambda is easy with Claudia API Builder. In that chapter, you also learned how to create a database for your pizza orders and created functions to store, retrieve, update, and delete them. But your application is capable of much more than that.

This chapter shows you how to connect your serverless application to an external HTTP service by enabling Aunt Maria's pizzeria to use the Some Like It Hot Delivery Company's API and offer more home delivery services. You will learn how to formulate an HTTP request from AWS Lambda, handle response errors, and set up a webhook with Claudia API Builder. You will also learn about the most common problems and pitfalls, how to solve them, and how to avoid encountering them in the first place.

4.1   Connecting to an external service

Ring, ring! Aunt Maria is on the phone again. She sounds pleased and thanks you for your current work, but you can sense that something is bothering her. It's not long until she asks you for a favor.

It's about the deliveries. Each time the pizzeria wants to deliver a pizza order, they need to phone the Some Like It Hot Delivery Company. That wasn't a problem until the recent rise in pizza orders (thanks to you!). But now the process is starting to take up more and more time, so Aunt Maria wants you to find an alternative. Luckily for you, the Some Like It Hot Delivery Company has an API. How can you connect to it?

As we discussed earlier, your serverless application can connect to any of the following:

- A database (DynamoDB, Amazon RDS)
- Another Lambda function
- Another AWS service (SQS, S3, and many others)
- An external API

The Some Like It Hot Delivery API belongs to the last category.

Serverless application connections

- *Connecting to a database*—As mentioned in the previous chapter, some applications require a more structured database, so sometimes DynamoDB is not the right tool for the job. AWS Lambda gives you many other options, and you can connect to almost any other database, including MySQL or PostgreSQL, via Amazon Relational Database Service (RDS).
  Amazon RDS is a web service that makes it easier to set up, operate, and scale a relational database in the cloud. It provides cost-efficient, resizable capacity for an industry-standard relational database and manages common database administration tasks. To learn more about RDS, visit https://aws.amazon.com/rds/.
- *Connecting to a Lambda function*—Sometimes you want to connect your Lambda function to another Lambda function, or to invoke itself. You can do this via an async call with the AWS SDK. This technique has many use cases—for example, Claudia Bot Builder uses it to deliver delayed Slack messages. We talk more about Claudia Bot Builder in part 2 of this book.
- *Connecting to another AWS service*—AWS offers a large variety of different services, including the Simple Queue Service (SQS), Simple Storage Service (S3), and many more. It's common to make connections to other AWS services (such as SQS and S3), but you can connect to third-party services using the AWS SDK, too. Some of those services are covered in later chapters of this book.

All these connections are supported by Claudia and are covered in this book. The first was covered in the previous chapter and the last is covered in this one. The chatbot chapters (8 through 10) cover connections to Lambda functions.

4.2   Connecting to the delivery API

Let's start with the `createOrder` handler, which is in the create-order.js file in your project's handlers folder. After the `createOrder` handler saves the order to your database, you want to contact the Some Like It Hot Delivery Company's API to schedule a delivery. The flow of your application should look like figure 4.1.

Before you start connecting the dots, take a quick look at the Some Like It Hot Delivery Company's API, described in the following section.

4.2.1   The Some Like It Hot Delivery API

Aunt Maria is happy with the professionalism of Some Like It Hot Delivery Company. For a reasonable price, they pick up and deliver the pizzas while they're still hot. Even their call center is good; the agents are polite and take orders quickly. But that's still a bottleneck—they don't have many agents, and despite the speed of their service, you

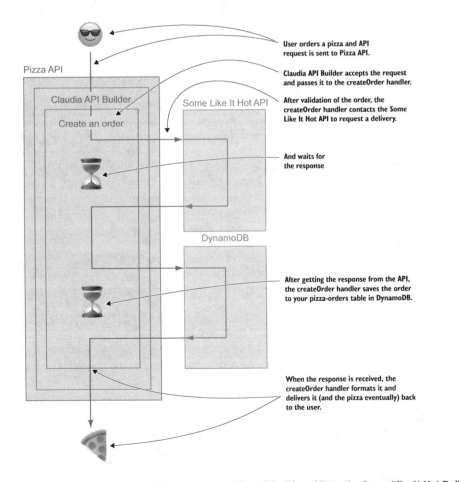

Figure 4.1   Connecting the createOrder handler of the Pizza API to the Some Like It Hot Delivery API

need to wait on the line for a free agent, which is a problem if you need to deliver a lot of pizzas every day.

You decide to look at their website to see if there's something that can simplify the workflow. Even a simple web form would be better than a phone call. Surprise, surprise—not only do they have a better solution, but they have a fully working API!

The API offers the following endpoints:

- `POST /delivery` creates a new delivery request and returns the delivery ID and a time estimation.
- `GET /delivery` returns all the scheduled deliveries for your restaurant.
- `GET /delivery/{id}` returns information on the status of a selected delivery.
- `DELETE /delivery/{id}` cancels the delivery, but only in the first 10 minutes following the creation of the delivery request.

It's not the best API ever, but it's good enough to allow you to automate the process.

> **THE SOME LIKE IT HOT DELIVERY API IS NOT A REAL API.** Keep in mind that the Some Like It Hot Delivery API is…fake. We created a mock API using Claudia and AWS Lambda so you can connect your test application. As you'll see, it returns mock data for the time and distance not related to the address you enter.
>
> The API is free and open source; to see the documentation and source code, visit https://github.com/effortless-serverless/some-like-it-hot-delivery.
>
> Feel free to use it—it will not set up any real deliveries!

We don't dive deep into the Some Like It Hot Delivery API documentation right now. Instead, you'll see the most important things about each API endpoint as you connect them.

4.2.2 Creating your first delivery request

As Aunt Maria described to you, when an order is placed she usually makes a phone call to create a delivery request. Instead, you'd like to create the delivery request automatically. Take a few seconds and, if you can, come up with a diagram of the flow.

When a customer orders a pizza, you need to

1 Validate the order.
2 Contact the Some Like It Hot Delivery API to see when the Some Like It Hot Delivery Company can deliver it.
3 Save the order to the database.

> **NOTE** Keep in mind that you are building a minimum viable product, so the application logic is simplified a bit. In a real-world application, this logic would need to take into account pizza prep time, working hours, and a few other things.

The flow is illustrated in figure 4.2.

Before implementing the flow from figure 4.2, you need to learn a bit more about creating a delivery request via the Some Like It Hot Delivery API. Let's look at that now.

The most important feature of the Some Like It Hot Delivery API is its POST /delivery route, which creates a delivery request. This API endpoint accepts the following parameters:

- pickupAddress—The pickup address for the order. By default, it'll use the address from your account.
- deliveryAddress—The delivery address for the order.
- pickupTime—The pickup time for the order. If the time isn't provided, the order will be picked up as soon as possible.
- webhookUrl—The URL for a webhook that should be called to update the delivery status.

The Some Like It Hot Delivery API returns the delivery ID, the pickup time for the order, and the initial delivery status, which is "pending." When the order is picked up, the Some Like It Hot Delivery API needs to make a POST request to your Pizza API webhook and send the new delivery status ("in-progress") along with the delivery ID.

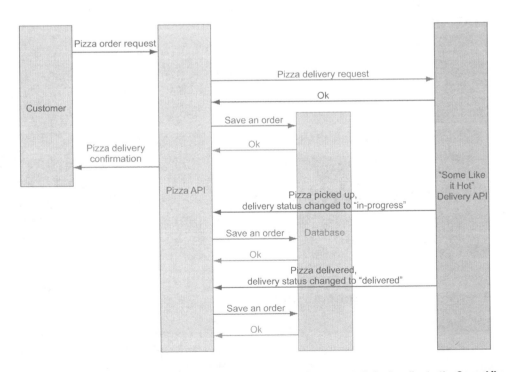

Figure 4.2   A detailed diagram illustrating the connection of the createOrder handler to the Some Like It Hot Delivery API and then the database

> ### Webhooks
>
> A webhook is just an endpoint on your API. Simply put, it is an HTTP callback: an HTTP POST request sent to you when something happens. You can think of it as a simple event notification via HTTP POST. A web application implementing webhooks will POST a message to a URL when certain events happen.

It's time to update your create-order.js handler. It needs to send a POST request to the Some Like It Hot Delivery API, wait for its response, and then save the pizza order to the database. But you need to add a delivery ID to the database, so you can update the status of the order when your webhook receives the data.

The updated create-order.js with the delivery request should look something like the following listing.

Listing 4.1   create-order.js updated to create a delivery request before saving the delivery to the database

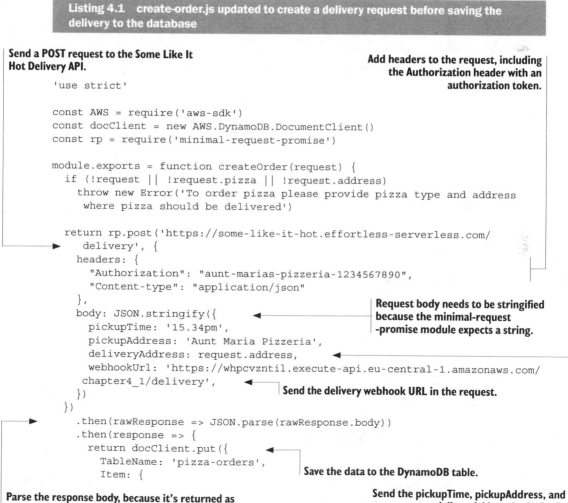

Send a POST request to the Some Like It Hot Delivery API.

Add headers to the request, including the Authorization header with an authorization token.

```
'use strict'

const AWS = require('aws-sdk')
const docClient = new AWS.DynamoDB.DocumentClient()
const rp = require('minimal-request-promise')

module.exports = function createOrder(request) {
  if (!request || !request.pizza || !request.address)
    throw new Error('To order pizza please provide pizza type and address
    where pizza should be delivered')

  return rp.post('https://some-like-it-hot.effortless-serverless.com/
    delivery', {
    headers: {
      "Authorization": "aunt-marias-pizzeria-1234567890",
      "Content-type": "application/json"
    },
    body: JSON.stringify({
      pickupTime: '15.34pm',
      pickupAddress: 'Aunt Maria Pizzeria',
      deliveryAddress: request.address,
      webhookUrl: 'https://whpcvzntil.execute-api.eu-central-1.amazonaws.com/
      chapter4_1/delivery',
    })
  })
    .then(rawResponse => JSON.parse(rawResponse.body))
    .then(response => {
      return docClient.put({
        TableName: 'pizza-orders',
        Item: {
```

Request body needs to be stringified because the minimal-request -promise module expects a string.

Send the delivery webhook URL in the request.

Save the data to the DynamoDB table.

Parse the response body, because it's returned as a string—notice promise chaining here.

Send the pickupTime, pickupAddress, and deliveryAddress in the body.

```
          orderId: response.deliveryId,
          pizza: request.pizza,
          address: request.address,
          orderStatus: 'pending'
        }
      }).promise()
    })
    .then(res => {
      console.log('Order is saved!', res)
      return res
    })
    .catch(saveError => {
      console.log(`Oops, order is not saved :(`, saveError)
      throw saveError
    })
}
```

> Because the delivery ID is unique, you can use it instead of generating a new one with the uuid module.

Note a few new things here:

- `minimal-request-promise`—As its name states, this is a minimal promise-based API for HTTP requests. You can pick the module you like the most. We recommend `minimal-request-promise` because of its minimal required implementation. For more details, you can take a look at its source code on GitHub: https://github.com/gojko/minimal-request-promise.
- `Authorization`—Making a request to an external service usually requires some kind of authorization, but because the Some Like It Hot Delivery API is not a real API, anything you pass in the `Authorization` header will work.
- `webhookURL`—The Some Like It Hot Delivery API needs an endpoint where it will send its delivery status updates.

As previously mentioned, a webhook is a simple API endpoint that accepts POST requests. There are two things you need to do:

1 Create a route handler for the webhook
2 Create a route called /delivery that accepts POST requests

Let's start with the first one. Go to the handlers directory in the root of your Pizza API project, and create a new file named update-delivery-status.js.

The webhook route handler flow should be as follows:

1 Your webhook should receive a POST request with its delivery ID and the delivery status in the request body.
2 Find the order in the table using the delivery ID you received from the Some Like It Hot Delivery API.
3 Update that order with a new delivery status.

But there's a tricky part here. DynamoDB has two actions: get and scan. The get command allows you to query the database only by key columns, whereas scan can query on any column. Another important difference is that scan loads up the whole table and then applies a filter on its collection; the get command directly queries the table.

These differences seem to be limiting, but in reality, you just need to do a bit more planning. Besides a single primary key, DynamoDB supports a composite key, too—it consists of a primary or hash key and a sort or range key, and requires the combination of those two to be unique. Another way to handle similar problems is to add a secondary index. To learn more about both approaches, see the official documentation: http://docs.aws.amazon.com/amazondynamodb/latest/developerguide/Introduction.html.

In your case, there's an even easier solution—the delivery ID is unique, and you'll get it before you store the order to the `pizza-orders` table, so you can use the delivery ID as an order ID. Doing so allows you to query the database by both order and delivery ID, because they are the same, and also to remove the `uuid` module, because you don't need it anymore.

Let's try to implement that. The following listing shows the code.

Listing 4.2   The update delivery status handler receives the data from the Some Like It Hot Delivery API and updates the order in the table.

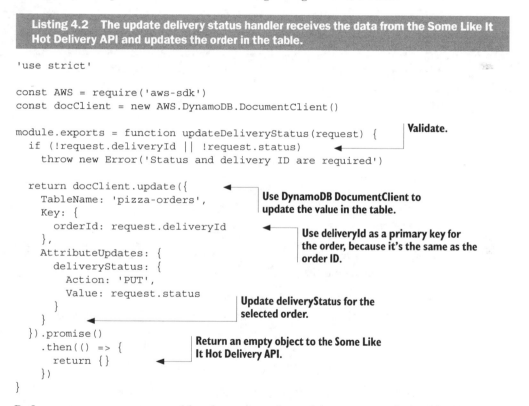

```
'use strict'

const AWS = require('aws-sdk')
const docClient = new AWS.DynamoDB.DocumentClient()

module.exports = function updateDeliveryStatus(request) {          Validate.
  if (!request.deliveryId || !request.status)
    throw new Error('Status and delivery ID are required')

  return docClient.update({
    TableName: 'pizza-orders',          Use DynamoDB DocumentClient to
    Key: {                              update the value in the table.
      orderId: request.deliveryId       Use deliveryId as a primary key for
    },                                  the order, because it's the same as the
    AttributeUpdates: {                 order ID.
      deliveryStatus: {
        Action: 'PUT',
        Value: request.status
      }                                 Update deliveryStatus for the
    }                                   selected order.
  }).promise()
    .then(() => {                       Return an empty object to the Some Like
      return {}                         It Hot Delivery API.
    })
}
```

Before you can test your webhook, you need to add a route to the api.js file in the root of your project. To do that you need to require your new handler at the top of the file by adding the `const updateDeliveryStatus = require('./handlers/update-delivery-status')` line. Then you need to add another POST route, the same way you did it in chapter 2. The following listing shows the last few lines of the updated api.js file.

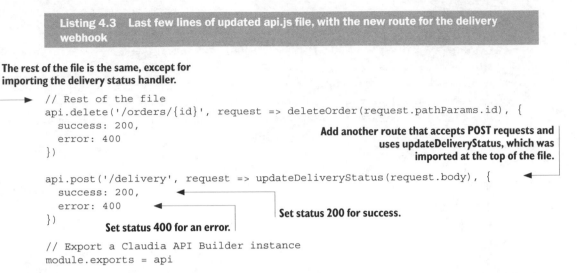

Listing 4.3   Last few lines of updated api.js file, with the new route for the delivery webhook

The rest of the file is the same, except for importing the delivery status handler.

```
// Rest of the file
api.delete('/orders/{id}', request => deleteOrder(request.pathParams.id), {
  success: 200,
  error: 400
})

api.post('/delivery', request => updateDeliveryStatus(request.body), {
  success: 200,
  error: 400
})
// Export a Claudia API Builder instance
module.exports = api
```

Add another route that accepts POST requests and uses updateDeliveryStatus, which was imported at the top of the file.

Set status 200 for success.

Set status 400 for an error.

Awesome—you have the webhook, and all the ingredients are finally in place. Let's taste the webhook—pardon, let's test it. To do so, you need to deploy your API using the `claudia update` command. After updating the API, use the same `curl` command you used in chapters 2 and 3 to test creating an order:

```
curl -i \
  -H "Content-Type: application/json" \
  -X POST \
  -d '{"pizza":4,"address":"221b Baker Street"}'
  https://whpcvzntil.execute-api.eu-central-1.amazonaws.com/chapter4_1/orders
```

> **NOTE** Don't forget to replace the URL in these `curl` commands with the URL you got from the `claudia update` command.

The `curl` command should return { }, status 200, so everything is fine. But what is happening in the background?

> **TIME IN THE SOME LIKE IT HOT DELIVERY API**   For easier testing, the Some Like It Hot Delivery API sets each order status to "in-progress" after one minute, and then to "delivered" after another minute—so the entire process, from "ordering" to "delivered pizza," takes two minutes. It would be awesome if that were the case in the real world too, right?

As you can see in figure 4.3, your Pizza API contacts the Some Like It Hot Delivery API first, then it saves the order to the `pizza-orders` table. Then, a bit later, the Some Like It Hot Delivery API contacts your webhook and updates the delivery status to "in-progress." And finally, it contacts your webhook again to set the status to "delivered."

That's it!

What else do you need to connect to the Some Like It Hot Delivery API?

Because you have a webhook, you don't need to contact the Some Like It Hot Delivery API to get the delivery status. But you do need to contact the API if you want to cancel a delivery request. That would be a nice exercise, and you can try to do that in

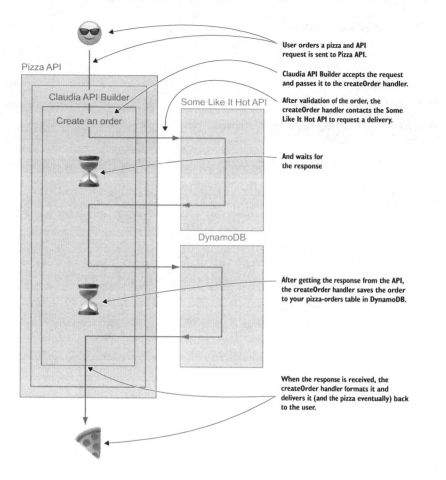

Figure 4.3   The flow from pizza ordering to delivery

section 4.4. But before the exercise, let's explore some of the common issues with async requests from AWS Lambda using Claudia.

4.3   *Potential issues with async communication*

As you've seen, handling asynchronous requests with AWS Lambda using Claudia is easy. But sometimes issues arise when you want to connect to an external service or do an async operation.

It's hard to summarize all the potential issues, but here are the most common errors people make:

- Forgetting to return a promise
- Not passing the value out of `.then` or `.catch` statements
- Not wrapping the external service in a promise if it doesn't support JavaScript promises out of the box
- Hitting the timeout before the async function finishes its execution

As you can see, most of the issues are promise-related. But let's take a look at them one by one.

4.3.1 *Forgetting to return a promise*

The most common problem with integration of an external service or an async operation is caused by omitting the `return` keyword. An example of this error is shown in the following listing. This issue is hard to debug because the code will run without an exception, but execution will be stopped before the async operation is done.

Listing 4.4   Breaking the code by not returning a promise

```
module.exports = function(pizza, address) {
  docClient.put({                            ◄─── This line is no longer
    TableName: 'pizza-orders',                    returning a promise.
    Item: {
      orderId: uuid(),
      pizza: pizza,
      address: address,
      status: 'pending'
    }
  }).promise()
```

Why is this a problem? As you can see in figure 4.4, if your async operation doesn't return a promise, Claudia API Builder won't know that the operation is asynchronous, and it will tell AWS Lambda that the function has finished its execution. It will also send `undefined` as the value of your function because you never returned anything meaningful.

The solution for this problem is easy: make sure you always return a promise, and if your code is not working, first check that all of your promises are returned.

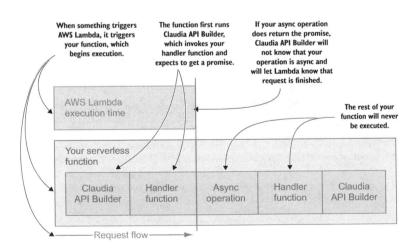

Figure 4.4   A visual representation of Lambda execution when an async operation doesn't return a promise

4.3.2   *Not passing the value from the promise*

This problem is almost the same as the previous one. The following listing shows an example.

Listing 4.5   Breaking the code by not returning a value from the promise

```
module.exports = function(pizza, address) {
  return docClient.put({
    TableName: 'pizza-orders',
    Item: {
      orderId: uuid(),
      pizza: pizza,
      address: address,
      status: 'pending'
    }
  }).promise()
  .then(result => {
    console.log('Result', result)
  })
```

> The promise is returned as it should be.

> But after logging the request you never return a value, so the next .then can't chain anything.

As you can see in figure 4.5, the main difference is that the async operation finishes its execution in this case, but the result is never passed back to your handler function, and your promise chain is broken. Again, `undefined` is returned as the result of your serverless function.

The solution for this problem is the same as for the previous one—make sure you always return the values.

4.3.3   *Not wrapping the external service in a promise*

Sometimes external or async services don't have native support for promises. In that case, another common mistake is not wrapping the operations in a promise, as you can see in the next listing.

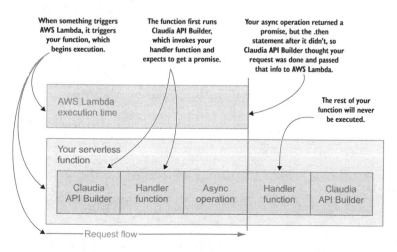

Figure 4.5   A visual representation of Lambda execution when the async operation doesn't return a value

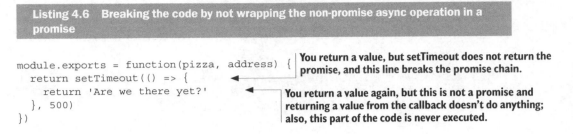

Listing 4.6   Breaking the code by not wrapping the non-promise async operation in a promise

```
module.exports = function(pizza, address) {
  return setTimeout(() => {
    return 'Are we there yet?'
  }, 500)
})
```

You return a value, but setTimeout does not return the promise, and this line breaks the promise chain.

You return a value again, but this is not a promise and returning a value from the callback doesn't do anything; also, this part of the code is never executed.

As you can see in figure 4.6, the problem is exactly the same as the first one.

But the solution is a bit different. As shown in the following listing, you need to return a new, empty promise. Then, execute an async operation inside it and finally resolve it when the async operation has finished its execution.

Listing 4.7   Fixing the broken code by wrapping the non-promise async operation in a promise

You create and return an empty promise, and now you have access to resolve and reject functions in its callback.

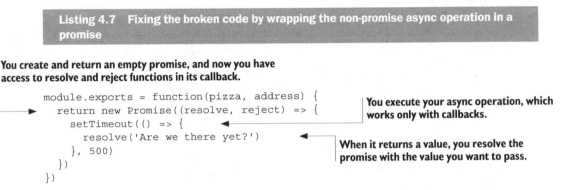

```
module.exports = function(pizza, address) {
  return new Promise((resolve, reject) => {
    setTimeout(() => {
      resolve('Are we there yet?')
    }, 500)
  })
})
```

You execute your async operation, which works only with callbacks.

When it returns a value, you resolve the promise with the value you want to pass.

4.3.4   *Timeout issues with long async operations*

This last common problem is one with AWS Lambda timeouts. As you may remember from chapter 1, the default execution time is three seconds. So what happens when your asynchronous operation takes more than three seconds, as in the following listing?

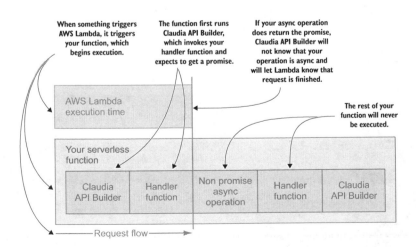

Figure 4.6   A visual representation of Lambda execution when the async operation is not wrapped in a promise

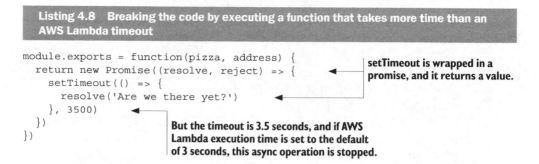

Listing 4.8 Breaking the code by executing a function that takes more time than an AWS Lambda timeout

```
module.exports = function(pizza, address) {
  return new Promise((resolve, reject) => {         ◄──  setTimeout is wrapped in a
    setTimeout(() => {                                    promise, and it returns a value.
      resolve('Are we there yet?')          ◄──
    }, 3500)    ◄──
  })                  But the timeout is 3.5 seconds, and if AWS
})                    Lambda execution time is set to the default
                      of 3 seconds, this async operation is stopped.
```

Well, as you can see in figure 4.7, it just stops, and your Lambda function never returns any value. The main difference here is that even Claudia API Builder isn't executed in this case. Imagine someone unplugging your computer during some operation—the effect is the same.

How do you fix this issue?

Unless you can optimize the speed of your async operation and be sure that your function executes in less than three seconds, the solution is to update the timeout for your function.

Claudia allows you to set the timeout only during the function's creation. To do that, invoke the `create` command with the `--timeout` option, like this:

```
claudia create --region eu-central-1 --api-module api --timeout 10
```

The value for this option is given in seconds.

If you already have a function, the best way to update it is by running the following AWS CLI command:

```
claudia update --timeout 10
```

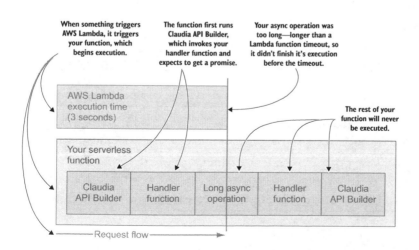

Figure 4.7 A visual representation of Lambda execution stopped by a timeout

For more information about this command, see the official documentation at http://docs .aws.amazon.com/cli/latest/reference/lambda/update-function-configuration.html.

After running the command, your function should be updated with the 10-second timeout. If you run the example from listing 4.9 again, it should work without a problem.

This list of potential issues is not complete, but the four we mentioned should cover the clear majority of them.

Now go play a bit more with the options and try to break your serverless API in a more creative way!

4.4   Taste it!

As you've seen, connecting external services is not that hard—so now, try to do it on your own.

4.4.1   Exercise

Remember that you can integrate cancelation of a delivery request using the Some Like It Hot Delivery API?

Your exercise for this chapter is exactly that—update the delete-order.js handler to cancel the delivery request via the Some Like It Hot Delivery API before it deletes the order from the database.

Before you start, here's some info about the DELETE method of the Some Like It Hot Delivery API:

- To delete the delivery request, you need to send a DELETE request to the /delivery/{deliveryId} route of the Some Like It Hot Delivery API.
- You need to provide the delivery ID as a path parameter in the URL.
- The full URL for the Some Like It Hot Delivery API is https://some-like-it-hot .effortless-serverless.com/delivery.
- An order can be deleted only if the status is "pending."

If that's enough information, go ahead and try it on your own.

In case you need additional tips, here are a few:

- You need to read the order from the pizza-orders table first in order to get its status.
- If the status is not "pending," throw an error.
- If the status is "pending," contact the Some Like It Hot Delivery API; only when you receive a positive answer should you delete an order from the pizza-orders table.

If you need more help, or you want to see the solution, check out the next section.

In case this exercise was too easy and you want an additional challenge, try to build the Some Like It Hot Delivery API you used in section 4.2.1. The solution for that exercise is not shown in the book, but feel free to compare your solution to the original source code at https://github.com/effortless-serverless/some-like-it-hot-delivery.

4.4.2 *Solution*

Let's start with the flow. As we said, first you need to contact the `pizza-orders` database table to see if the order has the "pending" status. Cancel it using the `DELETE` method of the Some Like It Hot Delivery API, and finally delete it from the `pizza-orders` table. See figure 4.8 for a visualization of the flow.

How should you update your delete-order.js handler?

It's easy. First, import the `minimal-request-promise` module, because you'll want to use it to contact the Some Like It Hot Delivery API.

Then update your `deleteOrder` function to read an order from the `pizza-orders` DynamoDB table. If no order with the specified ID exists, the function automatically throws an error and status 400 is returned to the customer. If the order does exist, check if the status of that order is "pending"; if it's not, you'll need to throw an error manually.

If the order status is "pending," use the `minimal-request-promise` module to send a `DELETE` request to the Some Like It Hot Delivery API. Remember that the order ID is the same as the delivery ID, so you can use that ID to delete the delivery request. An

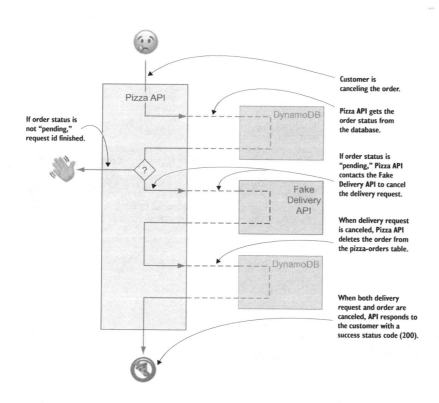

Figure 4.8 The delete order flow for the Pizza API

error from the API will automatically throw an error in your `deleteOrder` function, so the response status will be 400 as expected.

When the API successfully deletes the delivery request, you need to delete the order from the `pizza-orders` DynamoDB table—and that's it!

See the following listing for the complete delete-order.js handler's code after the update.

Listing 4.9   Deleting an order from the `pizza-orders` DynamoDB table

**Import the minimal-request
-promise module.**

**Get an order from the
pizza-orders table.**

```
const AWS = require('aws-sdk')
const docClient = new AWS.DynamoDB.DocumentClient()
const rp = require('minimal-request-promise')

module.exports = function deleteOrder(orderId) {
  return docClient.get({
    TableName: 'pizza-orders',
    Key: {
      orderId: orderId
    }
  }).promise()
    .then(result => result.Item)
    .then(item => {
      if (item.orderStatus !== 'pending')
        throw new Error('Order status is not pending')

      return rp.delete(`https://some-like-it-hot.effortless-serverless.com/
    delivery/${orderId}`, {
        headers: {
          "Authorization": "aunt-marias-pizzeria-1234567890",
          "Content-type": "application/json"
        }
      })
    })
    .then(() => {
      return docClient.delete({
        TableName: 'pizza-orders',
        Key: {
          orderId: orderId
        }
      }).promise()
    })
}
```

**If order status is not
"pending," throw an error.**

**Delete a delivery request via the
Some Like It Hot Delivery API.**

**Delete an order from the
pizza-orders table.**

**Both .then and .catch are removed because the
result will be sent directly as an API response.**

Summary

- With AWS Lambda, you can connect to any external service the same way you would from any regular Node.js app, as long as your async operations are correct.
- If you are connecting to an external API, make sure that your HTTP library supports promises, or wrap the operations manually.
- There are some potential problems with connecting to external services; most of the time they are related to a broken promise chain.
- Another common problem is with a timeout—if your Lambda function takes more than three seconds to complete, increase the timeout of the function.

Houston, we have a problem!

This chapter covers

- Reading console logs using CloudWatch
- The challenges of debugging serverless applications
- Debugging serverless APIs

By our nature, we—humans—aren't perfect. No matter what we do, there is always the possibility of making a mistake, even if we do our best not to make one. This is especially true when developing or interacting with software. Do you remember the last time when a mobile application you were using crashed or a website stopped responding? Chances are you have experienced this recently, and you had to refresh your browser or restart your app.

We all make mistakes, and applications crash on a daily basis. Though usually harmless, application bugs can sometimes result in huge losses. Let's take the example of a bug occurring in your pizzeria application that prevents you from creating orders. How would you find the bug in the first place? How does debugging work in serverless applications?

This chapter helps you learn how to find errors in your serverless applications, how to debug them, and what debugging tools you have at your disposal.

5.1 Debugging a serverless app

Because you're progressing quickly, Aunt Maria sends you a message saying that she's hired a mobile developer, Pierre. She wanted to increase the reach to her customers, and a mobile application for making pizza orders seemed like a good start. Pierre wanted to try out your serverless application. Unfortunately, as he tried creating a pizza order, the application returned an invalid response. Pierre complained to your aunt, and now you have your aunt on the phone. You're probably scratching your head thinking, "Where could I have gone wrong?" and "How can I debug this?"

In a traditional Node.js server application, you could just type in a `console.log ("some text")` command somewhere between the lines to log some text or objects to the console, or even type in `debugger` to activate a breakpoint in your code to debug your application. Afterwards you could start it locally and try it out, or log in to the server and tail your application log to debug it.

Logging in a serverless application is quite different compared to a traditional one. Although your serverless application consists of completely separated modules—an API Gateway and a Lambda function—you cannot run it locally and properly debug the whole application flow. Additionally, because your application is serverless, there isn't a server you can log into to tail its logs. Yes, this probably does sound weird and frustrating, but don't worry.

Each serverless provider has a tool to help you monitor and debug your serverless functions. For AWS, it's CloudWatch.

CloudWatch is the AWS service designed for tracking, logging, and monitoring your AWS resources. Think of it as a serverless version of your old server tail log, though capable of much more. As with other AWS services, CloudWatch is available in AWS CLI, and you'll use it from your terminal.

Because you are using AWS, CloudWatch is your default choice.

> **NOTE** You can run your serverless function locally, but that doesn't mean that it will execute the same way as when it's run by your serverless provider. Although Azure has an option to run the function in Visual Studio, and Google Cloud Platform has a Local Emulator for local debugging, neither serverless provider recommends using its function emulator for production usage, because both are in the alpha phase of development.

Here are several ways you can use AWS CloudWatch:

- Via the AWS web console from your browser
- Using the AWS CLI from your terminal
- With the AWS API
- With the AWS SDK (depending on your programming language)

You can use any of these you like, but in this book you will be working mostly with the AWS CLI because it is developer-friendly and you can invoke it from your local terminal.

CloudWatch is a simple service that captures logs and errors from your serverless functions. Whenever you log something in your function—for example, with a `console.log` in Node.js—those logs are automatically sent to AWS CloudWatch. AWS CloudWatch is responsible for their storage and grouping. You can access those logs via the AWS CLI in your terminal or using the AWS web console UI. For a visual understanding of this handling process, see figure 5.1.

> **NOTE** Capturing the logs in CloudWatch doesn't affect your Lambda response time. But the logs aren't available immediately; there is a delay of at least several seconds between the function call and when the logs are available in CloudWatch.

> By default, the CloudWatch logs are kept indefinitely, but you can configure how long you want to keep them for each log group.

> CloudWatch has a free tier, but the number of logs and the retention period can affect your monthly price. For more info, see https://aws.amazon.com /cloudwatch/pricing/.

5.2   *Debugging your Lambda function*

Now that you know what CloudWatch is, you'll use it to find the source of Pierre's problems. Pierre let you know that the error occurs when he tries to create a pizza order with a pizza type and a delivery address. You need to try to reproduce the issue while monitoring the logs using CloudWatch. You will put a log statement at the beginning of your create-order.js handler, redeploy your API, and ask Pierre to try again.

You should log the request with some prefix text—for example, "Save an order"—on the first line of your `createOrder` function, as shown in the following listing. Adding prefix text to your request logs will help you search the logs, but it is not required.

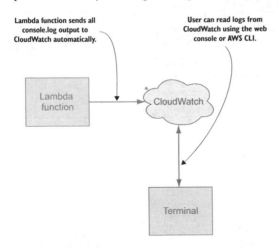

Figure 5.1   AWS Lambda sends console.log output directly to CloudWatch.

(The snippet in this listing shows just the beginning of the file; the rest of the file is unchanged.)

Listing 5.1 Updated create-order.js handler

```
'use strict'

const AWS = require('aws-sdk')
const docClient = new AWS.DynamoDB.DocumentClient()
const rp = require('minimal-request-promise')

module.exports = function createOrder(request) {        Log the request to the console and
  console.log('Save an order', request)    ◄─────────   add "Save an order" as prefix text.

  if (!request || !request.pizza || !request.address)
    throw new Error('To order pizza please provide pizza type and address
      where pizza should be delivered')
                                              The rest of the file remains unchanged.
  // ...    ◄──────────────────────────────
```

Pierre tries again, and receives the same error. Now you should search the logs for the "Save an order" text. Looping through CloudWatch logs for your Lambda function can be difficult, because there can be many entries with a bunch of metadata. Fortunately, you can do it faster with the AWS CLI and the `logs filter-log-events` command for filtering logs.

Because CloudWatch stores the logs in log groups, before running the `logs filter -log-events` command you'll need to find the name of your log group. To do this, you'll use the `logs` service of the AWS CLI once again—more precisely, the `describe -log-groups` command, as shown in the next listing.

Listing 5.2 `describe-logs-groups`

```
aws logs describe-log-groups --region eu-central-1
```

This command will return a response that includes `logGroupName`, similar to the next one:

```
{
    "logGroups": [
        {
            "arn": "arn:aws:logs:eu-central-1:123456789101:log-group:/aws/
    lambda/pizza-api:*",
            "creationTime": 1524828117184,
            "metricFilterCount": 0,
            "logGroupName": "/aws/lambda/pizza-api",
            "storedBytes": 1024
        }
    ]
}
```

NOTE Besides `filter-log-events`, the AWS CLI's `logs` service provides several other useful commands. If you want to see the full list of available commands, run `aws logs help` from your terminal.

Run the `logs filter-log-events` command from your terminal and provide the "Save an order" text as a filter, as shown in listing 5.3. You'll also need to specify an output format, which will be JSON again. See the next listing for the full code example.

Listing 5.3   Filtering CloudWatch logs with a selected log group and by the "Save an order" text

```
aws logs \
  filter-log-events \
```
Use the logs service from the AWS CLI.

Use the filter-log-events command to filter log events.

```
  --filter='Save an order' \
  --log-group-name=/aws/lambda/pizza-api \
  --region=eu-central-1 \
  --output=json
```
Provide filter text.

Show only filtered logs for the /aws/lambda/pizza-api log group.

Set JSON as the output format.

Running the command in listing 5.3 finally allows you to read console.log from your Lambda function. But, as you can see in listing 5.4, it returns it as a JSON with a lot of metadata that isn't relevant for your use case. The only info you care about is "message" from each of the events. Everything else from the response is metadata about the log streams you searched for and some additional info about the log messages.

Listing 5.4   Your Pizza API logs from CloudWatch with metadata

```
{
    "searchedLogStreams": [
        {
            "searchedCompletely": true,
            "logStreamName": "2017/06/18/
  [$LATEST]353ce211793946dba5bb276b0bde3e0e"
        }
    ],
    "events": [
        {
            "ingestionTime": 1497802509940,
            "timestamp": 1497802509920,
            "message": "2017-06-18T16:15:09.860Z\t4cc844ea-5441-11e7-8919-
  29f1e77e006c\tSave an order
            { pizza: 1,\n    adress: '420 Paper St.' }\n",
            "eventId": "334021121314455560391845663590530294774193374849061
  552",
            "logStreamName": "2017/06/18/[$LATEST]
  e24e0cab3d6f47f2b03005ba4ca16b8b"
        }
    ]
}
```
Tell the AWS CLI that you want only the message of the latest event.

Change the response format to text.

Also, the JSON output is not very readable when it's formatted as single-line text. You can improve readability by changing the output type to `text` and updating the filter to return just the message, as shown in the next listing.

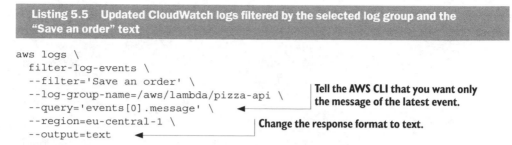

Listing 5.5 Updated CloudWatch logs filtered by the selected log group and the "Save an order" text

```
aws logs \
  filter-log-events \
  --filter='Save an order' \
  --log-group-name=/aws/lambda/pizza-api \
  --query='events[0].message' \        ◄——  Tell the AWS CLI that you want only
  --region=eu-central-1 \                    the message of the latest event.
  --output=text  ◄————                 Change the response format to text.
```

Running this command from the terminal returns a much cleaner response, similar to the one in the following listing.

Listing 5.6 The logged Pizza API message, without any metadata

```
2017-06-18T16:15:09.860Z    4cc844ea-5441-11e7-8919-29f1e77e006c
  Save an order { pizza: 1, adress: '420 Paper St.' }  ◄————  The log returns just
                                                               the message.
```

This output looks a lot cleaner and more useful. And would you look at that, Pierre made a typo! He was sending `adress` instead of `address` by mistake. Such a fuss about a simple spelling mistake, right? Well, at least you won't be the one on the phone explaining the issue to your aunt.

5.3 X-Ray your app

Debugging serverless applications is sometimes hard because it's not easy to visualize the data flow—but AWS has a tool to help you out. AWS X-Ray is a service that shows the data flow of your application and all its involved services in near real time. You can use X-Ray with applications running on EC2, ECS, Lambda, and Elastic Beanstalk. In addition, the X-Ray SDK automatically captures metadata for all API calls made to AWS services using the AWS SDK. Figures 5.2 and 5.3 show the visual representation of your Pizza API created with AWS X-Ray.

To enable AWS X-Ray for your Lambda function, you need to add a policy that allows X-Ray to interact with it, and you need to set the tracing mode to `Active` in your function configuration.

AWS X-Ray and AWS Lambda

AWS Lambda uses Amazon CloudWatch to automatically emit metrics and logs for all invocations of your function. But this mechanism might not be convenient for tracing the event source that invoked your Lambda function or for tracing upstream calls your function makes. That's where AWS X-Ray jumps in. X-Ray integration for AWS Lambda is seamless, because the AWS Lambda runtime already has an X-Ray daemon running.

This section shows just the basic integration of X-Ray and your Lambda function; if you want to learn more, visit the official guide at http://docs.aws.amazon.com/lambda/latest/dg/lambda-x-ray.html.

Figure 5.2   A visual representation of the "Create an order" flow of the Pizza API

> **NOTE**   You'll use the AWS web console for AWS X-Ray because you can't see the visual representation of your application from the terminal.

Let's see how to add a policy and to set the tracing mode to `Active` using the AWS CLI from your terminal. To attach the policy, you'll use the `iam attach-role-policy` command again, but now with `arn:aws:iam::aws:policy/AWSXrayWriteOnlyAccess`, as shown in listing 5.7.

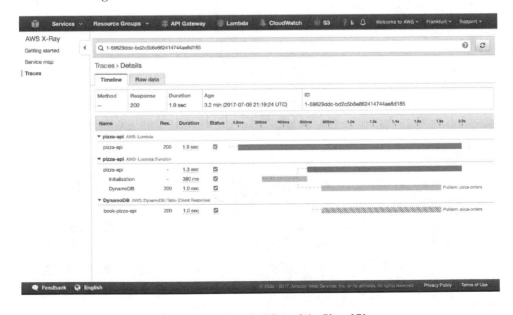

Figure 5.3   A detailed view of the "Create an order" flow of the Pizza API

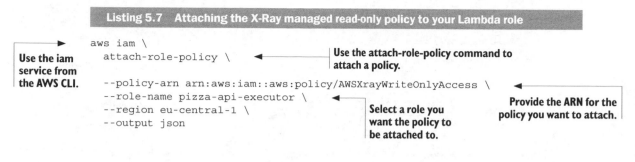

Listing 5.7 Attaching the X-Ray managed read-only policy to your Lambda role

Use the iam service from the AWS CLI.

```
aws iam \
  attach-role-policy \
  --policy-arn arn:aws:iam::aws:policy/AWSXrayWriteOnlyAccess \
  --role-name pizza-api-executor \
  --region eu-central-1 \
  --output json
```

Use the attach-role-policy command to attach a policy.

Provide the ARN for the policy you want to attach.

Select a role you want the policy to be attached to.

As you already know, that command returns an empty result when it's executed successfully.

The next step is to update the function configuration. You can do that with the `lambda update-function-configuration` AWS CLI command. This command expects a function name and options; in this case, you want to update `tracing-config` by setting its mode to `Active`. The following listing shows the full command.

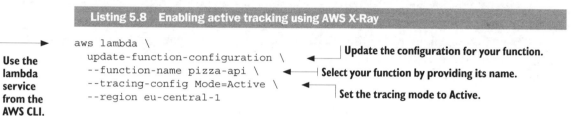

Listing 5.8 Enabling active tracking using AWS X-Ray

Use the lambda service from the AWS CLI.

```
aws lambda \
  update-function-configuration \
  --function-name pizza-api \
  --tracing-config Mode=Active \
  --region eu-central-1
```

Update the configuration for your function.

Select your function by providing its name.

Set the tracing mode to Active.

This command returns the Lambda function configuration as JSON output, as shown in the next listing. At this point, X-Ray displays your Lambda function flow, but by default you won't be able to see other AWS services your function is using, such as DynamoDB.

Listing 5.9 Response after activating the X-Ray tracing

```
{
    "TracingConfig": {
        "Mode": "Active"
    },
    "CodeSha256": "HwV+/VdUztZ782NBEqY9Dvzj3nxF6tigLOZPt8yyCoU=",
    "FunctionName": "pizza-api",
    // ...
}
```

Tracing mode is set to Active

Info about your function, including name, ARN, version and other function metadata

To be able to see other AWS services supported by X-Ray, you'll need to wrap the AWS SDK for Node.js in the `aws-xray-sdk-core` module. After installing the `aws-xray-sdk-core` module from NPM, update your create-order.js handler as shown in the following listing.

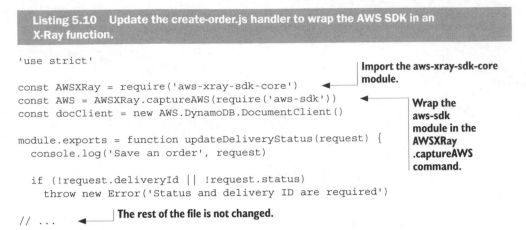

Listing 5.10   Update the create-order.js handler to wrap the AWS SDK in an X-Ray function.

```
'use strict'
                                                    Import the aws-xray-sdk-core
const AWSXRay = require('aws-xray-sdk-core')        module.
const AWS = AWSXRay.captureAWS(require('aws-sdk'))
const docClient = new AWS.DynamoDB.DocumentClient()        Wrap the
                                                           aws-sdk
module.exports = function updateDeliveryStatus(request) {  module in the
  console.log('Save an order', request)                    AWSXRay
                                                           .captureAWS
  if (!request.deliveryId || !request.status)              command.
    throw new Error('Status and delivery ID are required')

// ...        The rest of the file is not changed.
```

After you run the `claudia update` command to redeploy your API, X-Ray will be fully set up.

To see the visual representation of your function, go to the X-Ray section of the AWS web console. For this case, the URL is https://eu-central-1.console.aws.amazon.com/xray/home?region=eu-central-1#/service-map. Your URL may be different if you used a different region to deploy your function.

5.4   *Taste it!*

The exercise for this chapter is quite easy, but the next chapter brings in some more serious topics.

5.4.1   *Exercise*

Now that you've learned how to debug your serverless applications, let's revisit the code listings from chapters 3 and 4 and try to read their logs.

Your exercise for this chapter is to try to read the CloudWatch logs for all success and error messages from the create-order.js handler.

Because this is just a debug exercise, there will be no tips this time. In case you need help, feel free to take a peek at the solution in the next section.

5.4.2   *Solution*

In chapter 3, you updated the create-order.js handler to log success messages and errors. To read those logs with CloudWatch, use the `aws logs filter-log-events` command. As you learned in this chapter, this command requires a filter. As a reminder, success messages were logged with an "Order is saved!" prefix. For errors, you used the "Oops, order is not saved :(" prefix. Use both of these prefixes to help you to filter the logs.

The command to filter with the "Order is saved!" prefix is shown in the following listing.

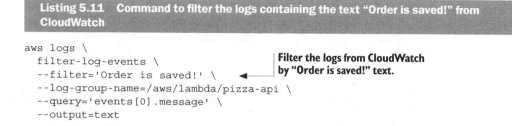

Listing 5.11 Command to filter the logs containing the text "Order is saved!" from CloudWatch

```
aws logs \
  filter-log-events \
  --filter='Order is saved!' \          Filter the logs from CloudWatch
  --log-group-name=/aws/lambda/pizza-api \    by "Order is saved!" text.
  --query='events[0].message' \
  --output=text
```

NOTE You can use the same command for the "Oops, order is not saved :(" text to filter the logs and read the errors. But because your message contains a comma and a colon, which are considered special characters, it's much safer to use just part of the text as a filter—for example, "order is not saved."

The responses for both commands will differ depending on the number of successful and failed orders in your system. If there aren't any errors, the output will display None.

Summary

- You need to use CloudWatch to read logs from Lambda functions.
- Instead of manually filtering the logs, you can use various commands from the AWS CLI.
- To visualize your function flow, you can use the AWS X-Ray service.

Level up your API 6

This chapter covers

- How authentication and authorization work in serverless applications

- Implementing authentication and authorization in your serverless application

- Identifying your users through social identity providers

Authentication and authorization are one of many challenges you face when developing distributed applications. The challenge lies in distributing the authorized user, along with its permissions, across all application distributed services and properly integrating third-party authentications.

This chapter shows you how to implement authentication and authorization in your serverless application by enabling it for Aunt Maria's customers and their pizza orders. You'll learn the difference between authentication and authorization in a serverless environment and how to implement a web authorization mechanism using AWS Cognito. Then you'll learn how to identify your users using a social provider—specifically, Facebook.

6.1 Serverless authentication and authorization

Aunt Maria and Pierre, her mobile developer whom you so fondly remember from the previous chapter, have informed you that your API call for pizza orders is showing all pizza orders to everyone, no matter who is asking. Only employees should be able to see all orders. Customers should be able to see only their own orders. Non-customers and non-employees should not be able to see any order.

Here's how you'll correct this issue:

1 Enable your application users to authenticate themselves in two ways:

   - Via email
   - Via Facebook

2 Create a user list for your API, and restrict each user to seeing only their own orders.

Authentication vs. authorization

You have probably noticed that the two different verbs—*authenticate* and *authorize*—look similar, especially if you're coming from a non-English speaking region, but they cover two different concepts. Combined with other concepts such as *user identity* and *permissions*, they can cause headaches.

Let's try to understand them using an example.

Think of your application as an enterprise company, which owns or rents an office building. Often, these office buildings include a building security that doesn't allow anyone except company employees to enter. Because the building security needs to know who is allowed to enter, companies usually provide security staff with an employee list along with their information, such as a photo.

If a person tries to enter the building, security stops them and asks for information about their **identity**. If the person doesn't provide any identifying information, security kicks them out, denying entry. If the person provides proper identity information, security checks it to confirm their identity. This process is called **authentication**.

If the person's identity is trusted, the person is *authenticated*. But now security checks whether the person trying to enter is on the company employee list. If the person is not on the list, security doesn't allow entry. If the person is on the employee list, their entry is allowed. This process is called **authorization**.

But can every company's employee spend money from the company's bank account? Unless the user is the company CEO, the answer is probably no (sometimes not even the CEO). The right to spend the company's money, or do something restrictive, is called a **permission**.

To summarize:

   - *Authentication*—Checking if the user is who they claim to be
   - *Authorization*—Checking if the user is allowed access
   - *Identity*—Information representing who the user is
   - *Permission*—The right given to a user to do something

Based on your experience with Express.js or other more traditional applications, you probably want to implement authentication as a part of your API and keep your users in a database table. Though that option is feasible, we recommend another method for serverless.

Most applications need authorization, and it's usually an email/password combination. Each authorization is implemented in a similar, if not identical, manner. Therefore, serverless providers have enabled almost literal plug-and-play authentication and authorization services to handle their vast serverless resources. In your case, Amazon has AWS Cognito—a user management and synchronization service that takes care of user authentication, authorization, access management, and user and data synchronization across services.

There are two main concepts in Amazon Cognito, each with a different responsibility:

- *User pools*—A service responsible for identity management. Alongside that, it also comes with a possibility of an out-of-the-box authorization. Put simply, it's a set of directories (*user pools*) for your users, with a capability of providing an authorization mechanism as well. For your front-end web and mobile application, you can implement the Cognito user pool authorization mechanism using AWS Cognito SDK.
  A user pool represents a single collection of users or a user directory.

- *Federated identities* (also called identity pools)—A service responsible for handling authentication providers and providing temporary authorization to AWS resources. Federated identities provide

  - Integration with social identity providers (such as Facebook, Google, and OpenId) and your Cognito user pool's authentication identity provider
  - Temporary access to your application's AWS resources for authenticated users

  Federated identities are directories of a single user's identities. Those identity pools keep track of each user logging in with different identity providers. To store actual user data, identity pools require Cognito user pools.

One of the key benefits of AWS Cognito is that it authorizes the requests before they hit your serverless application. It does that by setting the authorization on the API Gateway level. If the user is not authorized, it stops the requests before they hit your Lambda function and DynamoDB table, which can potentially save a lot of wasted time and money. Even though AWS Lambda is inexpensive, additional cost cutting is always welcome.

In the case of Aunt Maria's pizzeria, you need to have both Congito identity pools and Cognito user pools. An identity pool will allow you to integrate Facebook login, and it will also give you a temporary access to your Cognito user pool without hardcoding your AWS access token and secret in the front-end and mobile applications. A user pool will manage the database of users that can order a pizza.

For Aunt Maria's pizzeria, you need to enable your customers to authenticate via Facebook. As shown in figure 6.1, your Facebook authentication flow should have the following steps:

1. Ask the user to log in via Facebook in the web or mobile application.
2. When the Facebook access token is received, send that token to a Cognito identity pool that will grant the user temporary Cognito user pools access in the browser.
3. Use a Cognito user pool to log in or register your user. After successful login or registration, the user pool will return a JWT token.
4. Use that JWT token to contact the Pizza API when you want to create an order or list existing orders.

As shown in figure 6.2, the flow for authentication with email and password is similar:

1. Ask the Cognito identity pool for a temporary access to Cognito user pools.
2. Log in or register to the Cognito user pool using email and password. After successful login or registration, the user pool will return a JWT token.
3. Use that JWT token to contact the Pizza API when you want to create an order or list existing orders.

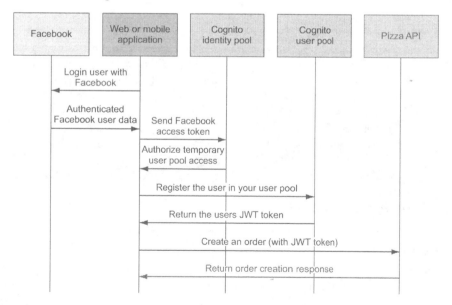

Figure 6.1   The responsibilities of user pools and identity pools

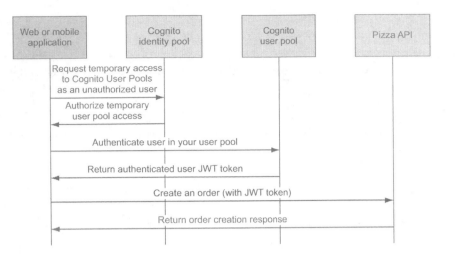

Figure 6.2   A visual representation of Facebook authorization using identity pools and user pools for your serverless Pizza API

Other paths to authorization

Within AWS, besides Amazon Cognito, there are other ways to protect your API, such as

- *Using IAM roles and policies*—The most basic authorization mechanism. To allow an API caller to invoke the API, you need to create IAM policies that permit the specified API caller to invoke the API method for which the IAM user authentication is enabled. In your case, that wouldn't be the optimal solution, because you have a single API on Gateway API and only certain routes that need to be protected.
- *Using custom authorizers*—Amazon API Gateway custom authorizers are Lambda functions that you enable to control access to your APIs using bearer token authentication strategies, such as OAuth or SAML. In practice, each time your API on API Gateway is invoked, your authorizer Lambda function is invoked as well. When the *authorization Lambda* confirms the access using authorization token, your handler Lambda function will be invoked.

6.2   Creating user and identity pools

To implement the authentication flow, as described in the previous section, you need to create both user and identity pools.

Start with a user pool. To create one, run the `aws cognito-idp create-user-pool` command from your terminal. The only required option for this command is the name for your new pool. In addition to the name, add the `--username-attributes` option, which specifies an email as a unique ID of your user pool. You may also want to customize the password policy by specifying the `--policies` option. The default password policy requires a mix of lowercase letters, uppercase letters, numbers, and special characters. The full command for creating a new user pool is shown in the next listing.

Listing 6.1 Creating a user pool

```
aws cognito-idp create-user-pool \
    --pool-name Pizzeria \
    --policies "PasswordPolicy={MinimumLength=8,RequireUppercase=false,
     RequireLowercase=false,
    RequireNumbers=false,RequireSymbols=false}" \
    --username-attributes email \
    --query UserPool.Id \
    --output text
```

Create the user pool.

Set a password policy.

Set the name for your user pool.

Define the email address as a unique user ID.

Print the user pool ID as text.

The output is the ID of your new user pool, because the query flag was provided. Keep this ID, because you'll need it later.

> **NOTE** For the sake of simplicity, this example uses only a small subset of Cognito features. There are many more options you can set for your user pool, such as automatic email or phone verification, a list of mandatory attributes. For more information, visit the official documentation at https://console.aws.amazon.com/cognito/home.

Your user pool needs to have at least one client so you can connect it. You can create a client via the aws cognito-idp create-user-pool-client command, as shown in the listing 6.2. To create a client, you need to pass your user pool ID, which you received from the previous command, and your client name. You'll test this setup with a simple web app, so you should create a client without a client secret (which means that you'll need to create another client for Pierre's mobile app in the future).

Listing 6.2 Creating a client for the user pool

```
aws cognito-idp create-user-pool-client \
   --user-pool-id eu-central-1_userPoolId \
    --client-name PizzeriaClient \
    --no-generate-secret \
    --query UserPoolClient.ClientId \
    --output text
```

Create the user pool client.

Do not generate the client secret.

Specify the user pool ID you received from the previous command.

Specify your client name.

Print out only the client ID as text.

This command prints out the client ID; save it because you'll need it in the next step.

Before implementing the Facebook authentication and permissions within your application, you need to visit the Facebook developer portal to create an application and obtain its ID.

> **NOTE** If you are not familiar with how Facebook applications work, a step-by-step tutorial is available in the Facebook developer documentation: https://developers.facebook.com/docs/apps/register.

If you aren't using Facebook and don't want to implement a Facebook login for your application, your application will work fine with the email and password login with minor modifications. We let you know which parts to modify.

The next step is to create an identity pool, which you can do using the `aws cognito -identity create-identity-pool` command from the AWS CLI, as shown in listing 6.3. To do so, provide the identity pool name, any supported login providers (in your case, Facebook), and a Cognito identity provider. For the `cognito-identity -providers` flag, you'll need to provide the provider name and client ID and indicate whether you need a server-side token check. The provider name is in the following format: `cognito-idp.<REGION>.amazonaws.com/<USER_POOL_ID>`. The client ID is what you received from the previous command, and you don't need server-side token validation, so that value is set to `false`.

Listing 6.3   Creating an identity pool

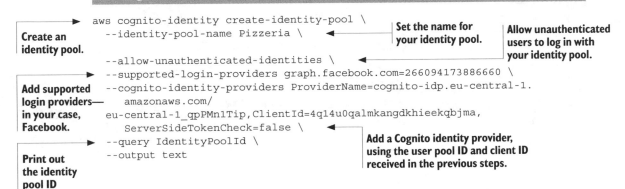

```
aws cognito-identity create-identity-pool \
   --identity-pool-name Pizzeria \
   --allow-unauthenticated-identities \
   --supported-login-providers graph.facebook.com=266094173886660 \
   --cognito-identity-providers ProviderName=cognito-idp.eu-central-1.
      amazonaws.com/
eu-central-1_qpPMn1Tip,ClientId=4q14u0qalmkangdkhieekqbjma,
      ServerSideTokenCheck=false \
   --query IdentityPoolId \
   --output text
```

Create an identity pool.

Set the name for your identity pool.

Allow unauthenticated users to log in with your identity pool.

Add supported login providers— in your case, Facebook.

Print out the identity pool ID as text.

Add a Cognito identity provider, using the user pool ID and client ID received in the previous steps.

After the identity pool is successfully created, you'll need to create two roles and assign them to authenticated and unauthenticated users. If you need help with role creation, see https://aws.amazon.com/blogs/mobile/understanding-amazon-cognito -authentication-part-3-roles-and-policies/.

> **TIP** If you struggle with role creation from the AWS CLI, single-click role creation and assignment is available from the web console. Go to your identity pool, click the Edit identity pool button, and then click the Create New Role link for both the authenticated and unauthenticated roles.

To set the roles, use the `aws cognito-identity set-identity-pool-roles` command, which expects the identity pool ID and roles for both authenticated and unauthenticated users, as shown in the following listing. Make sure you replace the <ROLE1_ARN> and <ROLE2_ARN> values with the ARNs of the two roles you just created.

Listing 6.4   Add roles to the identity pool

Provide the identity pool ID.

```
aws cognito-identity set-identity-pool-roles \
   --identity-pool-id eu-central-1:2a3b45c6-1234-123d-1234-1e23fg45hij6 \

   --roles authenticated=<ROLE1_ARN>,unauthenticated=<ROLE2_ARN>
```

Set the roles for the identity pool.

Add the roles for both authenticated and unauthenticated users.

This command returns an empty response if it successfully executes.

6.2.1 Controlling API access with Cognito

Now that you have user and identity pools, it's time to connect the authentication flow in your code.

Claudia, in combination with Claudia API Builder, supports all three authorization methods mentioned earlier: IAM roles, custom authorizers, and Cognito user pools. This book focuses on the last one, but the other two work in a similar way. For more information about them, see the official documentation for Claudia API Builder: https://github .com/claudiajs/claudia-api-builder/blob/master/docs/api.md#require-authorization.

> **NOTE** The Cognito identity pool is not used by Claudia or your Lambda function. It is used by the front-end applications to get temporary access to Cognito user pools without having to hardcode the AWS profile access and secret keys.

To enable Cognito user pool authorization, you'll need to register an authorizer using the `registerAuthorizer` method of the Claudia API Builder instance. This method requires two attributes: the authorizer name and an object with an array of Cognito user pool ARNs. The following is a simple example usage:

```
api.registerAuthorizer('MyCognitoAuth', {
  providerARNs: ['<COGNITO_USER_POOL_ARN>']
});
```

After the authorizer is registered, add an object with the `cognitoAuthorizer` key and the name you used to register your authorizer as a value, as a third argument to the route definition. Your route definition should look like this:

```
api.post('/protectedRoute', request => {
  return doSomething(request)
}, { cognitoAuthorizer: 'MyCognitoAuth' })
```

Apply the same to the routes in your api.js file. The routes will look similar to the ones shown in the following listing. All routes related to the orders will be protected with the Cognito authorizer, but routes for pizzas will stay public.

Listing 6.5 API with a custom authorizer

```
'use strict'

const Api = require('claudia-api-builder')
const api = new Api()

const getPizzas = require('./handlers/get-pizzas')
const createOrder = require('./handlers/create-order')
const updateOrder = require('./handlers/update-order')
const deleteOrder = require('./handlers/delete-order')

api.registerAuthorizer('userAuthentication', {        ◄──── Register a custom authorizer.
  providerARNs: [process.env.userPoolArn]        ◄──── Get the user pool ARN from an environment variable, and set it as the provider ARN.
})
```

```
// Define routes
api.get('/', () => 'Welcome to Pizza API')

api.get('/pizzas', () => {
  return getPizzas()
})
api.get('/pizzas/{id}', (request) => {
  return getPizzas(request.pathParams.id)
}, {
  error: 404
})

api.post('/orders', (request) => {
  return createOrder(request)
}, {
  success: 201,
  error: 400,
  cognitoAuthorizer: 'userAuthentication'
})
api.put('/orders/{id}', (request) => {
  return updateOrder(request.pathParams.id, request.body)
}, {
  error: 400,
  cognitoAuthorizer: 'userAuthentication'
})
api.delete('/orders/{id}', (request) => {
  return deleteOrder(request.pathParams.id)
}, {
  error: 400,
  cognitoAuthorizer: 'userAuthentication'
})
api.post('delivery', (request) => {
  return updateDeliveryStatus(request.body)
}, {
  success: 200,
  error: 400,
  `cognitoAuthorizer: 'userAuthentication'
})
```

Pass the whole request object, including its body and authorization data.

Enable authorization only on specific routes.

```
module.exports = api
```

The last piece of the authorization puzzle is updating the route handler to use the authorizer.

For example, to update your create-order.js handler you need to do the following:

- Update the handler to receive the full request object instead of just the body. You want to be able to read user data from the Cognito user pool; that information is provided in the request object, but outside of the body.
- Get the user data from the authorizer. It is available in the request context, in the authorizer object, under the key named `claims`.
- Update the code to get the user's address from the request body, if provided, or the default address of the authorized user if an address is not provided in the body.
- Save the Cognito username in the DynamoDB orders table.

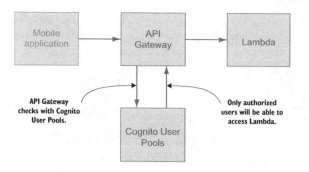

API Gateway
checks with Cognito
User Pools.

Only authorized
users will be able to
access Lambda.

**Figure 6.3   A visual representation of how access to
your API is controlled by API Gateway and Amazon Cognito
user pools**

Figure 6.3 shows how the API is restricted by API Gateway and Amazon Cognito
user pools.

The updated create-order.js handler is shown in the following listing.

Listing 6.6   create-order.js handler with authorization

```
'use strict'

const AWS = require('aws-sdk')
const docClient = new AWS.DynamoDB.DocumentClient()
const rp = require('minimal-request-promise')

function createOrder(request) {
  console.log('Save an order', request.body)
  const userData = request.context.authorizer.claims
  console.log('User data', userData)

  let userAddress = request.body && request.body.address
  if (!userAddress) {
    userAddress = JSON.parse(userData.address).formatted
  }

  if (!request.body || !request.body.pizza || userAddress)
    throw new Error('To order pizza please provide pizza type and address
      where pizza should be delivered')

  return rp.post('https://fake-delivery-api.effortlessserverless.com/
    delivery', {
    headers: {
      Authorization: 'aunt-marias-pizzeria-1234567890',
      'Content-type': 'application/json'
    },
    body: JSON.stringify({
      pickupTime: '15.34pm',
      pickupAddress: 'Aunt Maria Pizzeria',
      deliveryAddress: userAddress,
```

**The createOrder function
receives a full request object.**

**Get the user data added by the
authorizer from the context
object and then log it.**

**By default, use an address
from the request body.**

**If the address is not provided,
use the user's default address.**

**Pass the correct address to the
Some Like It Hot Delivery API.**

```
      webhookUrl: 'https://g8fhlgccof.execute-api.eu-central-1.amazonaws.com/
    latest/delivery',
    })
  })
    .then(rawResponse => JSON.parse(rawResponse.body))
    .then(response => {
      return docClient.put({
        TableName: 'pizza-orders',
        Item: {
          cognitoUsername: userAddress['cognito:username'],    ◄───┐ Save the
          orderId: response.deliveryId,                             │ username from
          pizza: request.body.pizza,                                │ Cognito to the
          address: userAddress,      ◄───── Save the correct address to the database.  database.
          orderStatus: 'pending'
        }
      }).promise()
    })
    .then(res => {
      console.log('Order is saved!', res)

      return res
    })
    .catch(saveError => {
      console.log(`Oops, order is not saved :(`, saveError)

      throw saveError
    })
}


module.exports = createOrder
```

After the code is updated, run `claudia update` to deploy your API. To test the working authorization, you'll need to implement the login/signup flow. The back-end part of adding the authorization was easy. But most of the work, including the integration of your user and identity pools, should be done on the front-end side. This part of the application is beyond the scope of this book, but you can see the working example code with a how-to guide on GitHub at https://github.com/effortless-serverless/pizzeria-web-app.

Before you run the code from that repository, however, you can confirm that unauthorized users will be rejected by running the following `curl` command:

```
curl -o - -s -w ", status: %{http_code}\n" \
  -H "Content-Type: application/json" \
  -X POST \
  -d '{"pizzaId":1,"address":"221B Baker Street"}' \     ◄──── Accept userData as an
  https://21cioselv9.execute-api.us-east-1.amazonaws.com/latest/orders   additional argument.
```

This command should return an error and a 401 HTTP status.

The back-end part for adding authorization is easy. Most of the work, including integration of your user and identity pools, should be done on the client-side. This part of the application is beyond the scope of this book, but you can see the working example code with the how-to guide on Github here: https://github.com/effortless-serverless/pizzeria-web-app.

6.3 *Taste it!*

Now that you know how authorizers work, it's time to try it on your own.

6.3.1 *Exercise*

Your exercise for this chapter is to update the delete-order.js handler to allow users to delete only their orders.

Here are a few hints, in case you need them:

- Authorization was added to the route in listing 6.5.
- Although the `deleteOrder` function currently accepts only `orderId`, you'll need to extend it to accept authorized user details, too.
- The `deleteOrder` method should use `cognito:username` from the `request.context.authorizer.claims` object to check if the current user is the order owner.
- If the user is not the owner, you should return an error.

> **Returning custom errors from Claudia**
>
> When an error is thrown, Claudia sends a 400 Bad Request status code to the customer, as you defined earlier. But if users want to delete orders that don't belong to them, you might want to return an HTTP error such as 403 Forbidden or 401 Unauthorized.
>
> In order to do so, you need to set a status code and response dynamically. Claudia API Builder enables you to do that by exposing an `ApiResponse` method in the API Builder instance. For example, to return a 403 status code you should use the following:
>
> ```
> return new api.ApiResponse({ message: 'Action is forbidden' },
> { 'Content-Type': 'application/json' }, 403)
> ```
>
> You can find more information about dynamic responses in the official Claudia API Builder documentation: https://github.com/claudiajs/claudia-api-builder/blob/master/docs/api.md#dynamic-responses.

In case you want an additional challenge, here are two more:

- Update an order's primary key to be a combination of the order ID and the owner's Cognito username. Doing so would allow you to directly search for and delete only orders owned by the authorized user.
- Modify the update-order.js handler in such a way as to allow users to update only their own orders.

6.3.2 *Solution*

First, you need to update your delete-order.js handler to accept both `orderId` and the authorized user data. You also want to get the order from the database and check if it belongs to the authorized user. The following listing shows the updated delete-order.js handler.

Listing 6.7   delete-order.js handler with authorization

```
'use strict'

const AWS = require('aws-sdk')
const docClient = new AWS.DynamoDB.DocumentClient()
const rp = require('minimal-request-promise')
                                                          Accept userData as an
                                                          additional argument.
function deleteOrder(orderId, userData) {   ◄─────┘
  return docClient.get({
    TableName: 'pizza-orders',
    Key: {
      orderId: orderId
    }
  }).promise()                                          Check whether the order is
    .then(result => result.Item)                        owned by the authorized user.
    .then(item => {
      if (item.cognitoUsername !== userData['cognito:username'])   ◄───┘
        throw new Error('Order is not owned by your user')    ◄───
                                                          Throw an error if the
      if (item.orderStatus !== 'pending')                 order is not owned by
        throw new Error('Order status is not pending')     the authorized user.

      return rp.delete(`https://fake-delivery-api.effortlessserverless.com/
      delivery/${orderId}`, {
        headers: {
          Authorization: 'aunt-marias-pizzeria-1234567890',
          'Content-type': 'application/json'
        }
      })
    })
    .then(() => {
      return docClient.delete({
        TableName: 'pizza-orders',
        Key: {
          orderId: orderId
        }
      }).promise()
    })
}

module.exports = deleteOrder
```

After updating your handler, you need to update the route to pass the correct data to the handler. The following listing shows an excerpt from api.js where the order ID and user data are passed to the delete-order.js handler. As you saw earlier, user data is available as claims in the request.context.authorizer object.

Listing 6.8   Updating the delete order route to pass user data to the handler

```
api.delete('/orders/{id}', (request) => {
  return deleteOrder(request.pathParams.id, request.context.authorizer.claims)
}, {
```

**Pass orderId and claims from the
authorizer object to the handler.**

```
  error: 400,
  cognitoAuthorizer: 'userAuthentication'
})
```

Now that your code is updated, simply run `claudia update` to deploy it. After its completion, you can use the front-end code from the https://github.com/effortless-serverless/pizzeria-web-app repository to implement retrieving the authorization token on your front-end application or to test. If you try to delete an old order using that token, it won't work because it was already created without authorization; the Cognito username won't match.

Summary

- You can authenticate users of your serverless application using Amazon Cognito.
- For many user groups with different permissions, use Amazon Cognito identity pools.
- Setting different authentication methods is easy; just remember that each authentication method has its own user pool.
- Using Claudia, you can speed up your whole AWS Cognito authentication setup.

Working with files

In addition to requiring processing and database storage, applications often also need file storage for static files. Static files are media such as photos, audio or video files, and text files (for example, HTML, CSS, and JavaScript files).

Serverless applications need to store static files, too. Keeping your whole application serverless implies that you need a storage solution that follows the same principles. This chapter takes a dive into serverless file storage possibilities and examines how to create a separate file processing function that uses the storage and provides requested files to your other Lambda—your serverless API.

7.1 Storing static files in a serverless application

In the case of your pizza application, it wouldn't be complete without the images of Aunt Maria's delicious pizzas. Your cousin Michelangelo (also known as Mike) already took awesome photos of all the pizzas, so you just need to store and serve these static files. AWS has a service for that as well: the Simple Storage Service (S3), which allows you to store the files—up to 5 TB—in a serverless manner.

Amazon S3 stores files in *buckets*—folder-like structures owned by an AWS account. Each file, or object, stored in a bucket has a unique identification key. S3 buckets support triggers for Lambda functions that allow you to invoke a certain Lambda when something happens in the bucket.

> **NOTE** We recommend that you understand the basics of Amazon S3 before reading this chapter. A good starting point is the official documentation available at http://docs.aws.amazon.com/AmazonS3/latest/dev/Welcome.html.

In S3 everything starts with the bucket, so you'll create one using the AWS web console, an API, or the AWS CLI, which is our preferred method. The `mb` command requires an S3 URI as an argument. An S3 URI is the name of your S3 bucket prefixed with `s3://`. If you want to specify the region, you can do that using the `--region` flag. In our example, we're naming the S3 bucket `aunt-marias-pizzeria` and specifying the region.

Run the following command at the CLI prompt:

```
aws s3 mb s3://aunt-marias-pizzeria --region eu-central-1
```

> **NOTE** Note that the bucket name must be unique across all existing bucket names in Amazon S3. Your command will fail if you use the same name you used in the previous code listing. To run the command successfully, change the name to something unique. For more information about S3 bucket naming conventions and rules, visit: https://docs.aws.amazon.com/AmazonS3/latest/dev/BucketRestrictions.html.

The response after running the command should be `make_bucket: aunt-marias -pizzeria`. If your bucket name isn't unique, you'll receive the following error, and you'll have to rerun the command with a different bucket name:

```
    make_bucket failed: s3://bucket-name An error occurred
  (BucketAlreadyExists) when calling the CreateBucket operation: The
    requested bucket name is
 not available. The bucket namespace is shared by all users of the system.
    Please select a
different name and try again.
```

Now that you have the bucket, you want to allow only certain users to upload files to it. But before that, you should think about the folder structure of your bucket.

> **NOTE** Amazon S3 buckets don't really support folders; everything in the bucket is just an object. But to simplify interactions with S3, Amazon displays folder-like object names as real folders in its web console. For example, an object named /images/large/pizza.jpg will be shown as the pizza.jpg image in the folder named large, which will be inside the images folder.

As you can see in figure 7.1, you should upload your images to an images folder. Sometimes raw images can be too big for a mobile application, so you should also have a thumbnails folder that will contain smaller versions of your images. Also, because there will be only a single menu.pdf file at a time, it doesn't need to be stored in the folder.

Now that you have the folder structure in place, you need to allow certain users to upload images to the bucket. The easiest way to do so is to generate a presigned URL that will be used for the image upload.

By default, all objects and buckets are private—only the user that created them can access them. A presigned URL allows a user that does not have access permissions to upload files to the bucket. This URL is generated by the user who has access to the bucket and who will grant temporary permissions to anyone that knows it.

Because this URL needs to stay secret, you'll create a new route in the Pizza API that will generate and return that URL. This route should also be protected; in this example you'll allow all authorized users to use this API endpoint, but in a real-world application you should have a special user group that can access certain API endpoints, such as an administrators group.

> **NOTE**   The user groups mentioned here are Cognito user groups within Cognito user pools. If you want to learn more about groups within Cognito user pools, see http://docs.aws.amazon.com/cognito/latest/developerguide/cognito-user-pools-user-groups.html.

To generate a URL, you need to create a new handler. To do so, use the `getSignedUrl` method of the `S3` class. This method accepts two arguments: the first is the name of the method that will be used via the signed URL (`putObject`), and the second is an options object. This options object requires the following parameters:

- The name of the bucket that this signed URL is accessing.
- The unique key that will be used for signing the URL. Because generating a unique key on your own isn't easy, you should use the `uuid` module. You used this module earlier, in chapter 3; just remember to reinstall it if you removed it from your package.json file. (You only need the version 4 UUID, so you'll directly require `uuid/v4`.)

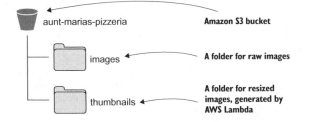

Figure 7.1   The recommended structure of your Amazon S3 bucket

- The access control list (ACL), which defines how the public can interact with the objects in your bucket. In your case you want everyone to be able to see the objects, so set it to `public-read`.
- The expiration time in seconds for the generated URL. Two minutes should be enough, so set it to 120 seconds.

After generating the options object, use the `getSignedUrl` method to sign the URL and then return it as a JSON object. Create a file named generate-presigned-url.js in the handlers folder of your Pizza API, as shown in the following listing.

Listing 7.1   Pizza API handler for presigned URL generation

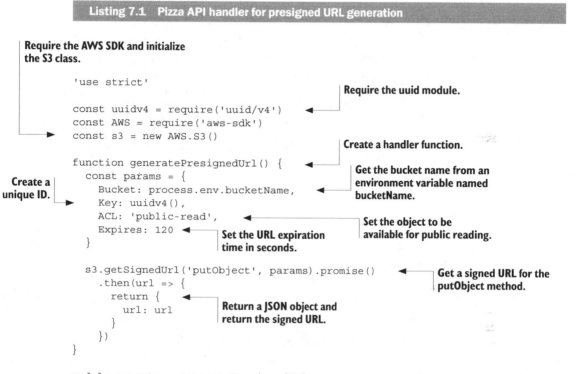

Require the AWS SDK and initialize the S3 class.

```
'use strict'

const uuidv4 = require('uuid/v4')      ◄── Require the uuid module.
const AWS = require('aws-sdk')
const s3 = new AWS.S3()

function generatePresignedUrl() {      ◄── Create a handler function.
  const params = {
    Bucket: process.env.bucketName,    ◄── Get the bucket name from an
    Key: uuidv4(),                         environment variable named
    ACL: 'public-read',                    bucketName.
    Expires: 120                       ◄── Set the object to be
  }                                        available for public reading.

  s3.getSignedUrl('putObject', params).promise()  ◄── Get a signed URL for the
    .then(url => {                                    putObject method.
      return {
        url: url                       ◄── Return a JSON object and
      }                                    return the signed URL.
    })
}

module.exports = generatePresignedUrl
```

Create a unique ID.

Set the URL expiration time in seconds.

Now that your handler is ready, to get the signed URL, you need to add a new route in your api.js file. You can name it /upload-url. As mentioned previously, you should protect this route in the same way the /orders routes are protected— only users authorized through the Cognito authorizer called `userAuthentication` should be able to get this URL. Listing 7.2 shows the end of the api.js file. The rest is unchanged; just remember to require the `getSignedUrl` handler at the top of the api.js file by adding the `const getSignedUrl = require('./handlers/generate -presigned-url.js')` line.

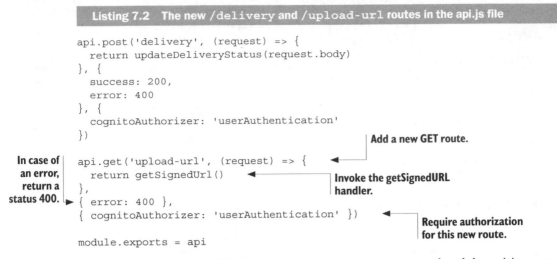

Listing 7.2   The new /delivery and /upload-url routes in the api.js file

```
api.post('delivery', (request) => {
  return updateDeliveryStatus(request.body)
}, {
  success: 200,
  error: 400
}, {
  cognitoAuthorizer: 'userAuthentication'
})
```

Add a new GET route.

```
api.get('upload-url', (request) => {
  return getSignedUrl()
},
```

In case of an error, return a status 400.

Invoke the getSignedURL handler.

```
{ error: 400 },
{ cognitoAuthorizer: 'userAuthentication' })
```

Require authorization for this new route.

```
module.exports = api
```

If you now update your API using the claudia update command and then visit your new route with an authorization token (received from the web application, as explained in the previous chapter), you'll receive the signed URL that can be used for uploading files to your bucket.

7.2   Generating thumbnails

Because each uploaded image can be quite large, and Aunt Maria also has a mobile application, you'll need to resize all the photos and create thumbnails. You don't want thumbnail creation to block your API in any way, so image processing is a perfect candidate for an independent microservice.

An independent service, in this case, represents a separate Lambda function that will trigger automatically when a new photo is uploaded to Amazon S3. The flow of the events (figure 7.2) proceeds as follows:

- User requests a new signed URL via /upload-url route of Pizza API.
- New photo is uploaded to the generated URL.
- Amazon S3 triggers your new Lambda function.
- Lambda function resizes the image and stores the thumbnail in the thumbnails folder.

The new Lambda function won't be triggered via an HTTP request, so you don't need Claudia API Builder. Instead, you'll need to export a simple handler function that will get the new object from S3 and then resize it using ImageMagick. ImageMagick is available in AWS Lambda by default; you do not need to install it before using it.

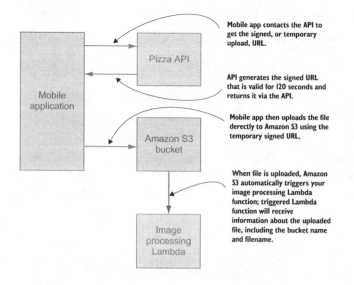

Figure 7.2   The image upload and processing flow

> ## ImageMagick
>
> ImageMagick is a free and open source software suite for displaying, converting, and editing raster image and vector image files. It consists of multiple command-line interfaces, and it can read and write more than 200 different image file formats.
>
> ImageMagick features include file format conversion, image scaling and transformations, color manipulation, composition, and many others.
>
> To learn more about ImageMagick, visit http://imagemagick.org.

The first step when creating a separate service is to create a new project. You need to

1 Create a new folder outside of your pizza-api folder (a good name for it would be pizza-image-processor).
2 Inside your new folder, initialize a new NPM package (`npm init`).

Your next step is creating a file that exports your service handler function. Because this is just an image processor and not an API, you don't need to use Claudia API Builder.

> **NOTE**   When you aren't using Claudia API Builder, you can't export your handler function using `module.exports` from your initial file. Instead, your "vanilla" Lambda requires you to do an `exports.handler` from your file.

This service will be small and could fit in a single file, but for easier maintenance and a more test-friendly approach, you'll split it into two files: the first is an initial file that just extracts the data from a Lambda event, and the second is the actual converter.

Your initial file needs a handler function that receives three arguments:

- The event triggered by the Lambda function

- The context of the Lambda function
- A callback that allows you to respond back from the Lambda function

In your initial file, you'll first check if a valid event record exists and, if so, if it is coming from Amazon S3. Because multiple services can trigger the same Lambda function, you also need to check if it's from your S3 storage. Then you need to extract your S3 bucket name and the filename with a path or an object key using a proper S3 query. Its response will be an image that you'll need to pass to the convert function.

NOTE The implementation of the convert function is promise-based, because Claudia API Builder is promise-based by default. You should keep the same coding style in all of your services, but if you prefer callbacks, this function can use them, too.

The initial code is shown in the following listing.

Listing 7.3   The initial file for your new image processor Lambda function

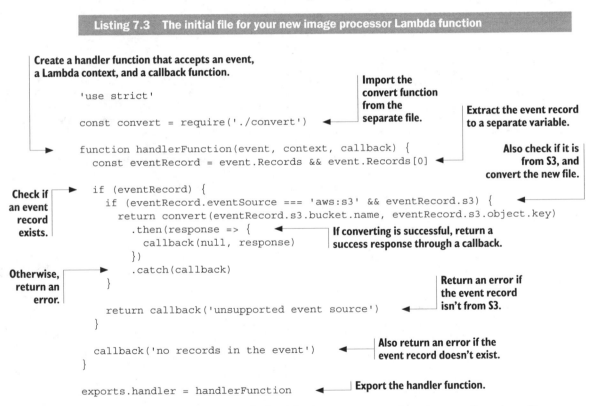

Create a handler function that accepts an event, a Lambda context, and a callback function.

Import the convert function from the separate file.

Extract the event record to a separate variable.

Also check if it is from S3, and convert the new file.

```
'use strict'

const convert = require('./convert')

function handlerFunction(event, context, callback) {
  const eventRecord = event.Records && event.Records[0]

  if (eventRecord) {
    if (eventRecord.eventSource === 'aws:s3' && eventRecord.s3) {
      return convert(eventRecord.s3.bucket.name, eventRecord.s3.object.key)
        .then(response => {
          callback(null, response)
        })
        .catch(callback)
    }

    return callback('unsupported event source')
  }

  callback('no records in the event')
}

exports.handler = handlerFunction
```

Check if an event record exists.

If converting is successful, return a success response through a callback.

Otherwise, return an error.

Return an error if the event record isn't from S3.

Also return an error if the event record doesn't exist.

Export the handler function.

Now that you have the initial file, it's time to create the convert function. Because this service is small, there's no need for a complicated folder structure: just create the convert.js file in the same project folder. As shown in figure 7.3, the flow of the convert function is as follows:

- S3 triggers your AWS Lambda and your initial file invokes the convert function.
- The convert function downloads the image from S3 and stores it locally in the /tmp folder.

- The image is converted using the `convert` command from ImageMagick, and a thumbnail is saved in the /tmp folder.
- The `convert` function then uploads the new thumbnail to the S3 bucket.
- The `convert` function resolves the promise that tells the initial file that the operation was successful.

As shown in figure 7.3, your `convert` function first needs to download the file from S3 using the `getObject` method of the `S3` class. This method accepts a bucket name and S3 file path and returns a promise that will, when resolved, return a response that contains the file body as a buffer.

Your convert.js file should export a `convert` function, which is a Node function that accepts a bucket name and an S3 file path as parameters and returns a promise. For the actual functionality, you need to import three core Node.js modules:

- `fs`, for manipulating your filesystem
- `path`, for file path manipulation
- `child_process`, for invoking an ImageMagick command

In addition to those three modules, you also need to install two additional packages from NPM: `mime`, a package that determines the uploaded file's MIME type, and `aws-sdk`. The AWS SDK is required for programmatic usage of the S3 service.

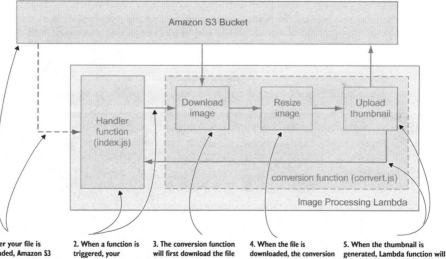

I. After your file is uploaded, Amazon S3 bucket will automatically trigger image processing Lambda function and pass the info about the file, including bucket name and filename.

2. When a function is triggered, your handler file will process the event and invoke the convert function with the bucket and image name, if the event is coming from Amazon S3; otherwise it will stop its execution.

3. The conversion function will first download the file from Amazon S3, using the AWS SDK and the bucket and filname that the main handler passed, and save the downloaded file to the local /tmp folder.

4. When the file is downloaded, the conversion function will execute ImageMagick's convert command, using Node.js's child_process.exec, which will create a thumbnail version of your image and store it in local /tmp.

5. When the thumbnail is generated, Lambda function will upload it from /tmp to /thumbnails folder of Amazon S3 bucket using the AWS SDK, and resolve the promise to tell the main handler function that the conversion was done successfully; handler will just send a callback to confirm that Lambda function is executed successfully.

Figure 7.3   The flow of the convert function

Your next step is saving the downloaded file. In your Lambda function, only the /tmp folder is writable. Therefore, you should create two folders inside your /tmp folder: one called images, where you'll store the downloaded images, and another called thumbnails, where you'll store generated thumbnails.

NOTE Before creating those folders, check to see if they already exist—AWS can reuse a single Lambda function, and the folders might have been created already.

When you are sure that the /images folder exists inside /tmp, use the `fs.writeFile` command with the same downloaded file as its argument to save to that folder. This method is asynchronous, but it doesn't return a promise, so you should wrap it in a promise.

Now that your file is saved locally, you can use ImageMagick to create a thumbnail. To do so, you need to use the `convert` command, which allows you to resize or convert image files. At the moment, you'll keep the same file format, so the only thing you should do is resize the given image. To do so, you invoke the `convert` command with the following command-line arguments:

- The path to the full image
- The `-resize` flag, which tells the command to resize the image
- A `120x120\>` value, which means that the image should be scaled so its larger dimension has a maximum of 120 pixels. Note the `\>` after the value, which tells the command to resize the image only if its larger dimension is greater than 120 px.
- The destination path

The complete command for creating an image named image.png as a 120 px thumbnail is the following:

```
convert /tmp/images/image.png -resize 120x120\> /tmp/thumbnails/image.png
```

To execute the command from your Lambda, you need to use the `exec` method of the `child_process` module that you imported at the top of the file. Although `exec` is asynchronous, it's not promise-based, so you'll need to wrap this function call in a promise.

---

exec vs. spawn

The Node.js core module `child_process` offers two methods for executing external commands: `exec` and `spawn`. Although both can do the same job, there's a slight difference between them.

`spawn` returns an object that contains `stdout` and `stderr` streams. This method is more suitable for commands that return larger output, or output that should be processed before the command is finished.

`exec` requires a callback function, which is triggered as soon as the command is fully finished. This callback returns an error, if one is raised, and also `stdout` and `stderr` outputs. By default, `exec` has a limit of 200 k of output, so it's more suitable for commands that don't return large output and whose final output is important whose but command progress is not.

For more information about both commands, see https://nodejs.org/api/child_process .html#child_process_asynchronous_process_creation.

As a final part of the `convert` function, you'll upload the file to the Amazon S3 bucket. You can do this using the `putObject` method of the `S3` class. This method returns a promise and requires the following:

- An options object with the bucket name
- The S3 file path
- The file body as a buffer
- The ACL
- The content type of your file

Because your image processor service can work with multiple file types, require the `mime` package at the top of your file to get the MIME type of your original image and set it as the content type of your thumbnail. If you don't provide this value, S3 will assume your file type is `binary/octet-stream`.

The following listing shows the full code of the convert.js file.

Listing 7.4 Convert images to thumbnails

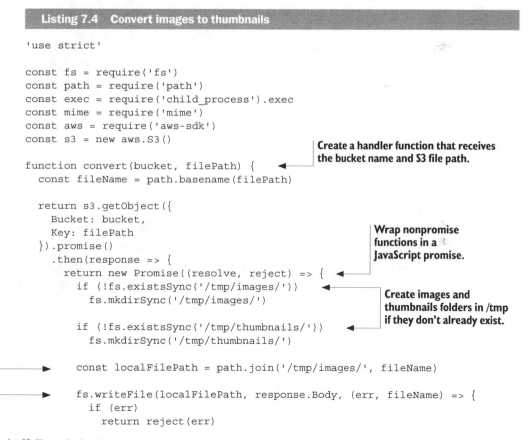

```
'use strict'

const fs = require('fs')
const path = require('path')
const exec = require('child_process').exec
const mime = require('mime')
const aws = require('aws-sdk')
const s3 = new aws.S3()

function convert(bucket, filePath) {          Create a handler function that receives
  const fileName = path.basename(filePath)    the bucket name and S3 file path.

  return s3.getObject({
    Bucket: bucket,
    Key: filePath                             Wrap nonpromise
  }).promise()                                functions in a
    .then(response => {                       JavaScript promise.
      return new Promise((resolve, reject) => {
        if (!fs.existsSync('/tmp/images/'))          Create images and
          fs.mkdirSync('/tmp/images/')               thumbnails folders in /tmp
                                                     if they don't already exist.
        if (!fs.existsSync('/tmp/thumbnails/'))
          fs.mkdirSync('/tmp/thumbnails/')

        const localFilePath = path.join('/tmp/images/', fileName)

        fs.writeFile(localFilePath, response.Body, (err, fileName) => {
          if (err)
            return reject(err)
```

Save the S3 file to the local path.

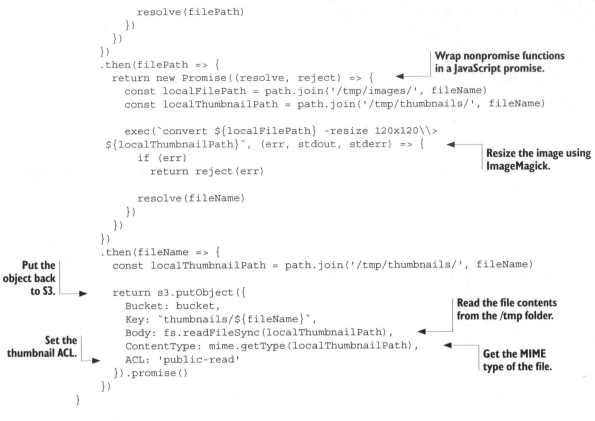

```
            resolve(filePath)
          })
        })
      })
      .then(filePath => {                          ◄─── Wrap nonpromise functions
        return new Promise((resolve, reject) => {        in a JavaScript promise.
          const localFilePath = path.join('/tmp/images/', fileName)
          const localThumbnailPath = path.join('/tmp/thumbnails/', fileName)

          exec(`convert ${localFilePath} -resize 120x120\\>
      ${localThumbnailPath}`, (err, stdout, stderr) => {   ◄─── Resize the image using
            if (err)                                            ImageMagick.
              return reject(err)

            resolve(fileName)
          })
        })
      })
      .then(fileName => {
        const localThumbnailPath = path.join('/tmp/thumbnails/', fileName)

        return s3.putObject({
          Bucket: bucket,
          Key: `thumbnails/${fileName}`,           ◄─── Read the file contents
          Body: fs.readFileSync(localThumbnailPath),     from the /tmp folder.
          ContentType: mime.getType(localThumbnailPath),  ◄─── Get the MIME
          ACL: 'public-read'                                   type of the file.
        }).promise()
      })
    }

    module.exports = convert
```

Put the object back to S3. (annotation pointing to `return s3.putObject({`)

Set the thumbnail ACL. (annotation pointing to `ACL: 'public-read'`)

7.2.1 *Deploying your S3 function*

Now that you've implemented your service, you need to use Claudia to deploy it. Interestingly, in this scenario you don't have an API. You'll invoke claudia create with a --region flag, just as you did in chapter 2 for your API, but instead of the --api-module flag, for a function without an API you'll use the --handler flag. You can see the command in listing 7.5. The --handler flag expects the path to your handler with a .handler suffix. For example, if you are using the handler export in a index.js file your path will be index.handler; if your handler is exported in a lambda.js file, you'll specify lambda.handler.

> **NOTE** The <insert-your-file-name>.handler is required by the --handler flag and, unfortunately, the --handler command can't catch any other option.

If you did a exports.somethingElse or module.exports in your main file, and then ran the command with the --handler index and --handler index .default flag, the command would fail, because it requires your main file to export a handler property. Therefore the --handler flag works only with an exports.handler.

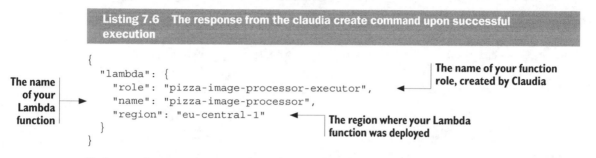

Select a region. → Create a new function.

```
claudia create \
  --region eu-central-1 \
  --handler index.handler
```

Specify the path for your handler function.

This command returns information about your Lambda function similar to that shown in the following listing, and it creates a claudia.json file in the root of your project.

The name of your Lambda function →

```
{
  "lambda": {
    "role": "pizza-image-processor-executor",
    "name": "pizza-image-processor",
    "region": "eu-central-1"
  }
}
```

The name of your function role, created by Claudia

The region where your Lambda function was deployed

Before trying your new service, there is one more step. You need to set a trigger for your Lambda function from your S3 bucket. Claudia has a command for that as well—`claudia add-s3-event-source`. This command has several flags, but you'll use the following two:

- `--bucket`—A required flag specifying your bucket name
- `--prefix`—An optional flag that allows you to specify a folder

NOTE　For the full list of options, see https://github.com/claudiajs/claudia/blob/master/docs/add-s3-event-source.md.

As shown in the following listing, you should specify `images/` as a prefix, because then the command will accept triggers only from the images folder.

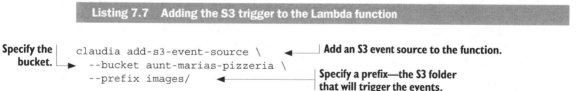

Specify the bucket. → Add an S3 event source to the function.

```
claudia add-s3-event-source \
  --bucket aunt-marias-pizzeria \
  --prefix images/
```

Specify a prefix—the S3 folder that will trigger the events.

A successfully added trigger returns an empty object as a response; otherwise, an error is shown.

One of the easiest ways to see if your new service is working is to manually upload a file to your S3 bucket's images folder. Try to do that, then wait a few seconds and check the thumbnails folder in your S3 bucket.

If you want to try out the complete flow of your API and the image processor, you can use the front-end application from https://github.com/effortless-serverless/pizzeria-web-app.

7.3   *Taste it!*

This chapter was pretty easy, but because it's the end of part 1 of this book, we've made the exercise more complicated as a bonus.

7.3.1   *Exercise*

Some images that Michelangelo prepares are big—10 megapixels or more. Because large file sizes can cause slow loading in both the web and mobile applications, you need to resize those images with a height or width larger than 1,024 px.

Here are a few tips:

- Use the `convert` function one more time to resize the file.
- Be careful during the resizing, because you are modifying the file that you are using for generating the thumbnail—maybe you shouldn't do both actions in parallel.
- Upload both files to S3 in the end.

7.3.2   *Solution*

As shown in listing 7.8, most of the code stays the same—you still need to download the image from S3 and store it in a /tmp folder, then you need to generate the thumbnail, and finally you need to upload it to S3.

But there are some differences. After you've downloaded the image from S3 and stored it on your local filesystem, you need to resize it before you create a thumbnail. Technically, you can resize after you create the thumbnail, but it's better to create the thumbnail from the smaller image than to use the original size.

After resizing the image and generating the thumbnail, you need to upload both files to Amazon S3. You can do this operation in parallel, so you should use `Promise .all` to parallelize the upload process.

Listing 7.8 shows the full code example for the sake of readability. Run `claudia upload` and try to manually upload a large image to your bucket to test your solution.

TIP   `claudia update` may appear slower than previous executions because of the size of `aws-sdk`. It's available on AWS Lambda by default, so to speed up your deployment, you should reinstall it as an optional dependency and run `claudia update` with the `--no-optional-dependencies` flag. Doing so removes optional dependencies from the zip file that is deployed to your Lambda function.

Listing 7.8   Convert images to thumbnails and resize big image to a reasonable size

```
'use strict'

const fs = require('fs')
const path = require('path')
const exec = require('child_process').exec
const mime = require('mime')
```

```
const aws = require('aws-sdk')
const s3 = new aws.S3()

function convert(bucket, filePath) {
  const fileName = path.basename(filePath)

  return s3.getObject({               ◄────┤ Download the file from S3.
    Bucket: bucket,
    Key: filePath                            Save the file to the
  }).promise()                               local /tmp folder.
    .then(response => {      ◄──────────┤
      return new Promise((resolve, reject) => {
        if (!fs.existsSync('/tmp/images/'))
          fs.mkdirSync('/tmp/images/')

        if (!fs.existsSync('/tmp/thumbnails/'))
          fs.mkdirSync('/tmp/thumbnails/')

        const localFilePath = path.join('/tmp/images/', fileName)

        fs.writeFile(localFilePath, response.Body, (err, fileName) => {
          if (err)
            return reject(err)

          resolve(filePath)
        })
      })
    })                              Resize the
    .then(filePath => {             original image.        Wrap the convert command in a
      return new Promise((resolve, reject) => {  ◄──────┤ JavaScript promise.
        const localFilePath = path.join('/tmp/images/', fileName)

        exec(`convert ${localFilePath} -resize 1024x1024\\>
    ${localFilePath}`, (err, stdout, stderr) => {  ◄──────┤ Execute the convert
          if (err)                                          command.
            return reject(err)

          resolve(fileName)
        })
      })                              Generate a thumbnail and save
    })                                it on the local filesystem.
    .then(filePath => {    ◄──────┤
      return new Promise((resolve, reject) => {
        const localFilePath = path.join('/tmp/images/', fileName)
        const localThumbnailPath = path.join('/tmp/thumbnails/', fileName)

        exec(`convert ${localFilePath} -resize 120x120\\>
    ${localThumbnailPath}`, (err, stdout, stderr) => {
          if (err)
            return reject(err)

          resolve(fileName)
        })
      })
    })
    .then(fileName => {    ◄──────┤ Upload the file to S3.
```

```
              const localThumbnailPath = path.join('/tmp/thumbnails/', fileName)
              const localImagePath = path.join('/tmp/images/', fileName)

              return Promise.all([          ◄──────  Return Promise.all, which
                s3.putObject({                        uploads both files to S3.
                    Bucket: bucket,
                    Key: `thumbnails/${fileName}`,
                    Body: fs.readFileSync(localThumbnailPath),
                    ContentType: mime.getType(localThumbnailPath),
                    ACL: 'public-read'
                }).promise(),
                s3.putObject({          ◄──────┤ Upload the image.
                    Bucket: bucket,
                    Key: `images/${fileName}`,
                    Body: fs.readFileSync(localImagePath),
                    ContentType: mime.getType(localImagePath),
                    ACL: 'public-read'
                }).promise()
              ])
          })
      }

      module.exports = convert
```

Upload the
thumbnail.

7.4   *End of part 1: Special exercise*

You've come to the end of part 1 of the book. You've learned the basics of creating a serverless API, and now it's time to put them to the test. Each part of the book ends with a special exercise where you'll test the skills you learned throughout that part. Each special exercise extensively challenges your gained knowledge and contains an advanced task for those who need an extra challenge.

This special exercise builds on what you've learned in this chapter—your goal is to create a new DynamoDB table `pizzas` that will keep your pizzas, add your static pizza list there, and then add a new API call for better pizza image handling. Contrary to the implementation you saw earlier in the chapter, this new API call should save the uploaded pizza image to S3, and then send the generated URL to your DynamoDB database to persist it as an extra column in your pizzas table. This means that each pizza will have its corresponding image URL.

NOTE   These special exercises have no hints, and we leave it up to you to test and verify your solution.

7.4.1   *Advanced task*

If that's too easy for you, this task brings another layer of complexity that is common in many applications. The task is to extend the pizza object to have more than one image assigned to it, and also allow the option to set one as the default.

NOTE   The special exercise advanced task always has a limited description.

Summary

- Serverless applications don't require serverless storage but need it to be fully serverless.
- When using AWS, S3 is the serverless storage service you need.
- Always try to separate your serverless application into smaller microservices—for example, for image processing you should always have a separate serverless function.
- Claudia.js helps you easily connect your Lambda to your S3 storage events.
- You can use ImageMagick within your serverless function to process your images and then store them to S3.

Part 2

Let's talk

Now that Aunt Maria has a functional application, it's time to bring the pizzeria closer to the younger population by having some fun with chatbots and voice assistants. Why would you use an app when you can ask Alexa to order a pizza for you?!

You'll start by building a simple Facebook messenger chatbot (chapter 8), connecting it to your current database and delivery service (chapter 9). Then you'll get to build an SMS chatbot for customers who aren't so tech-savvy, such as Uncle Frank, who want to order a pizza with a simple message (chapter 10). Finally, because your young cousin Julia bought an Amazon Echo Dot as a Christmas present for Aunt Maria, you'll build an Alexa skill that will allow everyone to order a pizza with voice commands.

When pizza is one
message away: Chatbots

This chapter covers

- Building a serverless chatbot

- How serverless chatbots work, and how Claudia
  Bot Builder helps

- Using a third-party chatbot platform (Facebook
  Messenger)

Serverless applications aren't always APIs or simple processing microservices. Software is evolving, and people are finding different ways to use it. We've come a long way from isolated desktop applications to websites and mobile apps, and recently we're starting to see an expansion of chatbots and voice assistants.

This chapter shows how you can interact with your users even more by building a serverless chatbot on Facebook Messenger and integrating it with your Pizza API. You'll also learn how chatbots work and how to easily implement them in a serverless way using Claudia.

8.1 Pizza ordering beyond the browser

While you were working on Aunt Maria's Pizza API, her niece Julia dropped by the pizzeria a few times to say hi. Julia is in high school and, of course, spends lots of time on her phone. Even though she's happy that you helped the pizzeria set up an online ordering service, she complains that it's not cool enough. You're way behind Aunt Maria's main competitor, Chess's pizzeria, which has a Facebook Messenger chatbot that helps their customers order pizzas without leaving Facebook. Because Julia's classmates are always chatting on Facebook Messenger, they use it all the time. Having a chatbot would definitely help Aunt Maria reach more young customers, so she asks if you could help with that.

WHAT IS A CHATBOT?   A *chatbot* is a computer program designed to simulate an intelligent conversation with one or more human users via text-based or auditory methods.

A short history of chatbots

For many, chatbots sound like a new hype thing, even though the idea is not new at all. Chatbots emerged in the middle of the 20th century as a result of attempts to enable human users to use computers in a more human-friendly way.

A chatbot interface is mentioned in the famous Turing test of 1950. Then there was ELIZA in 1966, a simulation of a Rogerian psychotherapist and an early example of primitive natural language processing (NLP). After that came PARRY in 1972, a simulation of a person with paranoid schizophrenia (and yes, of course, PARRY met ELIZA—see https://tools.ietf.org/html/rfc439.

In 1983, a book called *The Policeman's Beard Is Half Constructed* was generated by Racter, an artificial intelligence computer program that generated random English-language prose. Racter was later released as a chatbot.

One of the most famous chatbots was Alice (also known as A.L.I.C.E., the Artificial Linguistic Internet Computer Entity), released in 1995. It wasn't able to pass the Turing test, but it won the Loebner Prize three times. The Loebner Prize is an annual competition in artificial intelligence that awards prizes to the most human-like computer programs. In 2005 and 2006, the same prize was won by two Jabberwocky bot characters.

In 2014, Slackbot made chatbots popular again. In 2015, Telegram and then Facebook Messenger released chatbot support; in 2016 Skype did the same, and Apple and some other companies announced even more chatbot platforms.

Building a chatbot nowadays is often more of a marketing initiative, with the goal of reaching more potential customers on major social platforms without requiring them to visit another website or install a mobile application or a desktop program.

8.2   *Hello from Facebook Messenger*

Because you are going to build a pizza chatbot on Facebook Messenger, it's important to understand how users will send messages to your chatbot and how a Facebook chatbot works.

Facebook chatbots are support applications for Facebook pages, meaning that they aren't independent, separate applications, like games. Building a Facebook chatbot is done in four steps:

1 Set up a Facebook page for your chatbot.
2 Create a Facebook application that will serve your chatbot and connect it to your page.
3 Implement your chatbot and deploy it.
4 Connect your chatbot to your Facebook application.

To start interacting with your chatbot, users will need to open your Facebook page and send it a message. The page's Facebook application receives the message and sends a request to your chatbot with the user's message. Your chatbot receives and processes the message and returns a response to your Facebook application, which in turn responds in your Facebook page's message box.

A detailed visual overview of this messaging process is shown in figure 8.1.

Before you jump into thinking about how to implement your chatbot service, there is some good news. Besides its API Builder, Claudia also has a Bot Builder.

Claudia Bot Builder is a thin library that wraps Claudia API Builder. It abstracts away the various messaging platform APIs and provides a simple, unified API for building your chatbots. Claudia Bot Builder's purpose is to help you build chatbots on various messaging platforms, such as Facebook, Slack, Viber, and many more.

To start, you'll need to create a new folder at the same directory level as your pizza-api and pizza-image-processing folders. A good folder name would be pizza-fb-chatbot. After creating the folder, open it and initiate a new NPM project. Then you need to install Claudia Bot Builder as a project dependency. To do that, see appendix A.

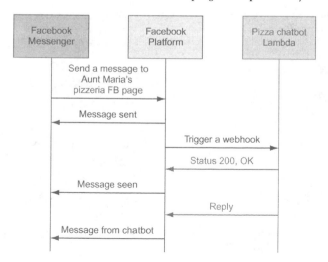

Figure 8.1   Chatbot message and reply flow

After installing the Bot Builder you'll need to set up your Facebook page and its Facebook application and connect them. For instructions on how to do that, see appendix B.

Now that you have the project set up, you can start with the actual implementation. You'll need to create an initial file for your chatbot, so create a bot.js file in the root of your pizza-fb-bot folder and open the newly created file in your favorite code editor.

At the top of the bot.js file, require Claudia Bot Builder.

> **TIP**   Unlike Claudia API Builder, Bot Builder is a module, not a class, so you do not need to instantiate it.

The Bot Builder, module is a function that requires a message handler function as its first argument and returns an instance of Claudia API Builder. The message handler function is the function that will be invoked when your chatbot receives a message. The easiest way to reply from your chatbot is to return a text message. Claudia Bot Builder will format this text message in the template required by the chat platform you are answering to—in your case, Facebook Messenger.

Because Claudia Bot Builder returns an instance of Claudia API Builder, as the last step you'll need to export the API Builder instance returned to you by the Bot Builder function.

Your bot.js file should look like the following listing.

Listing 8.1   A simple chatbot that says hello

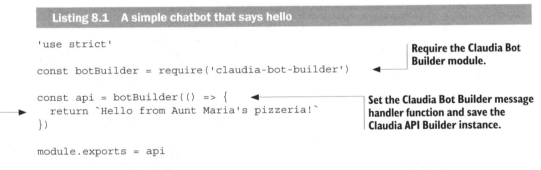

```
'use strict'

const botBuilder = require('claudia-bot-builder')       ◄──  Require the Claudia Bot
                                                              Builder module.

const api = botBuilder(() => {       ◄─────────  Set the Claudia Bot Builder message
  return `Hello from Aunt Maria's pizzeria!`             handler function and save the
})                                                       Claudia API Builder instance.

module.exports = api
```

Reply with simple text from the chatbot.

Deploying your chatbot is similar to deploying your Pizza API. As shown in listing 8.2, you need to run the `claudia create` command and provide your region and the `--api-module` option with the path to your initial file (without the extension). Your initial file is the bot.js file, so you need to provide `bot` as the API's module path. In addition to the region and the API module, you also need to provide the `--configure-fb-bot` option. This option will set up the Facebook Messenger chatbot configuration for you. Let's see it in action first, and we'll explain what happens in the background when you use this option later in this chapter.

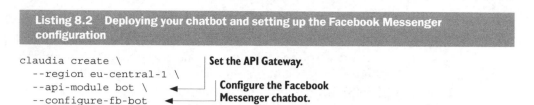

Listing 8.2   Deploying your chatbot and setting up the Facebook Messenger configuration

```
claudia create \                    Set the API Gateway.
  --region eu-central-1 \
  --api-module bot \                Configure the Facebook
  --configure-fb-bot                Messenger chatbot.
```

Running the `claudia create` command with the `--configure-fb-bot` option will make the command interactive. If the deployment of your API was executed successfully, this command will then ask you to provide your Facebook page access token and then print out the webhook URL with your verification token. (For a detailed explanation of the Facebook setup process, see appendix B.)

> **NOTE** When you deploy your chatbot, only users added to both the Facebook page and the Facebook app will be able to talk to it. To make your chatbot publicly available, you'll need to submit it for review. For more information on the review process, see https://developers.facebook.com/docs/messenger-platform/app-review/.

When you provide the Facebook page access token, your bot will be ready and immediately available for testing. To test your bot, go to your Facebook page and send a message to it. Your bot currently always replies with the static text "Hello from Aunt Maria's pizzeria!," as shown in figure 8.2.

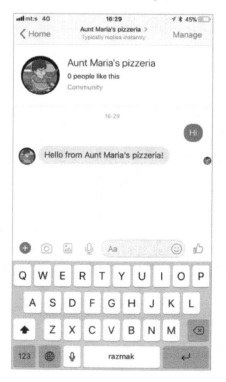

Figure 8.2   The first message from your chatbot

8.3   *What kinds of pizzas do you have?*

Building a chatbot in a few minutes is satisfying, but at this point your chatbot is pretty useless. To make it useful, you should allow customers to see all the available pizzas and place an order. Let's start with showing customers the list of pizzas.

If you remember from chapter 2, the currently available pizzas are stored in a static JSON file. As a temporary solution, copy that JSON file to your new project. First create the data folder, and then copy the pizzas.json file from your pizza-api folder to the data folder in the pizza-fb-chatbot project you created.

The next thing you want to do is show the pizza list as a chatbot reply. Defining the appropriate attitude and tone for your chatbot is beyond the scope of this book, so for now try to come up with some friendly message before you list the pizzas, such as "Hello, here's our pizza menu," and then ask users which one they want. To do this, you'll need to update your bot.js file.

First, import the list of pizzas from the pizzas.json file, which is in the data folder. Then update the `botBuilder` message handler function to return the pizza list and ask the user to pick one.

With Claudia Bot Builder, you can send multiple messages as responses to the user. To enable this capability, you need to return an array of messages instead of a single static text. Each message in the array will be sent separately, with the order determined by the order of the messages in the array.

Now you want to get the list of pizzas from the JSON file and convert each one to a string. To do so, you can map through the array of pizzas, get the name of each one, and then convert the array to a string using the `Array.join` function.

The updated bot.js code should look like the following listing.

Listing 8.3   Your chatbot replying with a pizza list

```
'use strict'

const pizzas = require('./data/pizzas.json')          ◄── Import the list of pizzas
                                                           from the JSON file.

const botBuilder = require('claudia-bot-builder')

const api = botBuilder(() => {          ◄── Return multiple messages as an array.
  return [
    `Hello, here's our pizza menu: ` + pizzas.map(pizza => pizza.name).
    join(', '),
    'Which one do you want?'          ◄── In the second message, ask
  ]                                        users which pizza they want.
})

module.exports = api
```

In the first message, list all the pizzas.

Deploy the updated bot with the `claudia update` command—no arguments needed. After a minute or so, your `update` command finishes and returns output similar to that in the following listing.

Listing 8.4   Response for the `claudia update` command

The ARN of your Lambda function

The name of your Lambda function

The Node.js runtime used for the function execution

The API Gateway URL

```
{
    "FunctionName": "pizza-fb-bot",
    "FunctionArn": "arn:aws:lambda:eu-central-1:721177882564:function:pizza-fb-
        bot:2",
    "Runtime": "nodejs6.10",
    "Role": "arn:aws:iam::721177882564:role/pizza-fb-bot-executor",
    "url": "https://wvztkdiz8c.execute-api.eu-central-1.amazonaws.com/latest",
    "deploy": {
        "facebook": "https://wvztkdiz8c.execute-api.eu-central-1.amazonaws.com/
            latest/facebook",
        "slackSlashCommand": "https://wvztkdiz8c.execute-api.eu-central-1.
            amazonaws.com/latest/slack/slash-command",
        "telegram": "https://wvztkdiz8c.execute-api.eu-central-1.amazonaws.com/
            latest/telegram",
        ...
    }
}
```

The role of your function

Webhook URLs for all the supported platforms

Try to send a new message to your chatbot and you'll see the updated answer, as shown in figure 8.3.

Figure 8.3   The updated response from your chatbot

8.4   Speeding up the deployment

As you probably noticed, updating your chatbot takes a bit more time than updating your API. That's because Claudia Bot Builder doesn't know if you changed the API configuration, so it rebuilds the webhook routes for all supported platforms. A detailed explanation of how Claudia Bot Builder works under the hood is given in section 8.6.

Fortunately, there is a way to skip the rebuilding step and speed up the deployment process. To do so, you can use the `--cache-api-config` option, which requires a stage variable name. When this option is provided, Claudia will create a hash of your API Gateway configuration and store it in a stage variable with the name you provided as the next argument in the `update` command. Each subsequent deployment will check if that variable exists, and compare the hash to see if the API Gateway configuration should be updated. This process speeds up the deployment, unless you add a new API route.

We recommend adding the `claudia update` command with the `--cache-api-config` option as an NPM script in your `package.json` file. If you do that, you should also install Claudia as a dev dependency, as explained in appendix A. Your package.json file should then look similar to the next listing.

Listing 8.5   package.json file with the updated script

```
{
  "name": "pizza-fb-chatbot",
  "version": "1.0.0",
  "description": "A pizzeria chatbot",
  "main": "bot.js",
  "scripts": {
    "update": "claudia update --cache-api-config apiConfig"   ◄─── Add the claudia update command as an NPM script.
  },
  "license": "MIT",
  "dependencies": {
    "claudia-bot-builder": "^2.15.0"
  },
  "devDependencies": {                    Install Claudia as a
    "claudia": "^2.13.0"   ◄───────────── dev dependency.
  }
}
```

The `--cache-api-config` option is useful when you aren't updating the API definition often, and it speeds up the deployment significantly. But Claudia Bot Builder creates webhooks for all platforms, and if you are building a chatbot for a single platform only, you don't need the webhooks for other platforms. From version 2.7.0, Claudia Bot Builder allows you to enable only the platforms you are using. To do so, you'll need to provide the options as the second argument to the `botBuilder` function. Claudia Bot Builder expects the options, if provided, to be an object. To enable only the Facebook Messenger platform, you need to add the `platforms` key in the options object, with an array with the string `"facebook"` as a value, as shown in the next listing.

To read more about selecting the platform, see https://github.com/claudiajs/claudia -bot-builder/blob/master/docs/API.md.

Listing 8.6 A chatbot with Facebook Messenger as the only enabled platform

```
'use strict'

const pizzas = require('./data/pizzas.json')

const botBuilder = require('claudia-bot-builder')

const api = botBuilder(() => {
  return [
    'Hello, here's our pizza menu: ' + pizzas.map(pizza => pizza.name).
    join(', '),
    'Which one do you want?'        Provide an options object as
  ]                                 the second argument in your
}, {                                botBuilder function.
  platforms: ['facebook']           Provide an array of platforms you want
})                                  to enable—in your case, just Facebook.

module.exports = api
```

If you run the `npm run update` command from your project directory now, you'll see that the deployment is significantly faster.

8.5   *Messenger templates*

Aunt Maria's chatbot is now capable of showing customers the available pizza list. But even though it does the job, customers may not understand what to do next.

Building a good chatbot experience is hard. Most users aren't accustomed to a textual interface, and a chatbot often requires some natural language processing and artificial intelligence—both are hard to set up correctly. For some spoken languages, it is almost impossible at the moment. Many chatbot platforms have acknowledged those problems and have simplified development and improved the user experience by adding support for some application-like interfaces, such as buttons and lists.

Facebook Messenger is one of those platforms, and its user interface elements are called *templates*. It offers several different templates, such as the following:

- *Generic*—Sends a message in the form of a carousel, or horizontally scrollable list, with cards that can have a title, subtitle/description, image, and up to three buttons
- *Button*—Sends a message with simple buttons (up to three) below the text
- *List*—Sends a message in the form of a vertical item list with names, descriptions, and images, and a call-to-action button
- *Receipt*—Sends an order confirmation or receipt to the user after a transaction

For the full list of supported templates, visit https://developers.facebook.com/docs/ messenger-platform/send-messages/templates/.

For your case, the generic or list templates seem like potential solutions. But the list template has a limitation on the list size—it needs at least two items and can display four at most. The generic template is more flexible; it can display 1 item, or up to 10. Because you want to display more than four pizzas, you should use the generic template.

To return a template instead of a text with the pizza list, you need to reply with a JSON object that has a specific structure. Doing so sounds simple enough, but these JSON objects can be quite big, and because you are going to display up to 10 pizzas, the readability of your code will be affected.

To improve the readability and simplify working with templates, Claudia Bot Builder has wrapped templates for some of its supported platforms (including Facebook, Telegram, and Viber) into template message builder classes. For Facebook, the template message builder is available through the `botBuilder.fbTemplate` object, which is a collection of classes for each of the supported templates.

NOTE To see Claudia Bot Builder's full list of template message builder classes, see https://github.com/claudiajs/claudia-bot-builder/blob/master/docs/FB_ TEMPLATE_MESSAGE_BUILDER.md.

As mentioned earlier, the generic template displays a horizontal scrollable carousel of items or elements. Each element is composed of an image attachment, title, optional description, and buttons to request user input. The generic template buttons can have different actions, such as opening a URL or sending a postback to your webhook. For the full list of button actions and more details about the generic template, visit https://developers .facebook.com/docs/messenger-platform/send-messages/template/generic.

In Claudia Bot Builder, the generic template is exposed through the `botBuilder .fbTemplate.Generic` class. You need to initialize the class without arguments and save the instance to the `message` constant.

Then you should add a carousel item, also known as a *bubble*, for each pizza. To do so, loop through the array of pizzas and for each one add a button using the `message .addButton` method of the `fbTemplate.Generic` class. This method requires the bubble title as an argument.

Then you'll add an image and a button for each pizza, which you can do via the `addImage` and `addButton` methods, respectively. For the `addImage` method, you need to provide a valid image URL, and the `addButton` method requires a button name and a value that will be passed when the button is tapped. For now, add a "Details" button and send the pizza ID as a value. You'll implement the button logic in the next chapter.

All class methods allow chaining, so you can chain them as follows:

```
message.addBubble(pizza.name).addImage(pizza.image).addButton('Details',
    pizza.id)
```

At the chain's end, you need to use the `message.get` method to convert the button to the JSON response Facebook expects. Because users will use the template button to order pizzas (you will implement this capability in the next chapter), you can replace the label with a "Which one do you want?" message with `message.get`.

The updated code for your bot.js file should look like the next listing.

Listing 8.7   The Bot Builder function that answers with the generic template

```
'use strict'

const pizzas = require('./data/pizzas.json')

const botBuilder = require('claudia-bot-builder')
const fbTemplate = botBuilder.fbTemplate

const api = botBuilder(() => {
  const message = new fbTemplate.Generic()

  pizzas.forEach(pizza => {
    message.addBubble(pizza.name)
      .addImage(pizza.image)
      .addButton('Details', pizza.id)
  })

  return [
    'Hello, here's our pizza menu:',
    message.get()
  ]
}, {
  platforms: ['facebook']
})

module.exports = api
```

Create a new fbTemplate constant that exposes the Facebook template message builder.

Create a new instance of the Generic template class.

Loop through the list of pizzas.

Add an image for each pizza.

Add a bubble for each pizza.

Add a button for each pizza and pass the pizza ID as its value when user taps the button.

After updating your bot.js file, run the npm run update command. As soon as it's finished, you can send a new message to your chatbot. The reply should look similar to the one in figure 8.4.

Figure 8.4   A chatbot response with the generic template

8.6   *How does Claudia Bot Builder work?*

Now that you have a nice-looking chatbot, it's time to see what Claudia Bot Builder did for you under the hood.

Most of the popular chatbot platforms use webhooks to notify your server that a new message was received. But each platform sends the data with a different structure, and also expects you to answer in a platform-specific way.

The main goal of Claudia Bot Builder is to abstract away the receiving and sending messages' platform-specific structure to a simple API. It uses Claudia API Builder to create webhooks for each supported platform. At the time of writing, Claudia Bot Builder supports 10 platforms (including Facebook Messenger, Slack, Amazon Alexa, and Telegram).

As shown in figure 8.5, the Claudia Bot Builder message-reply lifecycle looks like this:

1. The user sends a message via a messenger platform.
2. The platform API hits API Gateway via the webhook you provided in the platform settings.
3. API Gateway triggers your Lambda function, where the request is routed to the platform-specific API endpoint.
4. The request is parsed to a common format using the platform-specific message parser.
5. The parsed message is passed to your chatbot logic.
6. The answer from your chatbot logic is wrapped in a platform-specific format.
7. Claudia Bot Builder invokes the platform API with a wrapped reply.
8. The platform API sends the reply back to the user's messenger application.

You saw that the `botBuilder` function expects a message handler function, and you can also pass it an object with options as an extra parameter. The handler function is your chatbot logic, and the options object is used only for specifying the platforms used, to speed up the deployment.

The handler function is invoked with two arguments: the message object and the original Claudia API Builder request object.

The parsed message object contains the following properties:

- `text`—The text of the received message, extracted from a platform-specific message format. In most cases, if you want to reply to text messages, this is the only piece of information you'll need.
- `type`—The platform that received the message. For list of platforms, see https://github.com/claudiajs/claudia-bot-builder/blob/master/docs/API.md.
- `sender`—The identifier of the sender. It depends on the platform, but it is the user ID in most cases.

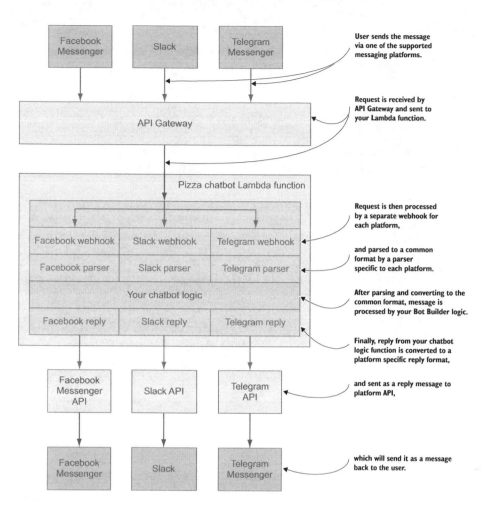

Figure 8.5 Claudia Bot Builder conversation flow

- postback—A Boolean property. This will be true if the message is the result of a Facebook postback (for example, tapping a generic template button). It will be undefined (falsy) for completely new messages or platforms that don't support postbacks.
- originalRequest—The original message object received by your webhook. This is useful if you want to do some platform-specific actions that are not provided by Claudia Bot Builder.

Finally, replying to a message from Claudia Bot Builder is as simple as replying from Claudia API Builder—if you want to reply with a text message, you need to return the string. You can also reply with a platform-specific template, either by using the message template builder or by returning a JSON object. To reply asynchronously, return text or an object at the end of the promise chain.

8.7   Taste it!

You've now seen the basics of implementing Facebook Messenger chatbots with AWS Lambda. It's not enough to win the Loebner Prize, but it's enough to have some fun. As in all the previous chapters, we've prepared an exercise for you.

8.7.1   Exercise

The goal of your first chatbot exercise is to show you how easy it is to create a chatbot.

Using the same Facebook page and application, create a chatbot that will echo the message text it received, in reverse.

Here are a few tips:

- Inspect the message parameter to get all its attributes and return the same text message the user sent.
- Use the built-in methods to reverse a string.

8.7.2   Solution

The solution, shown in the following listing, is simple and obvious.

Listing 8.8   A simple reverse echo chatbot

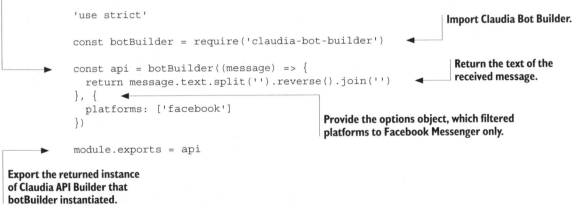

Invoke the botBuilder function with a handler function that expects the message attribute.

```
'use strict'

const botBuilder = require('claudia-bot-builder')

const api = botBuilder((message) => {
  return message.text.split('').reverse().join('')
}, {
  platforms: ['facebook']
})

module.exports = api
```

Import Claudia Bot Builder.

Return the text of the received message.

Provide the options object, which filtered platforms to Facebook Messenger only.

Export the returned instance of Claudia API Builder that botBuilder instantiated.

This Reverse-O chatbot is easy, but don't think future ones will be, too!

Summary

- Claudia enables you to deploy a chatbot for a few different platforms in a single command.
- Claudia Bot Builder is a wrapper around Claudia API Builder that returns an API instance.
- Claudia Bot Builder wraps the text reply in a format required by the platform you are answering to.
- You can build platform-specific template messages using Bot Builder templates.

Typing... Async and delayed responses

Being able to quickly build and deploy different applications is useful. As you've seen, building chatbots with Claudia Bot Builder is easy, and you can build a simple request/reply chatbot in just a few minutes.

But in the real world, chatbots need to do more complex operations than just reply with static data. You'll probably need to store customer information and request data, and perhaps do some calculations or even answer some unrelated questions. This chapter covers all of that: you'll learn how to make pizza orders from user requests, send delivery messages when the orders are ready, and integrate some basic natural language processing (NLP) to handle user input in a text format.

9.1   *Making chatbots interactive*

Your cousin Julia followed your progress and was excited when she saw you'd built the scrollable list of available pizzas. She's already started spreading the word at school about the amazing pizza chatbot—much better than the one from Chess's pizzeria. That's put you in the hot seat, but Aunt Maria is happy, because she's already seen increased website traffic as a result of that rumor.

The last thing you'd want now is to disappoint them, so you're going to finish the pizza ordering chatbot and add a few improvements to make your bot superior to Chess's.

9.1.1   *Tap to order: answering a postback*

Displaying a list with pizza pictures within a chatbot reply is great, because customers prefer a visual interface to a simple text reply. In the previous chapter, each pizza was displayed in a visual block that also had a Details button. If you were to tap it, though, it would do nothing.

Because your primary goal is enabling pizza ordering, you'll do the following:

1 Add an Order button below the Details one, as shown in figure 9.1.
2 Implement the pizza ordering by storing pizza order information in your database when the Order button is tapped.
3 Schedule an order feature.
4 Add NLP to your pizza chatbot, which will make your chatbot seem smarter and more human-like and encourage customer interaction. It will be able to answer any kinds of questions Julia's high school friends can think of.

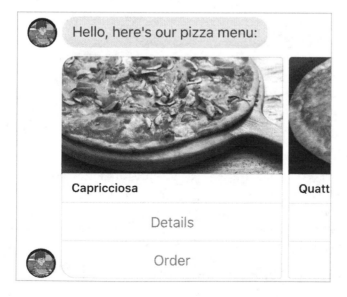

Figure 9.1   Chatbot reply with Details and Order buttons

Natural language processing

Natural language processing is a branch of artificial intelligence that deals with analyzing, understanding, and generating the languages that humans use naturally in order to interface with computers in both written and spoken contexts using natural human languages instead of computer languages.

If you want to learn NLP in practice, see Manning's *Natural Language Processing in Action* by Hobson Lane, et al: https://www.manning.com/books/natural-language-processing -in-action.

You are going to continue from the final chapter 8 listing as follows.

Listing 9.1   The current `botBuilder` function that answers with the generic template

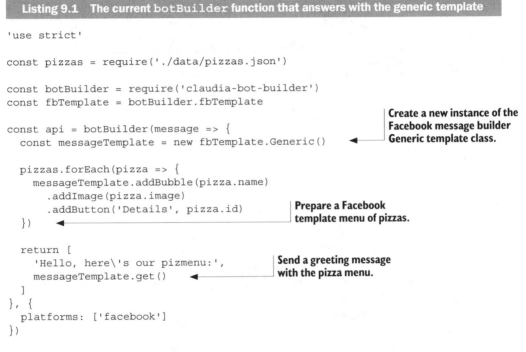

```
'use strict'

const pizzas = require('./data/pizzas.json')

const botBuilder = require('claudia-bot-builder')
const fbTemplate = botBuilder.fbTemplate

const api = botBuilder(message => {
  const messageTemplate = new fbTemplate.Generic()

  pizzas.forEach(pizza => {
    messageTemplate.addBubble(pizza.name)
      .addImage(pizza.image)
      .addButton('Details', pizza.id)
  })

  return [
    'Hello, here\'s our pizmenu:',
    messageTemplate.get()
  ]
}, {
  platforms: ['facebook']
})

module.exports = api
```

Create a new instance of the Facebook message builder Generic template class.

Prepare a Facebook template menu of pizzas.

Send a greeting message with the pizza menu.

As you can see from this code listing, the message attribute of the botBuilder function contains useful information about the request your chatbot received, such as whether the message was a button tap response or a text message.

To make your chatbot more useful, you should reply with the pizza details when the customer taps the Details button. Tapping the Order button should allow customers to order the selected pizza.

Now the flow of your chatbot will have three branches (figure 9.2):

- The user can see the details of the selected pizza.
- The user can order the selected pizza.
- If the user does anything else, show the initial message with the menu.

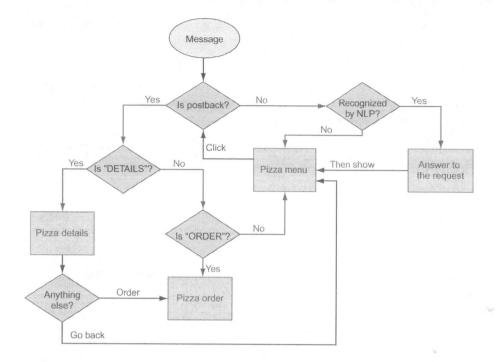

Figure 9.2   A visual representation of your chatbot flow

Customer button actions are replied to as postback messages.

To implement the flow from figure 9.2, you'll first need to check whether the message is a postback by checking if `message.postback` is `true` or `false`.

If the message is a postback, you'll check if the user wants to see the details of the pizza or to order it (let's call that *action*), and you'll also need the ID of the selected pizza. To save both values, you can update postback button value by serializing a JSON value or providing a string with both action and pizza ID, separated by a delimiter, such as pipe character (|). In the case of the pizza chatbot, doing the latter is easier because the chatbot's flow is quite simple. You can save the value in `ACTION|ID` format, where `ACTION` represents an uppercase action name (`ORDER` or `DETAILS` in your case) and `ID` represents the pizza ID.

If the message the chatbot received is a postback, its value will be in `message.text`. You'll split it by the pipe character (|) using the following built-in `String.split` method:

```
const values = message.text.split('|')
```

The new `values` array will have the action as its first item, and the pizza ID as the second. But ES6 destructuring can help with making this code more readable. If you replace the `const values` with `const [action, pizzaId]`, the first item of the new array will be stored directly to the `action` constant and the second to `pizzaId`.

Now that you've extracted both the action and the pizza ID, you need to check if the action is either `ORDER` or `DETAILS`.

In any case, you need to use the pizza ID to find a pizza from the `pizzas` array. To do so, you can use the built-in `Array.find` method like this:

```
const pizza = pizzas.find(pizza => pizza.id == pizzaId)
```

Note that this example uses `==` instead of `===`. That's because the `pizzaId` is of type `String`, because you got it from the `String.split` function, whereas the IDs from the `pizzas` array are integers.

Finding a pizza by its ID should take place with both `if` statements. It may seem redundant, but you might add an additional action that doesn't have a pizza ID in the future.

> **NOTE** If you moved the pizzas list to a DynamoDB table, you can stop here and try to connect your chatbot to the DynamoDB table the same way you connected your API in chapter 3. If you get stuck or aren't able to do it on your own, don't worry: the DynamoDB connection is repeated later in this chapter.

When your chatbot receives the `DETAILS` action, you can join all the pizza ingredients with commas and return the list of ingredients as a reply. But after receiving the pizza ingredients list, what should the customer do? What is the next conversation step?

Unlike in web applications, where the user can see the next available actions onscreen, the next step in a chatbot flow isn't always obvious to the user. If you return just a list of pizza ingredients, the user most likely won't know what to do next, and you may receive lots of unexpected user messages, like "Ew! Goat cheese!" and "What's your favorite kind of pizza?" or even "I love you," because human creativity is endless.

Even with NLP integration, chatbots are still far from being able to have a conversation on a human level, so the best thing you can do is add a nice, creative way of handling errors while trying to direct the user to the flow your chatbot can handle. Designing chatbot conversations is an interesting topic, but it is beyond the scope of this book.

The easiest way to direct users to the next chatbot action is to show them a visual menu with available options. This doesn't guarantee that the user will tap one of those buttons, but the menu will produce much better results than simply asking a question.

The two options you should show are the possibility to order the pizza the user just previewed, or to go back to the pizza list. To do so, you can use the `Button` class from `fbTemplate`. The `Button` class allows you to render a button template with up to three buttons, which look like the buttons from the generic template, and show a text reply. Using this class is similar to using the `Generic` class, so your reply should look something like the following:

```
return [
  `${pizza.name} has following ingredients: ` + pizza.ingredients.join(', '),
  new fbTemplate.Button('What else can I do for you?')
    .addButton('Order', `ORDER|${pizzaId}`)
    .addButton('Show all pizzas', 'ALL_PIZZAS')
    .get()
]
```

As you can see, the second button has the `ALL_PIZZAS` value, so this won't pass any of the `if` conditions you defined, and it will show the pizzas menu. Later, you can modify that flow to show a slightly different message depending on the previous conversation flow; for example "Not a big fan of mushrooms? Here are a few other pizzas you might like more."

> **NOTE** For more information about the `Button` class of `fbTemplate`, you can read the documentation at https://github.com/claudiajs/claudia-bot-builder/blob/master/docs/FB_TEMPLATE_MESSAGE_BUILDER.md.

In the case of an `ORDER` action, your chatbot should find a pizza by the ID and tell the user that the order was successful. You'll handle that case later in this chapter.

Finally, if the message isn't a postback, or if the action is neither `DETAILS` nor `ORDER`, you can return a generic template message similar to the one you used in chapter 8. The only difference is the addition of the Order button:

```
pizzas.forEach(pizza => {
  reply.addBubble(pizza.name)
    .addImage(pizza.image)
    .addButton('Details', `DETAILS|${pizza.id}`)
    .addButton('Order', `ORDER|${pizza.id}`)
})
```

Your updated bot.js file should look like the following listing.

Listing 9.2 Chatbot flow that accepts orders and details of selected pizza

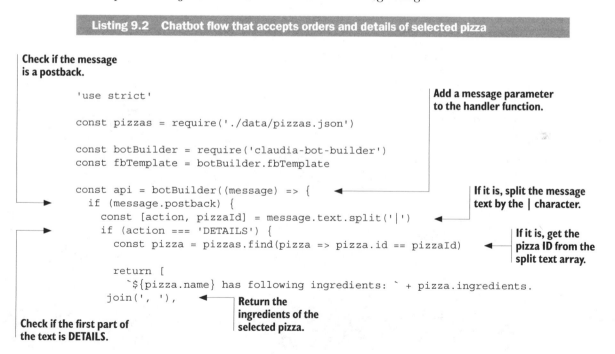

Check if the message is a postback.

```
'use strict'

const pizzas = require('./data/pizzas.json')

const botBuilder = require('claudia-bot-builder')
const fbTemplate = botBuilder.fbTemplate

const api = botBuilder((message) => {
  if (message.postback) {
    const [action, pizzaId] = message.text.split('|')
    if (action === 'DETAILS') {
      const pizza = pizzas.find(pizza => pizza.id == pizzaId)

      return [
        `${pizza.name} has following ingredients: ` + pizza.ingredients.
join(', '),
```

Add a message parameter to the handler function.

If it is, split the message text by the | character.

If it is, get the pizza ID from the split text array.

Return the ingredients of the selected pizza.

Check if the first part of the text is **DETAILS**.

Also return a menu so the user can navigate further.

In the `else` **block, check if the first part of the text is** ORDER.

```
        new fbTemplate.Button('What else can I do for you?')
          .addButton('Order', `ORDER|${pizzaId}`)
          .addButton('Show all pizzas', 'ALL_PIZZAS')
          .get()
      ]
    } else if (action === 'ORDER') {
      const pizza = pizzas.find(pizza => pizza.id == pizzaId)

      return `Thanks for ordering ${pizza.name}! I will let you know as soon
    as your pizza is ready.`
    }
  }

  const reply = new fbTemplate.Generic()

  pizzas.forEach(pizza => {
    reply.addBubble(pizza.name)
      .addImage(pizza.image)
      .addButton('Details', `DETAILS|${pizza.id}`)
      .addButton('Order', `ORDER|${pizza.id}`)
  })

  return [
    `Hello, here's our pizza menu:`,
    reply.get()
  ]
}, {
  platforms: ['facebook']
})

module.exports = api
```

And get the pizza ID again.

Then reply with the pizza ID to confirm the order.

If the message wasn't a postback, show the main menu.

Now run `claudia update` or `npm run update` to deploy the chatbot, and try the new flow, which looks similar to figure 9.3.

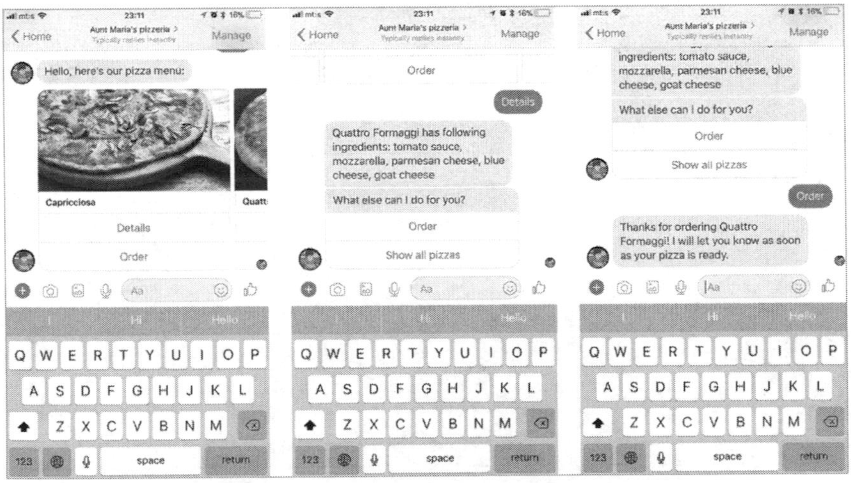

Figure 9.3   Screenshots of the three branches of chatbot flow

9.2 *Making the chatbot structure more scalable*

As with an API, managing the whole chatbot flow in a single file is not scalable. How can you improve the structure?

The chatbot doesn't have a router, but your `if...else` conditions act like a router, and their actions look like handlers. The easiest way to improve the structure is to keep the routing in the main file and move the handlers into separate files. You should have a main bot.js file and a handlers folder containing three handler files, one for each chatbot dialog branch. Your folder structure should be similar to figure 9.4.

Create the handlers folder within your pizza-fb-chatbot project, with the following three JavaScript files:

- order-pizza.js
- pizza-details.js
- pizza-menu.js

Then update your main bot.js file with the following changes:

- Remove the `require` for `fbTemplate` because it's no longer used in this file.
- Require three new handler functions from the files you just created.

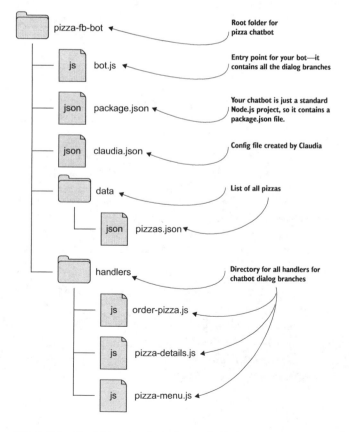

Figure 9.4 The folder structure of your chatbot

- Replace the pizza details and pizza ordering logic with the `pizzaDetails` and `orderPizza` handler functions, with the `pizzaId` as their argument.
- Replace the pizza menu generic template with the `pizzaMenu` handler.

After updates, the bot.js file should look like the following listing.

Listing 9.3   Main chatbot file

```
'use strict'

const botBuilder = require('claudia-bot-builder')        ◄──  Import the handler
                                                              functions.
const pizzaDetails = require('./handlers/pizza-details')
const orderPizza = require('./handlers/order-pizza')
const pizzaMenu = require('./handlers/pizza-menu')

const api = botBuilder((message) => {
  if (message.postback) {
    const [action, pizzaId] = message.text.split('|')      If the message is a postback
                                                           and the action verb is the
    if (action === 'DETAILS') {                            DETAILS text, invoke the
      return pizzaDetails(pizzaId)     ◄──                 pizzaDetails handler.
    } else if (action === 'ORDER') {
      return orderPizza(pizzaId)     ◄──    If the message is a postback and
    }                                       the action verb is the ORDER text,
  }                                         invoke the orderPizza handler.

  return [
    `Hello, here's our pizza menu:`,
    pizzaMenu()     ◄──    If the message is not a defined
  ]                       action, reply with the main menu.
}, {
  platforms: ['facebook']
})

module.exports = api
```

Now, open the handlers/pizza-details.js file. First, require the list of pizzas from the pizza.json file and the `fbTemplate` from Claudia Bot Builder by adding the following:

```
const pizzas = require('../data/pizzas.json')
const fbTemplate = require('claudia-bot-builder').fbTemplate
```

Then create the `pizzaDetails` function, which accepts one parameter: the `pizzaId`. This function should find a single pizza by the provided pizza ID from the `pizzas` array, and then return its ingredients and a button template message that allows the user to order the pizza or go back to the full pizza menu.

Finally, you'll need to export the `pizzaDetails` handler function by adding the line `module.exports = pizzaDetails` at the end of your file.

Your handlers/pizza-details.js file should look like the following listing.

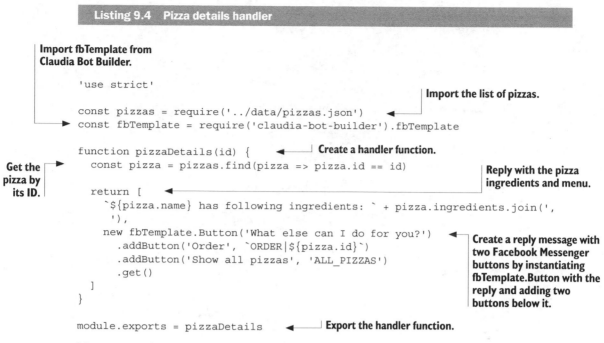

Listing 9.4 Pizza details handler

Import fbTemplate from Claudia Bot Builder.

```
'use strict'

const pizzas = require('../data/pizzas.json')          ◄—— Import the list of pizzas.
const fbTemplate = require('claudia-bot-builder').fbTemplate

function pizzaDetails(id) {          ◄—┘ Create a handler function.
  const pizza = pizzas.find(pizza => pizza.id == id)          Get the pizza by its ID.
                                                              Reply with the pizza
  return [          ◄—                                        ingredients and menu.
    `${pizza.name} has following ingredients: ` + pizza.ingredients.join(',
    '),
    new fbTemplate.Button('What else can I do for you?')          ◄—
      .addButton('Order', `ORDER|${pizza.id}`)
      .addButton('Show all pizzas', 'ALL_PIZZAS')
      .get()
  ]
}
```

Create a reply message with two Facebook Messenger buttons by instantiating fbTemplate.Button with the reply and adding two buttons below it.

```
module.exports = pizzaDetails          ◄—┘ Export the handler function.
```

Next, open the handlers/order-pizza.js file and do the same:

- Require the list of pizzas from the pizzas.json file.
- Implement an `orderPizza` handler function that will accept the pizza ID as a parameter.
- Find the pizza by its ID and return a text message as a result from the `orderPizza` function.
- Export the `orderPizza` function.

Your order-pizza.js file should look like the following listing.

Listing 9.5 Order pizza handler

Create a handler function.

```
'use strict'
                                                              Import the list of pizzas.
const pizzas = require('../data/pizzas.json')          ◄—

function orderPizza(id) {                                     Get the pizza
  const pizza = pizzas.find(pizza => pizza.id == id)          by its ID.

  return `Thanks for ordering ${pizza.name}! I will let you know as soon as
    your pizza is ready.`          ◄—  Reply with an order
}                                       confirmation.

module.exports = orderPizza          ◄—┐ Export the handler function.
```

After you update the pizza order handler, open the handlers/pizza-menu.js file and do the following:

- Import both the list of pizzas and the `fbTemplate`.
- Create the `pizzaMenu` handler function.
- Create a new generic template inside that function.
- Loop through all the pizzas from the pizza.json file and add bubbles for each of them in the generic template message.
- Return the message as the result.
- Export the `pizzaMenu` function.

Your pizza menu handler should look like the following listing.

Listing 9.6   Pizza menu handler

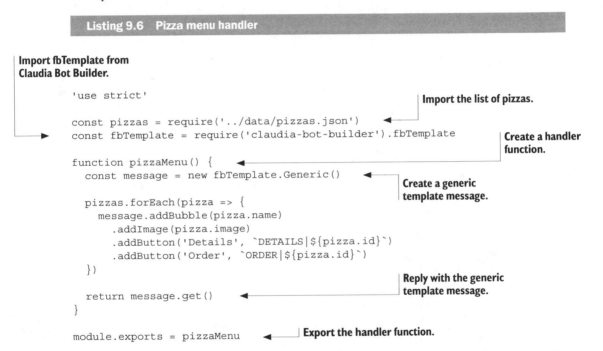

```
'use strict'

const pizzas = require('../data/pizzas.json')          ◄── Import the list of pizzas.
const fbTemplate = require('claudia-bot-builder').fbTemplate
                                                        Create a handler
                                                        function.
function pizzaMenu() {                          ◄──
  const message = new fbTemplate.Generic()      ◄──
                                                   Create a generic
                                                   template message.
  pizzas.forEach(pizza => {
    message.addBubble(pizza.name)
      .addImage(pizza.image)
      .addButton('Details', `DETAILS|${pizza.id}`)
      .addButton('Order', `ORDER|${pizza.id}`)
  })
                                                Reply with the generic
                                                template message.
  return message.get()       ◄──
}

module.exports = pizzaMenu    ◄──  Export the handler function.
```

Import fbTemplate from Claudia Bot Builder.

After you've updated all the files, run either the `npm run update` or the `claudia update` command to deploy your chatbot. When you send a message to your chatbot through Facebook Messenger, the response should stay the same, but now you have a more scalable and testable structure.

Other techniques for organizing your chatbot flow

Organizing your chatbot flow is not an easy thing to do. These examples are organized in a simple and easy way, but it's not scalable because of the many `if...else` conditions or `switch` statements, which are hard to maintain.

There are many alternatives—for example, by using an external library. Some of the external libraries allow proper control of your chatbot flow, such as Dialogue Builder, built atop of Claudia Bot Builder. See https://github.com/nbransby/dialogue-builder for more information about this library.

Another option is to use natural language processing for your chatbot flow. Building an NLP library is not an easy task, but fortunately there are many available NLP solutions, and some are relatively cheap. With NLP integration, you can organize your code around different entities and actions instead of having `if...else` loops (think of it as some kind of a router for conversation interface). Some of the NLP libraries also have session storage built-in. You'll learn more about NLP in section 9.6.

9.3 Connecting your chatbot to the DynamoDB database

To make the chatbot useful to your customers, you'll store pizza orders to your `pizza-orders` DynamoDB table.

As shown in figure 9.5, when your chatbot receives a message, it should connect to the same DynamoDB table your Pizza API is using and save the message. After that, it should reply with an order confirmation.

For the sake of simplicity, this chapter shows you only how to save the order in the database. A real-world chatbot should probably also allow the user to see the current order and cancel it.

Saving the order requires several changes to the order-pizza.js handler.

First, you can use the `DocumentClient` to connect to DynamoDB. To do so, you'll need to install the `aws-sdk` module from NPM as a dependency (or an optional dependency, if you want to optimize deployment speed). Then you need to import `aws-sdk` and create an instance of the `DocumentClient` by adding following code:

```
const AWS = require('aws-sdk')
const docClient = new AWS.DynamoDB.DocumentClient()
```

Now, instead of presenting the static text, you'll use the `docClient.put` method to save the pizza in the DynamoDB table.

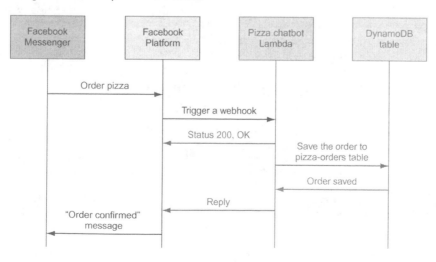

Figure 9.5   The chatbot flow with a DynamoDB connection

The main difference between your chatbot and your API is that you don't have the delivery address and the selected pizza in a single request. This means that you'll need to save partial data to the DynamoDB table and then ask the user for an address. Facebook Messenger platform doesn't save the state between sequential messages, so you'll need to save incomplete order state with some additional parameters in the `pizza-orders` table (which is done in this section) or in another DynamoDB table.

For the same reason, you won't be able to use the Some Like It Hot Delivery ID, so you'll need help from the `uuid` module again.

You'll save the following data in DynamoDB:

- `orderId`—Use the `uuid` module to generate the unique ID.
- `pizza`—Use the ID of the selected pizza.
- `orderStatus`—Use `in-progress` as a status, because this order is not finished.
- `platform`—Add `fb-messenger-chatbot` as a platform, because in the future your pizza bot might work on some other chat platforms.
- `user`—Save the ID of the user who sent the message.

When a pizza is successfully saved in the database, you want to ask the user for the delivery address. You can do this with a simple question, such as "Where do you want your pizza to be delivered?" You'll handle that later in this chapter.

You also want to handle errors, so you'll send a friendly message to the user in case of an error and show the pizza menu again.

When you've updated your code, the order-pizza.js handler should look like the following listing.

Listing 9.7   Order pizza handler connected to the DynamoDB database

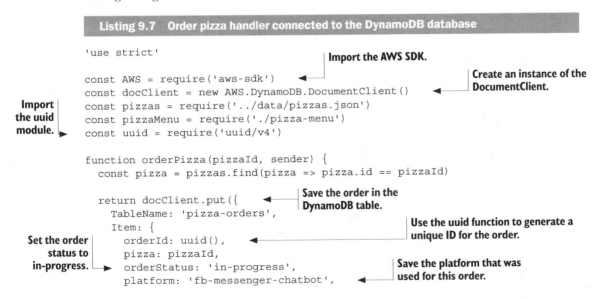

```
'use strict'
                                          Import the AWS SDK.

const AWS = require('aws-sdk')
const docClient = new AWS.DynamoDB.DocumentClient()        Create an instance of the
const pizzas = require('../data/pizzas.json')              DocumentClient.
const pizzaMenu = require('./pizza-menu')
const uuid = require('uuid/v4')
```
Import the uuid module.

```
function orderPizza(pizzaId, sender) {
  const pizza = pizzas.find(pizza => pizza.id == pizzaId)

  return docClient.put({                Save the order in the
    TableName: 'pizza-orders',          DynamoDB table.
    Item: {
      orderId: uuid(),                  Use the uuid function to generate a
      pizza: pizzaId,                   unique ID for the order.
      orderStatus: 'in-progress',
      platform: 'fb-messenger-chatbot',   Save the platform that was
                                          used for this order.
```
Set the order status to in-progress.

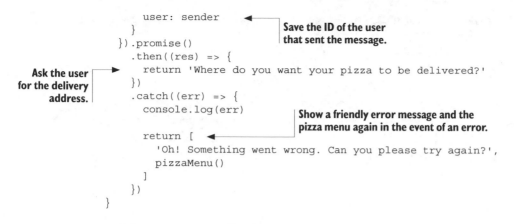

```
        user: sender
      }
    }).promise()
      .then((res) => {
        return 'Where do you want your pizza to be delivered?'
      })
      .catch((err) => {
        console.log(err)

        return [
          'Oh! Something went wrong. Can you please try again?',
          pizzaMenu()
        ]
      })
}
```

Save the ID of the user that sent the message.

Ask the user for the delivery address.

Show a friendly error message and the pizza menu again in the event of an error.

```
module.exports = orderPizza
```

In addition to the order-pizza.js handler, you'll also need to update the main bot.js file and pass the sender ID to the `orderPizza` function. The sender ID is available in the `message` object as `message.sender`; in the case of a Facebook Messenger chatbot, it represents a Facebook page-scoped unique user ID.

> **NOTE** The page-scoped user ID in a Facebook Messenger chatbot is different from a regular Facebook user ID, because Facebook tries to protect user privacy. To learn more about Messenger platform IDs, visit https://developers .facebook.com/docs/messenger-platform/identity.

The following listing shows the updated part of your bot.js file. This code goes just under the parsing of the `values` returned by your `message.postback`. The rest of the file is unchanged.

Listing 9.8   Update main chatbot flow

```
if (values[0] === 'DETAILS') {
  return pizzaDetails(values[1])
} else if (values[0] === 'ORDER') {
  return orderPizza(values[1], message.sender)
}
```

Pass the message sender as the second argument of your orderPizza function.

Now that your chatbot code is updated, you'll need to create a policy that allows the user that executes the Lambda function to interact with DynamoDB. Create a roles folder in your pizza-fb-chatbot folder and create a dynamodb.json file in it.

As shown in listing 9.9, the dynamodb.json file should allow the user to scan, get, put, and update items in DynamoDB. For now, your chatbot will not be able to update or cancel an order, but the `dynamodb:UpdateItem` action is required because the order will be updated after the user shares their address.

Listing 9.9   DynamoDB policy

```
{
  "Version": "2012-10-17",
  "Statement": [
    {
      "Action": [              ◄─────  Allow Scan, GetItem, PutItem, and
        "dynamodb:Scan",               UpdateItem actions in DynamoDB.
        "dynamodb:GetItem",
        "dynamodb:PutItem",
        "dynamodb:UpdateItem"
      ],
      "Effect": "Allow",
      "Resource": "*"
    }
  ]
}
```

Finally, run the `aws iam put-role-policy` command from the AWS CLI to add a policy from the roles/dynamodb.json file to the Lambda executor role. You can find the `role-name` in your claudia.json file. If you remember, on the initial deployment Claudia creates the claudia.json file in your project root to store some of your Lambda data. Claudia uses that data to do the later `update` deployments without requiring you to add any other parameters. The claudia.json file also stores your Lambda executor, which you need right now for your policy. Look for your `role-name` in it.

The `aws iam put-role-policy` command should look like the following listing.

Listing 9.10   Add a DynamoDB policy to the Pizza Bot role

```
aws iam put-role-policy \                                 Name of the Lambda executor role
  --role-name pizza-fb-chatbot-executor \    ◄─┘
  --policy-name PizzaBotDynamoDB \                         Document with
  --policy-document file://./roles/dynamodb.json   ◄─┘    policy definition
```
Name of
the policy ─►

When the `aws iam put-role-policy` command executes successfully, it returns an empty response, which means that the policy is in place. Your bot is ready for deployment.

> **NOTE** In the case of an unsuccessful execution of the `aws iam put-role-policy` command, the error usually states what the issue is. The most common errors are that the role does not exist or the `policy-document` is not in the specified location. If the role doesn't exist, try to run `claudia create` again with the already mentioned parameters. In case of an incorrect `policy-document` location, change the specified address so the `aws iam put-role-policy` picks it up from the right one.

Run the `npm run update` or `claudia update` command to deploy your chatbot, and then try to send a new message to your chatbot.

TIP As your codebase grows, frequently deploying can take up quite a chunk of your time and can become tiresome. You have probably noticed that you are deploying often in this book. But Claudia has a magic trick up its sleeve— it is able to speed up your deployment times. To enable this option, add `--no-optional-dependencies` to the NPM `update` script, which tells Claudia not to deploy any optional dependencies, such as the AWS SDK, which are already available within AWS Lambda:

```
"update": "claudia update --no-optional-dependencies"
```

9.4   *Getting the user's location from the chatbot*

As already mentioned, a pizza order is not complete without the address to which the pizza should be delivered. In a real-world project you'll want to build your chatbot to be as bulletproof as possible, so you'll probably need some natural language processing that will recognize addresses sent by users. But to keep this chapter simple, you'll use the built-in Facebook Messenger location share button.

As part of its platform, Facebook Messenger allows you to ask users to share their current location via a quick reply button. Tapping this button sends the coordinates with the rest of the payload. Claudia Bot Builder has support for that button in `fbTemplate`. You can add the button by adding the `.addQuickReplyLocation` method to any `fbTemplate` class.

Let's update the order-pizza.js handler. First require `fbTemplate` from Claudia Bot Builder by adding `const fbTemplate = require('claudia-bot-builder').fbTemplate` to the top of the file.

Then replace the reply where you ask the user to share their address with the `fbTemplate.Text` class and `.addQuickReplyLocation` method, as shown in the following listing.

Listing 9.11   Ask for the location after saving the order to the DynamoDB table

**Create an instance of the
fbTemplate.Text class.**

```
.then((res) => {
  return new fbTemplate.Text('Where do you want your pizza to be delivered?')
    .addQuickReplyLocation()
    .get()
})
```

**Convert the
template to
JSON.**

**Add a quick reply button for
location sharing.**

When your customer shares their location, the chatbot will receive its coordinates: its latitude and longitude. In addition to sending an address, the Some Like It Hot Delivery API also allows you to send position coordinates. (In a real-world example, you'd need to provide a lot more information, such as the floor, the apartment number, or at least a notes field for the delivery.)

In order to handle the location, you'll need to create a new handler function. To do so, create a save-location.js file in the handlers folder within your chatbot project. This handler should accept the `userId` and coordinates as parameters and use them to update the customer order.

To update the order, you'll need to import the AWS SDK, instantiate the `Document-Client`, and do the following:

1 Scan the database for the latest `in-progress` order for the specified customer using the `DocumentClient.scan` method, because the sender ID is not a part of the key.

2 Use the `orderId` from the returned result to update the order to the new status using the `DocumentClient.update` method.

For now, let's update the order status to `pending` and add the latitude and longitude coordinates where the pizza should be delivered.

The following listing shows what your save-location.js handler should look like.

Listing 9.12   Save location handler

Import the AWS SDK and instantiate the DocumentClient.

```
'use strict'

const AWS = require('aws-sdk')
const docClient = new AWS.DynamoDB.DocumentClient()

function saveLocation(userId, coordinates) {
    return docClient.scan({
        TableName: 'pizza-orders',
        Limit: 1,
        FilterExpression: `user = :u, orderStatus: :s`,
        ExpressionAttributeNames: {
            ':u': { S: userId },
            ':s': { S: 'in-progress' }
        }
    }).promise()
    .then((result) => result.Items[0])
    .then((order) => {
        const orderId = order.orderId
        return docClient.update({
            TableName: 'pizza-orders',
            Key: {
                orderId: orderId
            },
            UpdateExpression: 'set orderStatus = :s, coords=:c',
            ExpressionAttributeValues: {
                ':s': 'pending',
                ':c': coordinates
            },
            ReturnValues: 'ALL_NEW'
```

Annotations:
- **Create a handler function that expects userId and coordinates as parameters.**
- **Scan the pizza-orders table.**
- **Limit the result to only one item.**
- **Search only for orders sent by the selected user with the specified status.**
- **Define the customer (as sender) and status (in-progress) for the filter expression.**
- **Save the order ID in the local variable.**
- **Get only the first item from the response.**
- **Update the pizza-orders table.**
- **Specify the ID of an order that you want to be updated.**
- **Specify the update expression.**
- **Specify the update expression values.**
- **Return all the updated data.**

```
    }).promise()
  })
}
```

```
module.exports = saveLocation
```
◄———┘ **Export the handler function.**

Finally, you'll need to update your bot.js file to do the following:

1 Import the new save-location.js handler.
2 Invoke the new `saveLocation` handler function when the customer shares their location.

To import the new save-location.js handler, add the following snippet at the top of your bot.js file (for example, after the `pizzaMenu` handler function):

```
const saveLocation = require('./handlers/save-location')
```

To check if the customer shared their location, first you'll need to verify that the message is not a postback. After that check, use `message.originalRequest` to get the coordinates, if they exist. Coordinates are sent as an attachment, so you can access them via the `message.originalRequest.message.attachments[0].payload.coordinates` object.

The following listing shows the last few lines of your bot.js file.

Listing 9.13 Handle user location in the main chatbot file

**Check if the customer
shared their location.**

```
if (
    message.originalRequest.message.attachments &&
    message.originalRequest.message.attachments.length &&
    message.originalRequest.message.attachments[0].payload.coordinates &&
    message.originalRequest.message.attachments[0].payload.coordinates.lat
    &&
    message.originalRequest.message.attachments[0].payload.coordinates.long
) {
  return saveLocation(message.sender, message.originalRequest.message.
  attachments[0].payload.coordinates)
}
```
◄——— **Invoke the saveLocation function with the sender ID and coordinates.**

```
  return [
    `Hello, here's our pizza menu:`,
    pizzaMenu()
  ]
}, {
  platforms: ['facebook']
})
```

```
module.exports = api
```

After you update your bot.js file, deploy your chatbot using the `npm run update` command and then try it. The result should look like figure 9.6.

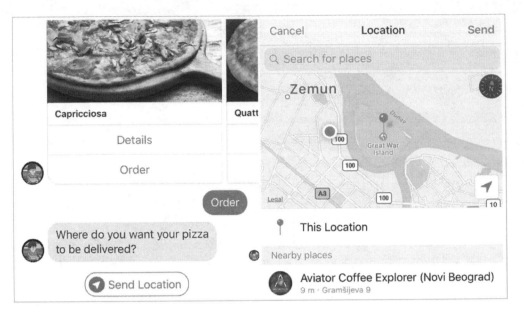

Figure 9.6   The chatbot with location sharing

9.5   *Scheduling a delivery*

The last piece of the "making your chatbot useful" puzzle is to connect it to the Some Like It Hot Delivery API. As shown in figure 9.7, after integrating with the API your chatbot flow should look like the following:

1 A customer taps the Order button to order pizza.
2 The order is saved to the database with the status `in-progress`.
3 Your chatbot asks the customer to share their current location.
4 The customer shares their location.
5 Your chatbot contacts the delivery API.
6 The delivery request is accepted, and the chatbot updates the database and replies to the customer.
7 When the order is picked up by the delivery service, its API triggers your webhook.
8 The chatbot notifies the customer.
9 When the order is delivered, the delivery API triggers the webhook again.
10 Your chatbot sends the final message to the customer.

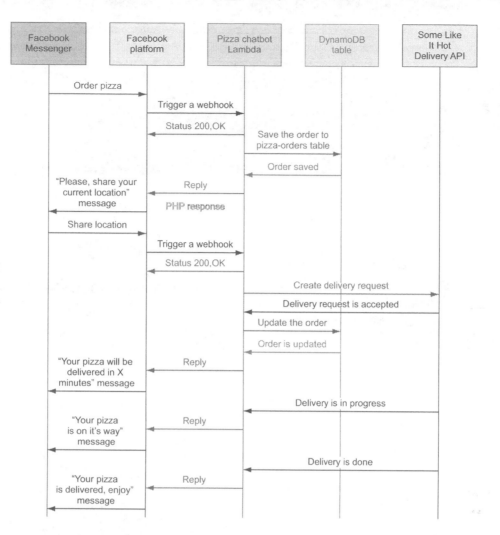

Figure 9.7   The chatbot flow with location sharing and the integration of the Some Like It Hot Delivery API

As you can see from the flow, there are two things to change in your chatbot:

- Update the save-location.js handler to send the request to the delivery API.
- Create a new webhook for the chatbot that will be sent to the delivery API.

Start with the easier part: the save-location.js handler update should be similar to the integration you did in chapter 4. You'll need to send a POST request to https://some -like-it-hot-api.effortless-serverless.com/delivery. The only difference is that you'll need to send deliveryCoords instead of deliveryAddress.

Another important difference is that you won't be able to update the order's primary key. Because you won't be able to use `deliveryId` as an `orderId`, you need to save the delivery ID in your DynamoDB table. As you probably remember from chapter 3, you used `deliveryId` as an `orderId` so you can find orders more efficiently when the delivery status is updated.

The following listing shows the modified section of your save-location.js handler with the integration of the Some Like It Hot Delivery API.

Listing 9.14   Save location handler

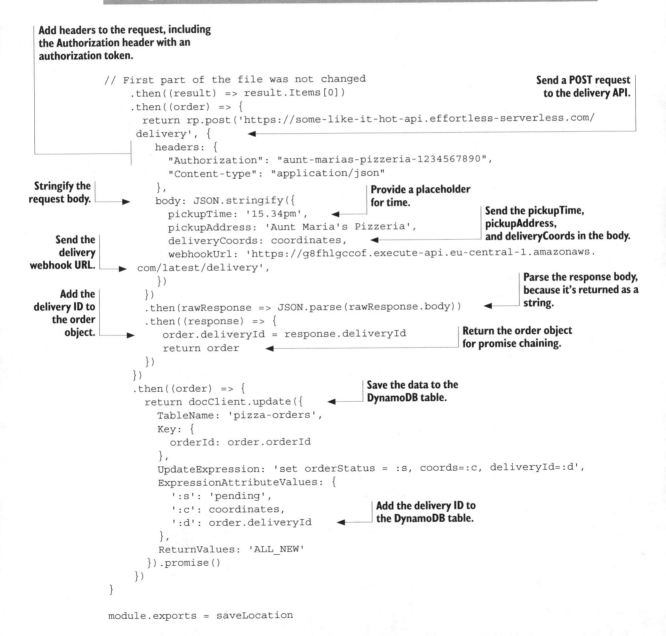

Now that you are saving the delivery ID in DynamoDB, you'll need to create a webhook that you send to the Some Like It Hot Delivery API. But how should you add the route to your chatbot?

As mentioned previously, Claudia Bot Builder exports an instance of Claudia API Builder. This means that the `botBuilder` function in your bot.js file returns a fully functional instance of Claudia API Builder.

Before adding the new route, you need to create a new handler for it. Create a file named delivery-webhook.js in your handlers folder. Within this handler you'll need to find the order by its delivery ID, which is passed by the delivery API, then update the order with the new status and send a message to the customer to let them know that the delivery status has changed. Full delivery webhook flow is shown in figure 9.8.

Finding and updating an order is similar to the find and update you did in the save-location.js handler file. The only tricky part is sending the message with the new status to the user.

To send a message from Facebook Messenger, you'll need to send an API request to the Facebook Messenger platform API. Each API request requires a user's page-scoped ID, the message that you want to send, and a Facebook Messenger access token.

You can send the API request the same way you send a request to the delivery API, or you can use the `claudia-bot-builder` library to send the message. This is an internal library, but you can require it by requiring the specific reply.js file as follows:

```
const reply = require('claudia-bot-builder/lib/facebook/reply')
```

By doing this, you'll require just the `reply.js` file, instead of a full Claudia Bot Builder, and store the function in a `reply` constant.

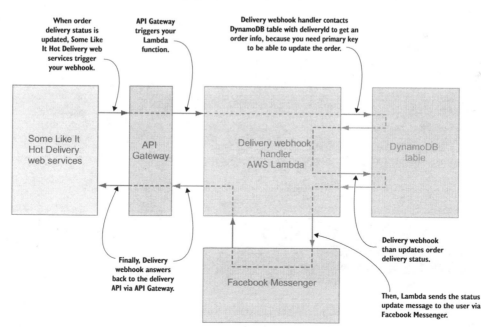

Figure 9.8   Delivery webhook flow

This `reply` function accepts three parameters: the sender ID, the message, and an access token.

You can get the sender ID from the database. The message is simply the message you want to send to the customer in the standard Claudia Bot Builder format. You can pass text, a template object, or an array of multiple messages. Finally, the Facebook Messenger access token is available as an API Gateway stage variable, and you can get it from the `request.env` object. You can pass the token to your handler function as its second parameter.

NOTE Facebook Messenger has certain limitations for sending messages to a user. You can't send a message to a user that is not a reply to a user message, and you can only send a reply to a message up to 24 hours after receiving it. To learn more about the limitations, visit https://developers.facebook.com/docs/messenger-platform/send-messages#messaging_types.

The full delivery webhook handler is shown in the following listing.

Listing 9.15   The delivery webhook handler

Import the reply function from Claudia Bot Builder.

Create a deliveryWebhook handler function that accepts the request object and access token as parameters.

Validate the basic request.

Scan the DynamoDB table by delivery ID.

Get only the first item of the response array.

Update the order status in the DynamoDB table.

```
'use strict'

const reply = require('claudia-bot-builder/lib/facebook/reply')

function deliveryWebhook(request, facebookAccessToken) {
  if (!request.deliveryId || !request.status)
    throw new Error('Status and delivery ID are required')

  return docClient.scan({
    TableName: 'pizza-orders',
    Limit: 1,
    FilterExpression: `deliveryId = :d`,
    ExpressionAttributeNames: {
      ':d': { S: deliveryId }
    }
  }).promise()
    .then((result) => result.Items[0])
    .then((order) => {
      return docClient.update({
        TableName: 'pizza-orders',
        Key: {
          orderId: order.orderId
        },
        UpdateExpression: 'set orderStatus = :s',
        ExpressionAttributeValues: {
          ':s': request.status
        },
        ReturnValues: 'ALL_NEW'
```

```
      }).promise()
    })
    .then((order) => {
      return reply(order.user, `The status of your delivery is updated to:
      ${order.status}.`, facebookAccessToken)
    })
}
```

Export the handler function. → `module.exports = deliveryWebhook`

Reply to the customer by providing the user ID, message, and Facebook Messenger access token.

Finally, you need to add a webhook route to your bot.js file. To do so, require the delivery-webhook.js handler at the top of the file with the following snippet:

```
const deliveryWebhook = require('./handlers/delivery-webhook')
```

Then you'll need to add the new POST /delivery route at the end of the file, just before the module.exports = api line. This route invokes the deliveryWebhook handler function with a request body and Facebook Messenger access token, and returns a status 200 as the success response or returns status 400 for an error.

The following listing shows the last few lines of your updated bot.js file.

Listing 9.16 Add a delivery webhook

```
  return [
    `Hello, here's our pizza menu:`,
    pizzaMenu()
  ]
}, {
  platforms: ['facebook']
})

api.post('/delivery', (request) => deliveryWebhook(request.body, request.env.
    facebookAccessToken), {
  success: 200,
  error: 400
})

module.exports = api
```

Return status 400 for an error.
Return status 200 for a successful delivery webhook request.
Add the POST /delivery route and invoke the deliveryWebhook handler when the route is triggered.

Now you need to deploy the chatbot using either npm run update or claudia update, and it will be fully functional.

9.6 Small talk: Integrating simple NLP

Building a more complex chatbot flow often requires some NLP integration. Building an NLP library from scratch is hard, and it's beyond the scope of this book. Fortunately, several libraries offer easy-to-integrate NLP features, which can help you to improve your chatbot experience. For example:

- Wit.ai (https://wit.ai), offered by Facebook, is an API that turns natural language (speech or messages) into actionable data.

- DialogFlow (formerly API.ai; see https://dialogflow.com), offered by Google, is a conversational user experience platform enabling natural language interactions for devices, applications, and services.
- IBM Watson (https://www.ibm.com/watson/) is an IBM supercomputer that combines artificial intelligence (AI) and sophisticated analytical software for optimal performance as a "question answering" machine. Watson also offers natural language processing for advanced text analysis.

Both Wit.ai and DialogFlow can be used for free with some limitations; IBM Watson has a free trial period.

Integrating any of these libraries into your chatbot is easy using their public APIs. All are good and recommended, but each has certain strengths and weaknesses that are not important at this point in the book. Claudia Bot Builder doesn't limit or interfere with any of their integrations.

Facebook Messenger also has built-in NLP, but unfortunately it offers only basic NLP features and basic recognition. If you integrate it with your chatbot, it can recognize greetings, thanks, and goodbyes. Besides that, it can also detect dates, times, locations, amounts of money, phone numbers, and emails. For example, in the case of date and time, expressions such as "tomorrow at 2pm" will be converted to timestamps.

NOTE   For more information about Facebook Messenger's built-in NLP, visit https://developers.facebook.com/docs/messenger-platform/built-in-nlp.

Though it is limited, Facebook Messenger's built-in NLP gives you everything you need to allow customers to order a pizza for a specific time or day. Because this is already a long chapter, you'll use this to make the chatbot reply to "thanks."

To do this, you'll need to do the following:

1 Enable the built-in NLP. The setup and configuration are described in appendix B.
2 Update your bot.js file to check whether the message is a postback. You don't want your NLP to get activated on your menu actions.
3 If the message is not a postback, check if the built-in NLP recognized the "thanks" expression. If yes, it should reply with "You're welcome!"; otherwise, you'll show the starting pizza menu.

The built-in NLP will add the recognized entities as an `nlp` key in your `message` object. Each entity returns an array of parsed entity values, and each entity has a `confidence` value and a `value`. The `confidence` value indicates the parser's confidence in its recognition (the probability that it is correct). It ranges between 0 and 1. The `value` attribute is the parsed entity value. In your case, if the entity is the word "thanks" it will always be `true`. You'll check if "thanks" exists, and if its `confidence` value is more than 0.8 (80%), you'll return a "You're welcome!" message.

The following listing shows the last few lines of the updated bot.js file.

Listing 9.17 Reply to "thanks" message

```
if (
    message.originalRequest.message.nlp &&
    message.originalRequest.message.nlp.entities &&
    message.originalRequest.message.nlp.entities['thanks'] &&
    message.originalRequest.message.nlp.entities['thanks'].length &&
    message.originalRequest.message.nlp.entities['thanks'][0].confidence >
    0.8
) {
    return `You're welcome!`            ◀──    Check if there is an nlp key
}                                               along with the entities, and
                                                within it a thanks entity.
return [
    `Hello, here's our pizza menu:`,
    pizzaMenu()
]                                       If no nlp response was captured,
}, {                         ◀───       return the pizza menu.
    platforms: ['facebook']
})

module.exports = api
```

9.7 *Taste it!*

Making your chatbot more interactive and a bit smarter is easy—but even though you want your customers to play around with your chatbot, it needs to quickly and efficiently fulfill a customer need.

9.7.1 *Exercise*

For this exercise, your primary goal is to show each of Aunt Maria's customers their last order in the user greeting message. When ordering from a specific restaurant chain, customers often tend to order the same food. The main goal of this exercise is to greet the customer with a reminder of their last order. In case you feel you can do something extra, an advanced exercise is presented after the primary exercise's solution.

9.7.2 *Solution*

The solution to this exercise is simple. You need to scan the order list for the customer's last order, using the sender ID in the `message` object, and for returning customers display the pizza they last ordered while saying that you hope they liked it.

Listing 9.18 Handle the user greeting in the main chatbot file

```
'use strict'

const botBuilder = require('claudia-bot-builder')

const pizzaDetails = require('./handlers/pizza-details')
const orderPizza = require('./handlers/order-pizza')
const pizzaMenu = require('./handlers/pizza-menu')
```

```
const saveLocation = require('./handlers/save-location')
const getLastPizza = require('./handlers/get-last-pizza')

const api = botBuilder((message) => {
  if (message.postback) {
    const values = message.text.split('|')

    if (values[0] === 'DETAILS') {
      return pizzaDetails(values[1])
    } else if (values[0] === 'ORDER') {
      return orderPizza(values[1], message)
    }
  }

  if (
      message.originalRequest.message.attachments &&
      message.originalRequest.message.attachments.length &&
      message.originalRequest.message.attachments[0].payload.coordinates &&
      message.originalRequest.message.attachments[0].payload.coordinates.lat
      &&
      message.originalRequest.message.attachments[0].payload.coordinates.long
  ) {
    return saveLocation()
  }

  return getLastPizza().then((lastPizza) => {
    let lastPizzaText = lastPizza ? `Glad to have you back! Hope you liked
      your ${lastPizza} pizza` : ''
    return [
      `Hello, ${lastPizzaText} here's our pizza menu:`,
      pizzaMenu()
    ]
  })

}, {
  platforms: ['facebook']
})

module.exports = api
```

Require the get-last-pizza module.

Invoke the module function and retrieve the customer's last pizza data.

Return the last pizza greeting text.

If there is a last pizza, construct the last pizza text.

The changes inside your main chatbot file are quite small, because you are just retrieving the exercise logic that should be contained inside your new get-last-pizza.js file.

Your get-last-pizza.js file should look like the following listing.

> **Listing 9.19   Get last pizza handler that retrieves the sender's last pizza from DynamoDB**

Import the AWS SDK.

```
'use strict'

const AWS = require('aws-sdk')
const docClient = new AWS.DynamoDB.DocumentClient()
const pizzaMenu = require('./pizza-menu')
const pizzas = require('../data/pizzas.json')
```

Create an instance of the DocumentClient.

Retrieve the list of available pizzas.

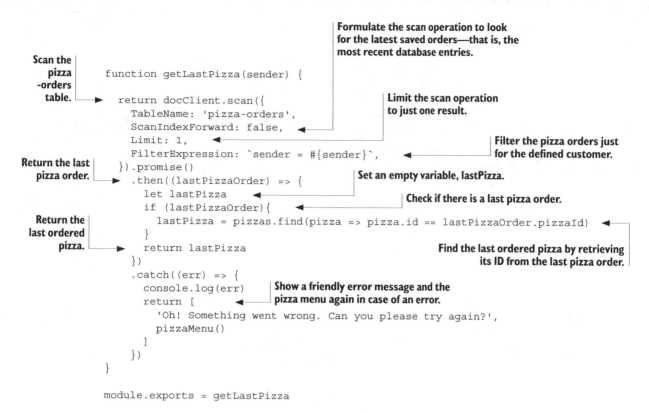

```
function getLastPizza(sender) {

  return docClient.scan({
    TableName: 'pizza-orders',
    ScanIndexForward: false,
    Limit: 1,
    FilterExpression: `sender = #{sender}`,
  }).promise()
    .then((lastPizzaOrder) => {
      let lastPizza
      if (lastPizzaOrder){
        lastPizza = pizzas.find(pizza => pizza.id == lastPizzaOrder.pizzaId)
      }
      return lastPizza
    })
    .catch((err) => {
      console.log(err)
      return [
        'Oh! Something went wrong. Can you please try again?',
        pizzaMenu()
      ]
    })
}

module.exports = getLastPizza
```

Annotations on the code:
- Scan the pizza-orders table.
- Formulate the scan operation to look for the latest saved orders—that is, the most recent database entries.
- Limit the scan operation to just one result.
- Filter the pizza orders just for the defined customer.
- Return the last pizza order.
- Set an empty variable, lastPizza.
- Check if there is a last pizza order.
- Return the last ordered pizza.
- Find the last ordered pizza by retrieving its ID from the last pizza order.
- Show a friendly error message and the pizza menu again in case of an error.

NOTE This solution covers the primary chapter exercise. No solution is provided for the advanced exercise, because it's meant to be a challenge.

9.7.3 *Advanced exercise*

For those who feel adventurous and want to implement something more difficult, this exercise is a good challenge. Its primary goal is to enable easy reordering of the customer's last pizza order. In the initial customer greeting, if the customer has previously ordered a pizza, you'll ask if the customer wants to order the same pizza again and provide two additional quick reply buttons as possible answers. If the customer taps "Yes, order again," you need to implement the same pizza order with the same address. If the customer taps "No, show me the menu," you'll need to show the menu of available pizzas.

Summary

- Postback message values are parsed as message.text and message.post. If the message is a postback, its post value will be true.
- Larger bot flows should be split into smaller files, either by a simple if...else or with a more sophisticated method.
- As with Claudia API Builder, chatbots built with Claudia Bot Builder can be connected to DynamoDB using DocumentClient.
- You can use a quick reply template to ask users to share their location.

Jarvis, I mean Alexa,
order me a pizza

This chapter covers

- Creating a serverless SMS chatbot

- The challenges of having different serverless chatbots

- Creating an Alexa skill using Claudia and AWS Lambda

Chatbots are useful for businesses because they significantly reduce the need for customer support while enabling your customers to interact with your applications in a convenient and interesting way. Serverless chatbots improve the equation even more, because you can support great user fluctuation, with many request peaks, without requiring server configuration. The only limitation of chatbots is that they're tied to their respective messaging platforms, and there are many, which vary greatly from market to market. For example, Facebook has been available for more than 10 years, but a significant percentage of people still don't use Facebook at all, and they may be your customers. How should you approach that?

On the other hand, human-computer interaction is constantly evolving, and recently we've witnessed the rise of voice assistants such as Apple's Siri, Amazon's Alexa, Google's Home, Microsoft's Cortana, and many others. Instead of writing to your chatbot, now you can just talk to it. And that technology is embraced completely

166

by the other, opposing end of your customer base: the tech-savvy pioneers, who easily adopt and promote new technologies. To target these two types of consumers, writing just one chatbot isn't enough. This chapter shows you how to handle both ends of the spectrum by creating both an SMS (Short Message Service) chatbot and an Amazon Alexa skill as serverless services using Claudia.js.

10.1 *Can't talk right now: sending an SMS with Twilio*

Aunt Maria's business has begun to flourish again, and that's great news! Pierre, her mobile application developer, has reported a big number of app downloads, and Julia's high school friends have spread the message about your Facebook chatbot, resulting in hundreds of orders coming in. Naturally, Aunt Maria is happy because you've helped get her business back on its feet, so she's asked you to come for a free dinner to meet with her and your Uncle Frank.

Uncle Frank is Maria's brother. He's an old, short, bulky guy, usually wearing his dark shirt, sleeves up to his elbows. He owns a well-known bar just down the street from the pizzeria. He loves to eat and frequently calls Maria to order pizzas for himself or his customers. But he's an old-school guy who doesn't bother that much with technology.

You go to the pizzeria and meet with Aunt Maria and Uncle Frank. They're happy, and Uncle Frank congratulates you. He's heard about your success, especially the case of your Facebook Messenger chatbot. But as the meal proceeds, you find that "there's no such thing as a free dinner." Aunt Maria and Uncle Frank explain that even though they think you've done a great job with the younger customers, you may not be reaching a significant portion of people, such as Uncle Frank's customers and friends, who are part of an older generation and don't have a Facebook account. Some don't have any social media accounts at all. Aunt Maria's pizzeria has become incredibly busy and at the moment she can't hire new workers just to answer the phone, so they ask if you can build an SMS chatbot. All her customers own mobile phones and know how to send text messages, so this might be a good solution. But where should you start?

Many cloud communications platforms are available, but Twilio is one of the best known and most widely used. Twilio enables customers to make and receive phone calls and text messages using its APIs.

> **NOTE** This chapter covers only text messaging (SMS) with Twilio; phone calls are out of the book's scope. To read more about Twilio, you can visit http://twilio.com.

Luckily, Claudia Bot Builder supports Twilio SMS chatbots, too. You can set up a Twilio chatbot as easily as the Facebook chatbot. To start smoothly, you'll first create a greeting SMS chatbot for Aunt Maria's pizzeria to get a grasp of the basic concepts. Then you'll continue with the complete pizza listing and ordering process.

First, create a separate project folder named sms-chatbot. Navigate to the folder, and inside it create a file called sms-bot.js.

NOTE You're probably wondering why you'd create a separate chatbot. Won't it have lots of logic duplicated with the Facebook chatbot? There are two reasons. First, SMS chatbots are substantially different from Facebook ones. They don't have interactive buttons, just simple text messages, so reusing the same logic would be problematic. The other reason is that you want your services to be independent and easier to maintain. Having both chatbots in one codebase would increase code complexity and reduce maintainability. Upgrading one would impact the other, and so on. Keeping the services separate also means that your SMS chatbot will be in another Lambda. If they were both in one Lambda and your Facebook chatbot crashed, your SMS chatbot wouldn't work either.

Because initially you are just writing a greeting bot, it will return only a single line of text stating "Hello from Aunt Maria's pizzeria!" First, you'll import Claudia Bot Builder to help you out with chatbot creation. Then you'll create your chatbot `api`, which will use the Claudia Bot Builder callback function to process messages. Within the function you'll return a single-line string, `Hello from Aunt Maria's pizzeria!`. After the function you'll need to specify an object containing `platforms` that represents an array of platforms you want your chatbot to support. Because you only want to support Twilio, you'll put `twilio` in the array. Your sms-bot.js file should look like the following listing.

> **Listing 10.1   A simple SMS chatbot that says hello**

```
'use strict'                                           Require the Claudia Bot
                                                       Builder module.
const botBuilder = require('claudia-bot-builder')   ◄

                                                Set the Claudia Bot Builder message handler
                                                function and save the Claudia API Builder instance.
const api = botBuilder(() => {                ◄
  return `Hello from Aunt Maria's pizzeria!`       Specify Twilio as an intended platform.
}, { platforms: ['twilio'] })               ◄

module.exports = api          ◄      Export the Claudia API Builder instance.
```

Reply with a simple text from your SMS chatbot.

This code is quite simple, but before seeing it in action, you'll need to create a Twilio account and provide a phone number from which it can send and receive SMS messages. After that, you'll set up the Programmable SMS service on your Twilio dashboard and assign it this phone number. For instructions about creating and setting up your Twilio account, see appendix B.

After that setup, you'll need to use Claudia to create your new AWS Lambda and deploy your SMS chatbot to it. To do so, you run the following command: `claudia create --region <your-region> --api-module sms-bot`.

As you probably remember, this command will return your newly created chatbot's URL. It should end with the `/twilio` suffix. Copy that URL and open your Twilio Programmable SMS service page, and paste it in the Inbound URL box. Don't forget to save your new Programmable SMS service configuration.

The last step remaining before trying your SMS bot is to run the command `claudia update --configure-twilio-sms-bot`. This command configures Twilio as your chatbot's platform. That's it.

Now try sending a "Hello" message to your Twilio phone number.

NOTE Due to mobile network traffic or network availability, receiving the initial response from your SMS chatbot may sometimes take up to 30 seconds.

10.1.1 An SMS pizza list

In the previous two chapters, your Facebook chatbot first returned a greeting message to customers. When the customer asked for the menu, the chatbot displayed a horizontal pizza list. The customer clicked a pizza item, and the ordering process started.

This seems to be a good reasoning model for other chatbot platforms, too, but SMS uses a different communication protocol that can't send images. You'll have to send your pizza list as text, with an explicitly specified text reply for ordering each pizza. For example, the specified reply to order a funghi pizza would be `FUNGHI`.

NOTE You can't send images via SMS; instead, you would have to use the Multimedia Messaging Service (MMS) to do that. Twilio provides support for MMS messaging, but it's limited to phone numbers in the United States and Canada. MMS also is not within the scope of this book. To read more about Twilio MMS, visit https://www.twilio.com/mms.

SMS sometimes also incurs hidden costs. Although in many countries it's almost free, in others it's still a bit expensive. If you're expecting thousands of users, the message cost can rise quickly. Therefore, try to minimize the number of sent SMS chatbot messages, while taking care not to break the message flow.

For your pizzeria SMS chatbot, minimizing messages means that you'll have to join certain steps. For example, at the start of the conversation, you should join the greeting and the pizza menu in a single message. It doesn't break the flow, and it's quite convenient for the customer. You need only to go through the pizza list and concatenate the pizza names, with their specified replies, into a single multiline string and send it back to the customers.

In the previous chapters you learned that you should separate your handlers for better application organization, so you'll extract the pizza menu greeting to a handlers folder from the start. You'll need to create a folder named handlers inside your project root folder, and inside it create a file named pizza-menu.js. Inside this file, you'll first import the static pizza list from the pizzas.json file into a `pizzas` variable. Then you'll create your `pizzaMenu` function, and within it a `greeting` variable with `Hello from Aunt Maria's pizzeria! Would you like to order a pizza? This is our menu:` as its value. Then you'll go through each of the loaded pizzas and concatenate to the `greeting` variable each pizza name with its short code on a new line. Finally, you should return the `greeting` variable as the result of your `pizzaMenu` function and export the function as your module. The full code is shown in the following listing.

Listing 10.2   The pizza menu greeting

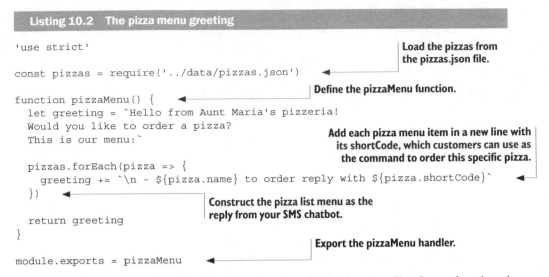

```
'use strict'

const pizzas = require('../data/pizzas.json')     ◄──  Load the pizzas from
                                                        the pizzas.json file.
function pizzaMenu() {     ◄──  Define the pizzaMenu function.
  let greeting = `Hello from Aunt Maria's pizzeria!
  Would you like to order a pizza?
  This is our menu:`                          Add each pizza menu item in a new line with
                                                its shortCode, which customers can use as
                                               the command to order this specific pizza.
  pizzas.forEach(pizza => {
    greeting += `\n - ${pizza.name} to order reply with ${pizza.shortCode}`   ◄──
  })     ◄──
                           Construct the pizza list menu as the
                           reply from your SMS chatbot.
  return greeting
}
                                              Export the pizzaMenu handler.
module.exports = pizzaMenu     ◄──
```

This handler always returns the pizza list when invoked. The pizza list shows the pizzas' names and short codes. To order, the user sends a text command instead of tapping a button, because interactions with an SMS chatbot are limited to text messages.

You then need to change your sms-bot.js file to invoke the `pizzaMenu` handler whenever a customer sends your chatbot an SMS. Because you don't have any other commands at this point, you can return just the imported `pizzaMenu` handler. It should look similar to the following listing.

Listing 10.3   The SMS chatbot entry

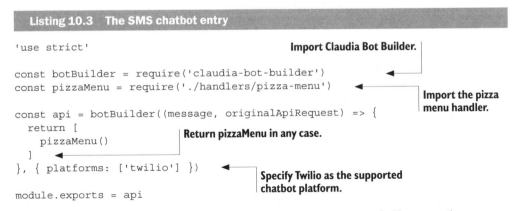

```
'use strict'                                  Import Claudia Bot Builder.

const botBuilder = require('claudia-bot-builder')     ◄──
const pizzaMenu = require('./handlers/pizza-menu')     ◄──
                                                          Import the pizza
                                                          menu handler.
const api = botBuilder((message, originalApiRequest) => {
  return [          Return pizzaMenu in any case.
    pizzaMenu()
  ]     ◄──
}, { platforms: ['twilio'] })     ◄──  Specify Twilio as the supported
                                       chatbot platform.
module.exports = api
```

Now, redeploy the project with the `claudia update` command. If you try it out, you should receive the greeting from the chatbot, along with the list of pizzas and their short codes.

10.1.2 *Ordering a pizza*

At this point, if a customer were to send your SMS chatbot a message, it would reply with a greeting and the pizza list. But if the customer were to send one of the pizza short codes as a response, the SMS chatbot would again reply with the pizza menu. In the following section, you'll enable your SMS chatbot to recognize the chosen pizza's short code and process the pizza order.

To start, you'll first need to check if the received message contains a pizza `shortCode`. You'll have to load the available pizzas inside your sms-bot.js file and check the message contents against each `shortCode`. If it finds a `shortCode`, it should ask the customer for the delivery address.

Your sms-bot.js file should now look like the following listing.

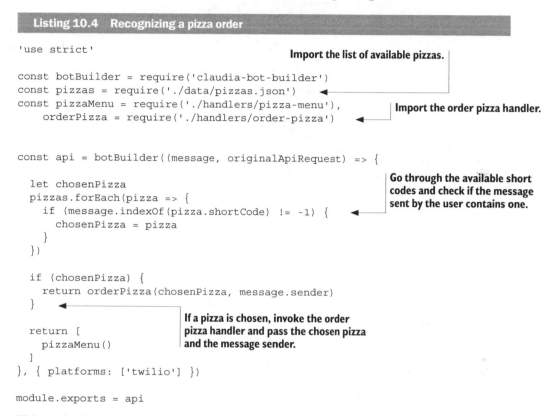

Listing 10.4   Recognizing a pizza order

```
'use strict'                                          Import the list of available pizzas.

const botBuilder = require('claudia-bot-builder')
const pizzas = require('./data/pizzas.json')   ◄
const pizzaMenu = require('./handlers/pizza-menu'),        Import the order pizza handler.
    orderPizza = require('./handlers/order-pizza')   ◄


const api = botBuilder((message, originalApiRequest) => {
                                                    Go through the available short
  let chosenPizza                                   codes and check if the message
  pizzas.forEach(pizza => {                          sent by the user contains one.
    if (message.indexOf(pizza.shortCode) != -1) {   ◄
      chosenPizza = pizza
    }
  })

  if (chosenPizza) {
    return orderPizza(chosenPizza, message.sender)
  }   ◄
                                   If a pizza is chosen, invoke the order
  return [                        pizza handler and pass the chosen pizza
    pizzaMenu()                   and the message sender.
  ]
}, { platforms: ['twilio'] })

module.exports = api
```

This code completes the first step, checking if the customer sent a pizza's short code and then passing the pizza and the sender (the customer) to the order pizza handler. The remaining step is writing the handler. The order-pizza.js handler should receive the chosen pizza object and the sender, and then store a new pizza order to the `pizza -orders` database table. For the new pizza order's `orderId`, you'll make use of the `uuid` module, and for the `pizza` you'll use the chosen pizza's ID. You'll set the `orderStatus` to `in-progress`, because you don't want the order to be delivered before you know the delivery address. Also, for `platform` you'll specify `twilio-sms-chatbot`, because if you're using the same database with multiple chatbots you want to have a way to differentiate the orders from each chatbot. Finally, you want to store the sender as the `user` attribute to be able to know which customer ordered it. The code for the order-pizza.js handler is shown in the following listing.

Listing 10.5   The order pizza handler

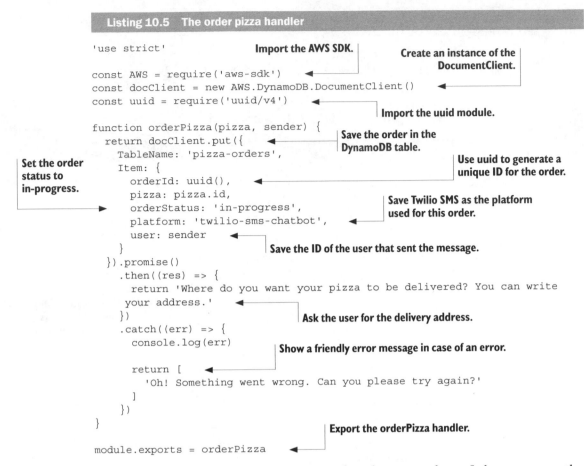

```
'use strict'                         Import the AWS SDK.
                                                          Create an instance of the
const AWS = require('aws-sdk')   ◄                          DocumentClient.
const docClient = new AWS.DynamoDB.DocumentClient()   ◄
const uuid = require('uuid/v4')   ◄
                                     Import the uuid module.
function orderPizza(pizza, sender) {
  return docClient.put({   ◄        Save the order in the
    TableName: 'pizza-orders',      DynamoDB table.
    Item: {                                        Use uuid to generate a
      orderId: uuid(),                             unique ID for the order.
      pizza: pizza.id,   ◄
      orderStatus: 'in-progress',      Save Twilio SMS as the platform
      platform: 'twilio-sms-chatbot',  used for this order.
      user: sender   ◄
    }                       Save the ID of the user that sent the message.
  }).promise()
    .then((res) => {
      return 'Where do you want your pizza to be delivered? You can write
      your address.'
    })                      Ask the user for the delivery address.
    .catch((err) => {
      console.log(err)
                            Show a friendly error message in case of an error.
      return [
        'Oh! Something went wrong. Can you please try again?'
      ]
    })
}
                            Export the orderPizza handler.
module.exports = orderPizza   ◄
```

Set the order status to in-progress.

`message.sender` in this case represents the phone number of the customer that requested the pizza. The missing piece of the puzzle at this point is the reply with the customer's address.

Handling SMS messages is not an easy task. SMS messages are plain text, so capturing the customer's address input is not provided as an additional option. With these limitations, you really have to think a lot about your implementation.

Currently, an order can only reach the `in-progress` status. Until you know the customer's address, you can't send the order to the delivery company. You'll need to obtain the address and save it—but at the moment, if the message does not contain a pizza's `short-Code`, your SMS chatbot will always reply with the greeting and pizza menu. You'll need to override that behavior and somehow manage to handle the address input properly.

Luckily, there is a solution. You are already storing the sender's phone number with the `in-progress` order, so you can first check if there is an `in-progress` order in your database with a matching phone number. If that's the case and there is no saved address, you can then save the sent message as the address. Figure 10.1 shows the message parsing process.

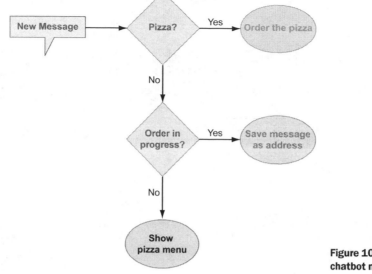

Figure 10.1 The serverless SMS
chatbot message parsing process

Understanding the process is the most important part, but you also need to learn how to implement it.

> **NOTE** In a real-world example, you probably shouldn't change the order status immediately, because the customer might have made a mistake or forgotten to respond and might now want to try to make a new order. To handle that, you may want to ask the customer for confirmation. If the answer is YES, you'll change the order status to pending; if it's NO, you'll delete the order from the database. Walking you through this process, however, is beyond the scope of the book.

First, you need to check for an in-progress order. It's best to have a separate handler file, check-order-progress.js, inside the handlers folder. Inside this file, implement the logic for scanning your DynamoDB table for an order that belongs to the sender and has an in-progress status. Because the DynamoDB scan command always returns an array of found items, you'll need to check if the scan result has any Items. If yes, return the first one. If not, return an undefined value, because nothing was found. Your check-order-progress.js file should look like the following listing.

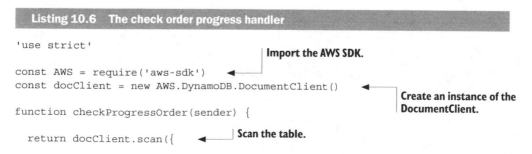

Listing 10.6 The check order progress handler

```
'use strict'
                                    Import the AWS SDK.
const AWS = require('aws-sdk')
const docClient = new AWS.DynamoDB.DocumentClient()
                                                        Create an instance of the
                                                        DocumentClient.
function checkProgressOrder(sender) {

  return docClient.scan({          Scan the table.
```

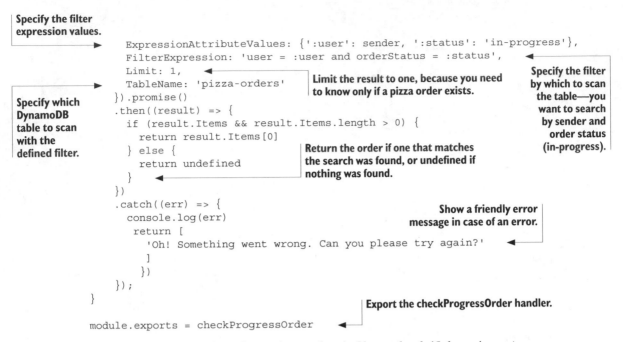

Specify the filter expression values.

```
ExpressionAttributeValues: {':user': sender, ':status': 'in-progress'},
FilterExpression: 'user = :user and orderStatus = :status',
Limit: 1,
TableName: 'pizza-orders'
}).promise()
.then((result) => {
  if (result.Items && result.Items.length > 0) {
    return result.Items[0]
  } else {
    return undefined
  }
})
.catch((err) => {
  console.log(err)
  return [
    'Oh! Something went wrong. Can you please try again?'
  ]
})
});
}

module.exports = checkProgressOrder
```

Limit the result to one, because you need to know only if a pizza order exists.

Specify which DynamoDB table to scan with the defined filter.

Specify the filter by which to scan the table—you want to search by sender and order status (in-progress).

Return the order if one that matches the search was found, or undefined if nothing was found.

Show a friendly error message in case of an error.

Export the checkProgressOrder handler.

Now you need to update the main sms-bot.js file to check if there is an in-progress order status and, if there is, save the location. If there isn't, show the pizza menu. To start, you'll first need to import the save-address.js and check-order-progress.js handlers. Then you'll use them to write the order status check. Your sms-bot.js file should look like the following listing.

Listing 10.7   The updated sms-bot.js file

```
'use strict'

const botBuilder = require('claudia-bot-builder')
const pizzas = require('./data/pizzas.json')
const pizzaMenu = require('./handlers/pizza-menu'),
  orderPizza = require('./handlers/order-pizza'),
  checkOrderProgress = require('./handlers/check-order-progress'),
  saveAddress = require('./handlers/save-address')

const api = botBuilder((message, originalApiRequest) => {

  let chosenPizza
  pizzas.forEach(pizza => {
    if (message.indexOf(pizza.shortCode) != -1) {
      chosenPizza = pizza
    }
  })

  if (chosenPizza) {
    return orderPizza(chosenPizza, message.sender)
  }
```

Import the check-order-progress.js handler.

Import the save-address.js handler.

```
    return checkOrderProgress(message.sender)
      .then(orderInProgress => {
        if (orderInProgress) {
          return saveAddress(orderInProgress, message)
        } else {
          return pizzaMenu()
        }
      })
  }, { platforms: ['twilio'] })
```

Check if there is an in-progress order for the current sender.

If there is an in-progress order, save the current order and save the current customer message as the address.

If there isn't an in-progress order, return the pizza menu.

```
module.exports = api
```

You're now missing only the save-address.js handler. Create the save-address.js file in the handlers folder, open it, and write the code to update an order in your DynamoDB table using the provided order ID as its key. You should also update the address and change the status from in-progress to pending. The handler is shown in the following listing.

Listing 10.8   The save-address handler

```
'use strict'

const AWS = require('aws-sdk')
const docClient = new AWS.DynamoDB.DocumentClient()

function saveAddress(order, message) {

  return docClient.put({
    TableName: 'pizza-orders',
    Key: {
        orderId: order.id
    },
    UpdateExpression: 'set orderStatus = :o, address = :a',
    ExpressionAttributeValues: {
      ':n': 'pending',
      ':a': message.text
    },
      ReturnValues: 'UPDATED_NEW'
  }).promise()
  });
}

module.exports = saveAddress
```

Specify the order to update by its orderId.

Specify the update expression.

Specify the update expression values.

Set the return value upon successful execution.

Export the saveAddress handler.

Now run the claudia update command and send a message to your Twilio phone number to try it out. That's it!

You've managed to build your first serverless SMS chatbot with Claudia.js and Twilio.

10.2   Hey Alexa!

Your SMS chatbot did its thing, and now even more people are ordering Aunt Maria's pizzas! Her pizzeria is getting crowded even on Mondays, so she's thinking of opening a second place in another neighborhood. Uncle Frank is happy, too, though he's a bit upset because he played with the SMS chatbot so much that his phone bill went sky-high.

Everything seems good—then your cousin Julia comes to you with a present, smiling smugly.

She gives you an Amazon Echo.

> ### Amazon Echo
>
> Amazon Echo is a voice-controlled home device. It's powered by Alexa, a smart voice assistant to whom you can talk and give commands, and that you can even use to order things online.

Julia explains that the she got it last Christmas, but was bored with it until she realized that you can use it to order pizzas. She wants Aunt Maria to dominate the market and surpass even Chess's pizzeria (probably because they don't give her free pizzas like Aunt Maria, but you go along). Julia thinks that having pizza-ordering voice commands for Echo before Chess's pizzeria does will help on the marketing side and win Aunt Maria many customers. It's not a bad idea, so you decide to help her out.

But what is Amazon Echo, and how do you use it? Julia shows you that you need to call the device "Alexa."

> ### Amazon Alexa availability
>
> Alexa was first used in the Amazon Echo and Amazon Echo Dot devices. It was announced in 2014, and it was inspired by the computer voice and conversational system onboard the *Starship Enterprise* from *Star Trek*. Alexa is now available on many devices, including the Amazon Echo family and Amazon Fire TV, and in mobile apps for most popular platforms, such as iOS and Android. Most of the devices require a *wake word* to start the Alexa conversation, but some will start an Alexa conversation on a button click.

The most interesting and powerful feature of Alexa is its custom *skills*. Skills are new commands that Alexa can learn, and they can be published to Amazon's Marketplace. At the time of writing, more than 20,000 custom skills are available in the Marketplace. These skills are analogous to computer applications.

Building a custom skill is quite simple. As shown in figure 10.2, an Alexa-enabled device forwards the audio file to the cloud, where Alexa parses it to a common format with *intents* and *slots* and then passes it as JSON to your Lambda function or HTTP webhook. Intents tell your skill what the user is trying to accomplish, and slots are the variables, or dynamic parts, of the given intent. Then your Lambda function or HTTP webhook replies with a JSON file that defines the Alexa voice reply that the user will hear. Before building your first skill, let's see how a skill works and how it differs from your Facebook Messenger and Twilio chatbots.

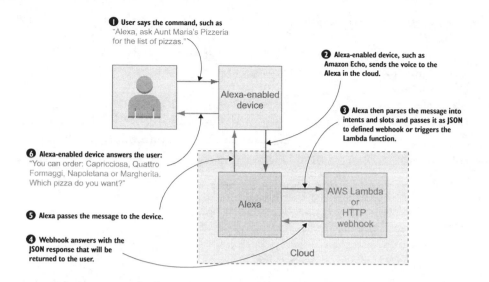

① User says the command, such as "Alexa, ask Aunt Maria's Pizzeria for the list of pizzas."

② Alexa-enabled device, such as Amazon Echo, sends the voice to the Alexa in the cloud.

③ Alexa then parses the message into intents and slots and passes it as JSON to defined webhook or triggers the Lambda function.

⑥ Alexa-enabled device answers the user: "You can order: Capricciosa, Quattro Formaggi, Napoletana or Margherita. Which pizza do you want?"

⑤ Alexa passes the message to the device.

④ Webhook answers with the JSON response that will be returned to the user.

Figure 10.2   A custom Alexa skill

Anatomy of an Alexa skill

Alexa and other voice assistants operate a bit differently from most of the chatbot platforms. Some notable differences are the following:

- Instead of just passing the message to your webhook, Alexa has a built-in natural language processing (NLP) engine, and it will pass only a parsed request to your webhook in the JSON format.
- Alexa conversation is command-based, and unlike most of the chatbot platforms, it doesn't allow free conversations. Your message must be recognized as one of the predefined commands for Alexa to understand and process it.
- Voice assistants typically require a wake word or phrase—a sound that tells them to expect a command immediately after.

As shown in figure 10.3, a typical Alexa command consists of the following:

1. Wake word
2. Launch phrase
3. Invocation name
4. Utterance with optional slots

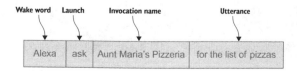

Wake word   Launch   Invocation name   Utterance

| Alexa | ask | Aunt Maria's Pizzeria | for the list of pizzas |

Figure 10.3   Alexa skill invocation

Other examples include "Alexa, start Aunt Maria's Pizzeria" and "Alexa, tell Aunt Maria's Pizzeria to order a pizza."

The default wake word is "Alexa," but it can be customized in the device settings. At the time of writing, available wake words are "Alexa," "Amazon," "Echo," and "Computer."

The launch phrase tells Alexa to trigger a certain skill. Launch phrases include "ask," "launch," "start," "show," and many others.

The invocation name is the name of the skill you want to trigger. To build a good skill, choosing a good invocation name is important.

NOTE   For some useful guidelines on invocation names, visit http://mng.bz/T6ly.

Finally, unless your launch phrase is "start," you need to tell Alexa what the skill should do. Those instructions are known as *utterances*. Having static utterances would not give you much flexibility, so Alexa allows you to add some dynamic parts to the instructions; those dynamic parts are called *slots*.

A user invokes the skill, and Alexa parses it and passes it to your AWS Lambda function or a webhook.

As shown in figure 10.4, once a voice command is processed by Alexa's NLP, it is converted to a recognized intent. If there are any slots in the invoked command, they are converted to objects that contain a slot name and value. Once a voice command is successfully parsed, Alexa builds a JSON object that contains the request type, intent name, and slot values along with other data, such as session attributes and metadata.

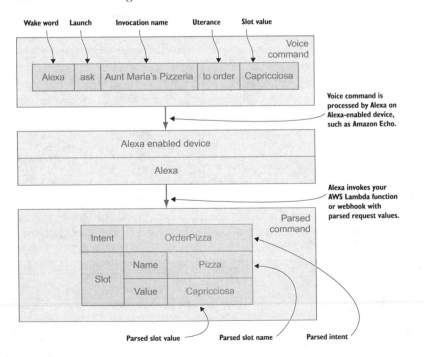

Figure 10.4   Alexa skill invocation and parsing flow

Alexa can receive a few request types (table 10.1).

Table 10.1 Alexa request types

Request type	Description
`LaunchRequest`	Sent when a skill is triggered with the "start" or "launch" phrases, such as "Alexa, launch Aunt Maria's Pizzeria"; does not receive custom slots
`IntentRequest`	Sent whenever a user message is parsed that contains an intent
`SessionEndedRequest`	Sent when a user session ends
`AudioPlayer` or `PlaybackController` (prefixes)	Triggered when a user uses any of the audio player or playback functions, such as pausing audio or playing the next song

Another important part of the Alexa command flow is the *session*. Unlike Facebook Messenger, Alexa can save some session data between commands, but you need to keep them in the session explicitly. An Alexa session is a conversation between a user and Alexa. If the session is active, Alexa waits for the user's next command after it replies. While the session is active, subsequent commands don't require a wake word, because Alexa expects a reply in the following few seconds.

Before building the Alexa skill, you'll need to design it. Designing voice assistant skills is not about the UI, of course, but about designing interactions and the intent schema. We cover that next.

10.2.1 *Preparing the skill*

The design is the most important part of building a skill. Voice assistants are often called "smart assistants," but in reality they're still far from HAL 9000 from *2001: A Space Odyssey*, and NLP capabilities are still a limiting factor.

Interaction design is beyond the scope of this book, but there are many good resources on the internet. As a good starting point, see Amazon's official voice design guide at https://developer.amazon.com/designing-for-voice/.

The skill you'll build in this chapter will be simple. It should do the following:

1 Allow the user to get the list of the available pizzas.
2 Allow the user to order the selected pizza.
3 Ask the user for a delivery address.

The basic flow of the skill you'll build is shown in figure 10.5.

To build an Alexa skill you need to prepare the following:

- Intent schema
- Custom slot types, if they exist
- List of sample utterances

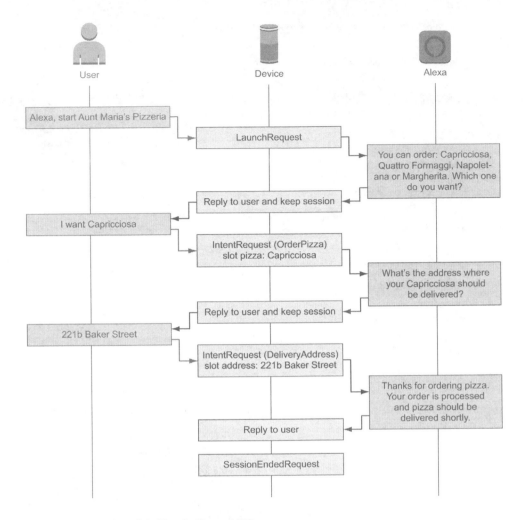

Figure 10.5   Aunt Maria's Pizzeria Alexa skill flow

NOTE   For instructions about setting up a new Alexa skill, connecting it to AWS Lambda, and entering the intent schema, custom slots, and sample utterances, see appendix B.

The *intent schema* is a JSON object that lists all the intents, or actions, that fulfill a user's spoken requests. Each intent can have slots, and each slot must have one type. Slot types can be custom or built-in. Amazon offers many built-in slot types, such as names, dates, and addresses. For the full list of built-in slot types, see https://developer.amazon.com/docs/custom-skills/slot-type-reference.html.

In addition to the built-in slot types, you can define *custom slot types*. A custom slot type consists of a name and a list of available values. The value list is a text file, in which each row represents a single value your custom slot type can have.

The *sample utterances* list is a set of likely spoken phrases mapped to the intents. It should include as many representative phrases as possible, and Alexa will use them to train its NLP for your skill. Similar to custom slot types, sample utterances are defined as a text file, where each sample utterance is entered on a new line. Each line starts with the intent that text should be parsed into, followed by a space and the sample text, as shown in figure 10.6.

Let's prepare everything you'll need, starting with the intent schema. This is a JSON object that contains an `intents` array with a list of intent objects. Each of the intent objects has an `intent` key, with the intent name as a value.

Your skill should have `OrderPizza` and `DeliveryAddress` intents, both with slots. `OrderPizza` should have a pizza name as a slot value, and `DeliveryAddress` should have an address as a slot value. There's a built-in slot type for addresses, but not for pizza names, so you'll need to create a custom slot type for these. Call it `LIST_OF_PIZZAS`— you'll define it later.

To add slots, both intent objects should have another key, `slots`, with a slots array as a value. The slots array will in both cases have just one slot object, with the slot name and type as a key-value pair.

For the `OrderPizza` intent, the slot name should be `Pizza` and the slot type should be `LIST_OF_PIZZAS`. For the `DeliveryAddress` intent, the slot name should be `Address`, and for the slot type you can use the `AMAZON.PostalAddress` built-in type, which accepts postal addresses.

Built-in slot types

The Alexa Skills Kit, which is a collection of APIs, tools, and documentation for building Alexa skills, supports several built-in slot types that define how data in the slot is recognized and handled. The provided types fall into the following general categories:

- Numbers, dates, and times
- List types

The first category contains slots that help you recognize numbers, such as `AMAZON.NUMBER` and `AMAZON.FOUR_DIGIT_NUMBER`, and date/time values, such as `AMAZON.DATE` and `AMAZON.DURATION`.

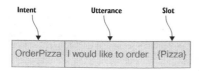

Figure 10.6   Sample utterances for an Alexa skill

In the second category, each slot type represents a list of items, such as addresses, actors, cities, animals, and many more. For example, the AMAZON.Animal slot will recognize animal species, the AMAZON.Book slot will recognize book titles, and the AMAZON.PostalAddress slot will recognize an address with a building or house number.

For more information, see https://developer.amazon.com/docs/custom-skills/slot-type -reference.html.

Let's also add one more intent: ListPizzas. This intent doesn't have any slots, and it should allow a user to ask Alexa for the list of all pizzas. It will trigger the same action as LaunchRequest.

When you've finished, your intent schema should look similar to the following listing.

Listing 10.9   Intent schema

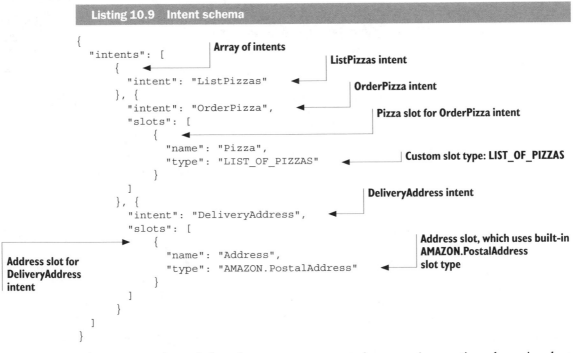

The next step is to define the LIST_OF_PIZZAS slot type. As mentioned previously, a custom slot type definition is a simple text file, where each possible slot value is on a separate line. Your LIST_OF_PIZZAS slot should be a list of all the pizzas, as shown in the following listing.

Listing 10.10   Custom slot type: LIST_OF_PIZZAS

```
Capricciosa
Quattro Formaggi
Napoletana
Margherita
```

The final step is to prepare the sample utterances list. This list is, again, a simple text file, where each of the sample utterances is on a separate line.

Each line should start with an intent name, followed by a space and a sample phrase; for example, `ListPizzas Pizza menu`. Having more than a few sample phrases is better, but Alexa will parse many other similar phrases, too. For example, if you define `ListPizzas Pizza menu`, Alexa will recognize phrases such as "Show me the pizza menu" or "What's on the pizza menu?"

Your sample utterances list should look similar to the following listing. You can leave some lines blank for readability.

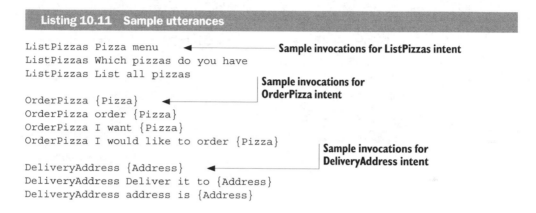

Listing 10.11 Sample utterances

```
ListPizzas Pizza menu            ◄──────────   Sample invocations for ListPizzas intent
ListPizzas Which pizzas do you have
ListPizzas List all pizzas
                                              Sample invocations for
                                              OrderPizza intent
OrderPizza {Pizza}               ◄───
OrderPizza order {Pizza}
OrderPizza I want {Pizza}
OrderPizza I would like to order {Pizza}
                                              Sample invocations for
                                              DeliveryAddress intent
DeliveryAddress {Address}        ◄───
DeliveryAddress Deliver it to {Address}
DeliveryAddress address is {Address}
```

10.2.2 *Ordering pizza with Alexa*

Now that you have the intent schema and sample utterances list, it's time to write the code for your Alexa skill.

As mentioned earlier, Alexa can trigger your API or AWS Lambda function. Claudia Bot Builder supports Alexa skills, and you can reuse the same AWS Lambda function you used for your Facebook Messenger or Twilio chatbot. But that adds an API Gateway layer between Alexa and your Lambda function, which increases cost and complexity. (It could also make maintenance easier in some cases, because you can reuse parts of the code.)

Your Alexa skill is simple at the moment, so let's create a separate AWS Lambda function for it. Creating this additional Lambda function doesn't have an initial cost—unlike with traditional servers, where you would need to pay for and set up an instance, both the setup cost and the deployment cost are zero.

Another big advantage of using Claudia Bot Builder is that it parses input in a common and simple format; it also removes the boilerplate for the answer. Input for the Alexa skill is automatically parsed into JSON, and for formatting the reply message, you can use the same thing that Claudia Bot Builder is using: `alexa-message-builder` is published as a separate NPM module, so you can use it without importing the full Claudia Bot Builder.

Create another folder at the same level as your pizza-api and pizza-fb-bot folders. You can name it pizza-alexa-skill to be consistent.

Then enter the folder and initialize an NPM project. Also install `alexa-message -builder` as a dependency by running the command `npm install alexa-message -builder --save`. Then create a file named skill.js and open it in your favorite editor.

Your skill.js file should be a standard AWS Lambda file that exports a handler function with `event`, `context`, and `callback` as parameters. It should also require the `alexa-message-builder` module you just installed.

Because you are not using Claudia Bot Builder, you need to check if the `event` your handler function receives is a valid Alexa request. You can check if `event.request` exists and if its type is `LaunchRequest`, `IntentRequest`, or `SessionEndedRequest`. Your skill will not have playback control or audio files, so you don't need to check `event .request` for those request types.

If the event is not a valid Alexa request, you need to return an error with the `callback` function.

Next, you need to add an `if…else` statement to determine which intent was triggered. You want to check the following states and provide the appropriate responses:

1 If `event.request.type` is `LaunchRequest`, or if it's `IntentRequest` with the `ListPizzas` intent, return the list of pizzas.

2 If the intent is `OrderPizza` and the `Pizza` slot is one of your pizzas, ask for the delivery address.

3 If the intent is `DeliveryAddress` and it has an `Address` slot, tell the user that the order is ready.

4 Otherwise, tell the user that there was an error.

If `request.type` is `IntentRequest`, you can get the intent from `event.request .intent.name`. If it has slots, they will be in the `event.request.intent.slots` object. For example, checking if the intent is `DeliveryAddress` and if the `Address` slot exists would look like this:

```
if (
  event.request.type === 'IntentRequest' &&
  event.request.intent.name === 'DeliveryAddress' &&
  event.request.intent.slots.Address.value
) { /* ... */ }
```

You can create an instance of `AlexaMessageBuilder` before your if…else statements with the following snippet:

```
const AlexaMessageBuilder = require('alexa-message-builder')
```

That snippet allows you to have just one callback after the if…else statements, by adding the following:

```
callback(null, message)
```

Then add the messages in each block of your if…else statements. For `LaunchRequest` and the `ListPizzas` intent, you should return the list of all pizzas, ask the user to pick one, and keep the session open. Keep in mind that the question you are asking must be clear and simple, so the user knows how to answer it in a way Alexa can process. For example, the code might look like this:

```
const message = new AlexaMessageBuilder()
  .addText('You can order: Capricciosa, Quattro Formaggi, Napoletana, or
    Margherita. Which one do you want?')
  .keepSession()
  .get()
```

The question used here is not perfect, because a user might answer with "the first one," and Alexa will not be able to understand this reply. It will be good enough to illustrate how the Alexa skill works, however.

Similar to Facebook Messenger templates, `AlexaMessageBuilder` is a class and its methods return `this` to allow chaining. To keep the session open, you can use the `.keepSession` method, and in the end you need to use the `.get` method to transform the reply to a plain JavaScript object with the format requested by Alexa.

Replying to the `OrderPizza` intent should be similar. You can reply with "What's the address where your pizza should be delivered?" and keep the session open. The main difference is that you want to save the selected pizza in the session attributes. You can do that by adding the following code:

```
.addSessionAttribute('pizza', event.request.intent.slots.Pizza.value)
```

At this point, your skill.js file should look similar to the following listing.

Listing 10.12   Alexa skill

```
'use strict'                                    Import the Alexa Message Builder library.

const AlexaMessageBuilder = require('alexa-message-builder')   ◄

function alexaSkill(event, context, callback) {   ◄
  if (
    !event ||                                     Provide the Lambda handler function.
    !event.request ||
    ['LaunchRequest', 'IntentRequest', 'SessionEndedRequest'].indexOf(event.
     request.type) < 0
  ) {    ◄
    return callback('Not valid Alexa request')    Check if the message is an Alexa
  }                                               event, and return an error if not.

  const message = new AlexaMessageBuilder()    ◄
                                                  Create an instance of
  if (                                            AlexaMessageBuilder.
    event.request.type === 'LaunchRequest' ||
    (event.request.type === 'IntentRequest' && event.request.intent.name ===
     'ListPizzas')
  ) {    ◄
    message                                    Check if the message is a LaunchRequest
                                               or the ListPizzas intent.
```

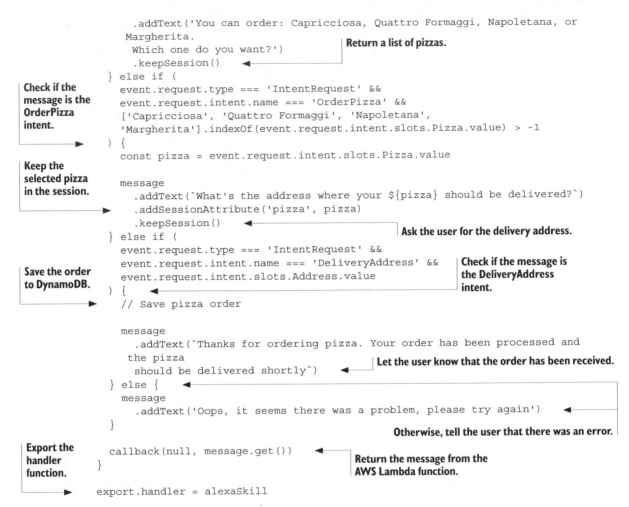

```
                .addText('You can order: Capricciosa, Quattro Formaggi, Napoletana, or
            Margherita.
                Which one do you want?')                    Return a list of pizzas.
                .keepSession()
        } else if (
            event.request.type === 'IntentRequest' &&
            event.request.intent.name === 'OrderPizza' &&
            ['Capricciosa', 'Quattro Formaggi', 'Napoletana',
            'Margherita'].indexOf(event.request.intent.slots.Pizza.value) > -1
        ) {
            const pizza = event.request.intent.slots.Pizza.value

            message
                .addText(`What's the address where your ${pizza} should be delivered?`)
                .addSessionAttribute('pizza', pizza)
                .keepSession()
        } else if (                                     Ask the user for the delivery address.
            event.request.type === 'IntentRequest' &&
            event.request.intent.name === 'DeliveryAddress' &&    Check if the message is
            event.request.intent.slots.Address.value             the DeliveryAddress
        ) {                                                      intent.
            // Save pizza order

            message
                .addText(`Thanks for ordering pizza. Your order has been processed and
            the pizza                                    Let the user know that the order has been received.
                should be delivered shortly`)
        } else {
            message
                .addText('Oops, it seems there was a problem, please try again')
        }
                                            Otherwise, tell the user that there was an error.
        callback(null, message.get())
    }                                       Return the message from the
                                            AWS Lambda function.
export.handler = alexaSkill
```

Check if the message is the OrderPizza intent.

Keep the selected pizza in the session.

Save the order to DynamoDB.

Export the handler function.

The next step is to deploy the Lambda function using the `claudia create` command. The two main differences in this case are the following:

- The supported regions are `eu-west-1`, `us-east-1`, and `us-west-1`.
- The default `latest` stage is not allowed, so you need to set some other version name, such as `skill`.

The command should look similar to the one in the following listing.

Listing 10.13   Deploy the skill with Claudia

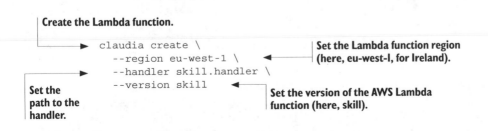

Create the Lambda function.

```
claudia create \
    --region eu-west-1 \            Set the Lambda function region
    --handler skill.handler \       (here, eu-west-l, for Ireland).
    --version skill
```

Set the path to the handler.

Set the version of the AWS Lambda function (here, skill).

After your Lambda function is deployed, you'll need to allow Alexa to trigger it. You can do that with the `claudia allow-alexa-skill-trigger` command. Don't forget to provide the version you defined with the `claudia create` command—in our example this is `skill`, so you'll need to run the `claudia allow-alexa-skill-trigger --version skill` command.

After you upload your Lambda function and allow Alexa to trigger the skill, make sure you follow the setup instructions described in appendix B. If you successfully configured your skill, you can simply say "Alexa, start Aunt Maria's Pizzeria."

10.3 *Taste it!*

Chatbots and voice assistants are fun! Now it's time for you to try to improve the skill on your own.

10.3.1 *Exercise*

Your exercise for this chapter is to send a welcome message on Alexa `LaunchRequest`. The message can be the following: "Welcome to Aunt Maria's Pizzeria! You can order pizza with this skill. We have Capricciosa, Quattro Formaggi, Napoletana, and Margherita. Which pizza do you want?"

To make this challenge a bit more fun, add a reprompt for both `LaunchRequest` and the `ListPizzas` intent. A reprompt is a repeated question that is sent if the session is still open but the user doesn't answer within a few seconds.

Tips:

- Split `LaunchRequest` and the `ListPizzas` intent into two if...else statements.
- Make sure to keep the session open.
- For reprompt usage, see the `alexa-message-builder` documentation: https://github.com/stojanovic/alexa-message-builder.

10.3.2 *Solution*

As you can see in the following listing, just a small part of the skill.js file should be changed. You need to separate `LaunchRequest` and the `ListPizzas` intent into separate `if` blocks and use the `.addRepromptText` method in both of the replies.

> **Listing 10.14 Modified skill.js file**

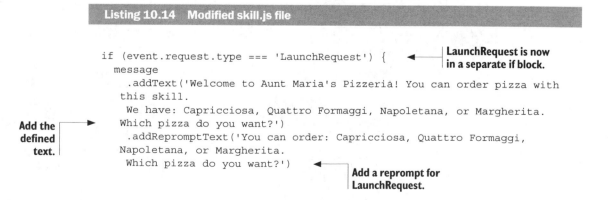

```
if (event.request.type === 'LaunchRequest') {          LaunchRequest is now
  message                                               in a separate if block.
    .addText('Welcome to Aunt Maria's Pizzeria! You can order pizza with
    this skill.
    We have: Capricciosa, Quattro Formaggi, Napoletana, or Margherita.
    Which pizza do you want?')
    .addRepromptText('You can order: Capricciosa, Quattro Formaggi,
    Napoletana, or Margherita.
    Which pizza do you want?')
```

Add the defined text.

Add a reprompt for LaunchRequest.

The ListPizzas intent is now in the else…if block.

```
        .keepSession()
    } else if (event.request.type === 'IntentRequest' && event.request.intent.
      name === 'ListPizzas') {
      message
        .addText('You can order: Capricciosa, Quattro Formaggi, Napoletana, or
      Margherita.
        Which pizza do you want?')
        .addRepromptText('You can order: Capricciosa, Quattro Formaggi,
      Napoletana, or Margherita.
        Which pizza do you want?')
        .keepSession()
    }
```

The rest of the file is not changed.

Add a reprompt for the ListPizzas intent.

After you've updated your code, deploy the code with the `claudia update` command and your skill will be ready for testing.

10.4   End of part 2: special exercise

You've now come to the end of part 2 of this book. You've learned many things related to serverless applications and chatbots, and it's time to consolidate that knowledge. The special exercise is to connect both your SMS chatbot and your Alexa skill to the database and the delivery service. Keep in mind that it's not possible to notify the user about pizza delivery status changes in Alexa.

NOTE   These special exercises have no hints.

Summary

- Claudia Bot Builder offers an easy and quick way to build SMS chatbots using Twilio.
- Providing a short and clear way for users to reply to your SMS chatbot is important because of its limitations.
- You can reuse chatbot code for multiple platforms, but sometimes splitting it into more Lambda functions is easier.
- Claudia Bot Builder supports Alexa skills, but because Alexa can trigger a Lambda function, you can save money and decrease latency if you deploy the skill without an API Gateway.
- Even though Alexa skills are easy to develop, designing the voice interaction in a bulletproof way is difficult.

Part 3

Next steps

Thanks to your work, Aunt Maria's pizzeria is blooming again. But even though everything works, frequent changes started causing occasional errors in the application. Now is the time to learn how automated testing works in serverless applications and how apply it to your Pizzeria API (chapter 11). Also, many customers inquired about online payments, so you'll need to integrate Stripe payments with AWS Lambda (chapter 12).

During your big family reunion, Aunt Maria bragged about her new online business. Her brother, your Uncle Roberto, asked if you can move his existing application to serverless. It's using Express.js and working well, but he's paying much more for it than Aunt Maria is, and it has scaling issues. Your assignment will be to learn and run his Express.js app in AWS Lambda (chapter 13). Then you'll learn more about migration of more complex existing apps to serverless (chapter 14).

Finally, you'll see how other real businesses are using serverless, how they migrated existing applications, and learn the benefits they've realized from it (chapter 15).

Testing, Testing, 1, 2, 3

This chapter covers

- Testing serverless applications—the approach
- Writing testable serverless functions
- Running automated tests locally

Application development is not an easy and carefree process. Even with careful implementation and checking, software bugs can slip through and put your company or your users at risk. In the past couple of decades, bug prevention and software testing have become imperative. As the old English proverb says, *an ounce of prevention is worth a pound of cure.*

Now with serverless, software testing seems to have gained a new layer of complexity. Having no server configuration, along with using AWS Lambda and API Gateway, can make testing your applications look scary. This chapter's goal is to show how, with just a minor change to your application testing approach, you can test your serverless applications as easily as you did those that were server-hosted.

11.1 Testing server-hosted and serverless applications

Recently, Aunt Maria has noticed that pizza ordering occasionally doesn't work for some customers—and Pierre, her mobile developer, has been reporting "ghost" bugs, sometimes even when displaying the pizza list. Aunt Maria is worried that she's losing some customers and has asked you to take a look. You can try to debug the Pizza API to find out where the issue is, but the bug might also be on the website or in the mobile app. Testing all the services manually each time an issue occurs is tedious, repetitive, and takes too long. The solution is to *automate* testing. Automated testing requires an initial investment to write the code that will test your application, but then you can rerun it to check your Pizza API whenever you alter its functionality, add a new feature, or encounter a new issue.

Automated testing is a big field, and there are many different automated test types, each taking a different approach: from testing small pieces (or *units*) of application code to complete application features and their behavior.

Taking your Pizza API as an example, the smaller unit tests will test just the execution of a single function within your pizza handlers, whereas the complete application tests (also known as *end-to-end, or E2E, tests*) will check the whole pizza listing and ordering flow from Aunt Maria's website.

Many more types of automated tests exist. They are often grouped into three layers based on their approach, from bottom to top:

- *Unit layer*—Tests that check the small (*unit*) application code pieces, such as single functions
- *Service layer*—Tests that check how those small code pieces work together, in *integration*; also called *integration* tests
- *UI layer*—Tests that check the complete application behavior from the UI perspective

In addition to those three automated test layers, there is another layer of manual testing, usually performed by Quality Assurance teams.

These testing layers have different test costs. A visual representation of the layers, along with their corresponding costs, is often called a *testing pyramid*. Usually, the testing pyramid consists of only the three automated test layers, but to gain a better understanding of the value and cost of each test type, you can also add the manual testing layer to the picture. With all four layers combined, the test pyramid looks like figure 11.1. The costs in the figure are based on testing server-hosted applications.

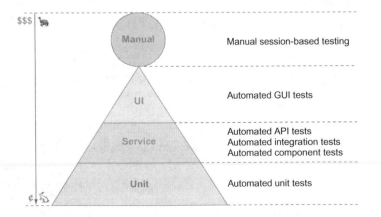

Figure 11.1   The testing pyramid

> **The test automation pyramid**
>
> The concept of the three-tier test automation pyramid was first mentioned by Mike Cohn in his book *Succeeding with Agile* (Addison Wesley, 2009). If you're interested in reading more about test automation, we highly recommend that book.

The figure shows that higher-level UI tests are more expensive than unit tests, because they test the whole application's behavior from the user's perspective, including visual details such as properly set inputs, displayed values, and so on. Besides being more expensive, the UI tests are also significantly slower because of the quantity of checks and the sheer volume of code executed.

In server-hosted applications, running automated tests usually requires a separate testing server, because you don't want to run the tests based on your production data. As a result, a big chunk of the server-hosted testing costs are infrastructure-related. That includes setting up a server with a setup identical to your production application, importing database data, developer time expended, and so on.

With serverless, the test-running costs are substantially reduced, mostly because there are no servers or server configuration. As a result, less developer time is invested. That reclaimed time can be used for more tests and more coverage. An updated testing pyramid for serverless applications, showing the difference in test costs, is presented in figure 11.2. We call this the *serverless testing pyramid*.

11.2 *How to approach testing serverless applications*

Developing serverless applications is great, because you don't have to worry about infrastructure. But from a testing perspective, that benefit now becomes a problem. Having no control over infrastructure requires you to rethink how to test. At first glance, you might think having no control over infrastructure means having no responsibility for whether AWS services are up or down, or if there is an AWS service down, or for

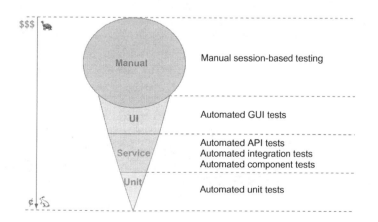

Figure 11.2   The serverless testing pyramid

network disconnects. But that instinct would be wrong. Even though you don't have control over infrastructure, that doesn't mean you're no longer responsible if it fails. Your customers won't know the difference between an AWS service malfunction and your application crashing. Youll be held responsible, and at the very least, you'll still need to check if your application is handling those cases well.

The following step-by-step approach can help you remember those cases while writing tests. Some of you might be using it in a different form already:

1 List all the different *concerns.*
   A concern represents a single function or a single piece of code responsible for one operation. In our example case, that might be calculating the discount for a pizza order.

2 Test each concern separately.

3 Look at how these concerns are working (integrating) with each other.
   It's like checking how a discounted price affects the amount you're charging the customer credit card.

4 Test each of their *integrations* separately, too.

5 List all the *end-to-end workflows.*
   An end-to-end workflow represents one complete feature workflow available within your application. An example of this is loading your site, listing pizzas, choosing one, ordering it, and paying for it. Listing all the workflows will give you a better and more complete overview of the application.

6 Test each of the defined end-to-end workflows.

This approach might seem logical, but the quantity of bugs in software applications nowadays tells us that something being logical doesn't mean that it's common practice.

> **NOTE** End-to-end tests for serverless applications are identical to those for server-hosted apps. Therefore, the last two steps are out of the scope of this book. Because you don't have access to Aunt Maria's website or mobile UI, writing the end-to-end tests isn't your responsibility. Regardless, these tests are important, because they test your serverless application as a whole product. To learn more about end-to-end testing, see https://medium.freecodecamp.org/why-end-to-end-testing-is-important-for-your-team-cb7eb0ec1504.

11.3   *Preparation*

A serverless Node.js application is still a Node.js application, and that means the tools you use for testing any other Node.js application will work for the Pizza API. This chapter uses Jasmine, which is one of the most popular Node.js testing frameworks, but you can use others, such as Mocha, Tape, or Jest.

> ### Jasmine testing framework
> Jasmine is a JavaScript testing framework. It doesn't depend on other JavaScript frameworks, and it doesn't require a DOM, so you can use it from both the browser and Node.js. Jasmine has a clean and obvious syntax that simplifies testing. To learn more about it, visit https://jasmine.github.io.

Jasmine tests are called *specs*, so we'll use the same name in the rest of this chapter. Spec is a JavaScript function that defines what a piece of your application should do. Specs are grouped in *suites*, which allow you to organize your specs. For example, if you're testing a form, you can have a validation suite, in which you'll group all specs related to form validation.

Jasmine uses *runner* to run your specs. You can either run all of your specs or filter them and run a specific spec or a specific suite. Before writing tests, you need to prepare your project for unit testing. To do so, you'll need to create a folder where you'll save your specs, and then to create a runner that will run your specs.

To follow Jasmine's naming convention, create a spec folder in your Pizza API project. This folder will contain all the specs for your Pizza API, including unit and integration specs. It will also include a configuration for Jasmine runner and some helpers, such as a helper for mocking HTTP requests. The application folder structure, with the specs you'll create in this chapter, is shown in figure 11.3.

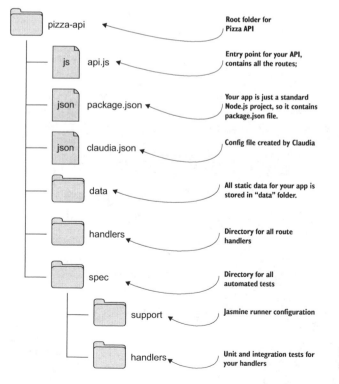

Figure 11.3 The Pizza API folder structure with specs

To configure your Jasmine runner, create a support folder in the specs folder of your Pizza API project. Inside that folder, create a jasmine.json file. This file represents runner configuration.

As shown in the following listing of this configuration, you need to define the location of your specs relative to the project root, and the pattern Jasmine will use to find spec files. In your case, it should be any file with a name that ends in "spec.js" or "Spec.js."

Listing 11.1   Jasmine configuration

```
{
  "spec_dir": "specs",          ◀———— Set the specs location to the specs folder,
  "spec_files": [                      relative to the root of the project.
    "**/*[sS]pec.js"           ◀———— All spec filenames end with "spec.js" or "Spec.js."
  ]
}
```

Next, define how Jasmine will run. You want to configure it to run with the configuration from the jasmine.json file and to give you an option to run only a specific spec or spec suite. And finally, you want it to run in verbose mode and to print the description of each spec as it runs.

To do so, create another file named jasmine-runner.js in the same folder, and open it with your favorite editor.

At the beginning of the file, require `jasmine` and `SpecReporter` from the `jasmine-spec-reporter` NPM package. Then create an instance of Jasmine.

The next step is to loop through the arguments passed in the command line. You can ignore the first two arguments because they are the path to Node.js and to your current file. For each remaining argument, check if they are `full` text and, if so, show the Jasmine spec reporter instead of the default reporter. If the argument is a filter, run only the specs that contain the provided filter.

Finally, load the configuration by using Jasmine's `loadConfigFile` method and launch the Jasmine runner with the provided filters.

Your jasmine-runner.js file should look like the following listing.

Listing 11.2   Jasmine runner

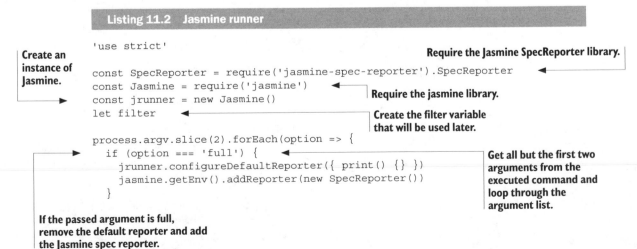

```
'use strict'                                          Require the Jasmine SpecReporter library.

const SpecReporter = require('jasmine-spec-reporter').SpecReporter  ◀——
const Jasmine = require('jasmine')  ◀——
const jrunner = new Jasmine()            Require the jasmine library.
let filter  ◀——                          Create the filter variable
                                          that will be used later.
process.argv.slice(2).forEach(option => {
  if (option === 'full') {  ◀——                        Get all but the first two
    jrunner.configureDefaultReporter({ print() {} })    arguments from the
    jasmine.getEnv().addReporter(new SpecReporter())    executed command and
  }                                                      loop through the
                                                         argument list.
```

Create an instance of Jasmine.

If the passed argument is full, remove the default reporter and add the Jasmine spec reporter.

Load the configuration from the jasmine.json file.

```
if (option.match('^filter='))
    filter = option.match('^filter=(.*)')[1]
})
```

If the passed argument is filter, save the filter value to the filter variable.

```
jrunner.loadConfigFile()
jrunner.execute(undefined, filter)
```

Launch the Jasmine runner with the provided filters.

At this point, you can run your specs using the `node spec/support/jasmine-runner.js` command. This will print the spec results to your terminal, with a green dot for each passing spec. To see the spec messages instead of green dots, you can run the `node spec/support/jasmine-runner.js full` command.

To simplify running your specs, you can add an NPM `test` script to your package.json file. This modification allows you to use the shorthand "test" to run your specs with the command `npm test`, or the even shorter `npm t` command. Add the following script to the package.json file:

```
"test": "node specs/support/jasmine-runner.js"
```

To run the specs with full message output, run the command `npm t-- full`. The `--` is required and must be followed by a space, because the options after it—in this case `full`—are not NPM options. Instead, they are passed to Jasmine directly.

> **TIP** You can improve your code with two other NPM scripts. First, if you have a linter, you can run it before your tests automatically if you add a `pretest` script to your package.json file. For example, if you're using ESLint, the command looks like this:
>
> ```
> "pretest": "eslint lib spec *.js"
> ```
>
> Also, if you're using the Node.js debugger, adding a `debug` script can be useful, as shown here:
>
> ```
> "debug": "node debug spec/support/jasmine-runner.js"
> ```
>
> Running this script will start your tests with the Node.js debugger. For more information about the debugger, see https://nodejs.org/api/debugger.html.

11.4 Unit tests

The foundation of the testing pyramid is the unit layer, which consists of unit tests. The goal of unit testing is to isolate each part of the application and show that the individual parts are working as expected.

The unit size depends on the application; it can be as small as a function or as large as a class or entire module. The smallest unit of code of the Pizza API that makes sense to isolate and test is a handler function. You can start with the `GetPizzas` handler.

The only external connection in the `getPizzas` handler is the connection to the pizzas.json file. Even though this is a static file, it represents an external connection that shouldn't be tested in a unit test. To prepare the handler for unit testing, you need to allow the handler function to receive a custom list of pizzas that will overwrite the list from pizzas.json. By doing this, you ensure your unit test will still work if the pizzas.json file is changed.

As shown in the following listing, you can do that by adding the `pizzas` parameter to your `getPizzas` handler, which defaults to the content of the pizzas.json file.

Listing 11.3   Updated `getPizzas` handler

Require the list of pizzas.

```
'use strict'

const listOfPizzas = require('../data/pizzas.json')

function getPizzas(pizzaId, pizzas = listOfPizzas) {
```

Pass the list of pizzas as the second argument, and set its value to listOfPizzas by default.

Now that your handler is ready for testing, you can start writing specs. To do so, create a file named get-pizzas.spec.js in the spec/handlers folder.

In this file, require your handler and create an array of pizzas. It should contain at least two pizzas with names and IDs, and it can look like the following code snippet:

```
const pizzas = [{
  id: 1,
  name: 'Capricciosa'
}, {
  id: 2,
  name: 'Napoletana'
}]
```

Now describe your spec using Jasmine's `describe` function. The description should be short and easy to understand; for example:

```
describe('Get pizzas handler', ()
        => { ... . })
```

TIP With Jasmine, you don't need to require the `describe`, `it`, and `expect` functions because they will be injected as global variables automatically. But if you're using a linter, don't forget to tell it that Jasmine functions are global, so it doesn't report them as undefined.

Your `describe` block should contain multiple specs. For a simple function, such as the `getPizzas` handler, you should test the following:

- Getting a list of all pizzas
- Getting a single pizza by ID
- An error for getting a pizza with an undefined ID

Each spec is a separate block defined by invoking the `it` function. This function accepts two parameters: the spec description and a function that defines your spec. Remember: descriptions should be short but clear, so you can easily understand what is being tested.

Each spec contains one or more *expectations* that test the state of the code. Expectations are actually the verifications, where you define what you *expect* the current value to be, compared with what that value is. Expectations are defined using `expect` statements.

NOTE For more information about using Jasmine with Node.js, see the official documentation at https://jasmine.github.io/api/2.8/global.html.

In your first spec, you want to check that the handler returns a list of all pizzas when a pizza ID is not provided. To do so, you need to invoke the handler without the first argument, but you also need to provide a list of pizzas as a second argument. You can do this by passing `undefined` and a list of pizzas to the handler, respectively. The spec can look like the following snippet:

```
it('should return a list of all pizzas if called without pizza ID', () => {
  expect(underTest(undefined, pizzas)).toEqual(pizzas)
})
```

To test the code with the existing pizza IDs, you should pass the IDs—1 and 2, respectively—and the list of pizzas, and expect the results to be equal to the first and second pizzas from your mocked array of pizzas. Your spec can look like this:

```
it('should return a single pizza if an existing ID is passed as the first
    parameter', () => {
  expect(underTest(1, pizzas)).toEqual(pizzas[0])
  expect(underTest(2, pizzas)).toEqual(pizzas[1])
})
```

For the last spec in the unit tests for the `getPizzas` handler, you can be as creative as you want in passing a nonexistent ID. For example, you should pass some edge cases such as numbers smaller and larger than the existing IDs, but you should also try to test some other values, such as strings or even other types.

The following example shows what your spec might look like:

```
it('should throw an error if nonexistent ID is passed', () => {
  expect(() => underTest(0, pizzas)).toThrow('The pizza you requested was not
    found')
  expect(() => underTest(3, pizzas)).toThrow('The pizza you requested was not
    found')
  expect(() => underTest(1.5, pizzas)).toThrow('The pizza you requested was
    not found')
  expect(() => underTest(42, pizzas)).toThrow('The pizza you requested was
    not found')
  expect(() => underTest('A', pizzas)).toThrow('The pizza you requested was
    not found')
  expect(() => underTest([], pizzas)).toThrow('The pizza you requested was
    not found')
})
```

Putting all this together, the following listing shows what your unit tests for the `getPizzas` handler should look like.

Listing 11.4 Unit tests for `getPizzas` handler

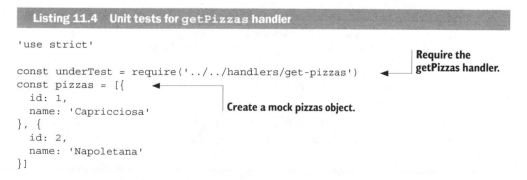

```
'use strict'

const underTest = require('../../handlers/get-pizzas')   ◀— Require the getPizzas handler.
const pizzas = [{                    ◀
  id: 1,                                   Create a mock pizzas object.
  name: 'Capricciosa'
}, {
  id: 2,
  name: 'Napoletana'
}]
```

Spec for the getPizzas handler invoked without an ID.

Describe the spec group.

Expect the getPizzas handler to return the list of all pizzas if an ID is not provided.

Spec for the getPizzas handler invoked with a nonexistent or invalid ID.

Spec for the getPizzas handler invoked with a valid and existing ID.

```
describe('Get pizzas handler', () => {
  it('should return a list of all pizzas if called without pizza ID', () => {
    expect(underTest(undefined, pizzas)).toEqual(pizzas)
  })

  it('should return a single pizza if an existing ID is passed as the first
      parameter', () => {
    expect(underTest(1, pizzas)).toEqual(pizzas[0])
    expect(underTest(2, pizzas)).toEqual(pizzas[1])
  })

  it('should throw an error if nonexistent ID is passed', () => {
    expect(() => underTest(0, pizzas)).toThrow('The pizza you requested was
      not found')
    expect(() => underTest(3, pizzas)).toThrow('The pizza you requested was
      not found')
    expect(() => underTest(1.5, pizzas)).toThrow('The pizza you requested was
      not found')
    expect(() => underTest(42, pizzas)).toThrow('The pizza you requested was
      not found')
    expect(() => underTest('A', pizzas)).toThrow('The pizza you requested was
      not found')
    expect(() => underTest([], pizzas)).toThrow('The pizza you requested was
      not found')
  })
})
```

Navigate to your project folder and run the npm test command from the terminal. The output after running this command, as shown in the following listing, will indicate that the spec failed.

Listing 11.5   Response after running specs

```
> node spec/support/jasmine-runner.js

Started
..F

Failures:
1) Get pizzas handler should throw an error if nonexistent ID is passed
  Message:
    Expected function to throw an exception.
  Stack:
    Error: Expected function to throw an exception.
        at UserContext.it (~/pizza-api/spec/handlers/get-pizzas-spec.
    js:26:40)

3 specs, 1 failure
Finished in 0.027 seconds
```

The failed spec prevents that bug from being deployed to the AWS Lambda function and creating an issue in production. It is important to test edge cases in your unit specs, because they can save you a lot of debugging from CloudWatch logs.

In this case, zero is passed as a pizza ID, and the `getPizzas` handler returned a list of all pizzas instead of an error, because zero is a false value in JavaScript and it will not pass the following part of the `getPizzas` handler:

```
if (!pizzaId)
  return pizzas
```

To fix this problem, update the problematic part of the `getPizzas` handler to check for an undefined `pizzaId`. For example, you can replace it with the following code:

```
if (typeof pizzaId === 'undefined')
  return pizzas
```

After updating your `getPizzas` handler, rerun the specs using the `npm test` command. The specs should pass now, and the output should look like the following listing.

> **Listing 11.6 Response after running specs that are passing**

```
> node spec/support/jasmine-runner.js

Started
...


3 specs, 0 failures
Finished in 0.027 seconds
```

Passed specs don't guarantee that your code is bug-free, but if meaningful specs are included in your code coverage, the number of production issues will be significantly lower. But how do you unit test handlers that can't be isolated easily—for example, handlers that have a direct connection to the DynamoDB table? That's where mock functions prove effective.

11.5 *Mocking your serverless functions*

In contrast to the `getPizzas` handler, most of the other handlers in the Pizza API interact with the database or send HTTP requests. To test those handlers in isolation, you'll need to mock all external interaction.

Mocking, primarily used in unit testing, refers to creating objects that simulate the behavior of real objects. Using mocks—instead of the external objects and functions the handler being tested interacts with—allows you to isolate the behavior of the handler.

Let's try testing a more complex handler, such as `createOrder`. Two things require mocking in the `createOrder` handler:

- The obvious functionality to mock is the HTTP request, because you don't want to contact the Some Like It Hot Delivery API from your specs. Some Like It Hot Delivery API is an external dependency that you don't own, and you don't have access to a test version. Any delivery request that you make in your tests can cause real-world production issues.
- You also want to mock the DynamoDB `DocumentClient`, because you want to isolate the test of the `getPizzas` handler from any dependency. If you test the fully integrated handler, you would need to set up a test database to test handler validation.

Mocking is important because unit specs are much faster to run than integration and end-to-end specs. Running your full spec suite takes a few seconds, instead of minutes or even hours in more complex systems. Also, unit specs are also much cheaper, because you don't need to pay for infrastructure when you want to check if your handler logic is working as expected.

After mocking HTTP requests and DynamoDB communication, the handler you're testing should work as described in figure 11.4.

To create a unit spec for the `createOrder` handler, create a file named create-order. spec.js in the specs/handlers folder of your Pizza API project. Then require this handler at the top of your spec file and add a Jasmine `describe` block, because you want to group your specs so you can easily read your Jasmine runner output.

At this point, your spec file should look like this:

```
const underTest = require('../../handlers/create-order')

describe('Create order handler', () => {
  // Place for your specs
})
```

Now let's mock the HTTP request. There are many ways to do that in Node.js. For example, you can use a full-featured module for mocking, such as Sinon (http:// sinonjs.org) or Nock (https://github.com/node-nock/nock), or even write your own.

In the spirit of Node.js and serverless development, we always recommend using small and focused modules, and `fake-http-request` is exactly that—a small Node.js module that mocks HTTP and HTTPS requests. You can install the module from NPM and save it as a development dependency by running the `npm install fake-http-request --save-dev` command.

In your new unit test, require the `https` module at the top of the file, too, because the `fake-http-request` module uses it for tracking mocked HTTP requests.

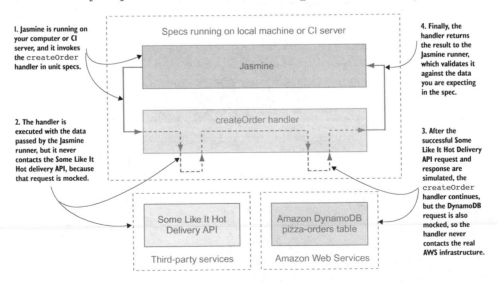

Figure 11.4   The unit test flow for the createOrder handler

NOTE You need to require the `https` module because the Some Like It Hot Delivery API requires an HTTPS connection. If you want to mock HTTP requests instead of HTTPS requests, you can require the `http` module instead of `https`.

To use the `fake-http-request` module, you'll need to use Jasmine's `beforeEach` and `afterEach` functions, which allow you to do something before and after each spec is executed. To install and uninstall the module, add the following snippet inside the `describe` block of your spec file:

```
beforeEach(() => fakeHttpRequest.install('https'))
afterEach(() => fakeHttpRequest.uninstall('https'))
```

Now that HTTPS requests are mocked, you need to mock the AWS `DocumentClient`. To do so, you'll need to require `aws-sdk` and then replace the `DocumentClient` class with a Jasmine spy. Remember to bind the `Promise.resolve` function; otherwise it'll have a different `this` and fail.

> **Jasmine spies**
>
> According to the Jasmine documentation, "Jasmine has test double functions called *spies*. A spy can stub any function and tracks calls to it and all arguments. A spy only exists in the `describe` or `it` block in which it is defined, and will be removed after each spec." To learn more about spies in Jasmine, visit https://jasmine.github.io/2.0/introduction. html#section-Spies.

Because the AWS SDK uses a prototype to create the `DocumentClient` class, you can replace the `DocumentClient` with your Jasmine spy by adding the following to the `beforeEach` block:

```
AWS.DynamoDB.DocumentClient.prototype = docClientMock
```

At this point, your create-order.spec.js file should look like the following listing.

Listing 11.7 Base of the `createOrder` handler unit test

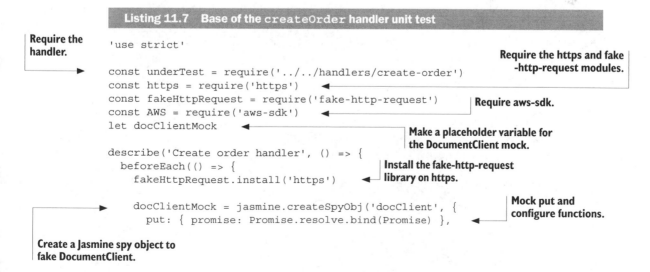

```
'use strict'

const underTest = require('../../handlers/create-order')
const https = require('https')
const fakeHttpRequest = require('fake-http-request')
const AWS = require('aws-sdk')
let docClientMock

describe('Create order handler', () => {
  beforeEach(() => {
    fakeHttpRequest.install('https')

    docClientMock = jasmine.createSpyObj('docClient', {
      put: { promise: Promise.resolve.bind(Promise) },
```

Require the handler.

Require the https and fake-http-request modules.

Require aws-sdk.

Make a placeholder variable for the DocumentClient mock.

Install the fake-http-request library on https.

Mock put and configure functions.

Create a Jasmine spy object to fake DocumentClient.

Replace the DocumentClient class with a Jasmine spy.

```
      configure() { }
    })
    AWS.DynamoDB.DocumentClient.prototype = docClientMock
  })

  afterEach(() => fakeHttpRequest.uninstall('https'))

  // Place for your specs

})
```

Uninstall the fake-http -request library.

Because the `createOrder` handler is more complex than the `getPizzas` handler, it requires more specs. To start with the most important parts, you should test the following:

- Sending a `POST` request to the Some Like It Hot Delivery API
- Reacting to both success and errors returned by the Some Like It Hot Delivery API
- Invoking `DocumentClient` to save an order only if the Some Like It Hot Delivery API request was successful
- Resolving the promise if both the Some Like It Hot Delivery API and `Document-Client` requests were successful
- Rejecting the promise if any integration fails
- Validating input

But you can add even more specs and test additional edge cases. To keep the page count of this chapter reasonable, we show you only the most important ones, and you can see a complete create-order.spec.js with all the important specs in the source code that goes with the book.

For the first spec, add an `it` block that will check if a `POST` request is sent to the Some Like It Hot Delivery API. Try to use a short and easily understood description; for example, "should send POST request to Some Like It Hot Delivery API."

In this spec, you want to invoke the `createOrder` handler with valid data, and then use the `https` module to see if the request is sent with the expected body and headers.

`fake-http-request` adds a `pipe` method to `https.request`, so you can use that method to check if the HTTPS request is sent with the expected values. For example, you can check if the number of sent requests is 1, because only one API request should be sent to the Some Like It Hot Delivery API. Also, you can check if the options passed to `https.request` were correct, including the method, path, body, and headers.

NOTE Keep in mind that the body is sent as plain text, and you need to stringify the object before checking if the body was correct; otherwise, your spec will fail because it will compare different types of data: object and string.

Your spec should look like listing 11.8.

TIP When comparing two large objects to see if just a few properties match, instead of writing all properties you can use `jasmine.objectContaining` and compare just a subset of the properties.

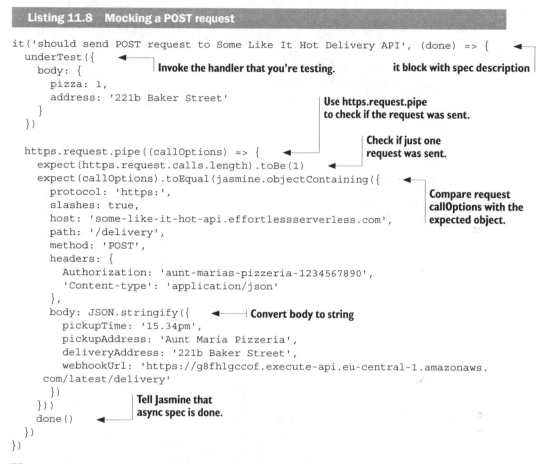

> **Listing 11.8 Mocking a POST request**

```
it('should send POST request to Some Like It Hot Delivery API', (done) => {
  underTest({
    body: {
      pizza: 1,
      address: '221b Baker Street'
    }
  })

  https.request.pipe((callOptions) => {
    expect(https.request.calls.length).toBe(1)
    expect(callOptions).toEqual(jasmine.objectContaining({
      protocol: 'https:',
      slashes: true,
      host: 'some-like-it-hot-api.effortlessserverless.com',
      path: '/delivery',
      method: 'POST',
      headers: {
        Authorization: 'aunt-marias-pizzeria-1234567890',
        'Content-type': 'application/json'
      },
      body: JSON.stringify({
        pickupTime: '15.34pm',
        pickupAddress: 'Aunt Maria Pizzeria',
        deliveryAddress: '221b Baker Street',
        webhookUrl: 'https://g8fhlgccof.execute-api.eu-central-1.amazonaws.
      com/latest/delivery'
      })
    }))
    done()
  })
})
```

Invoke the handler that you're testing.

it block with spec description

Use https.request.pipe to check if the request was sent.

Check if just one request was sent.

Compare request callOptions with the expected object.

Convert body to string

Tell Jasmine that async spec is done.

The next important test is whether the `DocumentClient` is invoked after a successful HTTP request. To test that, you need to simulate a successful response from the Some Like It Hot Delivery API by adding an `https.request.calls[0].respond(200, 'Ok', '{}')` line in the `https.request.pipe` method.

Because the `createOrder` handler returns a promise, you can use `.then` to check if the `DocumentClient` mock was invoked.

Remember to add `done()` after the `expect` statement, and also to invoke `done.fail()` if the promise was rejected; otherwise, your specs will run until Jasmine times out and fail.

The spec for testing the `DocumentClient` invocation should look like the following listing.

Listing 11.9   Testing `DocumentClient` invocation

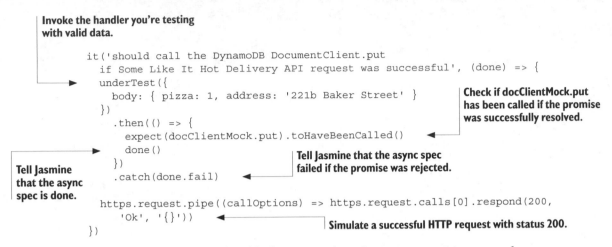

Invoke the handler you're testing with valid data.

```
it('should call the DynamoDB DocumentClient.put
  if Some Like It Hot Delivery API request was successful', (done) => {
  underTest({
    body: { pizza: 1, address: '221b Baker Street' }
  })
    .then(() => {
      expect(docClientMock.put).toHaveBeenCalled()
      done()
    })
    .catch(done.fail)

  https.request.pipe((callOptions) => https.request.calls[0].respond(200,
    'Ok', '{}'))
})
```

Check if docClientMock.put has been called if the promise was successfully resolved.

Tell Jasmine that the async spec failed if the promise was rejected.

Tell Jasmine that the async spec is done.

Simulate a successful HTTP request with status 200.

Another similar spec should show you that the `DocumentClient` mock was never invoked if the HTTP request failed. The differences between this spec and the previous one are

- The spec should fail if the promise was resolved.
- The spec should check that `docClientMock.put` has not been called.
- The `fake-http-request` library should return an error (with an HTTP status code greater than or equal to 400).

The spec for making sure that the `DocumentClient` mock is not invoked after a failed HTTP request might look like the following listing.

Listing 11.10   Testing that `DocumentClient` mock is not invoked if HTTP request fails

```
it('should not call the DynamoDB DocumentClient.put
  if Some Like It Hot Delivery API request was not successful', (done) => {
  underTest({
    body: { pizza: 1, address: '221b Baker Street' }
  })
    .then(done.fail)
    .catch(() => {
      expect(docClientMock.put).not.toHaveBeenCalled()
      done()
    })

  https.request.pipe((callOptions) => https.request.calls[0].respond(500,
    'Server Error', '{}'))
})
```

Tell Jasmine that the async test failed if the promise was resolved.

Check that docClientMock.put has not been called if the promise was rejected.

Respond with status 500.

If you run the `npm test` or `npm t` command, the specs should run successfully.

NOTE Consult the source code you got with the book to see the full specs file.

11.6 *Integration tests*

Integration tests are another test type; they are even more important for serverless functions that are larger than a few lines of code. Unlike unit tests, integration tests use real integrations with other parts of your system. But they still can and should mock some third-party libraries that you don't control. For example, you don't want your automated tests to interact with a payment processor.

As shown in figure 11.5, integration tests of the createOrder handler would still mock the Some Like It Hot Delivery API. Sending an HTTP request to a third-party API can affect real-world users, but it would have a real integration with the DynamoDB table prepared for testing.

The flow of the integration tests for the createOrder handler is as follows:

1 Create a new DynamoDB table before all the specs.
2 Mock only connections to the Some Like It Hot Delivery API before each spec.
3 Run a spec.
4 Remove the mock from the Some Like It Hot Delivery API HTTP request, and run the next spec if it exists (by going back to step 2).
5 Delete the test DynamoDB table when all specs are done.

TIP Creating and deleting the DynamoDB table can be done before and after each spec, but because both creating and deleting the database can take at least a few seconds, you can reuse the same table for all specs from the integration test suite to save time.

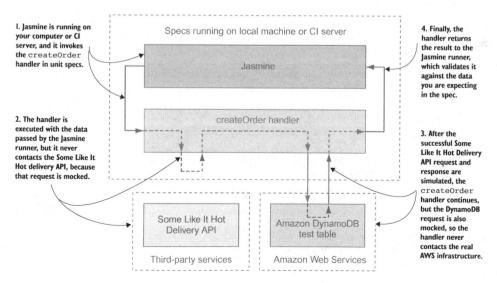

Figure 11.5 The integration test flow for the createOrder handler

Because there are just a few handlers, you can have both unit and integration tests in the same folder. Just make sure you name them in such a way that you can understand the difference easily. For example, integration tests for the `createOrder` handler can be in the create-order-integration.spec.js file.

As shown in the next listing, preparation for integration testing of the `createOrder` handler involves a few steps.

The first step is to require all the modules you need, such as the handler that you're testing and the `aws-sdk` (because you need the `DynamoDB` class), `https`, and `fake-http-request` modules.

Then you need to generate the name for your test, `DynamoDB`. You could use the same name each time, but a generated name will have a better chance of being unique. You also need to increase Jasmine's timeout to at least one minute, because creating and deleting a DynamoDB table can take a while, and the initial five-second timeout is not long enough.

> **NOTE** By default, Jasmine will wait five seconds for an asynchronous spec to finish before causing a timeout failure. If the timeout expires before `done` is called, the current spec will be marked as failed and suite execution will continue as if `done` had been called.

Next, you need to create a DynamoDB table before all tests using Jasmine's `beforeAll` function. Keep in mind that the creation of a DynamoDB table is asynchronous, so you'll need to use the `done` callback to tell Jasmine when the operation is finished. If you don't do that, spec execution will start before the table is ready.

You can use the `createTable` method from the `DynamoDB` class for this. It needs to have the same key definitions as your `pizza-orders` table, which means that it needs to have `orderId` as a hash key.

Because the `createTable` promise will resolve before the DynamoDB table is ready, you can use the `waitFor` method of the AWS SDK's `DynamoDB` class to be sure that the table exists before invoking the Jasmine `done` callback.

For deleting the table in Jasmine's `afterAll` function, the flow should be similar: delete the table using the `deleteTable` method of the `DynamoDB` class, and then use the `waitFor` method to be sure that the table is deleted. Finally, you invoke the `done` callback.

Mocking of HTTP requests to the Some Like It Hot Delivery API is similar to the mocking you did for unit tests. The only difference is that you want to mock only HTTP requests to this particular API; you want to allow other HTTP requests, because the `DynamoDB` class uses them to interact with the AWS infrastructure. To do so, you can pass an object that contains the request type—in your case, `https`—and regex matcher for the domain name to the `fakeHttpRequest.install` function.

At this point, your create-order-integration.spec.js file should look like the next listing.

Listing 11.11 Preparation for integration test for `createOrder` handler

Import aws-sdk.

Import the handler that you're testing.

Create an instance of the DynamoDB class.

Import the https and fake -http-request modules.

Generate the name of the test DynamoDB table.

Increase the timeout for the Jasmine runner to one minute.

Create a new DynamoDB table before all specs.

Wait for the tableExists status.

Delete the DynamoDB table after all specs are done.

Wait for the tableNotExists status before stopping the tests.

```javascript
'use strict'

const underTest = require('../../handlers/create-order')
const AWS = require('aws-sdk')
const dynamoDb = new AWS.DynamoDB({
  apiVersion: '2012-08-10',
  region: 'eu-central-1'
})
const https = require('https')
const fakeHttpRequest = require('fake-http-request')

const tableName = `pizzaOrderTest${new Date().getTime()}`
jasmine.DEFAULT_TIMEOUT_INTERVAL = 60000

describe('Create order (integration)', () => {
  beforeAll((done) => {
    const params = {
      AttributeDefinitions: [{
        AttributeName: 'orderId',
        AttributeType: 'S'
      }],
      KeySchema: [{
        AttributeName: 'orderId',
        KeyType: 'HASH'
      }],
      ProvisionedThroughput: {
        ReadCapacityUnits: 1,
        WriteCapacityUnits: 1
      },
      TableName: tableName
    }

    dynamoDb.createTable(params).promise()
      .then(() => dynamoDb.waitFor('tableExists', {
        TableName: tableName
      }).promise())
      .then(done)
      .catch(done.fail)
  })

  afterAll(done => {
    dynamoDb.deleteTable({
      TableName: tableName
    }).promise()
      .then(() => dynamoDb.waitFor('tableNotExists', {
        TableName: tableName
      }).promise())
      .then(done)
      .catch(done.fail)
  })
```

```
beforeEach(() => fakeHttpRequest.install({
  type: 'https',
  matcher: /some-like-it-hot-api/
}))
```

Install the fake-http-request module only for the Some Like It Hot Delivery API.

```
afterEach(() => fakeHttpRequest.uninstall('https'))

// Place for your specs
```

```
})
```

Now that you have integration tests set up, you need to update the `createOrder` handler to be able to receive the DynamoDB table name dynamically. You can do that by passing the table name as a second argument, or you can set the table name as an environment variable.

The easiest way is to pass the table name as the second argument. To do, so update your `createOrder` handler to accept the DynamoDB table name, but remember to set `pizza-orders` as the default value, so you don't break the existing code. Your `createOrder` handler function arguments should look like this:

```
function createOrder(request, tableName = 'pizza-orders') {
```

The last but most difficult step is to add the integration specs. The specs should check all the critical parts of the integration of your handler with any other part of the system or the infrastructure.

To keep the length of this chapter reasonable, we show you just the most important spec, which tests whether the data is written to the database as expected. You can see the full create-order-integration.spec.js file with more specs in the source code.

As shown in listing 11.12, to test if the order was saved to the database after the Some Like It Hot Delivery API response, you need to do the following:

1 Invoke the `createOrder` handler with the valid data and the test DynamoDB table name.
2 Mock the response from the Some Like It Hot Delivery API and return `deliveryId`.
3 When the `createOrder` handler promise is resolved, use the `DynamoDB` class instance to query the database for the item with the ID received from the Some Like It Hot Delivery API.
4 Check if the order info returned by `dynamoDb.getItem` is correct.
5 Mark the test as done.

Listing 11.12   Testing if order is saved to the DynamoDB table

```
it('should save the order in the DynamoDB table
  if Some Like It Hot Delivery API request was successful', (done) => {
  underTest({
    body: { pizza: 1, address: '221b Baker Street' }
  }, tableName)
```

Invoke the handler you're testing with the data and test table name.

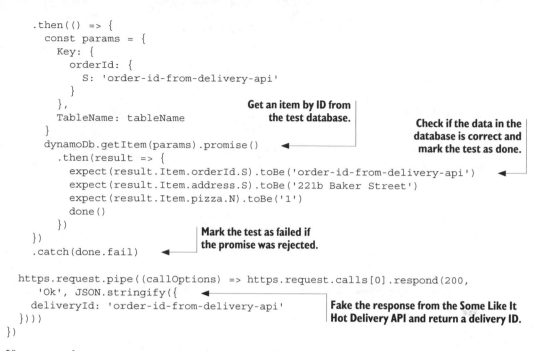

```
      .then(() => {
        const params = {
          Key: {
            orderId: {
              S: 'order-id-from-delivery-api'
            }
          },
          TableName: tableName
        }
        dynamoDb.getItem(params).promise()
          .then(result => {
            expect(result.Item.orderId.S).toBe('order-id-from-delivery-api')
            expect(result.Item.address.S).toBe('221b Baker Street')
            expect(result.Item.pizza.N).toBe('1')
            done()
          })
      })
      .catch(done.fail)

  https.request.pipe((callOptions) => https.request.calls[0].respond(200,
    'Ok', JSON.stringify({
    deliveryId: 'order-id-from-delivery-api'
  }))))
})
```

Get an item by ID from the test database.

Check if the data in the database is correct and mark the test as done.

Mark the test as failed if the promise was rejected.

Fake the response from the Some Like It Hot Delivery API and return a delivery ID.

If you run the `npm test` command again, you'll notice that it takes more time, but it should show all tests as passed, including your integration test.

> **TIP** If you have a large number of integration tests, having a DynamoDB test table predefined instead of creating it before running tests for the handler can speed up your test execution time.

You can check the AWS Web Console to make sure that the DynamoDB table is deleted successfully. Even after you've added a few more integration tests, your monthly AWS bill for the application built in this book should still be just a few cents.

11.7 *Other types of automated testing*

You've seen that unit and integration tests in serverless apps are similar to the same tests in non-serverless Node.js applications. As expected, the major impact is on the speed of setting up the infrastructure copy for the tests (setup is fast because there's no server configuration to do) and the price of the infrastructure (you don't have to pay for it when it's not in use).

There are many other types of automated tests, and serverless architecture affects some of them. For example, running load and stress tests doesn't make sense in a serverless architecture that is auto-scalable within documented limits. This applies unless your application is not fully serverless or you don't trust your serverless provider, which is a problem beyond the scope of this book.

Another type of automated test that can be affected by serverless architecture is GUI tests. It might not sound intuitive, but despite serverless being mostly focused on infrastructure, it can speed up GUI tests with its parallel execution and *headless browsers,* such as headless Chrome and Phantom.js. Headless browsers are regular web browsers, but they don't have a graphical user interface; instead, you run them from the command line. The ability to run automated GUI tests on Google Chrome running on AWS Lambda has already resulted in a lot of new tools that simplify GUI tests. But even more importantly, those tools speed up the tests by an order of magnitude and drop the price drastically. One of the tools that allows you to run GUI tests on AWS Lambda is Appraise, a visual-approval testing tool that uses headless Chrome to take a screenshot and then compares the screenshot with the expected output. To learn more about Appraise, visit http://appraise.qa.

11.8   *A step beyond: Writing testable serverless functions*

So far, you've learned the basics of testing serverless applications, but that doesn't mean you've covered all the potential edge cases. Let's take the example of our pizza order-saving handler.

Listing 11.13   The current pizza order-saving handler

```
function createOrder(request, tableName) {
  tableName = tableName || 'pizza-orders'
                                                        Load DynamoDB.
  const docClient = new AWS.DynamoDB.DocumentClient({
    region: process.env.AWS_DEFAULT_REGION
  })
  let userAddress = request && request.body && request.body.address;
  if (!userAddress) {
    const userData = request && request.context && request.context.authorizer
    && request.context.authorizer.claims;
    if (!userData)
                                                        Retrieve the
      throw new Error()                                 userAddress
    // console.log('User data', userData)               for pizza delivery.
    userAddress = JSON.parse(userData.address).formatted
  }

  if (!request || !request.body || !request.body.pizza || !userAddress)
    throw new Error('To order pizza please provide pizza type and address
      where
    pizza should be delivered')       Check if the required pizza order
                                      properties have been supplied.

  return rp.post('https://some-like-it-hot-api.effortlessserverless.com/
    delivery', {
    headers: {                                          Send a delivery request
      Authorization: 'aunt-marias-pizzeria-1234567890', to the Some Like It Hot
      'Content-type': 'application/json'                Delivery API.
    },
    body: JSON.stringify({
      pickupTime: '15.34pm',
      pickupAddress: 'Aunt Maria Pizzeria',
      deliveryAddress: userAddress,
      webhookUrl: 'https://g8fhlgccof.execute-api.eu-central-1.amazonaws.com/
      latest/delivery',
    })
```

```
    })
      .then(rawResponse => JSON.parse(rawResponse.body))
      .then(response => {
        return docClient.put({      ◄────────┤  Save the new pizza order to DynamoDB
          TableName: tableName,                  using its DocumentClient.
          Item: {
            cognitoUsername: userAddress['cognito:username'],
            orderId: response.deliveryId,
            pizza: request.body.pizza,
            address: userAddress,
            orderStatus: 'pending'
          }
        }).promise()
      })
      .then(res => {
        console.log('Order is saved!', res)
        return res     ◄──────────────────┤  Return the response when done saving.
      })
      .catch(saveError => {
        console.log(`Oops, order is not saved :(`, saveError)
        throw saveError
      })
}
```

This service looks fine—it's your handler for storing pizza orders. It is properly structured in a separate file and is straightforward and simple. It also doesn't do multiple things at the same time—but there is a catch. As you've seen, it's almost impossible to automatically test without invoking AWS DynamoDB. Even though this seems to be a good solution, you aren't covering all the edge cases. For example, what if one part of the AWS DynamoDB service changes abruptly and you don't manage to follow up? Or what if the DynamoDB service crashes? These conditions may occur only rarely, but taking the risks out of the equation is important. In addition to these, there are many more risks to consider. They can be categorized into four types. You may be wondering what sorts of risks those types cover, so here's a short list for the example of storing a single pizza order to DynamoDB:

- *Configuration risks*—Are you storing to the correct DynamoDB table? Does the role for the Lambda function have the correct access rights for the DynamoDB table?
- *Technical workflow risks*—How are you using and parsing the incoming requests? Are you handling both successful responses and errors well?
- *Business logic risks*—Are you properly structuring the pizza order?
- *Integration risks*—Are you reading the incoming request structure correctly? Are you storing the order to DynamoDB correctly?

You could test each of these as you did for the integration tests, but setting up and configuring the service each time you want to test for one of these risks isn't optimal. Imagine if testing automobiles was done that way. That would mean that every time you wanted to test a single screw or even a mirror in a car, you would have to assemble and then disassemble the whole car. Therefore, to make it more testable, the obvious solution is to break up your serverless function into several smaller ones.

If you're struggling with figuring out how to do this, or if it's your first time breaking apart any kind of service into smaller functions, you might not know where to start. Luckily, other people wanted to do it correctly and make their code more testable, too, which resulted in an architectural practice called *Hexagonal Architecture*, or the *ports and adapters* pattern.

Although the term "Hexagonal Architecture" sounds complex, it's a simple design pattern where your service code pieces don't talk directly to external resources. Instead, your service core talks to a layer of boundary interfaces. External services connect to those interfaces and adapt the concepts they need to those important for the application. For example, your `createOrder` handler in a Hexagonal Architecture wouldn't directly receive an API request; it would receive an `OrderRequest` object in an application-specific format that contains the `pizza` and `deliveryAddress` objects describing the ordered pizza and delivery address. An adapter would be responsible for converting between the API request format and the `createOrder` format. You can see a visual representation of this handler with the proposed Hexagonal Architecture in figure 11.6.

This architecture also means that your `createOrder` function won't call DynamoDB directly. Instead, it will talk to boundary interfaces that are specific for your needs. For example, you could define an `OrderRepository` object that could be any object with the function `put`. You would then define a separate `DynamoOrderRepository` object that implements that particular interface and talks to DynamoDB. You would do the same with the Some Like It Hot Delivery API.

This architecture allows you to test the integration of API requests and DynamoDB with your code without worrying how your service interacts with DynamoDB or the delivery service. Even if DynamoDB completely changes its API or you change from DynamoDB to some other AWS database service, your handler's core will not change, just the

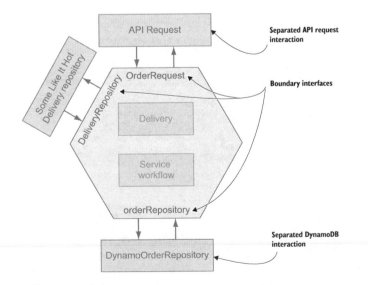

Figure 11.6   Hexagonal Architecture

DynamoOrderRepository object will. This improves testing of successful responses and internal error handling, and keeps your application code safe and consistent. Also, it shows what you need to mock in your integration tests.

To implement this architecture, you'll need to break your createOrder handler into several functions. You'll show only the one with DynamoDB. You'll need to pass the orderRepository as an additional parameter into your createOrder function. Instead of directly communicating with the AWS DynamoDB DocumentClient, you'll call the put on orderRepository. The next listing shows the applied orderRepository changes.

> **Listing 11.14   Updating pizza order saving handler with `orderRepository`**

```
function createOrder(request, orderRepository) {
```
◀ **Add the orderRepository parameter to the createOrder call.**

The initialization code for the AWS DynamoDB DocumentClient has been removed.

```
    // we have removed the code for initializing AWS DynamoDB, because that has
    moved inside the orderRepository

    let userAddress = request && request.body && request.body.address;
    if (!userAddress) {
      const userData = request && request.context && request.context.authorizer
    && request.context.authorizer.claims;
      if (!userData)
        throw new Error()
      // console.log('User data', userData)
      userAddress = JSON.parse(userData.address).formatted
    }

      // the previous code remains the same
      .then(rawResponse => JSON.parse(rawResponse.body))
      .then(response => orderRepository.createOrder({    ◀
          cognitoUsername: userAddress['cognito:username'],
          orderId: response.deliveryId,
          pizza: request.body.pizza,        Instead of calling docClient.put, you're now
          address: userAddress,             calling orderRepository.createOrder.
          orderStatus: 'pending'
        })
      ).promise()
    })
    // the rest of the code remains the same
}
```

This updated listing demonstrates how the createOrder handler has changed. Now, if you wanted to refactor or change your database service, you wouldn't need to edit your createOrder handler at all. Also, it's much easier to mock orderRepository compared with DynamoDB's DocumentClient. The only thing remaining is to set up the orderRepository. You can create it as a separate module, because you might want to use it in the other handlers as well. The next listing demonstrates the order-Repository setup.

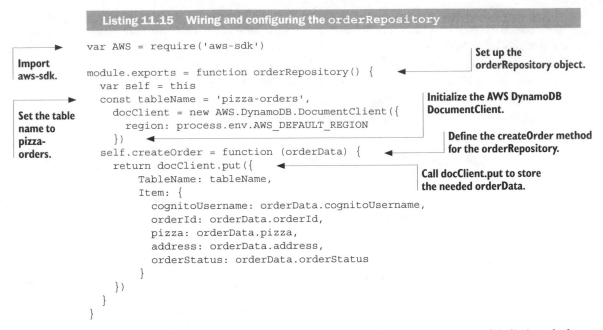

Listing 11.15   Wiring and configuring the `orderRepository`

Import aws-sdk.

Set the table name to pizza-orders.

```
var AWS = require('aws-sdk')

module.exports = function orderRepository() {
  var self = this
  const tableName = 'pizza-orders',
    docClient = new AWS.DynamoDB.DocumentClient({
      region: process.env.AWS_DEFAULT_REGION
    })
  self.createOrder = function (orderData) {
    return docClient.put({
      TableName: tableName,
      Item: {
        cognitoUsername: orderData.cognitoUsername,
        orderId: orderData.orderId,
        pizza: orderData.pizza,
        address: orderData.address,
        orderStatus: orderData.orderStatus
      }
    })
  }
}
```

Set up the orderRepository object.

Initialize the AWS DynamoDB DocumentClient.

Define the createOrder method for the orderRepository.

Call docClient.put to store the needed orderData.

Setting up boundary interfaces, such as the `orderRepository` from this listing, helps you to separate the logic of interacting with the specifics of AWS DynamoDB from the logic of saving pizza orders. Now, you can try to implement the other boundary interfaces (for DeliveryRequest and the API request) on your own.

Writing testable serverless functions makes your code simpler, easier to read, and easier to debug, and also removes the potential risks from your services. Thinking about testing first, before developing, can help you to avoid potential problems while at the same time providing high-quality serverless applications.

We hope that this chapter has provided you with enough knowledge and resources to at least make a start on testing your serverless functions. Now it's time for your exercises!

11.9   *Taste it!*

Automated tests are an important part of any application. Serverless applications are no different. We've prepared a small exercise for you, but you shouldn't stop there. Instead, you should go further and write more tests, until testing your serverless applications becomes part of your normal workflow.

11.9.1   *Exercise*

In Node.js applications, people often test API routes. You can do the same with Claudia API Builder. So, your next exercise is to test whether Claudia API Builder set up all the routes correctly. Here are a few tips on how to do that:

- You can use the `.apiConfig` method of Claudia API Builder to get the API configuration with the `routes` array.
- You can dynamically build specs by looping through the array of routes.

If you need an additional challenge, you can update your Pizza API to follow the Hexagonal Architecture guidelines, and then you can test the rest of your Pizza API service. This additional challenge isn't discussed in the next section, but you can take a look at the source code to see our solution.

11.9.2 *Solution*

To test the API routes, create a file called api.spec.js in the specs folder of your Pizza API project. Note that this file should not be in the handlers subfolder, because you're not testing handlers.

In this file, require the main api.js file and use Jasmine's `describe` function to add a description, which can be simple—for example, "API" or "API routes."

Then define the array of objects that contain paths and methods for those paths. Define paths without the leading slash (/), because Claudia API Builder stores them that way.

The next step is to loop through the array of routes and invoke Jasmine's `it` function for each. You can test whether the current route exists in the `underTest.apiConfig()` `.routes` array and if its methods are the same methods you defined in the `routes` array.

For the full api.spec.js file, see the next listing.

Listing 11.16   Testing API routes

```
'use strict'

const underTest = require('../api')      ◄─── Require the handler.

describe('API', () => {
  [        ◄──────────────────── Define an array of existing routes.
    {
      path: '',
      methods: ['GET']
    }, {
      path: 'pizzas',
      methods: ['GET']
    }, {
      path: 'orders',
      methods: ['POST']
    }, {
      path: 'orders/{id}',
      methods: ['PUT', 'DELETE']
    }, {
      path: 'delivery',
      methods: ['POST']
    }, {
      path: 'upload-url',
      methods: ['GET']
    }
  ].forEach(route => {
    it(`should setup /${route.path} route`, () => {
      expect(Object.keys(underTest.apiConfig().routes[route.path])).
      toEqual(route.methods)
    })
  })
})
```

Invoke the it function for each route from the array.

Test whether the route is defined with the expected methods.

If you run the `npm test` command again, the tests should all pass. If you want to run only tests for the API routes, you can run the `npm t filter="should setup"` command.

Summary

- As it is for any other serious application, automated testing is an important part of every serverless application.
- Serverless architecture affects traditionally slow and expensive tests, such as integration and GUI tests, by increasing the execution speed through parallel execution and decreasing the price of the testing infrastructure.
- Unit testing of Node.js serverless applications is almost the same as unit testing of nonserverless applications.
- Integration tests in serverless architectures should connect to real AWS services, because the price of the infrastructure is low.
- You should still mock some third-party services that you don't own, such as payment processors or, in the case of the Pizza API, the Some Like It Hot Delivery API.
- Serverless architecture is changing the way we test software, because the infrastructure cost and the risk shift to the integration between the serverless components.
- Designing serverless functions with testing in mind is important, and Hexagonal Architecture can help with that.

Paying for pizza

12

This chapter covers

- Processing payments with serverless applications
- Implementing payments to your serverless API
- Understanding the PCI compliance in payment processing

Enter your card number and your card's expiration date. Now, enter your card's security code. Everyone knows this sequence. Receiving payments for products or services is the most valuable step for almost every business. So far, you've been learning mostly how to develop serverless applications that provide useful services, such as pizza ordering and delivery. But you should also know how to receive payments from Aunt Maria's customers.

This chapter starts by analyzing how to enable online payments for Aunt Maria's pizzeria. You'll see how a payment travels from your customer, to your payment processor, and then to Aunt Maria's company. Then, you'll learn how to implement a payment service for Aunt Maria. Afterward, you'll examine the safety of your serverless payment service and discover how standards compliance helps with that.

12.1   Payment transactions

According to Aunt Maria, "Everything should revolve around customer needs." Her business has begun to expand, and she has received more than a hundred requests from customers to enable online payments in both the mobile and web applications. Therefore, she has asked you to help her implement accepting payments with the serverless Pizza API.

> **NOTE**   For some of you, enabling payments might sound scary because you've never done it before, whereas others may fear even a slight error causing havoc. This chapter's goal is to alleviate those fears and get you more comfortable with enabling payments, by teaching how payment processing works, how to interact with a payment processor, and how to create your serverless payment function.

Before implementing a payment service in your application, let's briefly touch on how payment transactions work internally.

A payment is a financial transaction between a customer and a seller. The customer pays money to the seller for needed products or services. If the customer doesn't have any money, the transaction isn't possible. If the customer has the needed amount, the cash is transferred to the seller, after which the purchased product or service is transferred to the customer. The transaction flow is shown in figure 12.1.

For credit and debit cards, the process is slightly different, because you're not dealing with raw funds (cash). A customer connects a payment card to the seller's card-reading device. The device checks if it's a valid credit card, reads the card number, displays the charge amount, and asks the customer for the card's confidential pin number to certify that the intended transaction is authorized. Then the device sends a request to the customer's bank to transfer the funds from the customer's account to the seller's. If there are sufficient available funds, the bank reserves the amount from the customer's account. This "reserving" process is also known as "charging" the customer. The bank creates a charge instead of immediately taking the money out of the account because there needs to be a delay in case a problem or an error occurs on either side. The flow for a credit or debit card transaction is shown in figure 12.2.

Online payments are different from in-person credit card payments processed with a card reader. First, because you can't use a physical card reader, you need a payment processor that can perform online payment processing. Second, again because you don't have a card reader, you need to verify the card with the payment processor directly. The verification process is necessary because you need to ensure that the card is valid and that it belongs to a valid authority (a bank, for example). Therefore, you need to send sensitive customer data to the payment processor for verification. If it's valid, you then

Figure 12.1   A diagram illustrating a cash transaction between a customer and a seller

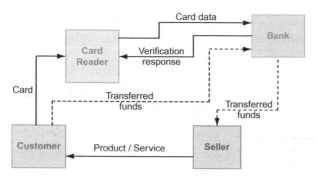
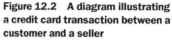

Figure 12.2   A diagram illustrating a credit card transaction between a customer and a seller

make a payment request. The third difference is that you can now optionally listen to possible payment status changes, as some charges may be checked by the customer's bank and rejected a few minutes later (figure 12.3), but for the sake of this chapter's length, this isn't covered.

The online payment process looks complicated, but from your side, it's quite simple. You have three responsibilities:

1 Securely send the payment information to the payment processor.
2 Create a charge on the card upon verification.
3 After a charge has been created, update the payment-related information.

Seems simple enough. Now that you've had a brief overview of the process, let's see how to implement it for Aunt Maria.

12.1.1   *Implementing an online payment*

As Aunt Maria has explained, when an order is placed, the customer can currently pay only when the pizza is delivered. Most customers are happy to do it that way, but she'd like to enable customer payment in advance with a card. To enable this capability, her web application needs a page with a payment form, where the customer types in the necessary information. After filling in the form, the customer taps Pay and a charge is made to the customer's credit card via a payment processor.

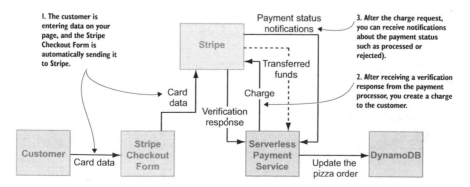

Figure 12.3   A diagram illustrating an online credit card transaction between a customer and a seller

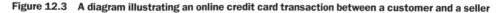

Try to visualize the steps of the payment transaction, corresponding to the transaction diagrams. The following actions need to happen:

1 Show the customer the form with the amount due.
2 After the customer taps Pay, invoke the function to charge the customer's card via the payment processor's API.
3 After a charge is created, update the order in the database.

> **NOTE** Keep in mind that you're building a minimum viable product, so the payment logic is simplified. In a real-world application, the payment would need to take into account a lot of other specifics, possibly even storing the payment history.

The flow is illustrated in figure 12.4.

Before you start implementing your payment service, you need to choose your payment processor. There are many online payment processors to choose from; in some cases, your bank can do it for you. But the ones that are most renowned and most used are *Stripe* and *Braintree*. We could have used either of these, but we chose Stripe: it's quick and easy to set up and provides multiple-platform support.

> **NOTE** For those of you who wanted to see Braintree, we assure you that the implementation differences are minimal, found in just the payment gateway libraries used and parameter names. If you're interested in that platform, you can choose Braintree instead and follow the same process.

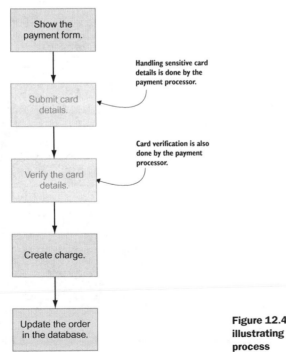

Figure 12.4   A detailed flow diagram illustrating your payment service process

Now that you've chosen your payment gateway, you need to set up your Stripe account and get your Stripe API keys (as described in appendix C, in the section "Setting up your Stripe account and retrieving Stripe API keys"). If you have a Stripe account already, please continue; if not, create one now.

Now that you've got your Stripe account set up, log in to Stripe and open the Stripe Test Dashboard in your browser (or type https://dashboard.stripe.com/test/dashboard in your browser's address bar). Click the "Accept your first payment" link, which opens a Stripe documentation page explaining how to set up card payments.

As the Stripe card payments setup page explains, there are two crucial steps:

1   Securely collect payment information using tokenization.
2   Use the payment information in a charge request.

NOTE   The wording of these steps may vary, but the concept remains the same: securely collect payment information and use the collected information to charge the customer.

These steps actually change the previously described payment service process flow. Instead of you requesting the customer's payment details and sending them to Stripe, you'll show only the Stripe payment form, which will send the sensitive payment information directly to Stripe. After the payment information is verified and stored, Stripe will send you a secure token—a hexadecimal string that represents this information. This secure token has a limited lifespan of a few minutes and can be used only once. You won't store the one-time token, but use it to charge the card. The updated flow is shown in figure 12.5.

As you can see from the flow, your responsibility has been reduced to a minimum. Your next step is to plan out what you need to implement. Let's take a look at this step-by-step.

1   *Show the payment form and send information to Stripe*—This means you're going to need to display an HTML page, so you'll need an HTML document or file.

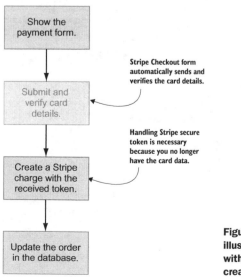

Figure 12.5   **The updated flow diagram illustrating the Stripe payment process with the use of its secure token to create a card charge**

Usually this is done on the front end of a web application, but you'll implement a basic page so you can test your service and see it in action. Stripe offers a couple of ways to create your own payment form:

- Mobile SDK
- Checkout
- Stripe.js and Elements

Because you want the form displayed in the browser, the Mobile SDK option doesn't suit you. Checkout is an already prepared, embedded HTML form, simple and quick to use, whereas using Stripe.js and Elements enables you to create your own style of form. Because you're using the form just to test, the best choice is the Checkout option.

2 *Receive the secure token from Stripe*—The Stripe payment form, in your case Checkout, requires a web service endpoint. This means that in addition to the payment form, you'll also need to implement a serverless payment API endpoint to receive the secure Stripe data. You'll create a serverless payment function that will receive the token.

3 *Create a charge using the secure token*—Upon receiving the token, your serverless payment service will invoke the Stripe API to charge the customer's card with the specified amount, currency, and token.

4 *Update the pizza order information based on the payment*—If the charge is successfully created, you'll need to find the customer's order in the DynamoDB table and update its status to paid (figure 12.6).

This all seems easy enough, so let's get started.

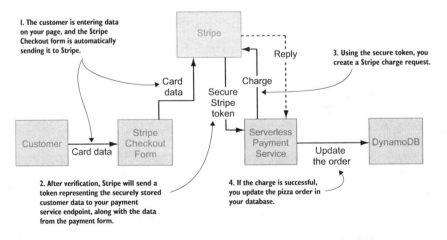

Figure 12.6   The flow diagram illustrating the Stripe payment process with the use of its secure token to create a card charge

12.2   *Implementing your payment service*

Your payment process consists of a payment service and an HTML document, so the first step is to choose which one to start with. We recommend that you start with the payment service, because you'll need to specify the URL of your deployed payment service on the Stripe Checkout form in the HTML document.

To start, create a new top-level project folder named pizzeria-payments and navigate to it in your terminal.

> **NOTE**   You may be wondering why you're creating a new, separate project. With serverless and AWS Lambda functions, we recommend that you write your services as independent functions or components. Having a loose coupling between your services provides the following benefits:
>
> - *Increased service stability*—If one of your services fails, the others will stay alive, unlike in a monolithic application, where one service crashing brings the whole application down.
> - *Increased maintainability*—Smaller services have a smaller scope, providing clarity and ease of maintenance.
> - *Reusability*—Each function can later be slightly modified or even completely reused by some other project your company might be working on.

While in the folder, create your NPM package.json file by running the command `npm init -y`. Then install the required Claudia API Builder and AWS SDK libraries by running the `npm install -S claudia-api-builder aws-sdk` command. Because you're using Stripe as a payment processor, you'll also need to run `npm install -S stripe` to install Stripe's open source Node.js SDK—a library to simplify making requests to Stripe.

Your payment service will receive a request with the Stripe secure token along with the other information required to charge the customer, such as the currency, amount, and the pizza order ID. It will then make a charge request to Stripe using the Stripe Node.js SDK and the received payment information. If the charge is successful, Stripe returns the charge made, so your service should then make another request to the DynamoDB table `pizza-orders` to update the pizza order corresponding to the provided order ID. After that, your service should return a success message.

Before we show you the implementation, take a few minutes to think about how you would write a testable serverless payment service using Hexagonal Architecture from the start. Which boundary objects will you need?

This exercise should bring you to the conclusion that you need three boundary objects:

- `PaymentRequest`—A boundary object with values coming from the Stripe charge request
- `PaymentRepository`—A boundary object with a `createCharge` method to create a charge in the DynamoDB `pizza-orders` database table
- `PizzaOrderRepository`—A boundary object with an `updateOrderStatus` method to update the DynamoDB `pizza-orders` database table

You're going to have the following four files in your service:

- The main service file, payment.js, which is the starting file, with an exposed POST endpoint built with Claudia API Builder
- A create-charge.js file, which is responsible for the business logic of creating a payment charge
- A payment-repository.js file, which is responsible for communicating with Stripe and has only one method, createCharge
- An order-repository.js file, which is responsible for communicating with AWS DynamoDB to update the pizza order with the new processed payment information

First, you'll create your payment.js file. In this file, you'll first define a charge request to Stripe containing the Stripe token, charge amount, and currency, and the order ID inside a metadata attribute. The reason for this request is because Stripe doesn't allow additional parameters to be sent through its calls. It allows only a metadata property to pass a string. Stripe does not look into that property. Then you need to invoke the createCharge function imported from the create-charge.js file. If it's successful, send a success message. If not, send a message containing the error report. The contents of the payment.js file are shown in the following listing.

Listing 12.1   The payment.js file with a POST endpoint to accept incoming Stripe requests

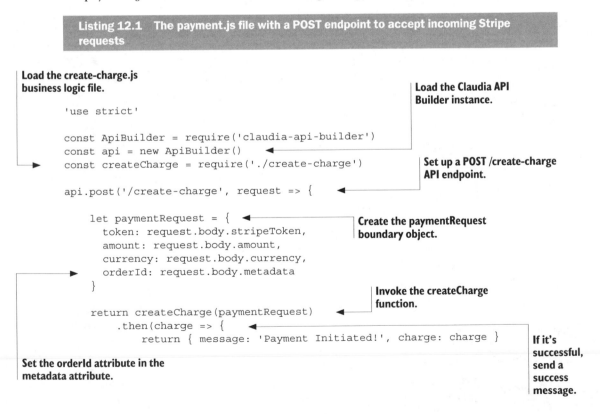

Load the create-charge.js business logic file.

Load the Claudia API Builder instance.

```
'use strict'

const ApiBuilder = require('claudia-api-builder')
const api = new ApiBuilder()          ◀── Load the Claudia API Builder instance.
const createCharge = require('./create-charge')

api.post('/create-charge', request => {          ◀── Set up a POST /create-charge API endpoint.

    let paymentRequest = {          ◀── Create the paymentRequest boundary object.
      token: request.body.stripeToken,
      amount: request.body.amount,
      currency: request.body.currency,
      orderId: request.body.metadata
    }
    return createCharge(paymentRequest)          ◀── Invoke the createCharge function.
        .then(charge => {
            return { message: 'Payment Initiated!', charge: charge }
```

Set up a POST /create-charge API endpoint.

Invoke the createCharge function.

If it's successful, send a success message.

Set the orderId attribute in the metadata attribute.

In the case of an error, send back a message with the error.

```
    }).catch(err => {
        return { message: 'Payment Initialization Error', error: err }
    })
})

module.exports = api
```

Export your payment service API.

Next, create the create-charge.js file inside the project root. It should first load the payment-repository.js file (for dealing with Stripe API protocols) and the order-repository .js file (for dealing with AWS DynamoDB pizza order protocols), then expose the function to accept a payment request. You should provide a payment description explaining the charge to the customer, then invoke the `paymentRepository.createCharge` function with the provided `token`, `amount`, and `currency` values to create a payment charge. When this is done, invoke the `orderRepository.updateOrderStatus` method with the provided `orderId` representing the ID of the order for which the payment was made. The contents of the create-charge.js file are shown in the following listing.

> **Listing 12.2 The create-charge.js file that contains the business logic**

Load the paymentRepository boundary object.

Load the orderRepository boundary object.

```
'use strict'
const paymentRepository = require('./repositories/payment-repository.js')
const orderRepository = require('./repositories/order-repository.js')

module.exports = function (paymentRequest) {
  let paymentDescription = 'Pizza order payment'
  return paymentRepository.createCharge(paymentRequest.token, paymentRequest.
    amount,
  paymentRequest.currency, paymentDescription)
    .then(() => orderRepository.updateOrderStatus(paymentRequest.orderId))
}
```

Provide a description for the charge.

Invoke the createCharge method.

Invoke the updateOrderStatus method.

Now let's continue with the implementation of the `createCharge` method in the payment-repository.js file. First, though, you need to organize the project properly, so create a repositories folder in your project root and navigate to it. Then create the payment-repository.js file, which defines an object containing a single method to create a Stripe charge by invoking the `stripe.charges.create` method. The parameters passed to the `stripe.charges.create` method are the `stripeToken` (the token corresponding to the customer transaction), the amount to charge the customer, the desired currency (the `amount` is in cents if the provided `currency` value is usd or eur), and a `description` of the transaction. The contents of the file are shown in the following listing.

Listing 12.3   The payment-repository.js file defining the `createCharge` method

Instantiate the Stripe SDK with your STRIPE_SECRET_KEY.

```
'use strict'
const stripe = require('stripe')(process.env.STRIPE_SECRET_KEY)

module.exports = {
  createCharge: function (stripeToken, amount, currency, description){
      return stripe.charges.create({          Invoke the stripe.
          source: stripeToken,                charges.create
          amount: amount,                     function to create a
          currency: currency,                 charge.
          description: description
      })
  }
}
```

The implementation of the Stripe protocol in the payment-repository.js file could easily be replaced with the implementation for Braintree or some other payment processor, but that's left as an exercise for the reader.

Now let's unwrap the last piece: the order-repository.js file, which is responsible for updating the status of the order in the `pizza-orders` DynamoDB table to `paid`.

Listing 12.4   The order-repository.js file that updates the order status in the DynamoDB database table

```
'use strict'
const AWS = require('aws-sdk')                    Load the DynamoDB
const docClient = new AWS.DynamoDB.DocumentClient()   DocumentClient.

module.exports = {
  updateOrderStatus: function (orderId) {         Define the updateOrderStatus
    return docClient.put({                        function with orderId as a parameter.
        TableName: 'pizza-orders',
        Key: {
          orderId: orderId
        },                                         Update the orderStatus of
        UpdateExpression: 'set orderStatus = :s',  the specified orderId key.
        ExpressionAttributeValues: {
            ':s': 'paid'                  Set the attribute
        }                                 value to paid.
        }).promise()
    }
}
```

By applying the principles of Hexagonal Architecture, not only did you make this payment service more testable, but you can now easily replace DynamoDB and try out Amazon Aurora or even the Amazon Relational Database Service (Amazon RDS).

The last step in implementing your payment service is to use Claudia to deploy your new API. In your terminal, while in the project root folder, run the following command to return the URL of your newly created API:

```
claudia create --region us-east-1 --api-module payment --set-env STRIPE_
    SECRET_KEY=<your-stripe-secret-key>
```

Copy and save the URL in a temporary document to use for the HTML form you're going to make. The only thing that remains is to create your HTML document.

Because you want this serverless payment service to be reusable and have a single purpose, you can't put the HTML document inside it. So, create a separate project folder named payment-form, and inside it create an HTML document named payment-form. html. In the HTML `body` element, you'll create a `form` element with the `action` attribute pointing to the URL of your newly created serverless payment service. Inside it, create a `script` element to load the Stripe Checkout form. This `script` element needs

- A `data-key` attribute (starting with `pk_test_`)
- A `data-amount` attribute, representing the amount you want to charge (in cents, for the USD or EUR currencies)
- A `data-name` attribute, showing the name of your Stripe payment window
- A `data-description` attribute, describing your Stripe payment transaction
- A `data-image` attribute, if you want to include a URL for a logo or image to display in the loaded form
- A `data-locale` attribute specifying the locale (you can set this to `auto` to display the form in the user's preferred language, if available)
- A `data-zip-code` attribute indicating whether to collect the customer's zip code (a Boolean value)
- A `data-currency` attribute, representing the currency short code for the transaction

The contents of the payment-form.html file are shown in the following listing.

Listing 12.5 The payment-form.html file representing the payment page

Create a new form element.

Create the script element to load the Stripe Checkout form.

The charge amount

Your Stripe public key

Your Stripe payment window name

The Stripe payment transaction description

```html
<html>
<head>
</head>
<body>
<form action="<paste-your-function-url-here>" method="POST">
  <script
    src="https://checkout.stripe.com/checkout.js" class="stripe-button"
    data-key="<your-stripe-public-key>"
    data-amount="100"
    data-name="Demo Site"
    data-description="2 widgets"
```

```
      data-image="https://stripe.com/img/documentation/checkout/marketplace.
       png"
      data-locale="auto"
      data-zip-code="true"
      data-currency="usd">
   </script>
</form>
</body>
</html>
```

The locale → `data-locale="auto"`

The zip code check → `data-zip-code="true"`

The URL for a logo or image to display in the loaded form. → `data-image=...png"`

The currency short code → `data-currency="usd">`

After you've created the payment-form.html file, open it in your browser. You'll see the Pay button from Stripe in the loaded window. Click it, and the Stripe payment form will appear with the $1 price defined in the example (`data-amount="100"`). The payment form that loads should look something like figure 12.7.

NOTE If you don't see the Pay button, make sure you followed all the steps outlined in this chapter. If you haven't obtained the Stripe API keys yet, please refer to "Setting up your Stripe account and retrieving Stripe API keys" in appendix C for instructions or, if you already have an account, log into the Stripe Dashboard and go to the API keys page at https://dashboard.stripe .com/account/apikeys.

To test your payment service in addition to the payment form, use the following data:

- A test card number of 4242 4242 4242 4242 (take a look at https://stripe.com/ docs/testing#cards, too)
- Any future month and year for the expiration date
- Any three-digit number for the card verification code

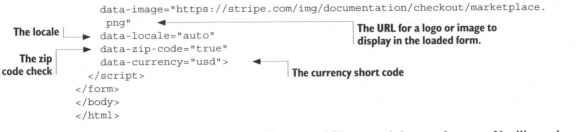

Figure 12.7   The payment form

- Any random zip code
- Any email address

Then tap "Pay $1".

That's it. After a moment or two, your payment should process. Take a look at your `pizza-orders` DynamoDB table, and you should see that the pizza order status was updated to `paid`. Also, be sure to look at your Stripe Dashboard (https://dashboard .stripe.com/test/dashboard) to see the payment. You can look at your CloudWatch logs, too, to see what went right or, in the case of errors, what went wrong.

As you can see, developing and maintaining a serverless payment service is quite easy with Claudia.js and Claudia API Builder. But what about security?

12.3 *Could someone hack your payment service?*

Having no control over your infrastructure or your environment may be troubling. How do you know there isn't a malicious service running in the background, stealing your customers' credit card details? And what about the risk of a big data breach or fraud that could ruin your business?

You can't know what's going on in the background with your serverless provider. These fears are plausible, because breaches or hacks can occur and wreak havoc in your organization. But two factors are often overlooked that can play a big part in security:

- Standards
- Competence

12.3.1 *Standards*

Having a safe and secure payment processing service is essential, not just for you but for your customers as well. Therefore, security is one of the top priorities in almost every company—at least on paper. Security is evolving constantly, with new issues discovered every day. Naturally, over time, most of the common best practices have converged into a standard, and a body for standards has appeared as well.

The standards body is the Payment Card Industry Security Standards Council, or *PCI SSC*, a security body responsible for defining and enforcing secure and safe payments and customer data handling practices. The main standard enforced for payment security is the Payment Card Industry Data Security Standard, or *PCI DSS*.

Services that adhere to the standard are termed *PCI DSS-compliant.*

WHAT IS PCI DSS COMPLIANCE?

PCI DSS sets the requirements for organizations and sellers to safely and securely accept, store, process, and transmit cardholder data during credit card transactions to prevent fraud and data breaches. Being PCI DSS-compliant means that you're securely handling cardholder data during a transaction.

You need to meet many requirements to be PCI DSS-compliant, such as setting up firewall configurations, encrypting transaction data, restricting physical access to data, implementing internal company security policies, and so on. To read more about it, download the standard directly from https://www.pcisecuritystandards.org/documents/ PCI_DSS_v3-1.pdf.

Currently, almost all the most-used serverless providers are PCI DSS-compliant, including

- AWS Lambda
- Microsoft Azure Functions
- Google Cloud Functions
- IBM OpenWhisk

To read more about PCI DSS compliance, see the main portal at https://www .pcisecuritystandards.org.

> **NOTE** Even though AWS Lambda is PCI-DSS compliant it doesn't mean that your service is automatically PCI DSS-compliant, too. Your serverless provider being compliant means that you don't have to think about the infrastructure layer for PCI compliance. But you still need to think about your codebase and company way of processing and handling payment-sensitive information.

12.3.2 Competence

Security breaches and frauds are almost always possible. Many companies and engineers question the security competence of their infrastructure providers, or in this case their serverless providers. Some even try to develop security themselves, despite the strictness required to achieve PCI compliance.

Even if this effort might be valid in some cases, if you're tempted to do this, give some thought to whether you or your company are likely to be more competent at securing your data or implementing security than the most-used serverless providers, such as Amazon AWS, Microsoft Azure, Google Cloud, or others.

The security responsibilities involved in payment processing are massive, and getting it wrong can cause a significant blow to you or your customers. Therefore, having a competent and PCI-compliant serverless provider should be one the top priorities when developing your serverless applications.

12.4 Taste it!

As you can see, implementing a serverless payment service is easy and doesn't take much time. But it's again time for you to try out what you've learned!

12.4.1 Exercise

Your exercise for this chapter is to create a new serverless function that will return a list of the charges you've previously created. You must do this by applying Hexagonal Architecture. Before you start, here's some information about Stripe's API:

- To retrieve all previously created charges, you'll need to use the Stripe `list-Charges` method; you can learn more about it at https://stripe.com/docs/ api#list_charges.

- You need to set it up with your STRIPE_SECRET_KEY and deploy the serverless function using Claudia's --set-env config option.
- The charge-listing service should return an empty list if there are no charges.

If that's enough information, go ahead and try it on your own. If you need additional tips, here are a few more:

- You need to create an API endpoint called GET /charges using Claudia API Builder.
- You need to create a ChargeRepository.

If you need more help, or you want to see the solution, check out the next section.

12.4.2 Solution

It's time to look at the solution. First, here's an overview of the whole flow.

When a request arrives at your GET /charges API endpoint, you should parse it and call the getAllCharges method of ChargesRepository. The getAllCharges method should call stripe.charges.create with no passed parameters. Afterward, it should parse the Stripe response object and return the list from the data attribute. This list should be sent as an array to the client.

First, create a project folder named charges. Inside that folder, run the command npm init -y and then the command npm install -S claudia-api-builder stripe. Then create the following two files:

- payment.js, in the project root
- payment-repository.js, in the repositories folder inside your project

The following two listings are the complete charge-listing code. First is the payment.js file, with a POST /charges endpoint to accept the incoming Stripe requests. The endpoint handler needs to call the paymentRepository.getAllCharges method to get all charges. If it's successful, it needs to return them, without any additional logic. If not, send a message back to the client, with the error property containing the error.

Listing 12.6 The payment.js file

Load your payment-repository.js file.

```
'use strict'

const ApiBuilder = require('claudia-api-builder')
const api = new ApiBuilder()
const paymentRepository = require('./repositories/payment-repository')

api.get('/charges', request => {

    return paymentRepository.getAllCharges()
        .catch(err => {
```

Load the Claudia API Builder instance.

Set up a GET /charges API endpoint.

If unsuccessful, send the error.

Invoke the paymentRepository. getAllCharges method.

```
                    return { message: 'Charges Listing Error', error: err }
            })
    })
})                                    ┌─ Export your charge-listing
module.exports = api  ◄───────────────┘  service API.
```

The following listing shows the content of the payment-repository.js file, responsible for retrieving all the Stripe charges you've made. It exposes a `getAllCharges` method, which invokes the `stripe.charges.list` method without any parameters, because you need to display all charges.

Listing 12.7   The payment-repository.js file

**Instantiate the Stripe SDK with
the STRIPE_SECRET_KEY.**

```
'use strict'
const stripe = require('stripe')(process.env.STRIPE_SECRET_KEY)

module.exports = {                          ┌─ Invoke the stripe.charges.list
  getAllCharges: function (){               │  method.
      return stripe.charges.list()  ◄───────┘
        .then(response => response.data)  ◄─┐ Return the response.data
  }                                         └ containing the list of charges.
}
```

Summary

- Knowing how to implement payments is essential for every application, regardless of whether it's serverless or not.
- Implementing payment processing as an independent serverless service is important, because you want it to be stable and independent from the other services within your application.
- Integrating Stripe with your payment service on AWS Lambda is easy.
- A nicely designed and independent payment service can later be reused by your other products or services.
- Having no control over your infrastructure is not an excuse for having less security.
- A good indicator of whether your payment service is safe is whether your serverless provider is PCI DSS-compliant.
- PCI compliance is necessary when using a serverless provider, because it provides the level of safety and security you need.

Migrating your existing Express.js app to AWS Lambda

This chapter covers

- Running Express.js applications in AWS Lambda and the serverless ecosystem

- Serving static content from an Express.js application

- Connecting to MongoDB from a serverless Express.js application

- Understanding the limitations and risks of Express.js apps in a serverless ecosystem

Express.js is the most important and most used Node.js framework. That's not without reason: Express.js is easy to use and has a large ecosystem of middleware that can help you build an API or server-rendered web application. But using Express.js still requires a server that will host the application, which means we're back to the problems this book tries to solve by using serverless technologies. Is there a way to keep your existing Express.js application and still have all the benefits of serverless?

The Express.js web application framework is basically an HTTP server. Serverless applications do not need HTTP servers, because HTTP requests are handled by API Gateway. But fortunately, there is a way to use an existing Express.js application in AWS Lambda with minor modifications. This chapter teaches you how to do that, and it also presents some of the most important limitations of serverless Express.js applications.

235

13.1   Uncle Roberto's taxi application

During your big family reunion, Aunt Maria brags about her new online business. It's better than ever, but she says best of all is that the new app just works—whether it needs to handle a single order or a few dozen at the same time, everything works.

Her brother, your Uncle Roberto, tells her she's lucky. He has many problems with his taxi company's app. The app itself is nice, but it crashes often when more ride requests than usual are coming in—for example, when it's raining. Unfortunately, his IT team is not very responsive in those situations, and he's losing customers and money.

Roberto asks how you performed your magic for Aunt Maria, and wonders if it would work for his app, too. You explain that it depends on the technology his app is using.

A few days later, you receive a message explaining that the taxi app is using Express.js and MongoDB. It's hosted on some small virtual private server that serves the RESTful API for the mobile app, and it uses server-rendered HTML pages for the admin panel. Overall, it sounds like a typical Express.js application. You agree to do some research and let Uncle Roberto know in a few days if you can do something to help him out.

13.2   Running an Express.js application in AWS Lambda

Before you start your investigation, you need to create a simple Express.js app. You'll use that app to test how Express.js works in AWS Lambda. To do so, create a new project folder and name it simple-express-app. Then initiate a new NPM project in it, and install Express.js as a dependency by running the `npm i express -S` command.

As a first test, you should create one file with one Express.js route, and try to run it in AWS Lambda. Create the file app.js in your simple-express-app folder.

In this file, require the `express` module and create a new Express app with it. Then add a `GET /` route that will return the text "Hello World." Finally, define the port the application will use and start the server using the `server.listen` function.

At this point, your app.js file should look similar to the next listing.

Listing 13.1   Express.js app

```
'use strict'
                         Create the Express.js application.
const express = require('express')
const app = express()

app.get('/', (req, res) => res.send('Hello World'))          Set the port to PORT passed via an
                                                             environment variable, or port 3000.
const port = process.env.PORT || 3000
app.listen(port, () => console.log(`App listening on port ${port}`))
```

Create the GET route that answers   Start the application on the defined port.
with the "Hello World" text.

Then run your simple Express.js app using the following command:

```
node app.js
```

Unless something else is running on port 3000, this command will start your local server. If you visit http://localhost:3000 in your web browser, you should see the "Hello World" text.

The easiest way to run the existing Express.js app in AWS Lambda is by using the `aws-serverless-express` Node.js module. This module requires only minor changes in the Express.js app you created.

To prepare your app for AWS Lambda and API Gateway, open your app.js file and replace the `app.listen` function with a simple export, as shown in the next listing. This export allows the Express.js wrapper in AWS Lambda to require your app.

Listing 13.2 Express.js app modified for AWS Lambda

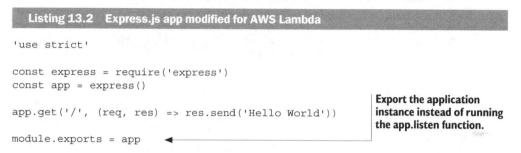

```
'use strict'

const express = require('express')
const app = express()

app.get('/', (req, res) => res.send('Hello World'))

module.exports = app   ◄────
```

> **Export the application instance instead of running the app.listen function.**

But doing this will break your Express.js app on localhost; you'll no longer be able to run a local version using the `node app.js` command.

To fix that issue, create another file in the project folder, and name it app.local.js. This file should require your Express.js app from the app.js file, and then invoke the `app.listen` function to start a local server on the port you provided.

Your app.local.js file should look like the following listing.

Listing 13.3 Running the wrapped Express.js app locally

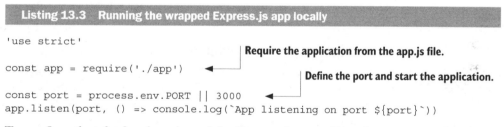

```
'use strict'

const app = require('./app')   ◄────

const port = process.env.PORT || 3000   ◄────
app.listen(port, () => console.log(`App listening on port ${port}`))
```

> **Require the application from the app.js file.**
>
> **Define the port and start the application.**

To confirm that the local version of the Express.js app still works as expected, run the following command:

```
node app.local.js
```

This command should show the "Hello World" text on http://localhost:3000 (unless you specified another port).

Now that the local version works, it's time to generate a wrapper for your Express.js app. The easiest way to generate the wrapper is by using the `claudia generate-server-less-express-proxy` command. This command requires the `--express-module` option with a path to your main file without the .js extension. For example, you should run the following command when your index file is app.js:

```
claudia generate-serverless-express-proxy --express-module app
```

NOTE   You need Claudia version 3.3.1 or higher to follow along with the rest of the code in this chapter.

This command generates a file named lambda.js and installs the `aws-serverless-express` module as a development dependency.

The file created by this command is a wrapper that runs your Express.js app in AWS Lambda. It is using the `awsServerlessExpress.createServer` function to start your Express.js app inside your Lambda function. Then, it uses the `awsServerlessExpress.proxy` function to transform an API Gateway request to an HTTP request and pass it to your Express.js app, and to transform and pass the response back to API Gateway.

The contents of the file are shown in the next listing.

Listing 13.4   AWS Lambda wrapper for Express.js apps

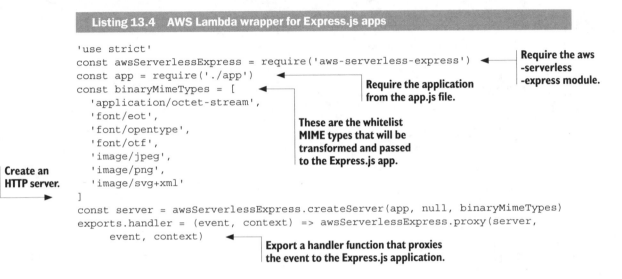

```
'use strict'
const awsServerlessExpress = require('aws-serverless-express')    ◄── Require the aws
const app = require('./app')    ◄── Require the application                -serverless
const binaryMimeTypes = [       from the app.js file.                       -express module.
  'application/octet-stream',
  'font/eot',
  'font/opentype',            These are the whitelist
  'font/otf',                 MIME types that will be
  'image/jpeg',               transformed and passed
  'image/png',                to the Express.js app.
  'image/svg+xml'
]
const server = awsServerlessExpress.createServer(app, null, binaryMimeTypes)
exports.handler = (event, context) => awsServerlessExpress.proxy(server,
    event, context)    ◄── Export a handler function that proxies
                           the event to the Express.js application.
```

Create an HTTP server.

The next step is to deploy your API to AWS Lambda and API Gateway. You can do that with the `claudia create` command, but with an important difference from the APIs used in the previous chapters: you need to invoke it with the `--handler` option instead of `--api-module`, and also with `--deploy-proxy-api`. This will set up a proxy integration, which means that all requests to API Gateway will be passed directly to your Lambda function.

To deploy your Express.js app, run the following command:

```
claudia create --handler lambda.handler --deploy-proxy-api --region eu-
    central-1
```

When the command executes successfully, the response should look similar to the next listing.

Listing 13.5   The deployment result

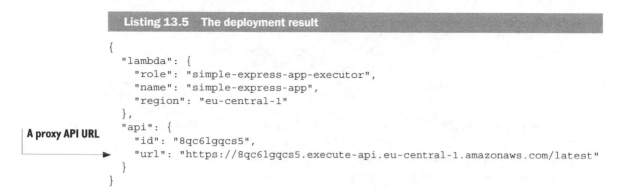

A proxy API URL

```
{
  "lambda": {
    "role": "simple-express-app-executor",
    "name": "simple-express-app",
    "region": "eu-central-1"
  },
  "api": {
    "id": "8qc6lgqcs5",
    "url": "https://8qc6lgqcs5.execute-api.eu-central-1.amazonaws.com/latest"
  }
}
```

As you can see, the response is extended with the `url` parameter. And if you visit the URL (in our case, it's https://8qc6lgqcs5.execute-api.eu-central-1.amazonaws.com/latest), you should see the "Hello World" text.

13.2.1   Proxy integration

As you learned in chapter 2, API Gateway can be used in the following two modes:

- With models and mapped templates for requests and responses
- With proxy pass-through integration

The first mode is useful for typed languages, such as Java and .Net, but because Claudia is focused only on JavaScript, it always uses the second approach. With this approach, API Gateway passes any requests directly to your AWS Lambda function, which is responsible for routing and managing the requests.

When you deploy a proxy API for Express.js app, Claudia does the following things for you:

- Creates a proxy resource with a greedy path variable of {proxy+}
- Sets the ANY method on the proxy resource
- Integrates the resource and method with the Lambda function

To learn more about proxy integration, see https://docs.aws.amazon.com/apigateway/latest/developerguide/api-gateway-set-up-simple-proxy.html.

13.2.2   How serverless-express works

The Express.js app is a small local HTTP server inside your AWS Lambda function, and the `serverless-express` module acts as a proxy between an API Gateway event and that local HTTP server.

When the user sends an HTTP request, API Gateway passes that request to your AWS Lambda function. In your function, `serverless-express` spins up the Express.js server and caches it for repeated invocations, and then transforms the API Gateway event to an HTTP request passed to the local Express.js app.

Then your Express.js app goes through its regular flow—the router routes the request to the selected handler, and all middleware functions are applied. When Express.js sends the response, the `serverless-express` module transforms it to the format that is expected by API Gateway, which then sends the reply back to the user. The request flow is depicted in figure 13.1.

Is running an HTTP server inside AWS Lambda an antipattern?

Serverless applications are still new, so patterns and best practices are still not fully formed. They change with each new feature. Running an HTTP server inside AWS Lambda sounds like an antipattern, and it has multiple downsides, such as increased execution time and function size. But it also has many upsides, such as preserving the existing codebase and avoiding vendor lock-in. Another reason why it can't be called an antipattern is that AWS Lambda with the GoLang runtime uses a similar approach to run the function.

13.3   Serving static content

Another scenario you want to test is serving static content from an Express.js app, because Uncle Roberto's admin panel works that way.

To do so, you need a simple static HTML page to test. Any page that includes at least one image and a simple CSS file will work for this test, because that will allow you to test a few different file types.

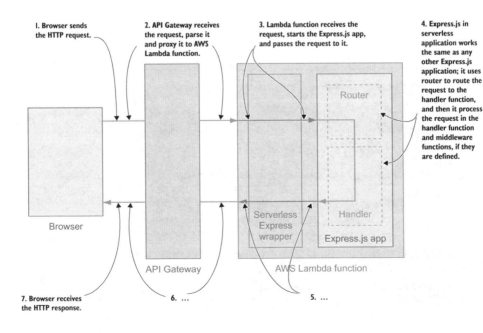

Figure 13.1   The flow of a serverless Express.js application

The first step is to create a new folder named static inside your Express.js project. Then create an index.html file that loads style.css, shows some title text, and shows an image such as the Claudia logo (claudiajs.png). Both the CSS and the logo image will be loaded from the static folder.

Your index.html file should look like the following listing.

Listing 13.6   The index.html file

```
<!doctype html>
<html>
  <head>
    <title>Static site</title>
    <link rel="stylesheet" href="style.css">         Load the CSS file.
  </head>
    <body>
    <h1>Hello from serverless Express.js app</h1>      This is the title text.
    <img src="claudiajs.png" alt="Claudia.js logo" />   Show the claudiajs.png image on the page.
  </body>
</html>
```

Next, add the Claudia logo to the static folder (you can find it in source code you got with this book or on the Claudia website), and create the style.css file in the same folder.

This CSS file doesn't need to do anything specific, but feel free to be creative. As a simple example, you can style the title to be in Claudia's blue color and to have a shadow, and center the logo below it. The next listing shows what your CSS file might look like.

Listing 13.7   The style.css file

```
body {
  margin: 0;
}

h1 {
  color: #71c8e7;
  font-family: sans-serif;
  text-align: center;
  text-shadow: 1px 2px 0px #00a3da;
}

img {
  display: block;
  margin: 40px auto;
  width: 80%;
  max-width: 400px;
}
```

Then, update the app.js file to serve the static content from the static folder. To do that, you should use the express.static middleware, and your code should look like the following listing.

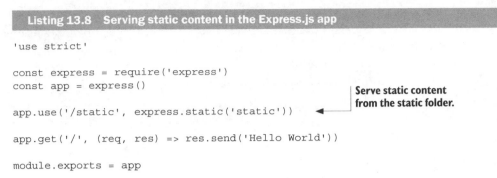

Listing 13.8   Serving static content in the Express.js app

```
'use strict'

const express = require('express')
const app = express()

app.use('/static', express.static('static'))
```
Serve static content
from the static folder.
```
app.get('/', (req, res) => res.send('Hello World'))

module.exports = app
```

Now that everything is ready, you can confirm that the Express.js app is working locally by running the command `node app.local.js` again, and visiting http://localhost:3000/static.

If everything is okay locally, update your app by running the following command:

```
claudia update
```

Wait for the command to finish, and load https://8qc6lgqcs5.execute-api.eu-central-1.amazonaws.com/latest/static/ in your browser. You should see your static HTML page with the Claudia logo, similar to figure 13.2.

NOTE A trailing slash is required for this URL. If you try to load the page without it (if you enter https://8qc6lgqcs5.execute-api.eu-central-1.amazonaws.com/latest/static), the page load will fail.

13.4 *Connecting to MongoDB*

So far, everything seems to work just fine with only minor modifications. But can you connect AWS Lambda to MongoDB?

You can connect AWS Lambda to any database, but if the database is not serverless, you'll run into problems when your function scales up and tries to establish too many database connections, because the database will not scale automatically.

To make sure your database can work with an AWS Lambda function, you have the following options:

- Make sure your database can scale quickly.
- Limit your AWS Lambda concurrency to something your database can handle.
- Use a managed database.

The first option requires DevOps and a good understanding of databases, both of which are beyond the scope of this book.

The second option works, but having more users than your concurrent execution limit would result in an error for each user after the limit is reached. If you want to learn more about managing AWS concurrency, visit https://docs.aws.amazon.com/lambda/latest/dg/concurrent-executions.html.

Figure 13.2   A static HTML page served from Express.js on AWS Lambda.

The last option is the easiest and probably the best one, so let's take a look at it. For MongoDB, which Uncle Roberto's app is using, you can use MongoDB Atlas, offered by MongoDB, Inc. It hosts the database on one of a few supported cloud providers, including AWS. For more information about MongoDB Atlas, see https://www.mongodb.com/cloud/atlas.

13.4.1 *Using a managed MongoDB database with your serverless Express.js app*

Your first step is to create a MongoDB Atlas account and create the database, as described in appendix C.

You need to modify the app.js file to connect to MongoDB. To do so, you'll need to install the `mongodb` and `body-parser` NPM modules as dependencies of your Express.js projects. The first allows you to connect to your MongoDB database, and the second allows your Express.js app to parse `POST` requests.

After you install the modules, you'll create a connection to the database. AWS Lambda functions are not really stateless, because the same container might be reused if your function is invoked again within the next few minutes. This means that everything outside of your handler function will be preserved, and you can reuse the same MongoDB connection.

For example, if you store your database connection outside of your handler function, you can check if the connection is still active with the following function:

```
cachedDb.serverConfig.isConnected()
```

If the connection is still active, you should reuse it. If the database connection is not active, you can create a new one using the `MongoClient.connect` function and cache it before returning the connection. Then you should activate the `body-parser` module using Express.js middleware.

Reusing the existing database connection is important, because each database has a maximum number of concurrent incoming connections. For example, a free MongoDB Atlas instance has a maximum of 100 concurrent connections, which means that having more than 100 Lambda functions connecting at approximately the same time will cause some failed requests. Reusing existing connections can help with this issue, and it can also lower the latency, because each database connection takes some time to be established.

The flow of the MongoDB connection from your Lambda function is shown in figure 13.3.

At this point, the beginning of your app.js file should look like the next listing.

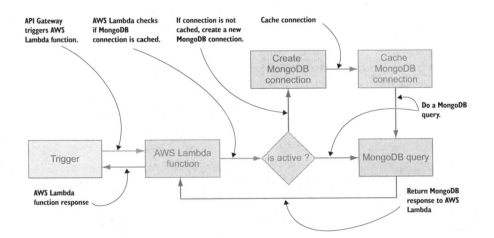

Figure 13.3   The flow of caching and reusing a MongoDB connection

Listing 13.9   Beginning of app.js file

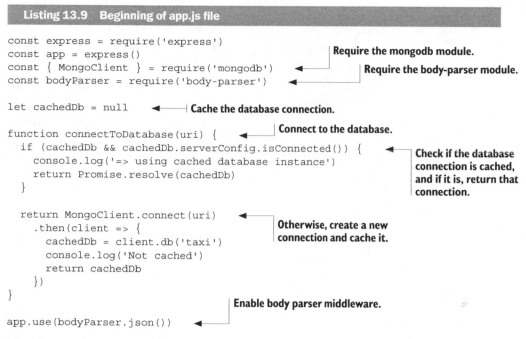

```
const express = require('express')
const app = express()                                    Require the mongodb module.
const { MongoClient } = require('mongodb')    ◄
const bodyParser = require('body-parser')     ◄          Require the body-parser module.

let cachedDb = null    ◄──── Cache the database connection.
                                       Connect to the database.
function connectToDatabase(uri) {   ◄
  if (cachedDb && cachedDb.serverConfig.isConnected()) {   ◄    Check if the database
    console.log('=> using cached database instance')             connection is cached,
    return Promise.resolve(cachedDb)                             and if it is, return that
  }                                                              connection.

  return MongoClient.connect(uri)   ◄
    .then(client => {                     Otherwise, create a new
      cachedDb = client.db('taxi')        connection and cache it.
      console.log('Not cached')
      return cachedDb
    })
}
                                       Enable body parser middleware.
app.use(bodyParser.json())   ◄
```

Now that you've connected your Express.js function to MongoDB, it's time to test your database connection. The easiest way to test the connection is by writing something to a MongoDB collection and then reading the collection to confirm that the item was saved.

To do so, you can add two routes that will be connected to your MongoDB database: one for writing the data, and one for reading the collection. For example:

- A POST /orders route, which will add a new order
- A GET /orders route, which will return all the existing orders

With these two new routes, the flow for creating and immediately reading orders will work like this:

1 A POST /orders request is received by API Gateway and passed to your AWS Lambda function.

2 The Lambda function starts the Express.js app.

3 The Lambda function then transforms the API Gateway request into an HTTP request to your Express.js app.

4 The Express.js app checks if a MongoDB connection already exists, and if not creates a new connection.

5 Your Express.js handler function stores the order in MongoDB and returns the response.

6 The Lambda function transforms the Express.js reply into the format that API Gateway expects.

7 API Gateway returns the response to the user.

8 The user sends a GET /orders request immediately after, and API Gateway passes it to your Lambda function.

9   The Lambda function transforms the request and passes it to an existing instance of the Express.js app.

10 The Express.js app checks if a MongoDB connection exists and, because it does, uses it to get all the orders from the database.

11 The Lambda function receives a response from Express.js, transforms it, and passes it to API Gateway.

12 The user receives the response from API Gateway with a list of the orders.

NOTE   Both the MongoDB connection and the Express.js app are cached. This happens once per cold start of the function.

This flow is illustrated in figure 13.4.

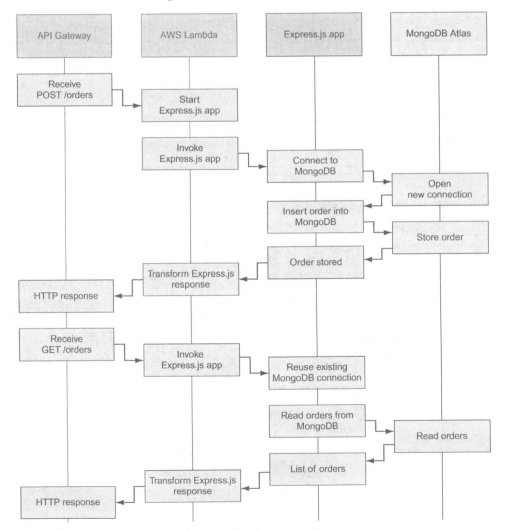

Figure 13.4   The flow for creating and reading orders from MongoDB

To connect new route handlers to the MongoDB database, you can use the `connect-ToDatabase` function you created in the previous step. Pass it the MongoDB connection string, which can be stored in an environment variable.

After the connection is established, in your `GET /orders` route you should use the `db.collection('orders').find().toArray()` function to get all the items from the `orders` collection and convert them to a plain JavaScript array. This command returns a promise, and when the promise is resolved, you can use the `res.send` function from Express.js to send a result or an error.

The only difference for the `POST /orders` route is that you should insert a new item into the database instead of getting an item from the database. To do that, use the `db.collection('orders').insertOne` function. An order can be a JSON object that contains an address only.

The routes to add to your app.js file are shown in the following listing.

Listing 13.10   Routes for getting and adding new taxi rides

```
app.get('/orders', (req, res) => {
  connectToDatabase(process.env.MONGODB_CONNECTION_STRING)     ◀── Get the database
    .then((db) => {                                                  connection.
      return db.collection('orders').find().toArray()    ◀── Find all orders and convert them to an array.
    })
    .then(result => {
      return res.send(result)
    })
    .catch(err => res.send(err).status(400))    ◀── If something failed, return
})                                                   an error with status 400.

app.post('/orders', (req, res) => {     ◀── Add a POST route.
  connectToDatabase(process.env.MONGODB_CONNECTION_STRING)
    .then((db) => {
      return db.collection('orders').insertOne({    ◀── Insert an order into
        address: req.body.address                        the database.
      })
    })
    .then(result => res.send(result).status(201))    ◀── If something failed, return
    .catch(err => res.send(err).status(400))              an error with status 400.
})
```

Add a GET route.

If successful, return the result.

Now that the MongoDB connection is ready, you can test it locally by running `node app.local.js`—but don't forget to pass the `MONGODB_CONNECTION_STRING` environment variable. For example:

```
MONGODB_CONNECTION_STRING=mongodb://localhost:27017 node app.local.js
```

If everything works fine locally, run the `claudia update` command with the `--set-env` or `--set-env-from-json` option, and pass the `MONGODB_CONNECTION_STRING`. For example, your command might look like this:

```
claudia update --set-env MONGODB_CONNECTION_STRING=mongodb://<user>:
<password>@robertostaxicompany-shard-00-00-rs1m4.mongodb.net:27017,
robertostaxicompany-shard-00-01-rs1m4.mongodb.net:27017,robertostaxicompany
-shard-00-02-rs1m4.mongodb.net:27017/taxi?ssl=true&replicaSet=
RobertosTaxiCompany-shard-0&authSource=admin
```

NOTE In the source code that accompanies this book, we used the other method to demonstrate the options you have: The MongoDB connection string is in the env.json file, and then we used `claudia update --set-env-from-json env.json` to pass it to the AWS Lambda function.

You have only one environment variable, so both options will work fine. But we recommend having a JSON file with the variables if you need more than one variable in your application, because that reduces the command length and decreases the chance of human error (for example, mistyping a variable name or value).

After your app is deployed, you can try sending a POST request to https://8qc6lgqcs5 .execute-api.eu-central-1.amazonaws.com/latest/orders to add a new order. You can also visit the same address in your browser to list all the orders: https://8qc6lgqcs5 .execute-api.eu-central-1.amazonaws.com/latest/orders.

13.5   *Limitations of serverless Express.js applications*

Now that you've tested all the most important cases, you can let Uncle Roberto know that his Express.js application will work in AWS Lambda. He'll be happy for sure, and you might end up with a lot of free taxi rides.

But before you do that, it's important to be aware that there are some limitations for serverless Express.js apps. Let's address the most important ones.

First, and probably most obvious, is that you can't use WebSockets in serverless Express.js apps. If Uncle Roberto is using WebSockets for real-time communication between his mobile app and the back end, serverless Express.js will not work as expected. Some limited support for WebSockets in AWS Lambda can be achieved through AWS IoT MQTT over the WebSockets protocol. To read more about the MQTT protocol, see https://docs.aws.amazon.com/iot/latest/developerguide/protocols.html#mqtt. For an example project using Claudia, visit https://github.com/claudiajs/serverless-chat.

Another limitation is related to the file upload functionality. First, if your application is trying to upload files to any folder except /tmp, the upload will fail, because the rest of the AWS Lambda disk space is read-only. Even if you're saving uploaded files to the /tmp folder, they will exist for a short time. To make sure your upload feature is working, upload files to AWS S3.

The next limitation is authentication. You can implement authentication in serverless Express.js apps as you do in any other Express.js app, for example using the Passport.js library, but you need to make sure that the session is not saved on the local filesystem. Or, if you use native Node.js libraries, you'll need to have them packaged into the static binary using an EC2 machine running Amazon Linux. To learn more about native libraries, also known as Addons, see https://nodejs.org/api/addons.html.

Also, API Gateway has stricter rules than traditionally hosted Express.js apps. For example, in Node.js and Express.js, you can send a body with a GET request; API Gateway will not allow you to do that.

Additionally, there are certain execution limits—for example, API Gateway has a timeout of 30 seconds, and AWS Lambda's maximum execution time is 5 minutes. If your Express.js app needs more than 30 seconds to reply, the request will fail. Also, if your Express.js app needs to answer the HTTP request and continue the execution, that will not work in AWS Lambda because AWS Lambda execution will stop as soon as the HTTP response is sent. This behavior depends on a `callbackWaitsForEmptyEventLoop` property of Lambda context; the default value for this property is `true`, and it means that the callback will wait until the event loop is empty before freezing the process and returning the results to the caller. You can set this property to `false` to request AWS Lambda to freeze the process soon after the callback is called, even if there are events in the event loop.

As long as you have these limitations in mind, your Uncle Roberto's taxi app will work fine in AWS Lambda.

13.6 *Taste it!*

It's time for a small exercise with Express.js.

13.6.1 *Exercise*

As an exercise, add a `DELETE /order/:id` route that will delete a request using the request ID that is passed as a URL parameter.

Here are a few tips that should help you:

- URL parameters are defined in the Express.js way (using `:id`), not in the API Gateway and Claudia API Builder way (using `{id}`).
- You can delete an item from MongoDB using the `collection.deleteOne` function.
- Make sure you convert the order ID to a MongoDB ID using the `new mongodb.ObjectID` function.

If you need an additional challenge, try implementing authentication in your Express.js app. (You can also try running an existing Express.js app in AWS Lambda, if you have one. There are no tips or a solution for this additional challenge in the next section.)

13.6.2 *Solution*

The solution for this exercise is similar to implementing the `POST /orders` route.

You need to add a new `DELETE` route to your app.js file, using the `app.delete` method. Then you need to connect to the database and use the `db.collection('orders').collection.deleteOne` function to delete an item from the `orders` collection. Because the order ID is passed as a string, you need to convert it to a MongoDB ID using the `new mongodb.ObjectID(req.params.id)` function.

Your new route should look like the following listing.

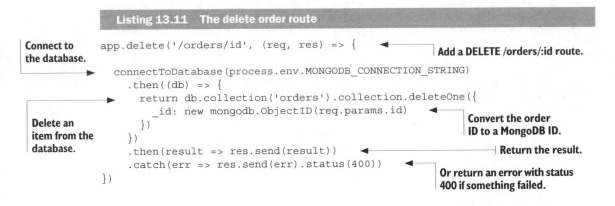

Listing 13.11 The delete order route

Connect to the database.

Add a DELETE /orders/:id route.

Delete an item from the database.

Convert the order ID to a MongoDB ID.

Return the result.

Or return an error with status 400 if something failed.

```
app.delete('/orders/id', (req, res) => {

  connectToDatabase(process.env.MONGODB_CONNECTION_STRING)
    .then((db) => {
      return db.collection('orders').collection.deleteOne({
        _id: new mongodb.ObjectID(req.params.id)
      })
    })
    .then(result => res.send(result))
    .catch(err => res.send(err).status(400))
})
```

After you deploy the function using `claudia update`, you can test the `delete` method using `curl` or Postman.

NOTE Make sure you set up the MongoDB connection string, by running the `claudia update` command with the `--set-env` or `--set-env-from-json` option.

Summary

- You can run Express.js apps in AWS Lambda using Claudia and the `serverless -express` module.
- You can serve static pages using serverless Express.js without additional modifications.
- For a MongoDB connection, use a managed MongoDB instance unless you want to manage the scaling by yourself.
- Cache a database connection in a variable outside of the handler function.
- There are certain limitations, such as when using WebSockets and for requests taking longer than 30 seconds.

Migrating to serverless

This chapter covers

- Learning how to approach migrating to serverless

- Structuring your app according to serverless provider characteristics

- Organizing your application architecture so it's business-oriented and able to grow

- Dealing with the architectural differences between serverless and traditional server-hosted applications

At some point, you'll start thinking about how to apply changes to your in-production serverless applications, migrate your existing apps, and assess the impact of your business needs on the migration.

You'll be concerned with the quantity of your serverless functions and how to organize and maintain them. You might also start wondering about your serverless provider's limitations, such as function "cold starts" and how they may affect your application. In this chapter, we recap the architecture of a serverless app and then examine some of these issues, helping you understand the basics of migrating to serverless and how to take serverless apps into production.

14.1 Analyzing your current serverless application

Before any migration to serverless, a good starting point is to look at an existing server-less application and the organization of its underlying services. Throughout the book, you've helped Aunt Maria and her pizzeria flourish, mostly due to the following server-less services you've created:

- *An API*—This API lists pizzas, takes pizza orders, and stores them in a serverless data-base. It connects to a delivery service, stores pizza images in a serverless storage, and also enables authorization.
- *An image-processing service*—This service converts pizza photos from large scale into thumbnails, preparing them for potential web or mobile usage.
- *A Facebook Messenger chatbot*—The chatbot can, on customer request, list pizzas, make pizza orders, and create delivery requests. It also has natural language processing, which you enabled, so it can respond to small talk initiated by your customers.
- *A Twilio SMS chatbot*—This chatbot can also list pizzas and take pizza orders.
- *An Alexa skill*—This Alexa skill enables the customer's Echo device to list Aunt Maria's pizzas and helps customers order pizzas.
- *A payment service*—This independent payment service is connected to Stripe and allows you to charge your online pizza customers for pizza orders.
- *Uncle Roberto's taxi application*—You migrated your Uncle Roberto's Express.js taxi application to serverless with ease. This application is not connected to Aunt Maria's, but it's worthwhile looking at its migration as a possible solution for one or more of your current applications.

Having a list like this is great, but to have a better understanding of an application and its service relationships, seeing them in a diagram is always more convenient. A complete diagram of the serverless services you've developed for Aunt Maria is shown in figure 14.1. Because Uncle Roberto's application is outside of Aunt Maria's system, it's not displayed.

The diagram shows exactly how your serverless services are working and how they are separated. But you may be wondering why Aunt Maria's services are structured like that, and how you can migrate your existing applications to serverless.

14.2 Migrating your existing application to serverless

Building serverless applications from scratch requires a mind shift. But once you start thinking in a serverless way, all the dots connect quickly. With the help of tools such as Claudia, development and deployment cycles are short and easy.

If you already have an application running and serving customers, it's unlikely that you'll just start from scratch. Instead, you have an app with a few thousand lines of code and a couple thousand daily active users, with a history of decisions caused by business requests or other issues that shaped your code in a specific way.

Can you and should you migrate such an application to serverless? The answer is not a simple one, because it depends on the specifics of your application, the structure of your team, and many other things. But in most cases, serverless can be beneficial for legacy applications.

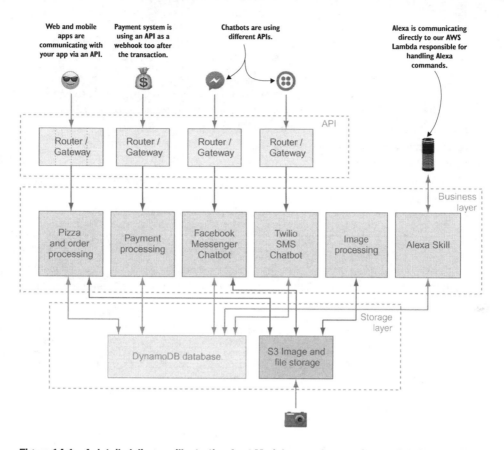

Figure 14.1 A detailed diagram illustrating Aunt Maria's serverless services and their relationships

Once you migrate your application, the serverless architecture will push you to keep it in good shape. It encourages further refactorings, because they can reduce costs; having a good and efficient codebase will become a business decision.

If you decide to try serverless, you might wonder how you should approach migration. The first and most obvious approach is to start small, with the less-important parts of your application that can be easily decoupled from the monolith.

One of our clients had a service that converted PDF catalogs into JPG images, so they could be annotated, linked, and served inside their mobile applications. The service was a part of their bigger monolithic application. When a PDF file was uploaded, the service processed the PDF, then generated a JPG image for each page, and notified almost 100,000 users via mobile push notifications that a new catalog was available.

The problem arose when they tried to upload a second big PDF catalog immediately after the first one. Users that received the push notifications started opening the app, but the same server had two things to do at the same time: serving API requests and converting files. Because PDF-to-JPG conversion is CPU-intensive, and the autoscaling process took two to three minutes, API requests often failed at the worst possible moment—when the users clicked the push notifications.

They had a few options, including having a separate server for PDF processing (which would be idle 99% of the time) or triggering autoscaling before they needed it. But the cost of the infrastructure was already too high, so they decided to migrate that service to AWS Lambda and make it 100% serverless.

Just a few days later, they had a fully operational PDF-to-JPG converter service that was independent from the API server. They were able to upload PDFs directly to AWS Simple Storage Service (S3), Amazon's serverless static file storage service, from their dashboard. S3 would then trigger their AWS Lambda function, which converted PDF files to JPG images using ImageMagick. You can read more about S3 integration with AWS Lambda in chapter 7, and you can read more about S3 service on its official website: https://aws.amazon.com/s3/.

Because PDF conversion is slow, and some of the PDF catalogs had a few hundred pages, they used the *Fanout pattern*: the first Lambda function receives the request and downloads the PDF file, then it triggers a new Lambda function for each page using an Amazon Simple Notification Service (SNS) event. When all pages are converted, the converter tool contacts the API, which sends push notifications to all the users. The flow of the converter service is shown in figure 14.2.

The Fanout pattern

In serverless architecture, *functions* are focused units that should have a limited scope and do one thing or perform a small number of actions around a single business unit. They are not good for processing long tasks or running background processes.

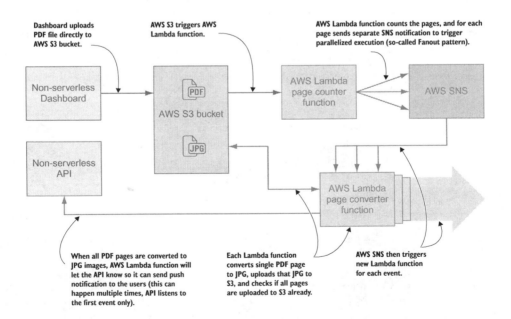

Figure 14.2 **Moving a small part of the application to serverless: PDF-to-JPG converter with Lambda Fanout pattern**

Because our applications often require processing large amounts of data or running long tasks, a new set of patterns started evolving around serverless functions. One of the most useful new patterns is *Fanout*. Fanout speeds up long processes or simulates background processes by splitting the work among many functions. The idea behind it is that one function receives the request, but then it invokes multiple other functions and delegates parts of the work to each of them.

This pattern is useful for slow processes, such as converting PDF files to JPG images, and for batch processing—for example, of CSV data and many other cases. In AWS, you can initiate fanout by using the AWS SDK or via another service, such as AWS SNS.

If moving one service to serverless goes well, your next step is to tackle the monolithic application step by step. You can use the technique we explained in chapter 13 and have your full Express.js app running in AWS Lambda. That's a good way to start using serverless, but don't think of it as a final solution. Moving your monolithic application to AWS Lambda won't make it faster and cheaper; it may be exactly the opposite. Going serverless requires a change in your development practices. We go over some of the most important challenges, such as cold starts, later in this chapter.

The other approach is to put API Gateway in front of your application and try to replace one route at a time with AWS Lambda functions or other serverless components that fit your needs (figure 14.3). Then you can observe the way your services work and optimize them.

Migrating routes to AWS Lambda functions is relatively easy; the hard part is migrating all the other parts of the application, such as authentication and authorization or databases. To migrate your whole application to serverless, you'll need to embrace the whole serverless platform, not just the functions.

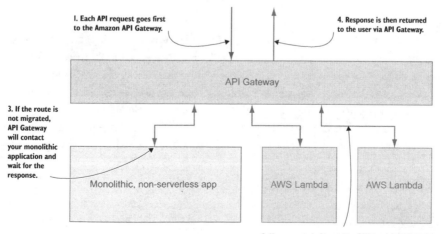

Figure 14.3 Migrating an API to serverless, step by step

14.3   *Embrace the platform*

Serverless architecture promises certain benefits, such as cheaper, faster, and more stable applications. But to get these promised benefits, you can't use just a subset of serverless by applying the same principles you would apply to nonserverless apps. Instead, you need to go all in and adjust your application to use all serverless services and let users connect directly to them.

Having a user connect directly to the database or the file storage is an antipattern. But with serverless in combination with other services, such as Cognito, this becomes a pattern that can reduce the cost of your infrastructure significantly.

This section discusses some of the questions we hear most frequently from people who are trying to migrate their existing applications to serverless.

14.3.1   *Serving static files*

Similar to traditional servers (as you saw in chapter 13), API Gateway and AWS Lambda can serve static files such as server-rendered HTML and images. But this increases the cost (and possibly latency) of those static files significantly when you scale, because each time a user wants to see the file, you'll pay per use for API Gateway for receiving the request and returning the response, and for AWS Lambda for processing the request and data transfer.

This cost may not seem like much, but API Gateway is significantly more expensive than Amazon S3. Also, serving static files from API Gateway and AWS Lambda can interfere with your limits and prevent more important requests from going through. So, how do you best serve static files in a serverless architecture?

You should let the user talk directly to Amazon S3 whenever possible. If you need to limit access to certain users, you can use Cognito to do that. If you want to grant only certain users permission to upload files, you can use a presigned URL (see chapter 7).

14.3.2   *Storing state*

Another important question is how to manage state in serverless applications. There's a popular misconception that AWS Lambda is stateless. But it's not, and treating it as stateless can cost you in terms of execution time and, of course, money.

Instead of treating serverless as stateless, you should design for *shared-nothing architecture*, according to Gojko Adzic, creator of Claudia and MindMup, a popular mind mapping tool. There is a virtual machine (VM) underneath each serverless function, but you don't know how long it will live or if the same VM will handle your next request.

Shared-nothing architecture

A shared-nothing (SN) architecture is a distributed computing architecture in which each node is independent and self-sufficient, and there is no single point of contention across the system. More specifically, none of the nodes share memory or disk storage. People typically contrast SN systems with systems that keep a large quantity of centrally stored state information, whether in a database, an application server, or any other similar single point of contention. To read more about shared-nothing architecture, see https://en.wikipedia.org/wiki/Shared-nothing_architecture.

AWS Lambda shouldn't be used for storing state, but it should be used for optimization. For example, in chapter 13 you started an Express.js app outside of your handler function; that way, you improved performance for all requests that reuse the same VM. For persistent state storage, you should use another service, such as DynamoDB or even S3, depending on the complexity of the state you want to save.

If you need a state machine, you might find AWS Step Functions helpful. With Step Functions, you can easily coordinate the components of distributed applications and microservices using visual workflows, and they allow you to have semi-persistent state. To learn more about Step Functions, see https://aws.amazon.com/step-functions/.

14.3.3 Logs

As you learned in chapter 5, CloudWatch has an out-of-the-box integration with other serverless components, such as AWS Lambda and API Gateway. But CloudWatch is not a great solution when you want to search for logs or just have a better overview.

Fortunately, there are other options that improve the experience of working with serverless logs, such as using a third-party solution or triggering Lambda functions or Elasticsearch from CloudWatch.

One of the most popular third-party solutions is IOpipe (https://www.iopipe.com), a metrics and monitoring service that allows you to see function performance metrics, real-time alerts, and distributed stack traces in a nice real-time dashboard. Setting up IOpipe is quite simple: you sign up for the service and get the client ID, then install the IOpipe module from NPM by running the command `npm install @iopipe/iopipe --save`. Then you need to wrap your handler with the `iopipe` function, as shown in the following listing.

Listing 14.1   Need Title FPO

```
const iopipe = require('@iopipe/iopipe')         ◄── Import the IOpipe module.

const iopipeWrapper = iopipe({                   ◄── Generate the wrapper function using your client ID.
  clientId: process.env.CLIENT_TOKEN
})

exports.handler = iopipeWrapper(                 ◄── Wrap your handler function with the IOpipe wrapper.
  function(event, context, callback) {
    // Your Code Here
  }
)
```

If you're using IOpipe with Claudia API Builder, that integration should look like the next listing.

Listing 14.2   Need Title FPO

```
const iopipe = require('@iopipe/iopipe')

const iopipeWrapper = iopipe({
  clientId: process.env.CLIENT_TOKEN
})
```

```
// Your routes

api.proxyRouter = iopipeWrapper(api.proxyRouter)
module.exports = api
```
◄─── Integrate IOpipe with your
AWS Lambda function using
api.proxyRouter.

Another option is to stream logs to an AWS Lambda function or Amazon Elasticsearch service. This option streams all logs and allows you to connect logs to other tools you would normally use, such as the Elastic stack. The Elastic stack—also known as the ELK stack—is a combination of three open source products (Elasticsearch, Logstash, and Kibana) that help you perform easy log analysis and visualization. To learn more about the Elastic stack, see https://www.elastic.co/elk-stack.

> **TIP** You can enable streaming logs to an AWS Lambda function or Amazon Elasticsearch service on a log stream (for a single log stream) or log group level (for all parts of the application) using CloudWatch log actions in the AWS web console. To learn more about how to stream logs to the Amazon Elasticsearch service, see https://docs.aws.amazon.com/AmazonCloudWatch/latest/logs/CWL_ES_Stream.html.

Which option is better?

The answer again is that it depends on your application, tools, and preferences. Third-party logging libraries give you additional value and data that is not available in CloudWatch. But as shown in figure 14.4, they also add additional latency to your function runtime. Most of the time, the runtime is just slightly longer, but because Lambda function pricing is per 100 ms, it might directly increase your bill.

Starting with third-party logging is probably a good idea, and then you can observe the effect and optimize it or replace it with built-in logging or, possibly, the Elastic stack.

14.3.4   *Continuous integration*

One of the big advantages of a serverless infrastructure is that you can have everyone on your team deploying to any environment with a single command. But that setup comes with a lot of potential issues, such as with running tests or doing a rollback if something fails.

Traditionally, some of the problems with frequent deployments are solved by continuous integration (CI). CI is a development practice that requires developers to integrate code into a shared repository several times a day. Each check-in is then verified by an automated build, allowing teams to detect problems early. CI therefore allows you to detect errors quickly and locate them more easily.

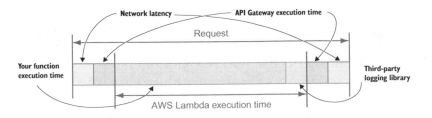

Figure 14.4   Request-runtime duration with the third-party logging option

Here are a few of the popular CI tools:

- Jenkins (https://jenkins.io)
- Travis CI (http://travis-ci.org)
- Semaphore CI (http://semaphoreci.com)

All of these tools can work with serverless apps on AWS without any problems. To integrate them, you'll need to commit a claudia.json file to your version control and run the `claudia update` command after each test suite runs successfully. Just make sure you add your AWS access key ID and secret access key to the environment variables.

In addition to the popular tools just listed, AWS offers a variety of integrated tools for using CI in your serverless app, including the following:

- CodePipeline, which is used to model, visualize, and automate the steps required to release your serverless application (http://docs.aws.amazon.com/ codepipeline/latest/APIReference/)
- CodeBuild, which is used to build, locally test, and package your serverless application (http://docs.aws.amazon.com/codebuild/latest/userguide/)
- AWS CloudFormation, which can be used to deploy your serverless application (http://docs.aws.amazon.com/AWSCloudFormation/latest/UserGuide/)
- CodeDeploy, which is used to gradually deploy updates to your serverless applications (https://docs.aws.amazon.com/codedeploy/latest/userguide/welcome .html)

NOTE Some of the tools available in the AWS platform don't work well with Claudia. For example, AWS CloudFormation is a free service that provides the tools for creating and managing the AWS infrastructure. That particular software application must be run on Amazon Web Services. It deploys AWS Lambda functions and other parts of your serverless application.

If your app grows to include a high number of different components, take a look at CloudFormation as a potential solution for managing the application.

14.3.5 *Managing environments: production and development*

Each time a Lambda function is published, it gets assigned a sequential build number. You can invoke a particular version and set the triggers to a particular build number, which makes it easy to roll back the deployment and use multiple versions at the same time.

In addition to the numeric build numbers, AWS Lambda also supports *aliases*. These named pointers to a particular numeric version make it easy to use a single Lambda function for development, production, and testing environments.

For example, during development, you can deploy a new Lambda version and mark it with the `development` alias, then push the `testing` alias to the same version and test it thoroughly. Finally, if your function works as expected, you can point the `production` alias to the same numeric version and put that version into production.

Because you can set most of the triggers to invoke an alias, as soon as your `production` flag is pointing to the new numeric version, production triggers will invoke it directly without additional changes.

> **NOTE** Some of the event sources, such as a CloudFront trigger for Lambda@ Edge, don't support aliases and require that you point to the numeric version of your Lambda function. In most of those cases, Claudia will automatically get the numeric version of your alias and assign the trigger to it. For more information about Lambda@Edge, see https://docs.aws.amazon.com/lambda/latest/ dg/lambda-edge.html. If you want to deploy Lambda@Edge using Claudia, see https://claudiajs.com/news/2018/01/04/claudia-3.html.

One of the most important things to keep in mind when you're building serverless functions that support different environments is to keep your function environment-agnostic. You should never hardcode the services your function accesses—for example, an S3 bucket or a DynamoDB table name. Instead, try to use the same bucket that sent the event or get the table name from the environment variables.

14.3.6 *Sharing secrets*

One of the key parts of successful serverless applications with multiple environments is managing app secrets. Throughout this book, we've managed secrets in two ways: as API Gateway stage variables and AWS Lambda environment variables. Both have their strengths and weaknesses, and which one you use will depend on your use case and preferences.

If you're using aliases to manage testing/production stages, Lambda environment variables are tied to a numeric version of your Lambda function, not the aliases, which means that all aliases that point to that same build version share the same environment variables. For example, if you point both `production` and `development` aliases to build 42 of your Lambda function, they can't have a different `TABLE_NAME` environment variable. See visual representation of how Lambda environment variables work in figure 14.5.

As opposed to Lambda environment variables, API Gateway stage variables are tied to the API Gateway stage so, as shown in figure 14.6, two API gateway stages can point to the same Lambda build number and have different variable values.

On a new deployment, Lambda environment variables are reused from previous versions, unless you provide the new set of variables. That means that variables from your development environment will be passed to production if you deploy it using `claudia update --version production` without overriding them using `--set-env` or `--set-env-from-json` flags. Also, to update Lambda environment variables, you need to provide all the active variables again, because each update overrides all existing variables. For example, if you want to change `TABLE_NAME` but keep the `S3_BUCKET` variable, you'll need to provide both of them again, or the `S3_BUCKET` variable will be lost. On the other hand, Claudia helps with that situation: it has an additional command `--update-env` you can use to update a single environment variable without having to specify the other environment variables.

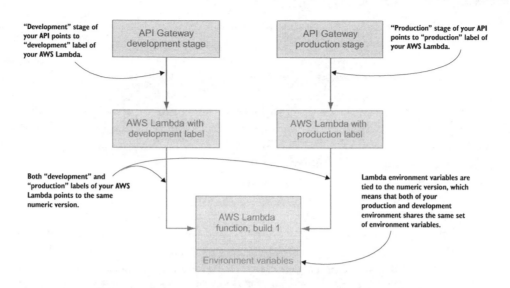

Figure 14.5 Visual representation of how Lambda environment variables work

API Gateway stage variables are preserved for each API Gateway stage, which means that if you push a new version to the development stage, it will still have all the stage variables from the previous version of the development stage. Or you can add one stage variable, and it will not affect other stage variables for the state you're updating or any other state.

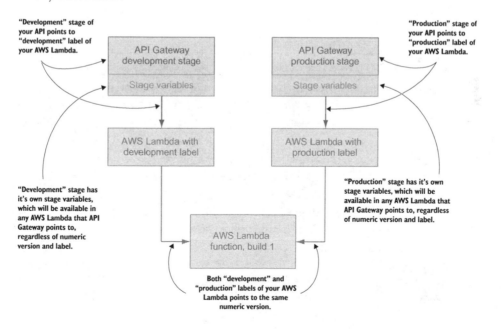

Figure 14.6 Visual representation of how API Gateway stage variables work

With API Gateway, you can update a single stage variable without overriding others.

But the Lambda environment variables have their strengths, too. For example, they are stored encrypted, which makes them more secure than API Gateway stage variables, which are not encrypted. They also can be used regardless of the event that triggered AWS Lambda.

The common weakness of both Lambda environment variables and API Gateway stage variables is sharing them between different Lambda functions. If you have many functions that should share secrets, such as DynamoDB table name, you can't do it without passing the same variable to each of them. For example, your `pizza-orders` DynamoDB table is used by the Pizza API, but it is also used by your Alexa skill, so you pass the name of the table to both of the Lambda functions.

That weakness can be solved using the AWS Systems Manager Parameter Store, which provides access to central, secure, durable, and highly available storage for application configuration and secrets. It also integrates with AWS Identity and Access Management (IAM), to allow fine-grained access control to individual parameters or branches of a hierarchical tree. One of the downsides of Parameter Store is an additional latency it introduces. To read more about AWS Systems Manager Parameter Store, see https://docs.aws .amazon.com/systems-manager/latest/userguide/systems-manager-paramstore.html.

14.3.7 *VPC (Virtual Private Cloud)*

When deciding whether to migrate to serverless, your company might have the challenge of complying with specific rules or laws—for example, rules for personal data storage and handling, or even special network security measures within the company itself. Those restrictions might prevent you from using AWS Lambda or other serverless resources.

Fortunately for these cases, serverless providers have a solution called the *Virtual Private Cloud* (VPC). A VPC is a service that allows you to create serverless resources within a virtual private network. It enables you to have complete control of your network environment, such as IP ranges, network gateways, and so on. Having your serverless resources in a virtual private network provides increased security and helps your company keep its resources in certain areas, regions, or countries. For example, if you're dealing with sensitive customer data (which may be required within the customer's country of residence), a VPC enables you to have your serverless resources within the same network as your data center in that country.

Simply put, a VPC enables you to have a virtual private network with your serverless provider resources (say AWS Lambda) and restrict access to these resources so that they are accessible from only the instances or resources in your VPC.

There are drawbacks to a VPC, however. A closed network has problems with cold starts, which are increased significantly, because AWS Lambdas are required to create elastic network interfaces (ENIs) to your VPC. Creating an ENI on a single request can easily add up to 10s to your cold starts. Also, by default, your Lambda function in a VPC doesn't have internet access, which can be configured using a network address translation (NAT) gateway. Therefore, you need to be careful when using them.

14.4   Optimizing your application

Going serverless can indeed reduce the cost of your application infrastructure, but only when it is done correctly. One of the most important things to understand is that serverless architecture is a new architecture, and some common best practices are not important anymore and can even be counterproductive. The cost savings of a serverless application are seen not just in the bill from AWS; a serverless application can also provide many savings because of shorter time to market, increased efficiency, and easier pivoting.

Although good practices and patterns are emerging, the only way to have a good serverless application is to continuously observe and optimize, which will reduce the cost of your application and improve the user experience.

14.4.1   Bundled or single-purpose functions

You may have noticed in Aunt Maria's serverless application diagram (figure 14.1) that her pizza listing and ordering API is a single serverless function doing multiple tasks. Isn't this a monolith within a function? Some may argue that it's an improper use of serverless functions. The argument is based on the FaaS (Function as a Service) concept that each of your functions should have a single purpose and that you shouldn't have monoliths in your serverless functions because of the benefits of looser coupling, reusability, and easier maintenance.

Others may argue that you could have joined some of the independent services into the same API—for example, the payment service. Because these services are not used that much, the cold starts may be slower; you'd be better off having a warmed-up serverless function and not making the user wait when paying for your services.

These are the viewpoints of opposing "tribes." Now, which approach should you take? First, you should remember the famous saying, "no size fits all." Although this may put you on the edge with both of those tribes, your goal is to create a customer-oriented service. You should have a rational approach, and it will always depend on the type of application you're building.

Initially, it's recommended that you divide your features based on domains, like the one in Aunt Maria's serverless application. Divide the features into a bundled "pizza-related" service and a payment service, and then separate functions for each of the additional services, such as chatbots or image processing. Later, when your system starts to grow, you should strive for single-purpose functions; in this case, you can separate the pizza listing and ordering application into two functions: one for showing a list of pizzas and the other for ordering those pizzas. Because your customer base will have grown, the cold starts are going to happen less and your response rate is going to be faster.

14.4.2   Choosing the right memory size for your Lambda function

Each of your serverless functions has a specified memory allocation. Even though serverless architecture promises no server configuration, certain tasks can require more memory or more computing power. Therefore, serverless providers give you the ability to specify how much memory to allocate. You may notice that we didn't mention CPU power here, because it's tied to memory size, meaning that if you want a larger CPU share, you must increase memory. For example, if you configured your Lambda function to have 2 GB instead of 1 GB of memory, it most likely will have more CPU power. For precise information and because it might change in the future, we suggest that you read more on the AWS documentation page about Lambda configuration at https://docs.aws.amazon .com/lambda/latest/dg/resource-model.html.

But specifying a bigger memory size also has a higher cost. That free 1 million requests per month can easily turn into just a hundred thousand if you increase the memory allocation for your Lambda to 1 GB. Choosing the right memory size for a Lambda is tricky. You can easily get pulled into one of the two following traps:

- Minimizing the memory size for your Lambda to minimize the cost by trying to guess how much memory or CPU power it will need.
- Maximizing the memory size for your Lambda to speed up all requests and subsequent computation, and also to be ready for any kind of potential increase in memory use.

Again, the best advice is that "no size fits all." You should try to use logging or a monitoring tool to inspect the function memory usage. For example, in CloudWatch logs you can find how much function memory you used and how long it took to finish, among many other details. Based on those facts, you may be able to get a proper estimate, but always try to base your estimate on various times of the day and also specific events.

14.5 Facing the challenges

With a new architecture comes a new set of challenges, but there are also old challenges that still apply in the same or in a slightly different way. With serverless, some of the new challenges are timeouts and cold starts. But you'll also have to deal with some old challenges such as vendor lock-in, security, and distributed denial of service (DDoS) attacks. This section discusses some of the most important challenges you'll face when migrating to serverless architecture.

14.5.1 Handling timeouts

One of the first challenges you might face when migrating is understanding serverless function limitations, one of which is the function timeout limit. Timeouts allow functions to safely shut down without wasting your money or the functions' time if for some reason they stop or block. The timeout limit forces you to think about how to finish your request in the specified timeframe. Although that might be a challenge in itself, the actual challenge is how you monitor, track, and debug issues when a timeout occurs. Also, you might not have a bug, but a certain service may take longer than expected to complete or return a response.

There are several ways to track this: the first and the simplest is to look at your Cloud-Watch logs, which log all your Lambda functions that time out. Doing so might not be useful though, because you still aren't handling the timeout itself. There is a better way to handle this. You want to be able to handle these timeout cases and at least log which service took too long or identify a bug. The solution is to create a *watchdog timer*, an essential service whose only purpose is to detect when your application or software is going to time out. It is a simple timer you put inside your Lambda function to check how much time your Lambda function has left. It calculates the remaining time based on your Lambda function timeout setting, which is defined in the Lambda function dashboard on the AWS Console website.

The watchdog timer detects when the function is reaching its timeout, as you need to handle situations when the function didn't finish everything on time. When the Lambda function is close to its timeout, the timer invokes another Lambda function. This other Lambda function's purpose is to log this event or handle it in some other way you might need. To implement this watchdog timer, you need to create a timer function that is constantly checking if there is less than one second until the Lambda function timeout, and to invoke another Lambda in that situation and send it the current function context. Then you can log the new timeout event details or just track this timeout occurrence.

As an alternative to another AWS Lambda function, you can also use some third-party error-handling services, such as Bugsnag (https://www.bugsnag.com) or Sentry (https://sentry.io).

14.5.2 *Cold starts*

Another challenge you'll face with serverless applications is function latency, also known as *cold start*. Because AWS manages scaling and containers for you, each function has additional latency when invoked the first time. This is because a container needs to start, and your function needs to be initialized. After the first invocation, your function will stay *warm* for a certain amount of time (a few minutes at most), so it can handle the next requests faster (figure 14.7).

A cold start doesn't happen only the first time your function is invoked, however. If you have multiple parallel or nearly parallel executions, a cold start will occur for each, because AWS may spin up multiple VMs to handle all your requests (figure 14.8).

How do you fight cold starts? You can't avoid them completely. You can try pre-warming a certain number of your functions, but that adds an additional layer of complexity

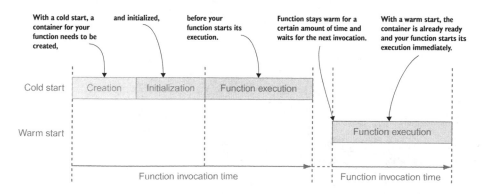

Figure 14.7   Cold versus warm start of the function

and forces you to try to predict the number of requests you'll have under peak load. Another and probably better option is to keep your functions as small as possible (up to a few megabytes), because the cold start is faster if the application can initiate faster.

Also, with serverless, the choice of programming language and the set of libraries you use directly affects the price of your application hosting, so it becomes an important business decision. Running Node.js or Golang functions will cost you significantly less than using Java for writing your functions, because of faster initialization.

14.5.3 *DDoS attacks*

Serverless completely changes the business model by charging for time used instead of time reserved. That is a marvelous change, but you may wonder about handling DDoS attacks. These attacks send a large volume of junk data to your application so your application servers can't scale quickly enough to respond to valid customer requests, thereby preventing your servers from providing service to your customers. Now, because your serverless provider handles scaling and load balancing for you automatically, you might think that a DDoS attack would bankrupt you. The chances of that happening, however, are virtually nonexistent because your serverless provider (AWS, for example) is able to do a much better job of providing security and stability in the face of such attacks than typical server-hosted providers.

In addition to this, you can also specify the following:

- Max throttling on the API Gateway level (for more information, go to https://docs.aws.amazon.com/apigateway/latest/developerguide/api-gateway-request-throttling.html)
- Max concurrency of your AWS Lambda functions (for more information, go to https://docs.aws.amazon.com/lambda/latest/dg/concurrent-executions.html)
- Setting CloudWatch alarms to be notified about possible unknown spikes

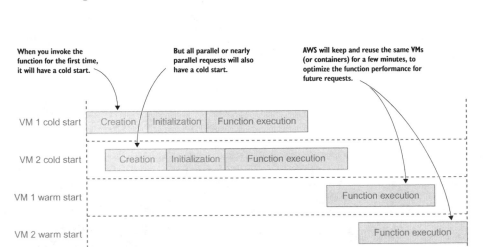

Figure 14.8   Cold starts affect all VMs during parallel requests.

NOTE With serverless, DDoS attacks are instead called DDoW (distributed denial of wallet) attacks. Because serverless providers charge you for each request, increasing your bill translates to "denying your wallet."

14.5.4 *Vendor lock-in*

When going serverless, one of the main concerns is vendor lock-in. It's easy to become reliant on your serverless provider's resources and their corresponding APIs. This may not sound so bad, but the issue comes when you want to move from one serverless provider to another. The original provider's resources will no longer be available to you, and that might necessitate a complete refactoring or even a rewrite of your application.

In some cases that may be a blocker. Businesses don't want to tightly couple with a single resource provider, requiring them to submit to any potential changes in pricing or resource stability and availability. The counter-argument for server-hosted applications is that no matter which provider you use, you can always install the same versions of the needed databases or tools on your servers.

But there is an occasional confusion of concerns. When analyzing vendor lock-in, two distinct layers sometimes get confused and mixed together:

- Infrastructure
- Service

Coupling in the *infrastructure layer* refers to the coupling of your application to a specific infrastructure, whereas coupling in the *service layer* refers to the coupling of your application to a specific software service (a database, file store, search service, and so on).

When going serverless, you might be tempted to start comparing servers and serverless computing services (such as AWS Lambda). But this is in fact comparing apples to oranges, because a serverless computing service belongs to the service layer, whereas a server belongs to the infrastructure layer. You might be asking yourself what the difference is or why you should care. The main point is that AWS Lambda doesn't fill the previous role of the server.

Even with an understanding of this separation of concerns, some might think, "But I'm still locked in to a vendor. This doesn't change anything, because I'm still required to use AWS resources when using AWS." This is correct, but this understanding reveals two benefits that were hiding in plain sight:

- Switching serverless providers/vendors is like switching your MySQL database to a PostgreSQL one.
- Applying Hexagonal Architecture instead of directly interacting with the serverless resources can almost completely remove all potential vendor lock-in issues.

When switching serverless providers, the rules that apply are the same as when migrating one service to another—and you can safely migrate a single serverless service to another just by changing the interaction with its API.

There are serverless frameworks that abstract away the serverless provider specifics, but by using them you'll then be locked in to your serverless framework, instead of the vendor lock-in with your serverless provider. Also, you'll still be tied to your serverless provider, because you'll still be expecting that the responses and messages coming from your serverless provider services are going to be in the serverless provider's format. For example, if you're using AWS Kinesis and you're expecting the Kinesis message format in your code, you're still locked in to a vendor; you won't be able to just jump in to a Google or someone else's alternative.

For that reason, Claudia.js does not abstract away serverless provider details and therefore is AWS-specific.

The recommended method for mitigating this "vendor lock-in" is to apply Hexagonal Architecture, where you'll be defining boundary objects whose sole purpose will be to interact with the specifics of the serverless provider's resource APIs. Your business logic will stay intact, meaning that switching to another serverless provider will just require a change in the boundary object protocol logic.

14.6 *Taste it!*

The exercise for this chapter is simple, but it's not easy: migrate one of your existing Node.js applications to serverless.

Unfortunately, there's no solution you can copy and paste. But we're sure it will be fun, and much more importantly, it will have a great business impact, both on your application and on the way you're going to develop applications from now on. Good luck!

> **TIP** When migrating your application to serverless, you might want to check out the AWS Serverless Application Repository, an open marketplace of serverless applications and components. You might be able to find an existing component you can simply plug in to your new serverless app. To learn more about the Application Repository, see https://aws.amazon.com/serverless/serverlessrepo/.

Summary

- Running your existing application in AWS Lambda and API Gateway is a good start when migrating to serverless, but it can end up costing you more if you don't fully embrace the platform.
- You can migrate your application to serverless by putting an API Gateway in front of it, and then moving the routes one by one to serverless.
- To get the full benefits of serverless, such as lower cost and faster development time, you'll need to use all serverless services.
- With serverless, the choices you make with programming languages, libraries, and when to refactor become business decisions and risks, because they directly affect the cost of your infrastructure. Therefore, continuous observation and optimization are important for a successful serverless application.
- Serverless is a new architecture that requires a new set of patterns and best practices.
- Migrating to serverless brings a new set of challenges, such as cold starts and handling timeouts. But some of the old challenges still apply—some more than ever, such as vendor lock-in.

Real-world case studies

We've come to the end of this serverless journey. Through this book, you've learned what serverless is, how to use it in a new application, and how to migrate your existing applications to a serverless architecture. But we know that there is one important question you want to ask: Who is using serverless in production?

Hearing about companies using a new approach in production is always useful, along with the problems they've encountered and how it's worked for them. In this case, another interesting question is why these companies felt serverless with Claudia.js was the right solution for them.

To answer that question, we chose two companies to ask about the challenges they'd faced, how and why they decided to go serverless, their architecture before and after going serverless, and the approximate costs.

Many companies are using serverless in production, and it was hard to pick the two best examples. But because you can read many success stories from enterprise companies using serverless on the AWS blog, we chose two companies that have successful products with small teams behind them. We think serverless allows you to move and scale quickly with a small team and a relatively low infrastructure cost, and we decided to show you how CodePen and MindMup are doing just that.

15.1   CodePen

CodePen (https://codepen.io) is a popular web application for creating, showcasing, and testing snippets of user-created HTML, CSS, and JavaScript. It's an online code editor and open source learning environment where developers can create code snippets (creatively named "pens"), test and share them with other developers, and work collaboratively.

The CodePen developers had already done an episode on their podcast regarding their serverless applications with Node and Claudia.js. Alex Vazquez, one of the founders of CodePen, said that they extensively use AWS Lambda with Claudia for preprocessors, so we contacted Alex for an interview. The following is a description of what we learned.

15.1.1   Before serverless

CodePen allows developers to write and compile HTML, CSS, and JavaScript live in the editor. To do so, it needs to be able to display the developer's code; if the developer is using preprocessors (such as SCSS, Sass, and LESS for CSS, and even Babel for JavaScript), it needs to preprocess it, too.

Therefore, the initial CodePen architecture was based on two monolithic Ruby on Rails applications—the main website and another application dedicated to preprocessors—and a single, relatively small database service.

You can see the CodePen architecture before moving to serverless in figure 15.1.

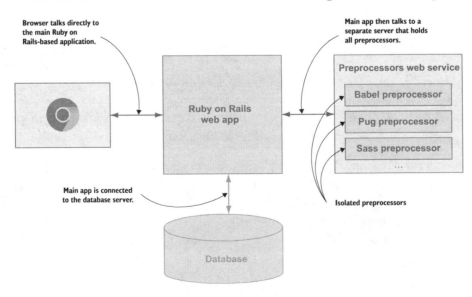

Figure 15.1   The CodePen architecture before migrating to serverless

CodePen aims to allow its users to run their own code as frequently as they want. Another goal of CodePen is for people to get excited about code examples they find on the site and for pens to go viral—but there are moments that it gets "too awesome." Naturally, CodePen gets huge spikes for different pens, and they can be impossible to predict. For these situations, CodePen needs to be able to scale quickly. Also, most CodePen users use CodePen free of charge, so it needs both a quick and an inexpensive way to make sure that it can serve all its users.

The team behind CodePen is small and distributed around the world, and they have one DevOps engineer. Because CodePen is running other people's code, they're always striving to keep security at a maximum. So, they started investigating how to separate the users' code execution for security purposes. That was the first time they heard about AWS Lambda: their DevOps engineer, Tim Sabat, suggested it as a possible solution. Initially, the CodePen developers rejected the idea because they didn't really see the point, thinking it would be a hassle to set up and configure. They already had preconfigured servers, and it didn't seem as though they needed individual Lambda services.

But one day they had a need to format code on demand using a new tool, and this "Lambda concept" seemed like a perfect solution for this task, especially with Claudia.js as its deployment tool. Alex said that they learned a lot about all the different things you can do with serverless functions, such as using API Gateway to set up a full HTTP API, connecting to S3, and setting up cron jobs. It suddenly dawned upon the team how powerful serverless applications are.

15.1.2 Serverless migration

CodePen runs a lot of preprocessors. Each of the preprocessors is dedicated to processing a specific code type, whether it's HTML, CSS, or JavaScript. They also perform differently, have different CPU and memory requirements, and should run asynchronously. You can see how the preprocessors work in figure 15.2.

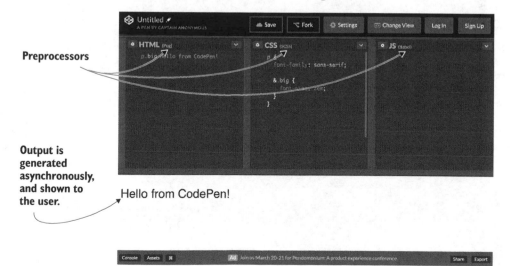

Figure 15.2   CodePen preprocessors

As you can see, each preprocessor does a different job, and one's execution could affect another's. Therefore, when the developers analyzed their current architecture, they realized that separating them was important for both performance and security reasons. Running all the individual preprocessors on the same server made it much harder to optimize each one and to determine where any bugs were. They decided that it made a lot of sense to split them up and run individual AWS Lambda functions, like their previous "code-prettifying-on-demand" service.

The team decided to completely refactor their monolithic Ruby on Rails preprocessor application, dividing it into a single serverless function called the *router* and many other individual preprocessor serverless functions. The router's job is to invoke the needed preprocessor functions, each of which has the goal of preprocessing a certain code type.

Using Claudia, the team realized that even their front-end engineers could help with the migration, taking the strain off the lone DevOps engineer. CodePen's lead front-end developer, Rachel Smith, was able to handle the whole refactor of the router to AWS Lambda, which has enabled CodePen to serve more than 200,000 concurrent requests during peak times. At the same time, Alex and the other developers refactored and migrated the individual preprocessors. You can see the resulting architecture in figure 15.3.

After migrating to serverless, CodePen still has the main monolithic Ruby on Rails application, but instead of a monolithic preprocessor application, it has the router serverless function and about a dozen serverless preprocessor functions. The router is available over API Gateway and uses the AWS SDK to directly invoke every serverless function it needs. It receives an array of tasks to accomplish in the payload. For example, one of the preprocessors is Babel; it has a default version, and the payload sent to the router states the version of Babel that it needs. The router knows which Babel

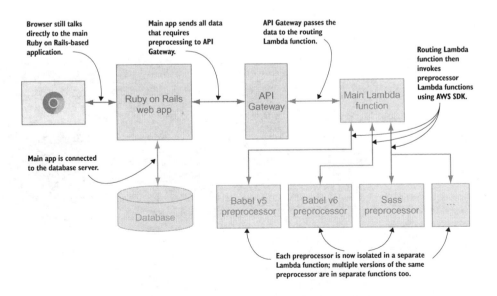

Figure 15.3   CodePen architecture using serverless

versions are available, because each of the preprocessor Lambda functions comes with an associated version number. The design follows the Command pattern, where you provide the command to run and the router knows which Lambdas it needs to invoke.

NOTE The Command pattern is a behavioral design pattern where an object is used to encapsulate all information needed to perform an action or an event trigger. It is one of the design patterns explained in the popular book *Design Patterns: Elements of Reusable Object-Oriented Software.* You can read more about the Command pattern here: https://en.wikipedia.org/wiki/Command_pattern

In addition to the performance and security benefits, separating the monolithic preprocessor application into serverless functions means that as CodePen grows, it will be trivial to add more preprocessors as serverless functions and make them available to users. For the CodePen developers, that's the biggest benefit: before, everything was stuck in the "mini-monolith," as they called their previous Ruby on Rails preprocessor application, and changing or adding new features wasn't easy.

Marriage of AWS Lambda and Claudia

Alex said that AWS Lambda and Claudia came together as a perfect solution for CodePen. Most of the development team's problems and issues were resolved, and the AWS Lambda/Claudia combination allowed them to do a lot more with their existing skillsets. Before, the front-end engineers had to wait for the DevOps engineer to write the scripts, set up the servers and tools, and automate all the tasks required for a deployment. With AWS Lambda and Claudia, the front-end developers are now enabled to do everything themselves. The CodePen founder we spoke to stated that the level of integration ranges from "We really love Claudia and AWS Lambda" to "We're married to Claudia and AWS Lambda." That takes their relationship to a whole other level.

15.1.3 Cost of the infrastructure

Costs have decreased significantly for CodePen after going serverless, because it had to reserve instances up front before; now it pays based on demand. The load fluctuates, so when there isn't a lot of traffic, it's great that CodePen isn't charged for extra capacity. Additionally, with API Gateway caching, CodePen was able to save even more money. Compared with paying for reserved servers, AWS Lambda costs are cheap.

Additionally, one important consideration most people don't factor in is the amount of time spent managing servers and the inherent complexity. To see what a difference it made, CodePen even tried changing all of their Lambdas to the maximum (3 GB) memory. Everything was even faster, because it was running on great hardware (better than was required, really). The monthly cost went up $1,000, which is a lot, but even at that level it was still affordable—and according to Alex Vasquez, even the additional cost for the maxed-out AWS Lambdas didn't compare with the cost of the developer time required to set up and deploy a server.

THE RIGHT LAMBDA SIZE

CodePen doesn't have a standard for defining the size of its serverless functions. The monoliths and the functions (if they get bigger) are separated using the *logical unit* approach. This approach specifies that, for example, if an image manipulation is needed, a serverless function will be created that includes everything related to that image manipulation.

Likewise, for an audio manipulation, a serverless function dedicated to that audio type will be created.

In CodePen's case, the preprocessors are the logical units: Babel, Autoprefixer, Sass, LESS, and so on. For each one, an individual Node.js serverless function has been created. This allows for deployment of multiple versions of a specified preprocessor. Breaking up the functionality even further doesn't make sense for CodePen, because the functions would become difficult to manage with all the directories and repositories.

Additionally, each CodePen serverless function must have a specific memory allocation. The general CodePen serverless function memory allocation is 512 MB. Babel is the only preprocessor that has a slow start time, so it is allocated 1,024 MB.

15.1.4 *Testing and challenges*

CodePen mostly has unit tests, written with Jest. Because both CodePen's serverless functions are written in Node.js with Claudia, their front-end engineers are also able to write tests. There aren't many integrated tests, but there are many defined test cases—mostly for debugging or manual testing of the entire system.

ADDITIONAL SCALING

AWS Lambda's default limit for the number of concurrent requests is 1,000, and because of the unpredictable traffic patterns to its site, CodePen managed to hit this limit.

After sending a simple request to AWS, CodePen received an upgrade to 5,000 concurrent requests almost immediately.

COLD STARTS

The asynchronous nature of CodePen's preprocessors softens the impact of their serverless function cold starts. It doesn't affect their operations or the user experience. CodePen also relies heavily on API Gateway cache. They create a unique URL for every defined data set because API Gateway can cache only unique URLs.

MONITORING

For monitoring their serverless system, the CodePen team use only CloudWatch. For error reporting, they use HoneyBadger and its Node.js SDK. The entire system is monitored, and whenever a timeout or an error occurs, it is reported to HoneyBadger.

SECURITY

CodePen uses JSON Web Token (JWT) for security. The token is generated by the monolith and shared to the client so that the client can easily authenticate the requests sent afterward to the router serverless function.

15.2 *MindMup*

MindMup (https://www.mindmup.com) is a popular mind mapping web application written primarily in JavaScript. According to Gojko Adzic, one of the company's co-founders, MindMup serves almost half a million active users monthly with just a two-person team. To accomplish that, they started using serverless on AWS extensively, which significantly reduced their costs. More importantly, serverless pushed them to improve the architecture and is now allowing them to move quickly and experiment more.

> **Mind maps**
>
> A *mind map* is a diagram used to visually organize information. It's hierarchical and shows relationships among pieces of the whole. A mind map is often created around a single concept, drawn as an image in the center of a blank page, to which associated representations of ideas such as images, words, and parts of words are added. Major ideas are connected directly to the central concept, and other ideas branch out from those. To learn more, visit https://en.wikipedia.org/wiki/Mind_map.

15.2.1 *Before serverless*

From its inception in 2013, MindMup was optimized for a small team, relatively cheap infrastructure, and rapid development. At the beginning, the developers chose to combine Heroku with AWS to build an infrastructure that required minimal maintenance but was still scalable.

> **Heroku**
>
> Heroku is a cloud Platform as a Service (PaaS) supporting several programming languages that is used as a web application deployment model. It was released in June 2007 as one of the first cloud platforms. Back then, it supported only the Ruby programming language, but it now supports Java, Node.js, Scala, Clojure, Python, PHP, and Golang. As a polyglot platform, it lets developers build, run, and scale applications in a similar manner across all the languages.
>
> To learn more about Heroku, visit https://www.heroku.com.

MindMup had one Heroku app that was the system core; it served a single-page web app and an API. The API was in charge of authentication, authorization, providing data, and subscriptions. MindMup began as a free service, but after almost two years, the creators added a paid option for collaboration. To support paid users, they needed a simple but scalable database, so they added AWS DynamoDB.

Along with the single-page application for mind map creation, one of the most important parts of MindMup is *exporters*—a feature that allows users to export mind maps they've created in different file formats, such as PDF, Word, or even as a Power-Point presentation. They had lots of converters, and usage and memory consumption for each of them varied. For example, the PDF exporter was used all the time and required a lot of CPU and memory for file generation. The text exporter required only a small amount of resources, and the Markdown exporter was used much less frequently. Also, different exporters required different applications:

- For PDF, they needed Ghostscript, a software suite for PDF manipulation.
- For Word, they used Apache POI, a library that provides Java libraries for reading and writing files in Microsoft Office formats.
- For other exporters, they needed Ruby and Python.

To export mind maps in different formats, they used AWS S3 file storage. But instead of uploading files from the API, they uploaded files directly from the browser to an AWS S3 bucket, using signed URLs generated by the API. Notifications about newly uploaded conversion request files were then pushed to an AWS Simple Queue Service (SQS) queue. They had one SQS queue per conversion file type and a few applications to read from the queue and convert the file to the specified file type.

The converter applications were Heroku apps, but supporting lots of independent exporters required almost 30 dynos (Heroku's lightweight Linux-based containers), which was too expensive. To reduce the cost, they bundled the exporters into a few Heroku apps; each app was a group of all the exporters that required the same programming language, because Heroku dynos require programming language selection on setup. The MindMup architecture at that point was similar to figure 15.4.

Bundling exporters reduced the cost of the infrastructure, but it also brought certain issues, such as the following:

- There was less isolation and more situations where different libraries could collide.
- Adding a new exporter required a lot of coordination because it required a new app and a new SQS queue. SQS queues were not too expensive, but they were an additional layer of complexity.
- Because it was all bundled, performing small experiments was difficult.
- Updating packages for different Heroku apps with different programming languages was difficult to manage.

Also, there was bit of a scandal with the way Heroku was doing routing—it routed requests to a random dyno instead of to a free one, even if the random dyno was already busy. To learn more about this incident, see https://genius.com/James -somers-herokus-ugly-secret-annotated.

At that time, exporters were the biggest pain point of the MindMup architecture.

15.2.2 *Serverless migration*

In January 2016, the developers were planning to add a new exporter, and they were looking at AWS Lambda because they had seen that files saved in S3 could invoke Lambda functions. As an experiment, Gojko created an exporter in Node.js with a bash script to automate the deployment of a new Lambda function. They liked how it worked,

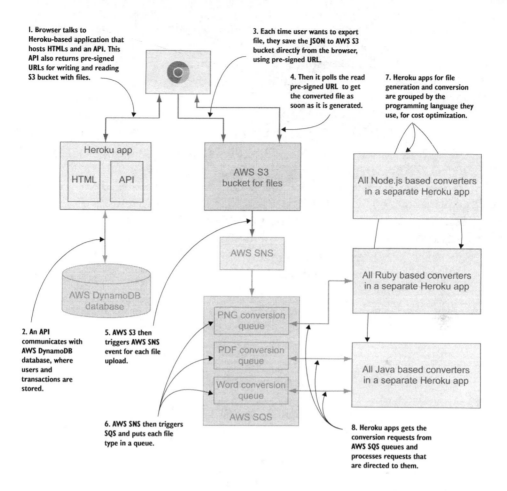

Figure 15.4   The MindMup architecture before migration to serverless

and in contrast with Heroku, which required them to reserve capacity, the AWS Lambda model was pay-per-use. That meant they could conceivably have a separate function for each exporter. At that moment, they decided to start gradually moving all the exporters to AWS Lambda, one by one.

Gojko saw that for the first exporter he had 30 lines of Node.js code and more than 200 lines of bash script. He realized that the risk had shifted from the code to the deployment and that he needed a tested tool to be able to fully migrate to serverless. The ecosystem of serverless tools wasn't developed enough, however, so he decided to "roll his own" solution—which later was open-sourced and published as Claudia.js.

Because the MindMup website was a monolith that served an API and performed server-side rendering, the developers decided to start moving each of the API services to AWS Lambda functions. Migration of an API could be done through API Gateway, but they used this opportunity to rewrite and refactor some of the legacy code and to fix the three-year-old codebase that had grown "in many weird ways," according to Gojko.

As the migration progressed, they ended up with a single application on Heroku that was responsible for rendering the index.html file. They replaced it with a static site on an AWS S3 bucket, with AWS CloudFront as a CDN and caching layer. The only exporter that was left on Heroku was the PowerPoint exporter, written in Java. It ran fine for some time, but they eventually moved that to AWS Lambda, too.

The entire migration took about a year of slow rewriting, and MindMup was a fully serverless application in February 2017. Everything was divided into small Lambda functions that are organized in logical units, and a single function is not necessarily doing just one small thing. In the current architecture, the MindMup website is loaded from AWS S3 and CloudFront. A browser communicates directly with the so-called *Gold API*, which is a Lambda function behind an API Gateway. The Gold API is connected to the DynamoDB database, and it is used by Stripe and PayPal webhooks.

The Gold API also generates presigned URLs that allow a browser to write files directly to an S3 bucket and to poll the bucket to check if the files were generated. When a file is uploaded to the S3 bucket, it triggers an SNS notification, which then triggers the converters.

The biggest difference is with the exporters, because each exporter—regardless of how many requests it handles—is in its own Lambda function.

> **TIP** Isolating each exporter in its own Lambda function also allows MindMup to optimize costs: they can have some of the exporters in Lambda functions with minimum memory (128 MB) but use more memory for exporters that require it.

When a file is converted, an exporter directly stores the result to an S3 bucket, and the browser gets the converted file.

Even more Lambda functions are used for analytics purposes, triggered by the different parts of the system (for example, by an API or by one of the exporters) via SNS notifications. Those Lambda functions process the data and store it to a few different services, such as S3 buckets and DynamoDB tables.

There's also an authorization component in front of an API that communicates with the static website and the Gold API Lambda function. MindMup uses Cognito for Google sign-in, but they also have a custom authorizer for the rest of the app.

The current MindMup architecture is shown in figure 15.5.

Although MindMup is fully serverless now, the team is constantly working on improvements. For example, one of the next steps is to add scalable real-time collaboration support, using Kinesis streams and AWS Lambda functions.

15.2.3 *Cost of the infrastructure*

One of the most amazing things about MindMup's serverless migration was the improvement in application infrastructure cost. A comparison of the infrastructure costs and the number of users for December 2016 and December 2015 showed that the user base had grown by about 50%, whereas the costs had decreased by about 50%. At

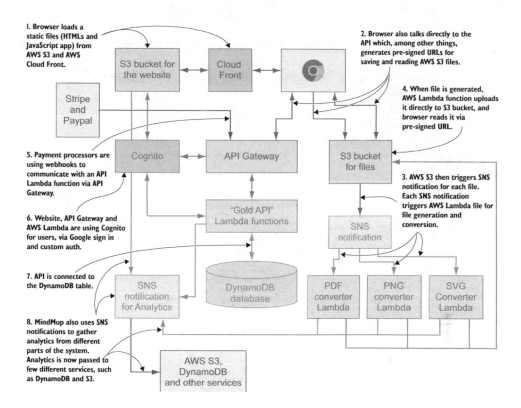

1. Browser loads a static files (HTMLs and JavaScript app) from AWS S3 and AWS Cloud Front.

2. Browser also talks directly to the API which, among other things, generates pre-signed URLs for saving and reading AWS S3 files.

4. When file is generated, AWS Lambda function uploads it directly to S3 bucket, and browser reads it via pre-signed URL.

5. Payment processors are using webhooks to communicate with an API Lambda function via API Gateway.

6. Website, API Gateway and AWS Lambda are using Cognito for users, via Google sign in and custom auth.

7. API is connected to the DynamoDB table.

8. MindMup also uses SNS notifications to gather analytics from different parts of the system. Analytics is now passed to few different services, such as DynamoDB and S3.

3. AWS S3 then triggers SNS notification for each file. Each SNS notification triggers AWS Lambda file for file generation and conversion.

Figure 15.5 MindMup architecture using serverless

that point, they decided to drop Heroku and SQS completely; they moved everything to AWS, reduced data transfers, and reduced latency. With Heroku, they had been paying for reserved capacity. That changed when they went serverless. The Gold API was the gateway for everything else, and it had been their main bottleneck. As a serverless function, it scales automatically, so it's no longer a bottleneck.

In September 2017, MindMup had around 400,000 active users. Their total monthly AWS bill was $102.92 USD. See table 15.1 for cost breakdown by services.

Table 15.1 Applications

AWS Resource	Monthly cost
Lambda	$0.53 USD
API Gateway	$16.41 USD
DynamoDB	$0 USD
CloudFront	$65.20 USD
S3	$5.86 USD
Data transfer	$4.27 USD

They managed to reduce the cost because they let the front-end application talk to some services, such as S3, directly, without putting an API between the browser and S3. This affects the cost because different AWS services have different pricing models. For example:

- AWS charges for the number of requests, execution duration, and memory consumption.
- API Gateway charges for the number of requests and for data transfer.
- Amazon S3 charges only for data transfer.

In a traditional application, you would upload images through the API, but by doing this, you would incur costs for data transfer in S3 and API Gateway and for the number of requests, request duration, and memory consumption in AWS Lambda. In a serverless application, you can get the presigned URL for S3 from an API, which takes less than 100 ms and requires minimal memory. You can then upload the file directly to an S3 bucket from the front end and pay for only that data transfer.

15.2.4   *Testing, logs, and challenges*

Knowing that Claudia is well covered with automated tests, it was interesting to hear from Gojko how they test MindMup. As expected, MindMup has a lot of unit and integration tests. Everything is separated into libraries, and they use Hexagonal Architecture extensively.

Tests are written using the Jasmine framework. Each of the Lambda functions has many unit tests, and a few integration tests where needed. For most of the Lambda functions, they have a lambda.js file that does almost nothing, and is responsible just for wiring other components. This lambda.js file is rarely covered with tests because it contains only three to four lines of code. Then they have the main.js file, which is the main file for that Lambda function; it receives an event from lambda.js and processes it. This main.js file is connected to different libraries (for example, `FileRepository`), configured, and passed from the lambda.js file.

The biggest chunk of their testing is unit tests for the main.js file. They also have integration tests that connect main.js with the `MemoryRepository`. The `FileRepository` is tested with both unit and integration tests, but separately, because it's a separate library.

The testing flow of the typical AWS Lambda function is depicted in figure 15.6.

For some of the exporters, they also conduct visual tests using Appraise, a tool for visual approval testing that we mentioned in chapter 11. To learn more about Appraise, see http://appraise.qa/.

For logs, MindMup uses CloudWatch. They also track errors, payment information, and access; for example, front-end exceptions are tracked through Google Analytics. They store some events in S3 so they can search them. They do not need real-time logging with extensive search capabilities.

It's important to note that MindMup uses labels for the environments, which is a bit contrary to AWS best practices. MindMup labels functions for development; those functions then talk to a development S3 bucket, DynamoDB table, and so on. Moving from

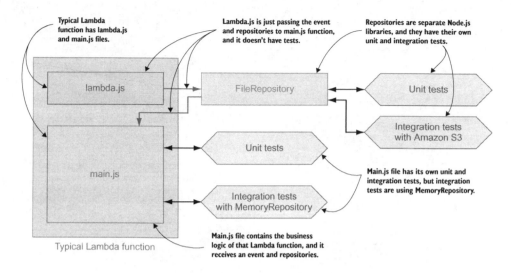

Figure 15.6   The testing flow of the typical AWS Lambda function

development to production requires only a label update. It's safer to have different accounts for different environments, but the small size of the team is what makes this approach feasible and MindMup able to grow faster.

Summary

- Serverless architecture allows you to build a scalable product fast with a small team and an inexpensive infrastructure.
- The combination of Claudia and AWS Lambda allows front-end developers to develop and deploy production-ready services without extensive back-end knowledge.
- Going serverless can lead to a significant cost reduction if you optimize your application for the platform.
- With serverless, risk shifts from the code to deployment and integrations, and it's important to cover those things with tests.
- Using Hexagonal Architecture reduces code complexity and allows you to test your serverless application more easily.
- Migration to serverless can be used to refactor a whole legacy application.

As well as learning a lot about the benefits of serverless, we hope you enjoyed Aunt Maria's company throughout this book, and haven't become too hungry while reading it. Bon appétit!

appendix a
Installation and configuration

This appendix provides details on how to install and configure Claudia and other libraries for its ecosystem: Claudia API Builder and Bot Builder.

This appendix, like this book in general, assumes that you are familiar with the basics of the AWS platform and that you have an account. If that assumption is incorrect, we strongly recommend that you create an account and try to become more familiar with AWS in general, and with its user and permission system in particular, before reading on. You can create an account on the AWS website: https://aws.amazon.com. To better understand users and roles, the official documentation is a good starting point: http://docs.aws.amazon.com/IAM/latest/UserGuide/id.html.

A.1   *Installing Claudia*

Claudia is a regular Node.js module, published on NPM.

To install Claudia and make the `claudia` command available in your terminal, run the following:

```
npm install claudia -g
```

Another option is to install Claudia as a development dependency to your Node.js project by running the following command in your project:

```
npm install claudia --save-dev
```

In this case Claudia will not be installed globally, so you can't use it from your terminal. Instead, you need to run it as an NPM script. The following listing shows the minimal version of package.json with Claudia installed as a development dependency, and with the required NPM scripts.

Listing A.1   Example of package.json file with local version of Claudia

```
{
  "name": "pizza-api",
  "version": "1.0.0",
  "description": "",
  "main": "api.js",
  "scripts": {
    "create": "claudia create --region eu-central-1 --api-module api",
    "update": "claudia update"
  },
  "keywords": [],
  "license": "MIT",
  "devDependencies": {
    "claudia": "^4.0.0"
  },
}
```

NPM script for creating the API in the eu-central-I region

NPM script for updating the API

Claudia saved as a development dependency

After updating the package.json file with the content from listing A.1, you can create your Lambda function and API Gateway definition by running the `npm run create` command from the terminal in your project folder, or update it by running the `npm run update` command.

The full process of Claudia installation is also explained on the Claudia website: https://claudiajs.com/tutorials/installing.html.

A.1.1   *Configuring Claudia prerequisites*

Despite its easy installation, Claudia has one prerequisite: keys for the AWS profile.

If you haven't created an AWS profile yet, see the next section.

Claudia uses the AWS SDK for Node.js to function, and that SDK requires AWS profile keys. There are a few ways to configure the keys. The easiest is to create an .aws folder in the home directory on your operating system. Then create the credentials file inside that folder, without an extension, with the following content:

```
[default]
aws_access_key_id=YOUR_ACCESS_KEY
aws_secret_access_key=YOUR_ACCESS_SECRET
```

The name of your AWS profile

The access key ID for your AWS profile

The secret access key for your AWS profile

> **NOTE** Make sure that you replace the `YOUR_ACCESS_KEY` and `YOUR_ACCESS_SECRET` values with the actual keys.

If you named your profile with any other name than the default, you need to provide that profile name to Claudia. You can do that by passing the `--profile` flag with a profile name (for example, `claudia update --profile yourProfileName`) or by setting an `AWS_PROFILE` environment variable (for example, `AWS_PROFILE=yourProfileName claudia update`).

For a full guide on configuring the AWS SDK for Node.js, visit http://docs.aws .amazon.com/sdk-for-javascript/v2/developer-guide/configuring-the-jssdk.html.

A.1.2 Creating an AWS profile and getting the keys

To create a new AWS profile for Claudia, go to the AWS web console (https://console .aws.amazon.com) and log in.

Then go to the Users tab of the IAM section (https://console.aws.amazon.com/iam /home#/users). Click the Add User button to create a new user, as shown in figure A.1.

To add a new user, you need to go through a four-step process. First, you need to name your user (*claudia* is a good name for your first user) and set its access type. Because you'll use it only through the AWS CLI and AWS SDK for Node.js, select the Programmatic Access option. Click the Next: Permissions button (see figure A.2).

For the second step, you need to add permissions to your user. Select the Attach Existing Policies Directly tab, as shown in figure A.3. Then use the input field to search for the policies you want to add.

The recommended policies you need for this book are

- *IAMFullAccess*—Required if you want Claudia to automatically create execution roles for your Lambda function (which is recommended for beginners). The other option is to do that on your own and pass the existing role name using the `--role` flag when issuing the `claudia create` command.
- *AWSLambdaFullAccess*—Required for Claudia deployments.
- *AmazonAPIGatewayAdministrator*—Required for Claudia API Builder and Claudia Bot Builder.

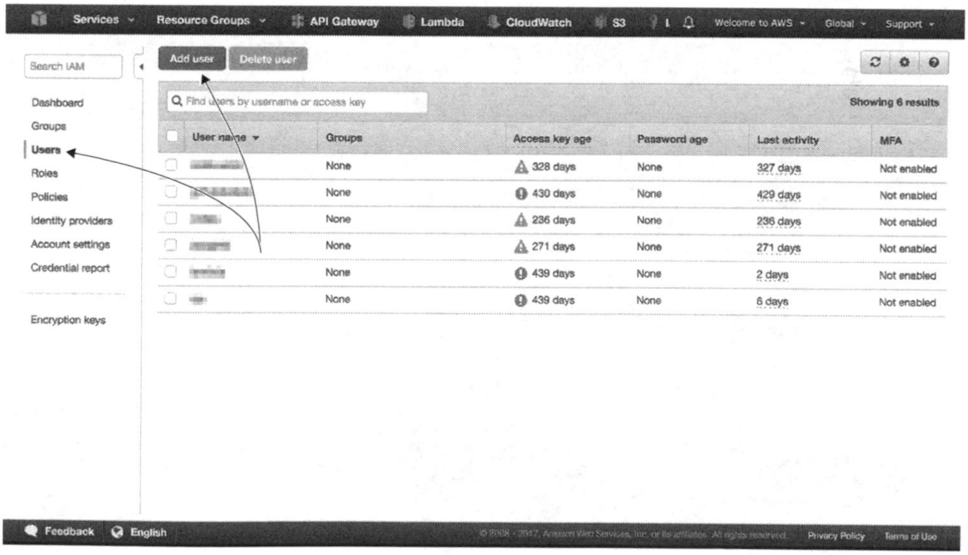

Figure A.1 The Users tab of the IAM section of the AWS web console

- *AmazonDynamoDBFullAccess*—Required for managing a DynamoDB database.
- *AmazonAPIGatewayPushToCloudWatchLogs*—Optional; used for logging full requests and responses from API Gateway.

Production apps require careful selection; this topic is beyond the scope of this book, but we recommend that you learn more about AWS roles and policies before deploying more serious applications to production.

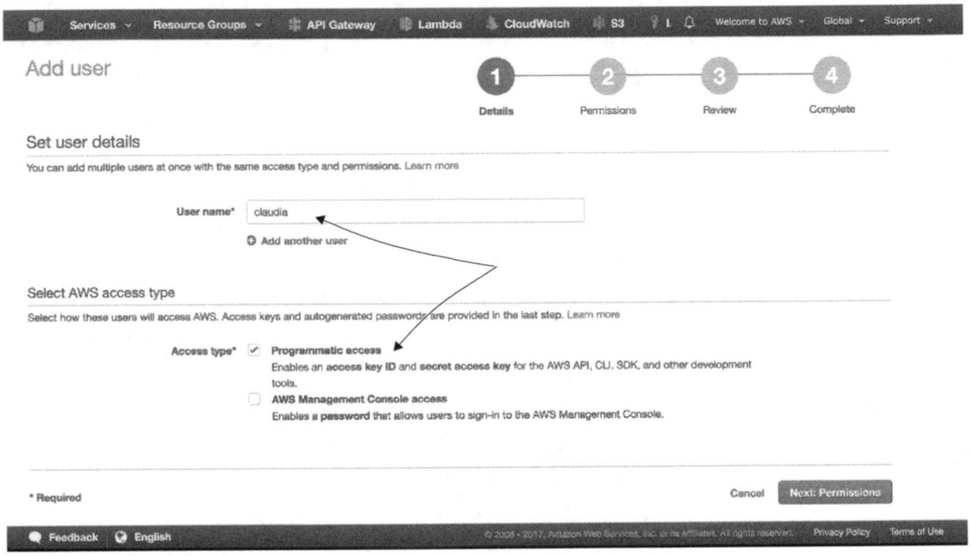

Figure A.2 The first step of adding an AWS user: setting the user details

Figure A.3 The second step of adding an AWS user: setting user permissions

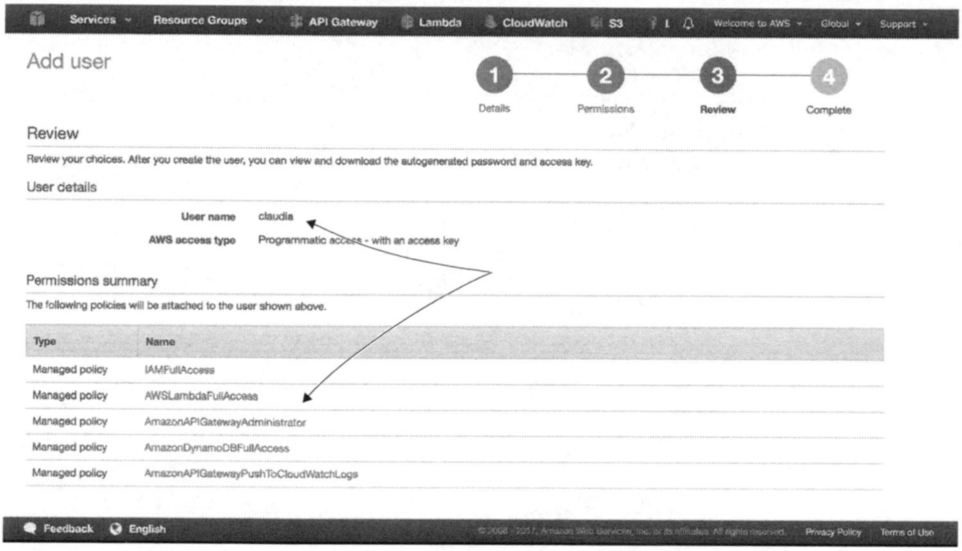

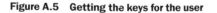

Figure A.4   The third step of adding an AWS user: review

The third step is reviewing your new user, as shown in figure A.4. If all the information seems right, click the Create User button at the bottom of the page to create your new user.

You finish with the confirmation step, as shown in figure A.5. This step is important because it gives you an access key ID and a secret access key for your new user.

Now that you have your access key ID and secret access key, you can go back to the previous section and set them up.

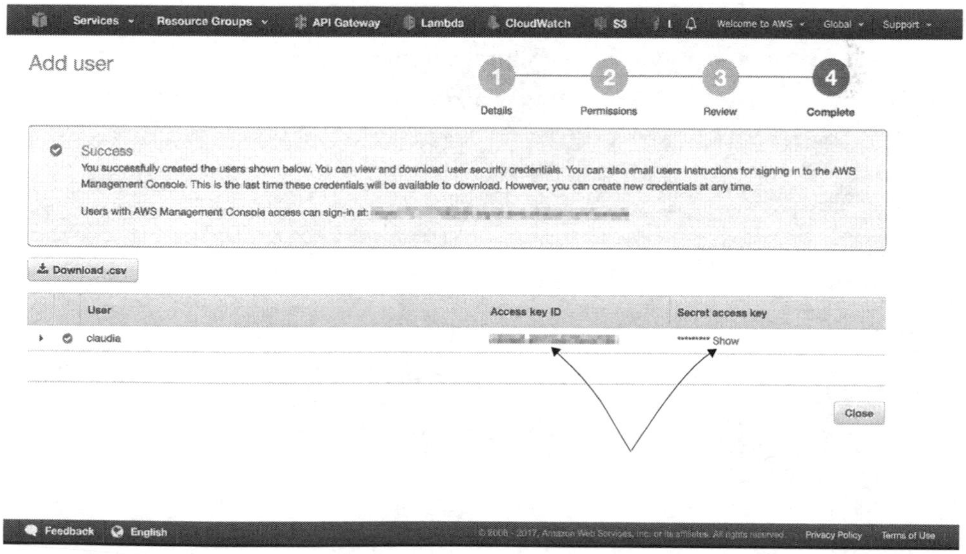

Figure A.5   Getting the keys for the user

A.1.3   *Installing Claudia API Builder*

Claudia API Builder is available on NPM as a package. It doesn't require any configuration, so to install it, save it as a dependency in your Node.js project by running the following command:

```
npm install claudia-api-builder --save
```

The version we used for the examples in this book is 4.0.0.

A.1.4   *Installing Claudia Bot Builder*

Similar to the API Builder, Claudia Bot Builder is a regular NPM package that doesn't require any special configuration. To install it and save it as a dependency of your project, run the following command:

```
npm install claudia-bot-builder --save
```

The version we used for the examples in this book is 4.0.0.

A.2   *Installing the AWS CLI*

The AWS Command Line Interface (CLI) is a unified tool to manage your AWS services. This book uses the AWS CLI for many things, including creating roles and permissions and accessing the DynamoDB tables.

To install the AWS CLI on Windows, visit https://aws.amazon.com/cli/ and download the Windows installer.

If you are a Mac or Linux user, you need to have Python version 2.6.5 or later, with pip. With Python, you can run the following command to install the AWS CLI:

```
pip install awscli
```

For more information about the AWS CLI, visit https://aws.amazon.com/cli/.

To confirm that the command works, run `aws --version`.

The version we used for the examples in this book is

```
aws-cli/1.11.138 Python/2.7.10 Darwin/16.7.0 botocore/1.6.5
```

appendix b
Facebook Messenger, Twilio, and Alexa configuration

This appendix provides details on how to set up the following items required by chapters 8, 9, and 10:

- A Facebook Messenger page and application
- A Twilio account
- An Amazon Alexa account and skill

NOTE All the services we use are under active development, and at some point the user interface or even certain steps might change. If the UI you see is different from the screenshots we provide here, please visit the official documentation for the service in question. Links are given in the text.

B.1 Facebook Messenger setup

Configuration of the Facebook Messenger chatbot for chapters 8 and 9 requires the following steps:

1 Create a Facebook page.
2 Create a Facebook app.
3 Create a Facebook Messenger chatbot using Claudia Bot Builder.
4 Enable built-in natural language processing (NLP).

B.1.1   Creating a Facebook page

To create a Facebook page, visit https://www.facebook.com/pages/create/. This page will show you a list of categories, which looks like figure B.1. You need to choose the type of page you want to create.

> **NOTE** If the screenshots shown here do not match what you see on the site, consult Facebook's help article for creating pages at https://www.facebook .com/business/help/104002523024878.

You can choose any category; we picked "Cause or Community" because it requires minimal configuration. When you select the "Cause or Community" tile, Facebook asks you for the name of your page. Name your page "Aunt Maria's pizzeria," like we did in figure B.2, and click Get Started.

After you name your page, Facebook asks you to upload profile and header pictures and fill in some additional data. When you've completed or skipped all the steps, your new Facebook page should look like figure B.3.

B.1.2   Creating a Facebook app

The next step is to create a Facebook application. To do so, go to https://developers .facebook.com, and from the My Apps menu, choose Add a New App, as shown in figure B.4.

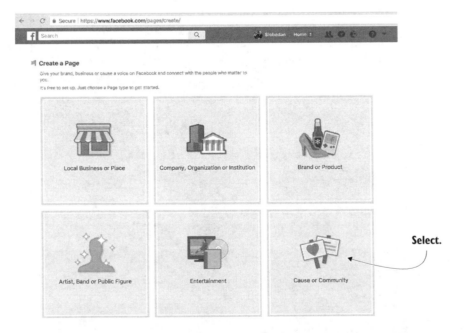

Figure B.1   Create your Facebook page.

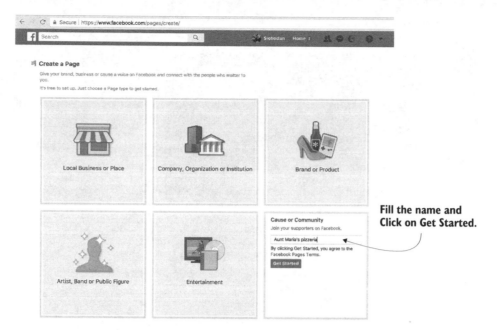

Figure B.2   Select the page category and name your page.

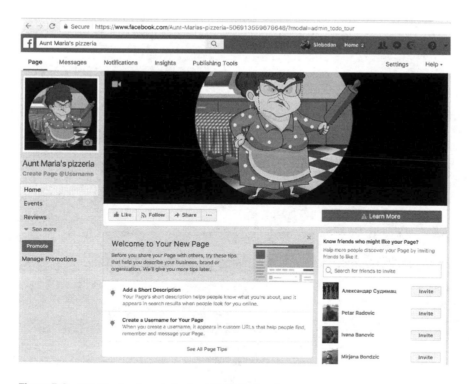

Figure B.3   The Facebook page for Aunt Maria's pizzeria

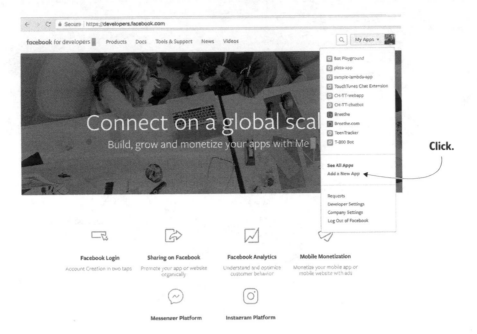

Figure B.4   The Facebook developers portal

> **NOTE**   If the screenshots shown here do not match what you see on the site, consult Facebook's help article for creating apps at https://developers.facebook.com/docs/apps/register.

A pop-up titled "Create a New App ID" appears, as shown in figure B.5, asking you for your app's name and your email address. Fill in the form (use "Aunt Maria's pizzeria" for the application name) and click the Create App ID button to create a new Facebook application.

A screen listing some recommended products appears. When you hover over products with your mouse cursor, two buttons appear: Read Docs and Set Up. Find the Messenger product and hover over it with your mouse, as shown in figure B.6. Click Set Up.

Clicking this button takes you to the Messenger Platform settings screen, which looks similar to figure B.7.

Do not close this browser page; you'll need it again in a few moments.

B.1.3   Creating a Facebook Messenger chatbot using Claudia Bot Builder

Now that you have both a Facebook page and a Facebook application, it's time to create a chatbot.

> **NOTE**   Before performing the next step, make sure you have Claudia installed globally, as described in appendix A. Also, you need to have an NPM project initialized and Claudia Bot Builder installed as a dependency, as explained in the same appendix.

Finally, you need to have the code for your chatbot ready, as shown in listing 8.

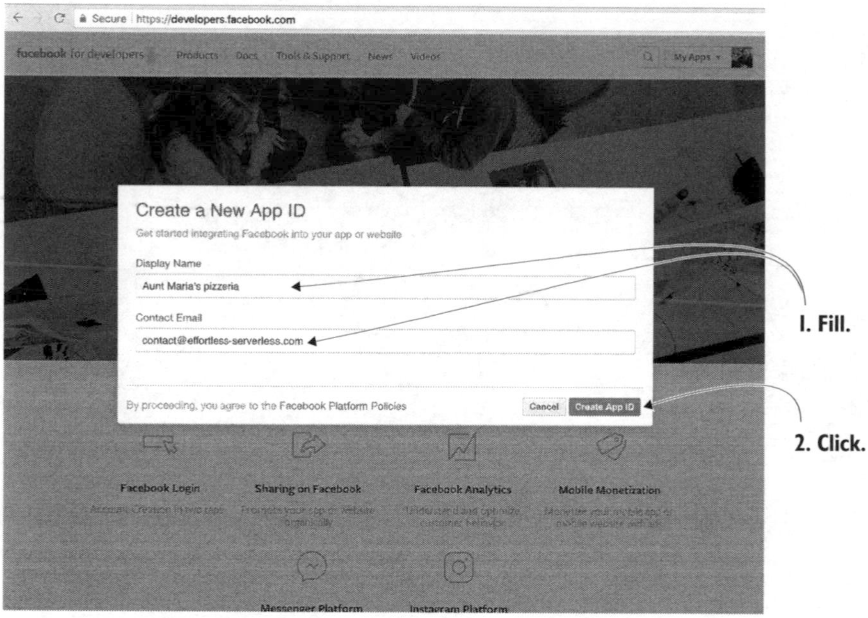

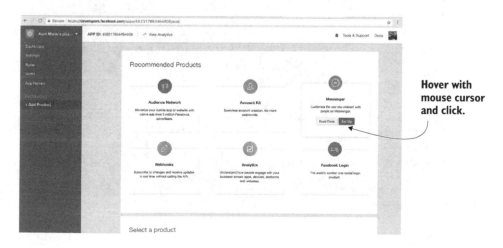

Figure B.5 Creating a new Facebook application

Open your terminal and navigate to your project folder. Then run the command from listing A.1 to create your AWS Lambda function and configure your chatbot.

> **NOTE** Multiline commands like the one shown in the next listing may not work on every OS. If they are not supported by your OS, type the command on a single line—just make sure you remove the backslashes (\\), which are there to tell the terminal that the command continues on another line.

Figure B.6 The list of recommended products

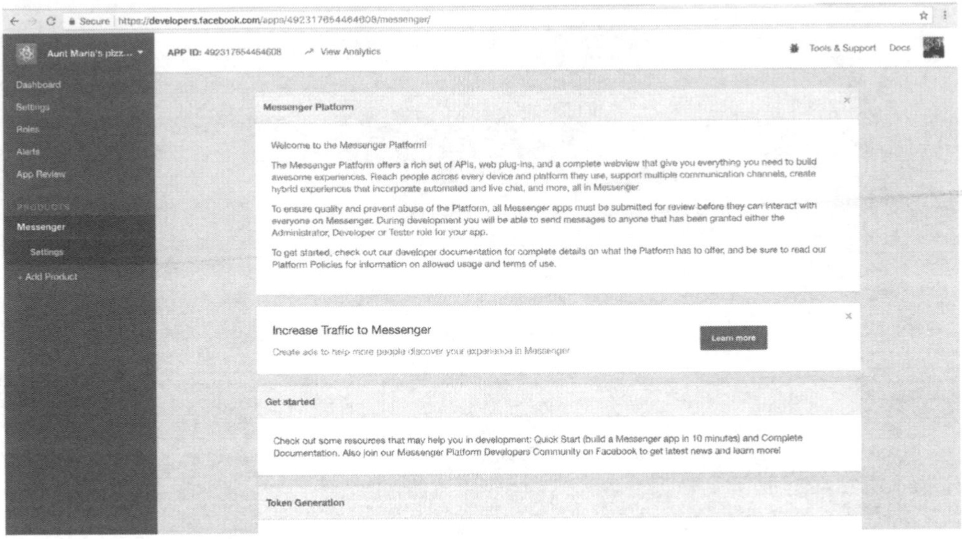

Figure B.7   The Messenger Platform settings screen

```
claudia create \
    --region eu-central-1 \         ◄────┤ Select your region.
    --api-module bot \         ◄────
    --configure-fb-bot                   Select your main file (this listing assumes
                                         you named it bot.js, as in chapter 8).
   ─────►
  Tell Claudia that you want to configure a
  Facebook Messenger chatbot.
```

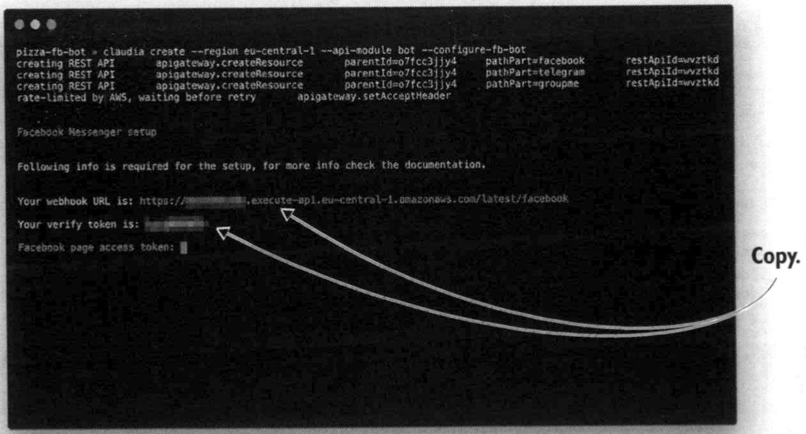

Figure B.8   Facebook Messenger bot setup with Claudia Bot Builder

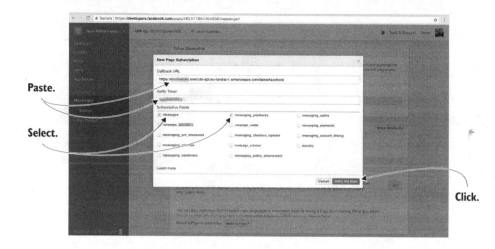

Figure B.9 Set up the webhook and verification token

Unlike a regular Claudia deployment, the command with the `--configure-fb-bot` option is interactive. After your code is deployed to an AWS Lambda function, the command will print the webhook URL and verify token you'll need to configure your chatbot, as shown in figure B.8. You'll need those values for the next step.

Keep the terminal open, because the process is not done yet.

Go back to the Messenger Platform settings screen in your browser (figure B.7), and click the Setup Webhook button in the Webhooks section. This button opens a pop-up similar to the one in figure B.9. In this pop-up, use the values that the terminal printed for you in the previous step to fill out the webhook URL and verify token. In the Subscription Fields section, select the "messages" and "messaging_postbacks" options. Then click the Verify and Save button.

After a moment, the pop-up closes and you see your webhook configured, as in figure B.10.

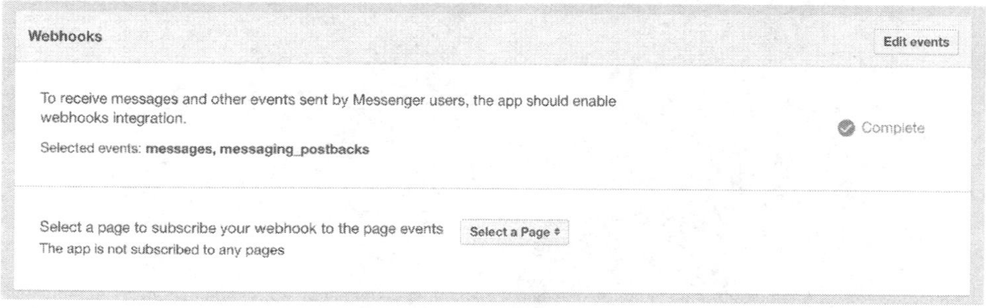

> **Webhooks**   Edit events
>
> To receive messages and other events sent by Messenger users, the app should enable
> webhooks integration.   ✓ Complete
>
> Selected events: **messages, messaging_postbacks**
>
> ---
>
> Select a page to subscribe your webhook to the page events   Select a Page ◆
> The app is not subscribed to any pages

Figure B.10 Webhook activation confirmation

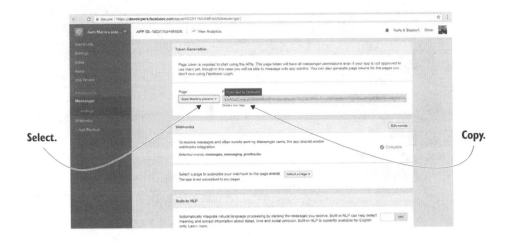

Select.   Copy.

Figure B.11   Generate the page token.

The next step is to get your Facebook page access token. To do so, go to the Token Generation section of the settings screen, select the page you created from the drop-down menu, and copy the token, as shown in figure B.11.

Go back to your terminal, paste the access token from the previous step, and press Enter, as shown in figure B.12.

The interactive command then asks you for the Facebook app secret. The app secret is required because it is used to verify that a message is being received from your chatbot, not from some other source. Your secret will be stored in an API Gateway stage variable.

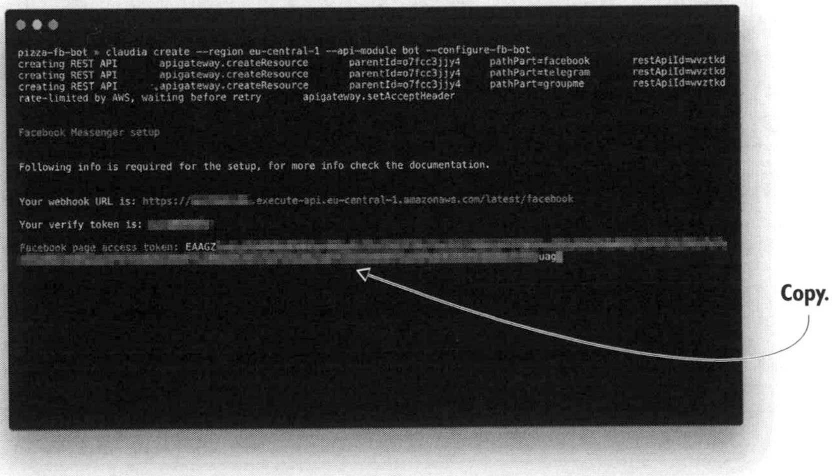

Copy.

Figure B.12   Configure the page token.

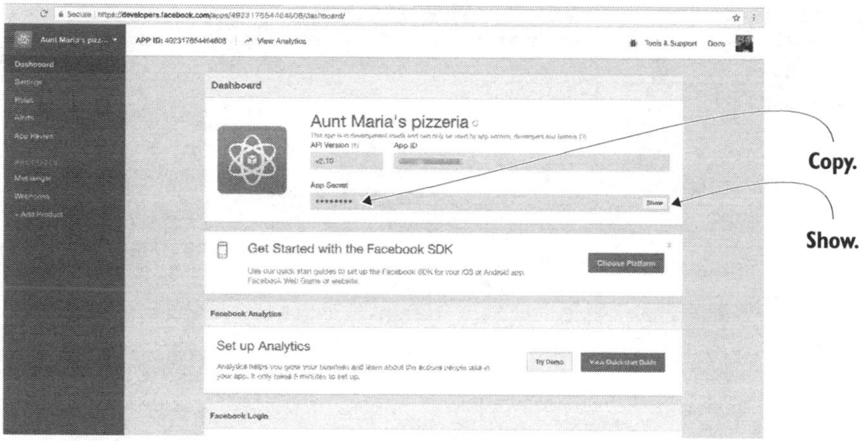

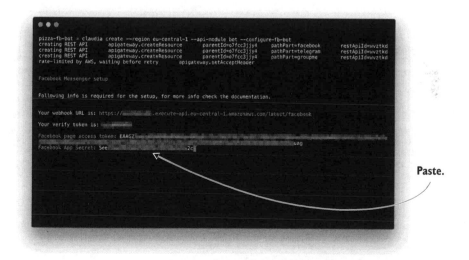

Figure B.13 Copy the app secret.

To get your Facebook app secret, go back to your browser, and select the Dashboard tab in the Facebook app's menu on the left. Click the Show button next to the App Secret field, as shown in figure B.13. Copy this value, and go back to your terminal window.

Paste your App Secret and press Enter, as shown in figure B.14.

When the command finishes after a few moments, you should see a response similar to listing B.1.

Figure B.14 Configure the app secret.

Listing B.1   Bot creation response

```
{
  "lambda": {
    "role": "pizza-fb-bot-executor",
    "name": "pizza-fb-bot",
    "region": "eu-central-1"
  },
  "api": {
    "id": "wvztkdiz8c",
    "module": "bot",
    "url": "https://wvztkdiz8c.execute-api.eu-central-1.amazonaws.com/
    latest",
    "deploy": {
      "facebook": "https://wvztkdiz8c.execute-api.eu-central-1.amazonaws.com/
      latest/facebook",
      "slackSlashCommand": "https://wvztkdiz8c.execute-api.eu-central-1.
      amazonaws.com/latest/slack/slash-command",
      "telegram": "https://wvztkdiz8c.execute-api.eu-central-1.amazonaws.com/
      latest/telegram",
      "skype": "https://wvztkdiz8c.execute-api.eu-central-1.amazonaws.com/
      latest/skype",
      "twilio": "https://wvztkdiz8c.execute-api.eu-central-1.amazonaws.com/
      latest/twilio",
      "kik": "https://wvztkdiz8c.execute-api.eu-central-1.amazonaws.com/
      latest/kik",
      "groupme": "https://wvztkdiz8c.execute-api.eu-central-1.amazonaws.com/
      latest/groupme",
      "line": "https://wvztkdiz8c.execute-api.eu-central-1.amazonaws.com/
      latest/line",
      "viber": "https://wvztkdiz8c.execute-api.eu-central-1.amazonaws.com/
      latest/viber",
      "alexa": "https://wvztkdiz8c.execute-api.eu-central-1.amazonaws.com/
      latest/alexa"
    }
  }
}
```

AWS Lambda info

API Gateway info

Webhooks for all supported platforms,
including Facebook Messenger

This response prints out all the webhooks, but you don't need them because Claudia
has already set everything up for you. Claudia also automatically subscribed your chatbot to your page, as shown in figure B.15.

Now try to find your page in Facebook Messenger. You should see something similar
to figure B.16.

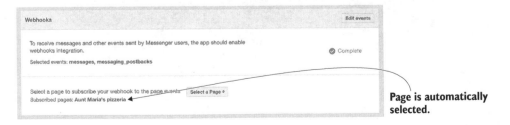

Page is automatically
selected.

Figure B.15   Your chatbot is subscribed to the page.

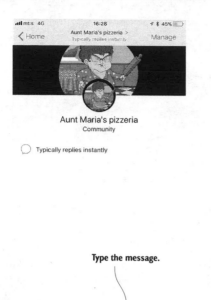

Figure B.16   The Facebook Messenger bot start page

And if you message the bot, it should reply as shown in figure B.17.

Figure B.17   The Facebook Messenger bot's answer

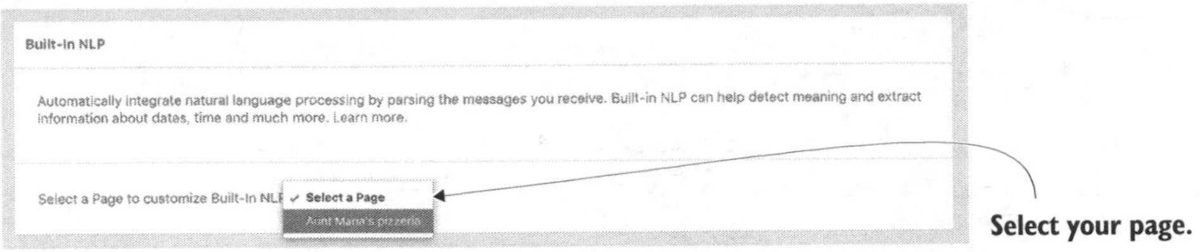

Select your page.

Figure B.18   Select the page to enable built-in NLP.

B.1.4   *Enabling built-in NLP*

To enable built-in NLP, go back to the Messenger Platform settings screen in the Facebook developers portal, and scroll down to the Built-In NLP section. Then select your Facebook page in the Select a Page to Customize Built-In NLP drop-down, as shown in figure B.18.

Now you can enable built-in NLP, select the default language, and see advanced settings. For the pizzeria application, you'll use English, so you need to enable built-in NLP as shown in figure B.19.

B.2   *Twilio setup*

Configuration of the Twilio SMS chatbot for chapter 10 requires the following steps:

1 Sign up for a Twilio account.
2 Get a Twilio number.
3 Set up your Twilio Programmable SMS service.
4 Create a Twilio SMS chatbot using Claudia Bot Builder.

NOTE   Twilio has a free trial period, so you won't need to pay right away, but after a certain period of time it will ask you to pay for the service.

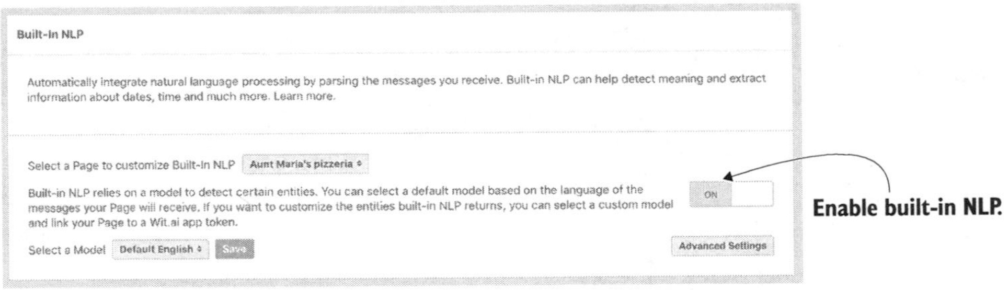

Enable built-in NLP.

Figure B.19   Enable built-in NLP.

B.2.1 *Creating a Twilio account*

If you already have a Twilio account, jump to the next section, "Getting a Twilio number."

To sign up for a Twilio account, visit https://www.twilio.com/try-twilio. Type in the required account details. You'll also see four drop-down fields, as in figure B.20.

In the drop-downs, make the following choices:

1 For the product you're going to use, choose SMS.
2 For what you're going to build, choose SMS Support.
3 For the language you're going to use, choose Node.js.
4 For potential monthly interactions, choose Less Than 100,000 (or if you're already planning for more, feel free to choose a higher value).

After you fill out all of the fields, Twilio asks you to verify that you're a human by sending you a verification SMS. You need to type in your mobile phone number, and you'll receive an SMS with the authentication code. Type in that code on the following screen.

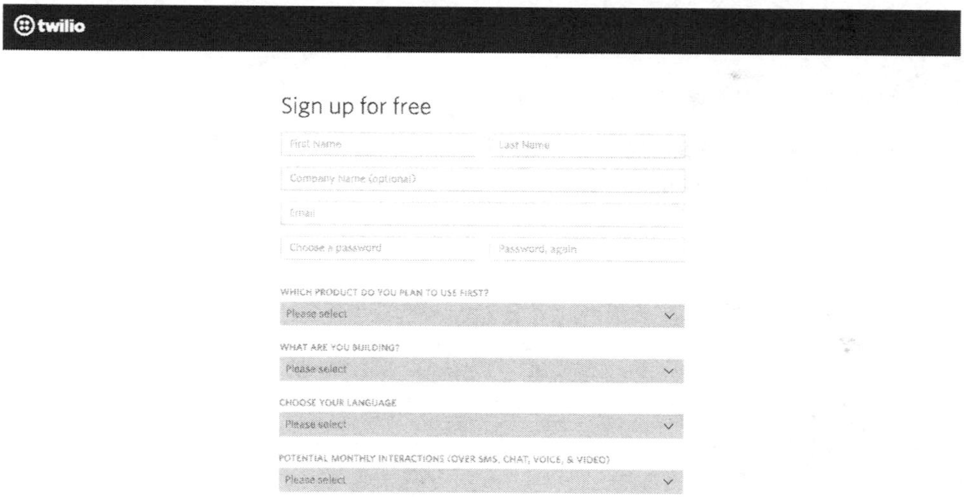

Figure B.20 Sign up for a Twilio account.

Upon successful verification of your number, Twilio asks you to create a new project. You can see that page in figure B.21.

Fill in the project name and click Create Project, and your project is created. You'll then see the Programmable SMS project page, shown in figure B.22.

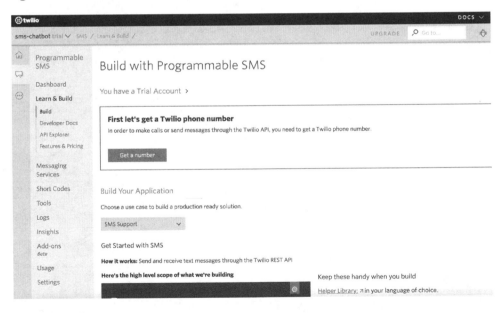

Figure B.21   Create a new Twilio project.

Figure B.22   Your Programmable SMS project page

B.2.2 Getting a Twilio number

If you already have a Twilio number, jump to the next section, "Setting up your Twilio Programmable SMS service."

Otherwise, on the Programmable SMS project page, click the Get a Number button. You'll see a modal with a phone number suggested by Twilio. If you don't like this number, or you just want a different one, you can click the Search for a Different Number link in the modal. When you're okay with the phone number, click Choose This Number.

When Twilio finishes processing your new number request, you'll see a "Congratulations" modal with your chosen phone number. Click Done, and Twilio opens up your Programmable SMS project page with the Learn & Build tab selected.

B.2.3 Setting up your Twilio Programmable SMS service

Your Twilio SMS chatbot should be able to both automatically send and receive messages. To enable this messaging, you need to configure it in your Programmable SMS project page as a Messaging Service. You can find the Messaging Services menu item in the navigation menu on the left side of the project page (see figure B.23).

Open that tab, and click Create New Service. A pop-up window appears, asking you for the friendly name of your service and the use case. Set the name as "Aunt Maria's Pizzeria chatbot" and the use case as "Mixed."

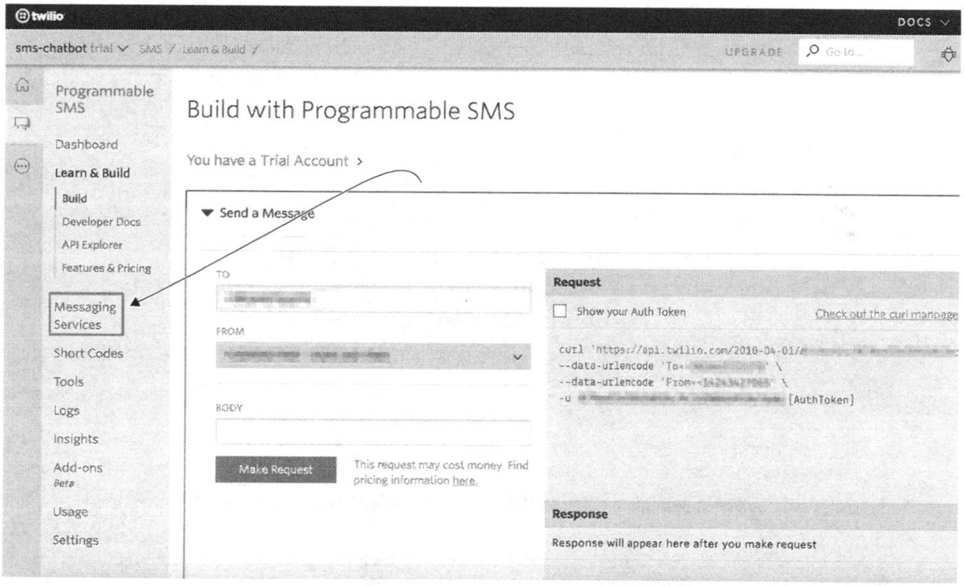

Figure B.23   The Messaging Services option in the Programmable SMS project navigation menu

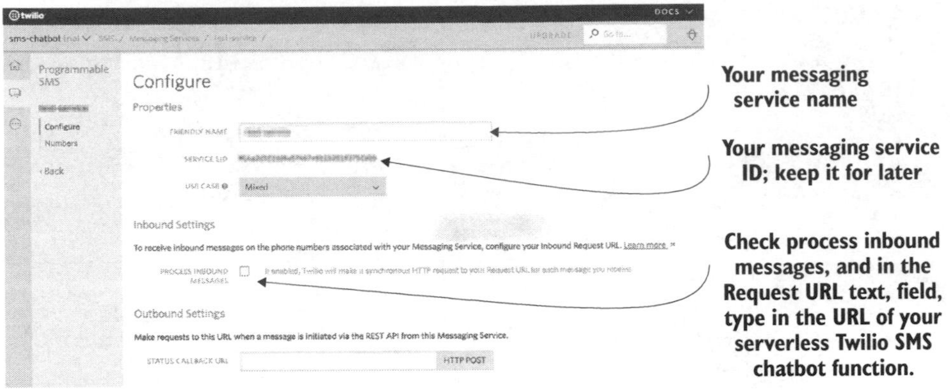

Figure B.24   Configure your Messaging Service.

The configuration page for your newly added Messaging Service opens, as shown in figure B.24.

On this page, select the Process Inbound Messages options. Two text fields appear:

- Request URL
- Fallback URL

In the Request URL text field, paste or type in the URL of your serverless Twilio SMS chatbot you created with Claudia Bot Builder. Then click Save.

Next you need to add to this service the Twilio number you requested in the previous section. To do that, click the Numbers link in the left navigation menu of the Messaging Services tab.

In the Numbers page, click the Add an Existing Number button. A pop-up appears, as shown in figure B.25.

In this pop-up, you can see your list of available Twilio numbers. If you don't have one, please go back to the previous section, "Getting a Twilio number."

To add one or more of these numbers, use the checkboxes to select them, and then click Add Selected. The numbers appear in the list on the Numbers page.

If you've also pasted the URL of the serverless Twilio SMS chatbot function you created into the Request URL field, that's it—you've properly set up your Twilio account

Figure B.25   Add your Twilio number to your Messaging Service.

Figure B.26 The Amazon Alexa dashboard

and Programmable SMS project. Congratulations! You can now try out your SMS chatbot by sending an SMS to your selected Twilio number.

B.3 *Alexa skill setup*

To set up an Alexa skill, go to https://developer.amazon.com/alexa and log in with your Amazon account. Then click the Add Capabilities to Alexa link, as shown in figure B.26.

The Alexa Skills Kit screen appears, a place where you can find documentation and tutorials for designing, building, and launching Alexa skills. You can also create new skills here. To do so, click the Start a Skill button, as shown in figure B.27, which takes you to the Create a New Alexa Skill screen.

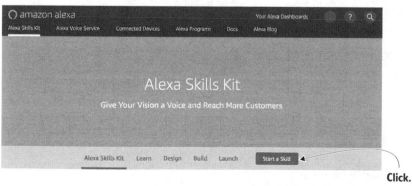

Figure B.27 The Alexa Skills Kit

The first part of the process is the Skill Information section. In this section you can select the skill type, set the name and invocation name of your skill, and configure global fields such as Audio Player, Video App, and Render Template.

The Custom Interaction Model type is selected by default; keep it selected because it allows you to build a new custom skill. Besides this type, you can build a Smart Home skill, a Flash Briefing skill, or a Video skill (for Amazon Echo Show or other visual Alexa devices).

Set both the name and invocation name to "Aunt Maria's Pizzeria," make sure that all the global fields are off, and click the Save button, as shown in figure B.28. Click the Next button to go to the next section.

The next screen is the Interaction Model settings. For this screen, you need the intent schema, custom slot, and sample utterances you built in chapter 10.

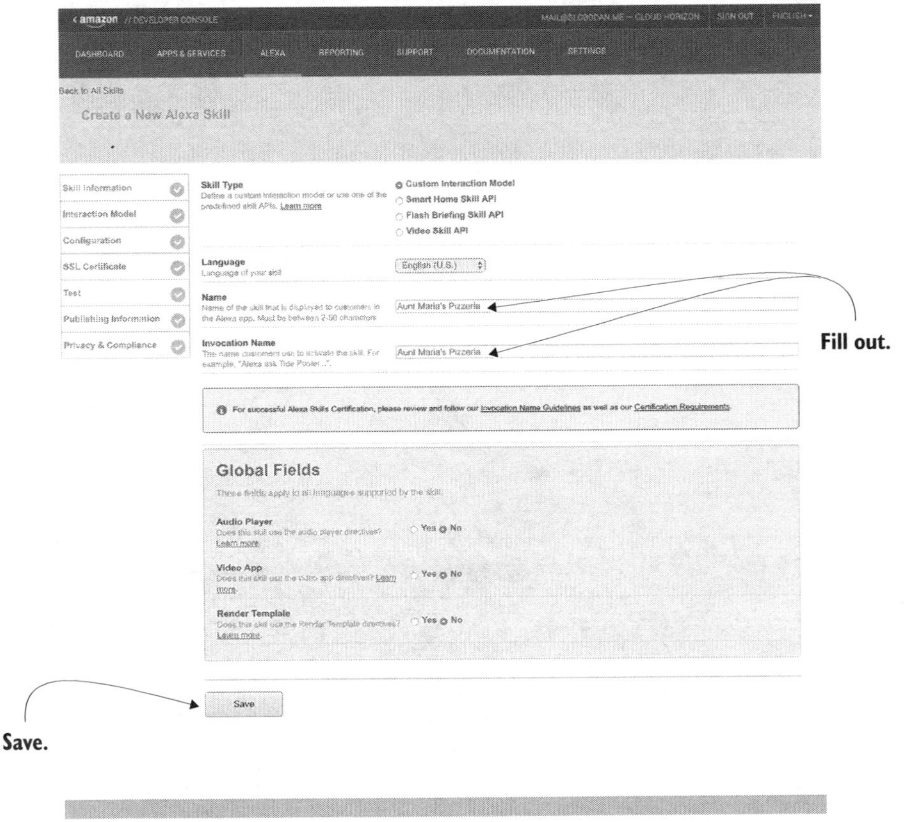

Figure B.28 Setting up your skill

First, paste the intent schema you built (listing 10.9) into the Intent Schema text field. Then fill out the Custom Slot Types form, adding a custom slot name (LIST_OF_ PIZZAS) and using the values from chapter 10 (listing 10.10). Then click the Add button, as shown in figure B.29.

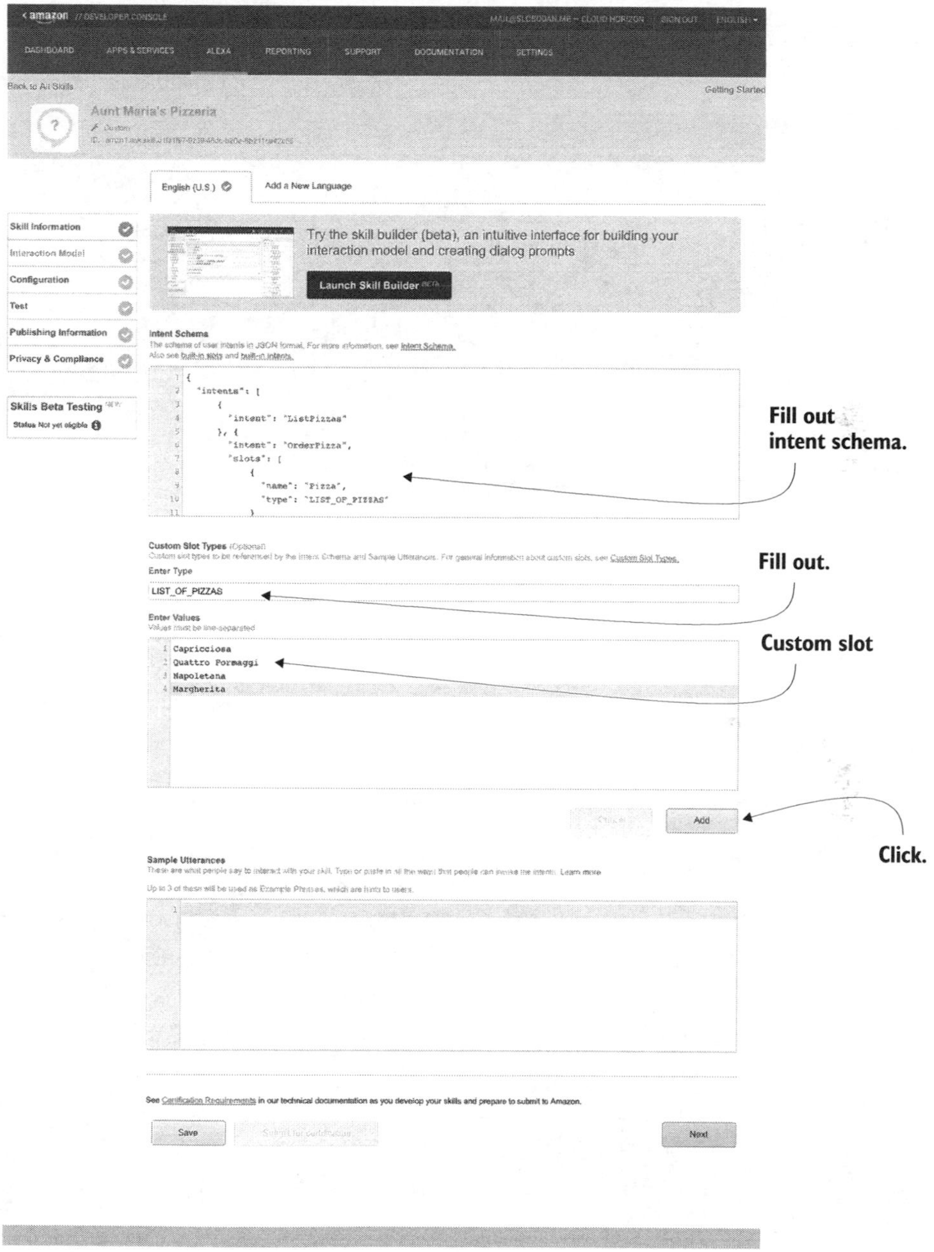

Figure B.29   Configuring the interaction model

After adding your custom slot type, fill out the custom utterances from chapter 10, then click the Next button, as shown in figure B.30.

The next screen is the Configuration section, where you set up your skill's webhook or AWS Lambda function. Before you complete this step, deploy your code to a Lambda function if you haven't done that already. Keep your browser page open while you are doing this, because you'll need to go back to the Configuration section of the Create a New Alexa Skill page in a few moments.

To deploy your Lambda function, open your terminal, navigate to your Alexa skill code folder, and run the following command:

```
claudia create --region eu-west-1 --handler skill.handler --version skill
```

Figure B.30 Adding the sample utterances

This command deploys your code to AWS Lambda in the eu-west-1 region (only us-east-1 and eu-west-1 regions are supported by Alexa), and sets the version to skill.

After a few moments, you'll see the standard claudia create response, similar to this one:

```
{
  "lambda": {
    "role": "pizza-alexa-skill-executor",
    "name": "pizza-alexa-skill",
    "region": "eu-west-1"
  }
}
```

Before you can use the Lambda function for your Alexa skill, you need to allow it to be triggered by Alexa. To do so, run the following command:

```
claudia allow-alexa-skill-trigger --version skill
```

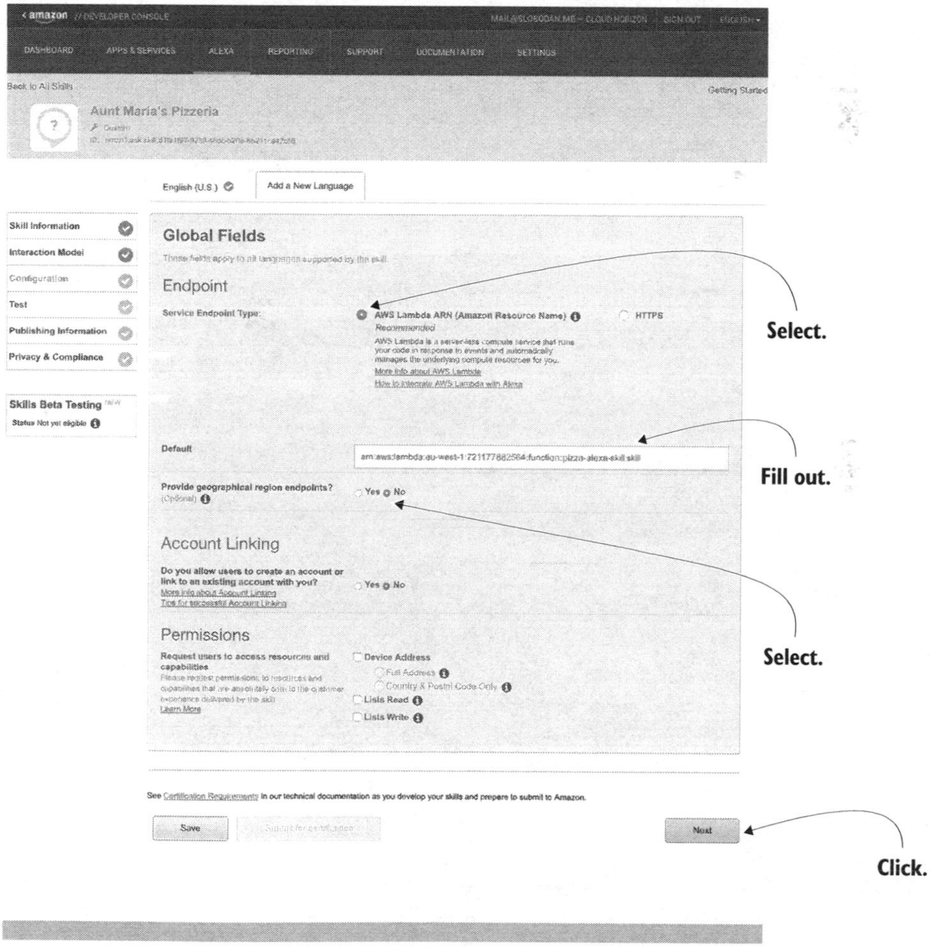

Figure B.31   Skill configuration

This command allows the `skill` version of your Lambda function to be triggered by Alexa. After a few moments, you'll see a response similar to this one:

```
{
  "Sid": "Alexa-1518380119842",
  "Effect": "Allow",
  "Principal": {
    "Service": "alexa-appkit.amazon.com"
  },
  "Action": "lambda:InvokeFunction",
  "Resource": "arn:aws:lambda:eu-west-1:721177882564:function:pizza-alexa-
      skill:skill"
}
```

Copy the Lambda ARN (`Resource` in the JSON response in your terminal), then go back to the skill configuration page in your browser. Select AWS Lambda ARN as the Service Endpoint Type and paste the ARN of your Lambda function into the input field below, as shown in figure B.31.

You are not building a skill that will have multiple geographical region endpoints (for example, different regions for the US and UK), so select No as the response to the "Provide geographical region endpoints?" question, and then click Next.

After your skill is configured, the Test screen appears. This screen is where you can test your skill, for example by entering an utterance in the Service Simulator and then listening to the response by clicking the Listen button, as shown in figure B.32. Your skill is also active on your Alexa device, so you can also say, "Alexa, start Aunt Maria's Pizzeria."

This skill is now available on your Alexa device, but if you want to make it available for everyone, you need to submit your skill for certification, as explained here: https://developer.amazon.com/docs/custom-skills/submit-an-alexa-skill-for-certification.html.

Figure B.32   Testing your skill

appendix c
Stripe and MongoDB setup

This appendix covers

- Setting up your Stripe account and retrieving Stripe API keys
- Installing and configuring MongoDB

C.1 Setting up your Stripe account and retrieving Stripe API keys

Creating and configuring a Stripe account and obtaining the API keys is required for chapter 12 when you create your serverless payment service. The process consists of the following steps:

1 Sign up for a Stripe account.
2 Retrieve your Stripe API keys.
3 Create the serverless Stripe payment service using Claudia API Builder.

If you have a Stripe account but haven't retrieved your keys yet, skip to the section "Getting your Stripe API keys."

C.1.1 Creating a Stripe account

Creating a Stripe account is quick and easy. Open your browser and go to https://stripe.com. Click Create Account, which takes you to the Stripe registration page.

Type in your email address, full name, and password. After you submit the form, Stripe asks you to add a mobile recovery number. We recommend you do so in case you forget your password.

After that, your account is created, but don't forget to confirm your email address—Stripe will not allow you to accept live payments until you do this. That's it; you have your very first Stripe account!

C.1.2   *Getting your Stripe API keys*

When you want to use Stripe to accept payments in your applications, you are required to use Stripe's API. Stripe needs to be able to identify you when you're using its API. To identify your account, Stripe gives you a pair of secret hashed keys that are meant to be used in all communications with its API. These keys are automatically generated for you by Stripe when you initially create your Stripe account.

Once you've created your account, as described in the previous section, you need to retrieve your API keys. To do that, open the Stripe Dashboard at https://dashboard.stripe.com.

From the navigation menu, choose the API option (see figure C.1).

The API page contains two tables, for standard API keys and restricted API keys (figure C.2). You want standard API keys; they are the most commonly used and the key type you'll use for your serverless payment service.

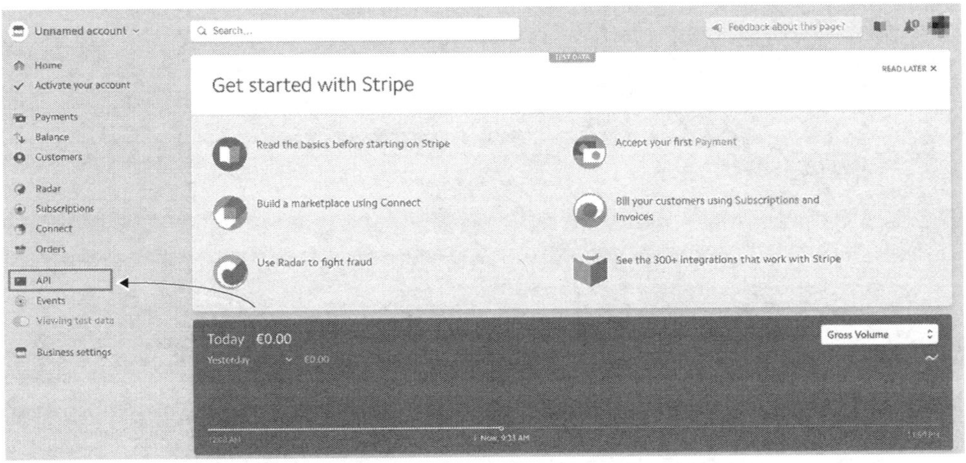

Figure C.1   The Stripe Dashboard

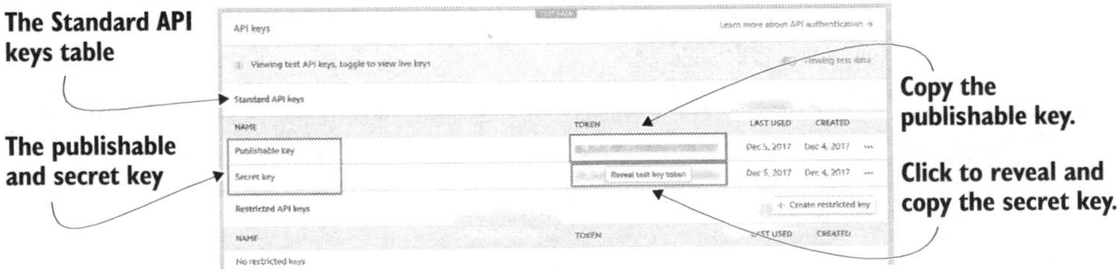

Figure C.2   The standard API keys table

As mentioned before, two standard API keys are automatically generated for you when you create your account: a publishable key and a secret key. The publishable key can be used as a public key in your front-end web or mobile applications. It may be publicly seen, as it is something as your email. But either way, you don't want everyone to have it.

The secret key provides your applications or APIs access to Stripe resources. This is what lets Stripe know it's you using its resources. It's similar to a password, and you must hide it from everyone—but don't worry, if you suspect someone might have seen it, you can regenerate both the public and secret key.

Copy both keys to a blank document on your computer for ease of access now, but be sure to delete the document after you finish chapter 12.

> **WARNING** Keep your secret key safely secured and hidden on your server only. Take the utmost care with your secret key, because it can be used to access or even manipulate your Stripe account.

C.2 Installing and configuring MongoDB

MongoDB Atlas is a cloud-hosted and managed MongoDB service, engineered and run by the same team that built the database. In this section you'll create and configure a free instance of MongoDB, which is sufficient to follow along with the code examples from chapter 13 and to run a small real-world application.

C.2.1 Creating an account

To learn more about the product and create a MongoDB Atlas account, go to https://www.mongodb.com/cloud/atlas in your browser (see figure C.3).

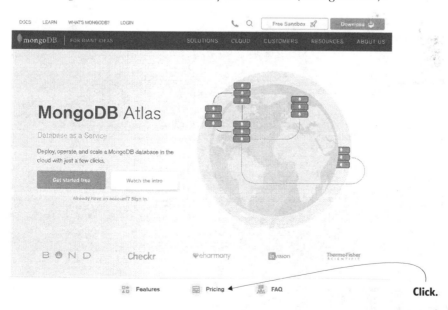

Figure C.3 The MongoDB Atlas landing page

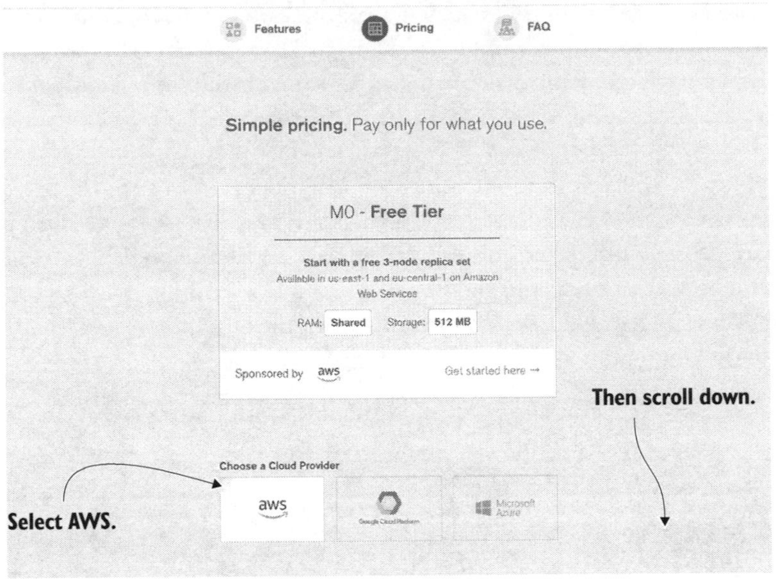

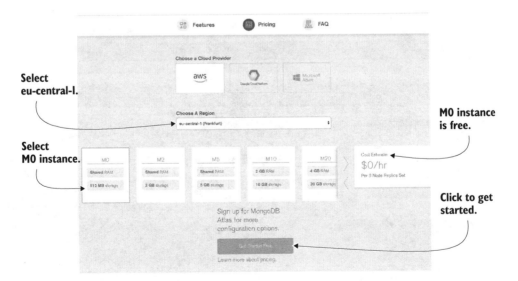

Figure C.4   Choose a cloud provider on the Pricing tab.

Click Pricing to open the Pricing tab, where you can choose a cloud provider, region, and instance size. Select AWS, as shown in figure C.4, and then scroll down.

Below the cloud provider section, select the region you used for your Lambda function (we used eu-central-1). Then choose the M0 instance, which costs $0 per month, and click Get Started Free, as shown in figure C.5.

Figure C.5   Choose a region and instance size.

In the sign-up form that appears, fill out the required fields and click Continue, as shown in figure C.6. MongoDB Atlas does not require your credit card details for a free account, so clicking Continue creates your account and take you to the configuration page.

C.2.2 Configuring your cluster

After you create an account, you need to create your first cluster. A database cluster is a collection of databases that is managed by a single instance of a running database server. As shown in figure C.7, you need to add a cluster name (for example, "RobertosTaxi-Company"). Make sure the price is still $0, and then click the Confirm & Deploy button.

Now that your cluster is created, you'll be able to see your MongoDB Atlas dashboard. The next step is to create a new user for your MongoDB database. To do so, select the Security tab and then click the Add New User button, as shown in figure C.8.

In the Add New User pop-up, enter a username (for example, "roberto") and password for your new database. Then show the advanced options in the User Privileges section. This allows you to select more granular permissions for your new user. To add the user for a single database only, select readWrite from the drop-down on the left, and then enter the database name in the database field as shown in figure C.9. Because your database doesn't exist yet, you can enter "taxi" and the database will be automatically created for you. When you're done, click Add User.

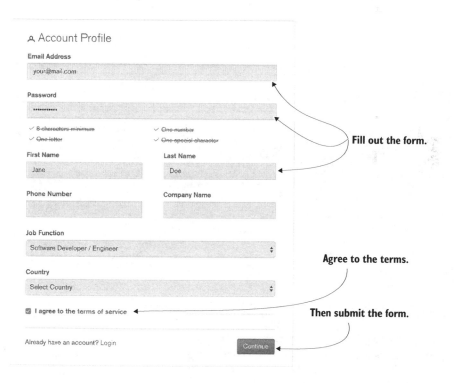

Figure C.6   Create your MongoDB Atlas account.

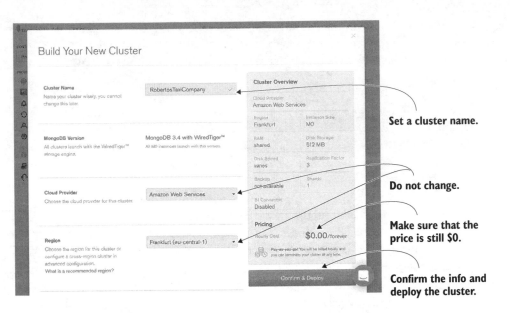

Figure C.7   Build a cluster.

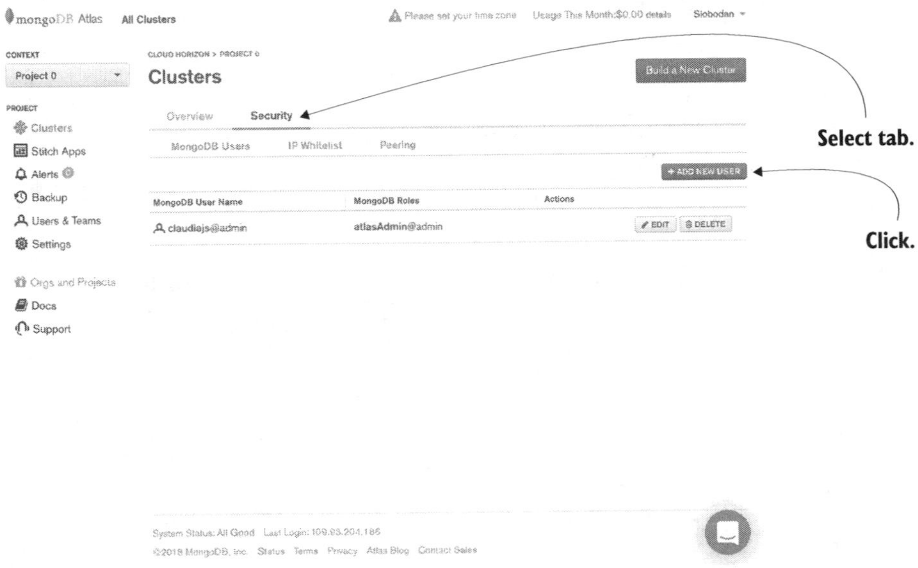

Figure C.8   The Security tab of the MongoDB Atlas dashboard

After creating your new user, you return to the Security tab of the MongoDB Atlas dashboard. The last step in the database configuration is to get the connection string. To do so, select the Overview tab, and then click on the RobertosTaxiCompany cluster, as shown in figure C.10.

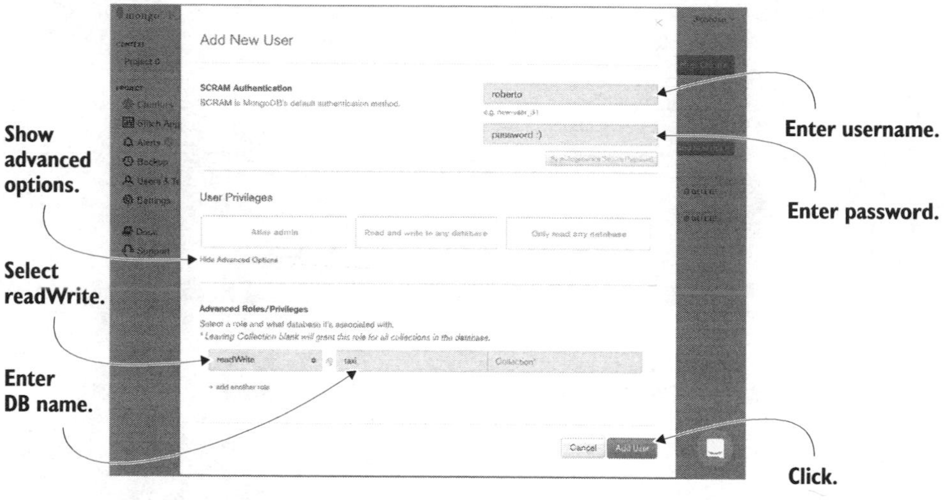

Show advanced options.

Select readWrite.

Enter DB name.

Enter username.

Enter password.

Click.

Figure C.9   Create a new user.

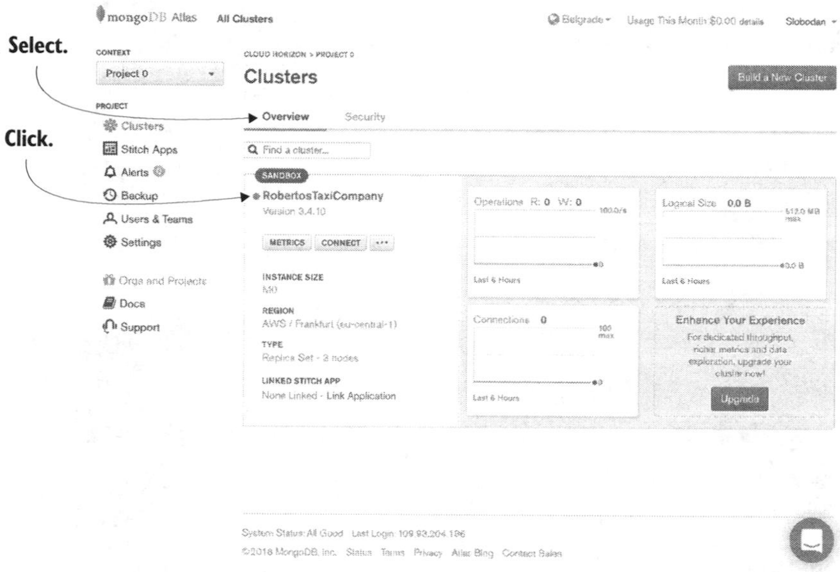

Select.

Click.

Figure C.10   The cluster overview

As shown in figure C.11, click the Connect button to open the connection pop-up.

To be able to create a connection string, you need to whitelist at least one IP address that will communicate with your MongoDB cluster. To do so, click the Add Entry button, as shown in figure C.12.

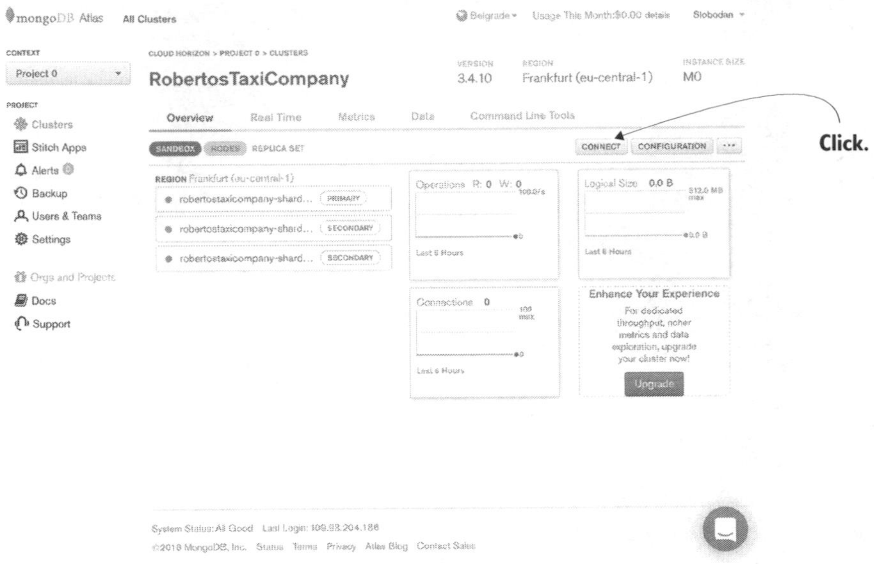

Figure C.11   The RobertosTaxiCompany cluster overview

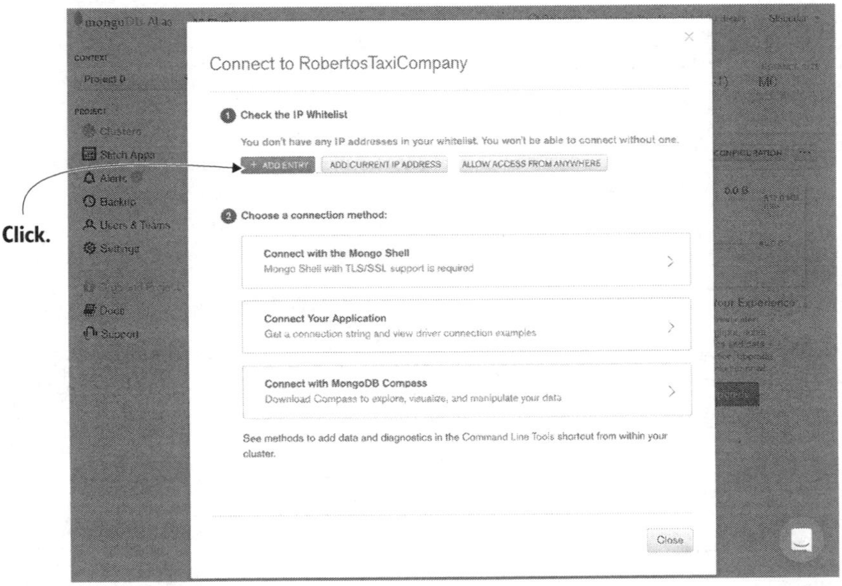

Figure C.12   Connect to your cluster.

But because you don't know all the IP addresses that AWS Lambda will use, you need to open your MongoDB cluster to all IP addresses by adding the `0.0.0.0/0` value to the IP address field. Then add a description and click the Save button, as shown in figure C.13.

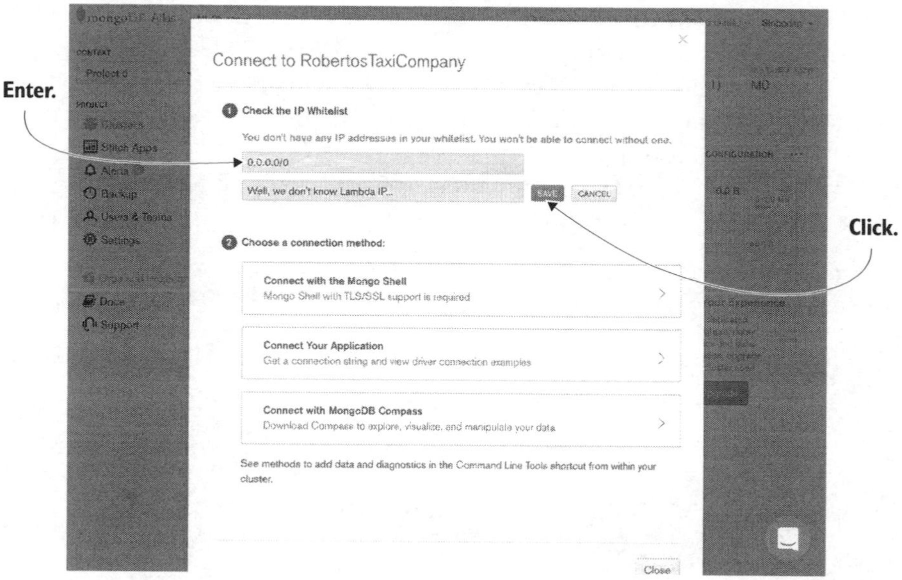

Enter.

Click.

Figure C.13 Whitelist all IP addresses because you don't know the AWS Lambda IP addresses.

The last step is to select the connection method. Select Connect Your Application, as shown in figure C.14, because you want to get a MongoDB connection string.

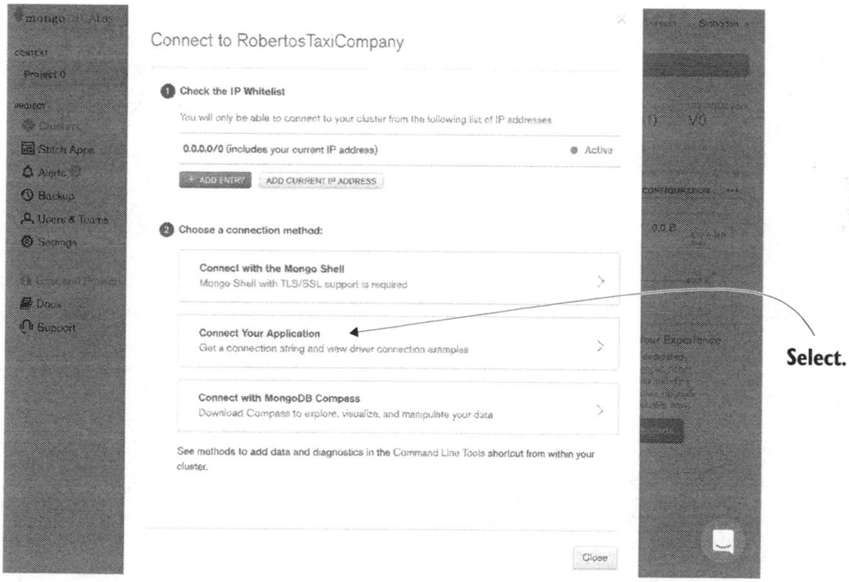

Select.

Figure C.14 Get a connection string (step 1).

A connection string is shown in the pop-up (see figure C.15). Click the I Am Using Driver 3.4 or Earlier button, because this is the driver you'll use in chapter 13, and then copy the connection string. Make sure you update the username value in the connection string to "roberto" (or whatever you used) and the password value to the password you entered when you created the new user.

Now that you have a MongoDB connection string, you'll be able to deploy and test the Express.js application from chapter 13.

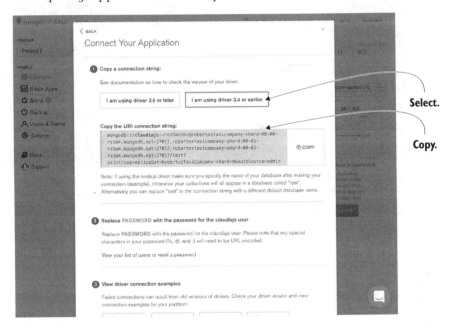

Figure C.15 Get a connection string (step 2).

appendix d
The pizza recipe

One pizza consists of several ingredients. Each of those ingredients has a specific place in your pizza timeline. The pizza ingredients can be separated into three categories:

- Dough ingredients
- Topping ingredients
- Spices/Sauce ingredients

Pizza dough ingredients seem very simple—isn't dough just flour and water? But don't be fooled; the pizza dough is the most important and the most difficult part. It has numerous variations based on the following:

- Shape
- Thickness
- Color
- Chewiness
- Additional variations (such as border crust filled with melted cheese—a blasphemy for Italians)

For the dough of one pizza based on this recipe, you will need the following ingredients:

- 2 cups of flour (250g)
- 1 teaspoon of yeast (5g)
- ½ cup of mildly warm water (120ml)
- A pinch of salt
- ½ tablespoon of sugar (6g)
- ½ tablespoon of olive oil (7ml)

Mix half of the mildly warm water needed with yeast, sugar, and a spoon of flour. Mix it all thoroughly and let it rise at warm room temperature for about half an hour.

Add the salt, olive oil, and the water and yeast mixture, plus the rest of the water to the remaining flour. Mix it all up nicely. Knead it for about 10 minutes by hand. You can also use a machine if you have one.

Put a handful of flour in an empty clean pot. Spread the flour evenly and then put the mixture in the floured pot.

Put your oven heating to the max.

> **WARNING**   If you're not sure how your oven behaves on max temperature, then put it at 220°C. Some ovens may behave weirdly at their max setting—we don't want you to start a kitchen fire.

While the oven is heating up, prepare your sheet pan. Cut a piece of parchment paper (baking paper) in the size of your sheet pan. Separate the pan and parchment paper and put the sheet pan inside the oven to heat. When its well heated, it's time to work again with the dough.

Without any kneading or mixing, stretch the dough to the size of the parchment paper and then put it on the paper. Spread the olive oil over it. Now, put your topping ingredients on it. You can be as creative as you like when it comes to toppings, but to get you started, here's a reminder of what goes on Aunt Maria's pizzas. First goes the famous Aunt Maria's tomato sauce.

> **NOTE**   If you're wondering about Aunt Maria's sauce or the recipe, well, that's a family secret that can never be revealed! You can use a regular tomato sauce instead, though.

Now place several pieces of mozzarella cheese on top and then spread around several pieces of pepperoni, then olives, and just a bit of oregano.

> **WARNING**   Always be careful not to put too many topping ingredients on any kind of pizza!

Take out the heated sheet pan and put your pizza on the parchment paper. Quickly put it back inside the oven.

It's going to take about 5–10 minutes for the pizza to bake fully. The correct timing depends on your oven but the indicators to look for are when the pizza's edges start getting golden or brownish. If you prefer, pour on a bit of olive oil.

index